THE PALESTINIAN REFUGEES IN JORDAN

1948-1957

THE
PALESTINIAN
REFUGEES
IN JORDAN
1948–1957

AVI PLASCOV

FRANK CASS

First published 1981 in Great Britain by
FRANK CASS AND COMPANY LIMITED
Gainsborough House, Gainsborough Road,
London, E11 1RS, England

and in the United States of America by
FRANK CASS AND COMPANY LIMITED
c/o Biblio Distribution Centre
81 Adams Drive, P.O. Box 327, Totowa, N.J. 07511

British Library Cataloguing in Publication Data

Plascov, Avi
   The Palestinian refugees in Jordan, 1948-1957
   1. Palestinian Arabs–Jordan–History
   2. Refugees, Arab
   I. Title
   301.45'19'27569405695   DS153.55.P34

ISBN 0-7146-3120-5

Typeset by A-Line Services, Saffron Walden, Essex
Printed in Great Britain by
Robert Hartnoll Limited Bodmin Cornwall

To my wife Tovi

Contents

Illustrations
Between pages 78 and 79

The first years: a refugee camp at South Shunah, Trans-Jordan, 1949

Second phase: mud-built shelters at Ayn al-Sultan camp near Jericho

A camp with jerry-built shacks

A new era: asbestos and concrete shelters at Fawwar camp

Dahaysha camp in 1949, and 20 years later

Jabal Husayn camp

UNWRA distributing flour to the refugees

Education: Madaba (East Bank) elementary school

Preface

There is perhaps no aspect of the Arab-Israeli conflict that is more complex and more emotionally charged than the problem of the Palestinian refugees. The atmosphere surrounding the discussion has led to confusion, so that the facts have become unclear and the problems more difficult to treat, even for those studying the Palestinians.

Despite the extensive research into Palestinian affairs under the British Mandate, and the interest shown in the Palestinian issue in the 1960s, the developments of the 1950s seem to be relatively neglected. Certainly this is true with regard to the refugee section of the Palestinian society — the subject of this study. The present work concentrates on the various aspects concerning the Palestinian refugees — *after* they had fled or were expelled — in the country which adopted most of them, namely Jordan. Topics such as the refugee exodus, the number of refugees, their abandoned property, the various programmes to resettle them and the dispute over the River Jordan water, though researched in depth, are here only alluded to briefly.

The issues examined form an intricate web where each one has some bearing on the other. Therefore it sometimes proved difficult to isolate certain subjects when discussing particular areas. As no clear dividing line can be drawn to ascertain who is truly a refugee, the widest definition has been used in this work, that is, *he who considers himself to be one.* Although this approach widens the scope of the study, it avoids any pointless and artifical divisions between the different categories of refugees, and helps to concentrate on the refugee element of the Palestinian Community. This of course is another problem, since one cannot really isolate the Refugee Problem from the Palestinian Question. Therefore the regime's policy towards the Palestinians as a whole was carefully studied, being part of its "Refugee Policy".

The period covered is the first ten years following the 1948 War, perhaps the most significant period for the Palestinians in general and the Refugees in particular. The discussion sometimes extends beyond this period to give some sense of perspective and to provide continuity with the new era of the 1960s.

Note on Sources

Prior to my field research, much time was spent reading published UN reports* and consulting valuable secondary sources — some of which are essentially propaganda or sheer polemics. As one soon discovered, propaganda plays an important part in daily politics amongst the refugees, and this kind of material was useful since it helped in understanding refugees' reactions. However, most reviewed secondary sources did not contribute directly to the body of the work, which relies chiefly on rarely seen primary sources. The variety of these unpublished sources enabled me to compare and evaluate interpretations and avoid basing information on a single source. The unrevealed sources include: Jordanian Secret Police, Army and Government documents relating mainly, though not exclusively, to the West Bank; Red Cross correspondence; UNRWA documents; underground political publications; refugee petitions to the Agencies and the government, etc. — all contained in the respective archives I was allowed to visit. Private papers, diaries and photographs were also carefully studied.

The local daily press was another indispensable source of information especially on refugee affairs, since such topics were hardly ever censored. Special attention was paid to the short-lived dailies and weeklies which were later banned and were therefore difficult to trace. These were found in the Jerusalem and Tel Aviv University Libraries, the Israel State Archives and obtained from private individuals. Other Arab newspapers could provide additional information, when they did not reflect a hostile attitude to the Jordanian regime. The content of the area's radio transmissions were studied as they revealed the various governments' policies. These radio broadcasts were used to influence the opinion of the masses (though the transistor radio did not come into popular use in the period under review).

Part of the field research included interviews, talks and meetings carried out in the West Bank, Israel, the U.S.A., England and Switzerland. These were held with Palestinian refugees and non-refugees, Jordanians, former government officials, local and international Red Cross and UNRWA workers, etc. These interviews were liable to contain various kinds of distortions. The Palestinians are under occupation, insecure and striving for a homeland of their own. For this reason, when asked to reflect on the developments of the 1950s some Palestinians tended to rewrite the history of the period. So wishful thinking, self-criticism, exaggeration, slander, speaking "for the record" and forgetfulness, combined with deep suspicion, only added to the danger of accepting at face value what was said. The study was carried out immediately after the 1973 War, a time of intense P.L.O. activity when different declarations came from all quarters; this also had a

*Owing to the manner and the circumstances under which they were written and the differences between them and the examined classified records, UN *published* reports, relating to the subject under study, could hardly be treated as primary sources.

bearing on the attitude of interviewees. However, the interviews provided an extremely useful source: they enabled various gaps in the record to be filled, shed light on developments and elucidated the meaning of different documents. In addition, they were invaluable for the understanding of people's reactions and attitudes. The findings were checked by repeating the questions in different forms. Some of the people involved were interviewed a number of times, and were also confronted with secret documents relating to them or signed by them. Other data was collected through correspondence. Some of the sources cannot be revealed as people gave the interviews on the condition that they would remain unnamed. And since much of the material, if attributed, could open old wounds, no names have been listed.

The field research took over two years and included extensive visits to all official and unofficial UNRWA West Bank Refugee Camps, refugee concentrations in tribes, villages, townlets, towns and Frontier Villages and UNRWA's installations and projects. Covering the ground in this way contributed towards a deeper understanding of the various problems. Unfortunately it proved impossible to go to the East Bank of the Hashimite Kingdom of Jordan. This potential handicap was compensated for by two factors. Firstly, in the period under review, the bulk of the refugees were concentrated in the West Bank. Secondly, a wide coverage of the subject was gained from the following combination of sources: The British Red Cross files, some UNRWA documents and government correspondence, interviews with people who served or lived in the East Bank, and of course the local press which reported on the kingdom as a whole.

The sources listed at the end of this book include the names of those archives consulted and the media researched by the author. For a comprehensive reading list and names of most interviewees, please see the author's University of London SOAS dissertation, which was used as a basis for this book.

The official maps which appear in the Appendices (hitherto unpublished) provide a previously unrecognized dimension to the story of the Palestinian refugees.

Acknowledgments

I would like to make a few respectful and grateful acknowledgments to Professor P. J. Vatikiotis, who helped me throughout the five years of this study; to Dr Abbas Kelidar for his tremendous help and encouragement, and my teacher, Prof. Uriel Dann of the Tel Aviv University, whose guidance I always sought.

A number of people have contributed to the research with their own time and expertise, giving me the benefit of their advice and supplying me with valuable material. A special word of thanks is in order to Antranig (Tony) Bakarjyan, the late Hazim al-Khalidi, the late Henry Knesevitz, Fransis Rahil and Dr Shawkat Kaylani, some of whom perhaps would disagree with part of my analysis. Needless to say, all remaining errors are my own.

Special thanks are due to UNRWA for all the facilities they gave me, and to all the local and international workers whose unfailing encouragement and advice I received.

I would like to express my deep gratitude to those working in the Israel State Archives for their patience and help, and to all those many other workers in the archives and libraries I consulted.

I am most grateful to Z. Bar-Lavi (Biver), T. Bakarjyan, A. Susser and the late H. Knesevitz, all of whom read the work, for their useful criticism and comments.

My sincere thanks to I. Rozenfeld for the help given in the preliminary stages of the field research; to Ilana and Dr Harry Levy who helped with the section on the relief operation which is not included, (but is to be published at a later stage); to R. Firth, Dr R. Jeffries, S. Miller and H. Silman for their invaluable help in the final editing of the work, and of course to Cheryl Mariner for her valuable assistance and tireless efforts in typing this study.

Finally I thank my in-laws, Sima and Shmuel Mandelsberg for their trust and aid, my parents Dora and Benjamin for their love and patience, and my wife for her devotion and encouragement, without which this work would never have come to fruition.

This work could not have been written without the financial support of: The Anglo-Jewish Association; B'nai B'rith Leo Baeck (London) Lodge, and the Hillel Foundation—Sydney Green Memorial Bursary (Ealing); Israel Foundations of Trustees (The Ford Foundation); The University of London Central Research Fund; Rotary Foundation of the Rotary International U.S.A. and the Herman de Stern Stiftung—Merkaz Vera Solomons (Foundation). Accordingly my deep gratitude to those responsible for this assistance.

London   A.P.

Due to the high cost of printing, it has been decided to eliminate diacritical marks in transliteration, except in a few cases where ambiguity could arise.

List of Abbreviations

A.C.	Area Commander
A.H.C.	Arab Higher Committee for Palestine
A.I.D.	United States Agency for International Development
A.P.G.	All-Palestine Government
B.C.C.	British Council of Churches
C.C.P.	U.N. Conciliation Commission for Palestine
C.L.	UNRWA Camp Leader
C.O.S.	Chief of Staff
D.G.	District Governor (Ministry of Interior) *Mutasarrif*
F.O.	Foreign Office
FV	Frontier Villages
G.R.C.	The General Refugee Congress (Ramallah)
H.G.R.C.	The Haifa and Galilee Refugees Committee in Nablus
H.K.J.	Hashimite Kingdom of Jordan
I.C.R.C.	International Committee of the Red Cross
J.C.P.	Jordanian Communist Party
J.D.	Jordanian Dinar
J.M.H.A.	Jerusalem Municipality Historical Archives
L.D.C.	The Lydda Displaced Committee in Nablus
L.P.	Islamic Liberation Party
L.R.C.S.	League of Red Cross Society
M.B.	Muslim Brotherhood Association
M.D.R.	Ministry of Development and Reconstruction
M.E.A.	Middle Eastern Affairs
M.E.J.	Middle East Journal
M.P.	Member of Parliament
N.E.	New East (*ha-Mizrah he-Hadash*) (*Quarterly*)
N.E.C.C.R.W.	*Near East Churches Council for Refugee Welfare*
N.E.R.S.	*Near East Radio Station (Sharq al-Adna)*
N.G.	*National Guard*
N.L.L.	*National Liberation League (Communist)*
N.S.P.	The National Socialist Party
P.A.W.A.	Palestine Arab Workers Association
Q.A.M.	The Arab Nationalist Movement
Q.S.P.	The Syrian Nationalist Party
R.C.H.	The Refugee Congress in the Hebron Region
R.O.	Region Officer (Ministry of Interior) *Qaymaqam*
S.A.JUPR	*Israel, State Archives–Unpublished Jordanian Records*
T.C.	*Town Council*
UNESCO	*United Nations Educational, Scientific and Cultural Organization*
U.N.E.S.M.	*United Nations Economic Survey Mission*

U.N.E.S.O.	*United Nations Economic and Social Office*
U.N.R.P.R.	*United Nations Relief for Palestinian Refugees*
UNRWA	*United Nations Relief and Works Agency for Palestine Refugees*
W.C.C.	*World Council of Churches*
W.H.O.	*United Nations World Health Organization*
YMCA	*Young Men's Christian Association*

Introduction

Conflicting Aspirations and their Realization

Abdullah's long-cherished goal, the creation of a Greater Syria which he envisaged as his empire,[1] had shaped his policies since he appeared in the area. Far from being content with the poor backward area of Trans-Jordan—specially created for him by the British—he longed to widen his domain and establish himself as a supreme ruler in the Arab world. Persisting in his efforts, Abdullah tried anxiously to persuade the British, as well as the Syrians, of their need for an expanded kingdom under his rule. He based his claim on his family origin (being a descendent of the Prophet which he felt entailed certain rights[2]), his loyalty to the Allies throughout the Second World War and the fact that he was the ruler of part of the area known then as Southern Syria. Despite all his efforts, he received a hostile response from the newly independent Syria and most other Arab countries, who were exasperated by his moves. Meanwhile, because of the rapid developments in Palestine towards the end of the British Mandate, Abdullah sought to ensure that the area allocated for the independent Arab State would become part of his sphere of influence.[3] He regarded his desired unified Arab Kingdom, to be achieved by the merging of Palestine and Trans-Jordan,[4] as the nucleus of an extended State. His attempts to stop the 1936 disturbances, along with other Arab leaders, were motivated by his desire to assume the role of mediator, showing Britain his growing influence. This kind of intervention resulted in the Arabization of the conflict between Arabs and Jews in Palestine. It was favoured by the British Administration, which hoped that the Arab rulers' moderate attitudes would have some impact on the local Arab community and undermine the Mufti, Hajj Amin al-Husayni's influence.

Abdullah had a common interest with the Nashashibi faction in Palestine, some of whom supported the idea of a unified geographical Syria, unlike their opponent the Mufti, the leader of the Husayni faction, who was struggling for an Arab State throughout Palestine. The absence of the Mufti made it easier for Abdullah to persuade the British, who held the deciding position, that he was the only one who could defend Arab and British interests in Palestine.

One of the British plans for a solution to the Palestinian Question proposed in September 1945 by the Foreign Office (F.O.), was a Federal union of three component parts: a Jewish area, an Arab area of Palestine (but not including the Jerusalem enclave) and Trans-Jordan—all under an Arab King. Yet the Cabinet soon ruled against it[5] and later referred the issue to the UN, advocating the establishment of a Trusteeship system in accordance with the San Francisco Charter.

The 1947 UN Partition Plan was vehemently rejected by all Arab governments and especially the Mufti-led Arab Higher Committee for Palestine (A.H.C.), since it involved the establishment of a Jewish State on what was regarded by the Arabs as their land. Although they were a small group, the Communists on both sides wholeheartedly supported the basic principles laid down by Partition.[6] Despite serious misgivings, the Jewish leadership also preferred the solution offered by this plan to no Jewish State at all, since it gave an immediate answer to the desperate predicament of thousands of homeless Jewish survivors of the Holocaust.

Yet it soon became obvious to all concerned that a peaceful settlement in Palestine was impossible because of the diametrically opposed national objectives. Tension increased between the two sides. Violence, arson, murder and counter reprisals conducted by irregular Arab and Jewish forces took place daily. An American last-minute attempt to establish a trusteeship failed and open war became inevitable. With the termination of the British Mandate on May 15, 1948 and the simultaneous proclamation of the State of Israel, the Arab invasion began, though for the inhabitants of Palestine hostilities had already commenced earlier.

A. NEUTRALIZING THE PALESTINIANS

Prior to their assault there was no unified Arab scheme in operation. The plan which had been proposed to satisfy both the demands and expectations of the Arab masses and also to serve as a threat to the Jews and to pressurize the West, was not supported by all Arab statesmen. Its implementation only exposed the differences among the Arab leaders, and those between them and the Palestinian leadership nominated by the Arab League. Regardless of all public or secret resolutions, the Arab countries had no intention of either granting the Palestinians any decisive role in the imminent war or any say in the political fate of Palestine.[7] For that matter it could further be argued that each Arab ruler dismissed any practical or immediate possibility of creating an Arab Palestine, certainly in the form envisaged by the Mufti.

The Palestinians were doomed to be crushed beneath the cumulative pressure of the pragmatic interests of particular Arab rulers, British interests, their own disunity and weakness, and the outcome of the war.

But what prevented the Arabs in Palestine from developing a united stand on the future of Palestine? Why and how were they denied a say as to their political future? Although the so-called 1936-9 Great Rebellion contributed enormously to raising the spirit of local Arab patriotism, it hardly outweighed the individualistic bias of the Palestinians.[8] The rivalry between different factions inevitably produced strong suspicion, fluctuating loyalties and continued competition, and considerably weakened the cohesive forces within the Palestinian community. The Palestinians were exhausted by their political feuds, fragmented internally and lacked a recognized leadership, since many of their leaders were deported, jailed or abroad. The renewal of the struggle in Palestine following the second World War was marked by the shifting of the political initiative from the Palestinian Arabs to the Arab States. Thus at the peak of its 'success', when it achieved the change in British policy towards the Jewish Question and the future of Palestine — expressed in the White Paper of 1939 – the Palestinian leadership began to lose its limited political power. The A.H.C. could not carry out any of its decisions, since it was completely dependent on the consent of the Arab regimes. It was unable to rely on local support and became a tool in the hands of those rulers who promised arms, ammunition and money whether or not they intended to provide it.

The mutual accusations concerning these consignments to the local population shed light on the deep-rooted suspicion and personal conflicts of those behind the local forces. Hajj Amin endeavoured to strengthen only those para-military bodies which accepted his authority. Local Arab centres where he did not enjoy full support were not supplied with arms, and had to purchase them in a flourishing black market where prices were soaring.

For their part, the Arab countries did not wish to see a strong Mufti, since he wanted to take advantage of the situation to further his own interests independently of the Arab League. The Palestinian Arabs could not really defend themselves without outside help, since they were poorly armed with a motley selection of weapons, and operated in small semi-organized forces under a divided command. They were led to believe that the Arab League would defend them. But the Iraqi and other Arab forces who arrived in some of the Arab towns to protect their inhabitants indulged in looting, theft and rape. They did very little to organise local defence, and by their violent behaviour, helped to weaken the Palestinians' determination, causing many of the rich and the more able to leave the towns and seek refuge abroad.

The same applied to the League's improvised force, "The Arab Army of Deliverance" *(Jaysh al-Inqadh al-Arabi),* under Fawzi Qauqji's command. The troops, composed of soldiers and volunteers who entered Palestine in January 1948, faced no British counter measures and succeeded initially in causing damage to the Jewish defenders. They failed, however, to crush the small Jewish forces and to occupy certain settlements as they had expected. The composition of this makeshift force, with its considerable mercenary element, together with the soldiers' pre-occupation with plunder, their lack of fitness, training and equipment, the quarrels amongst its different commanders and above all the disputes over its control and tasks, all served to reduce its military power and competence.

Whilst the killing and injury of Jews intensified the collective struggle of the Jewish community for an independent State, similar events on the other side, such as the Dayr Yasin village massacre had no such cohesive effect, in fact they had a detrimental impact on the already handicapped organizational capacity of the local Arabs. The intention of the wide publicity given by the Arab media to this slaughter was to reinforce the resistance of the Palestinian Arab populace to the Jews. As it turned out, it had the opposite effect. This news together with other rumours terrified the inhabitants, who feared a similar fate. Feeling betrayed by their absent local political leaders, with many of the villages' defenders operating away in the hills, the remaining local Arab population was unorganized and defenceless. This left them unable to muster any real military opposition to the Jews, although they did at times pose some danger to isolated Jewish settlements. The Israelis initially feared the power of the Arab population, but were to discover throughout the 1948 war that their local enemy was relatively passive in military terms, and reliant on the regular Arab forces from outside. Many of them soon fled out of fear, to nearby eastern protected Arab villages. There they joined many of their relatives and friends who had previously escaped in the bloody period of the first half of 1948.

The Palestinians' experiences made them realize that they would be safer elsewhere in spite of the publicity given to Qauqji's "achievements and conquests", the dubious "ability" of the Palestinian-led forces, and the presence of regular Iraqi troops. The increasing desertion of Arab areas reached new heights after Haifa and Jaffa fell into Jewish hands. This made it easier for the Israeli army to establish its position and advance its forces during the course of the coming war.

Qauqji's failure proved beyond doubt to the Arab leaders that the war they were about to launch would not be a "march into Palestine", and that the Jewish forces, for which they had so little regard, were far more formidable than they had thought.

Conflicting interests aside, it was felt that a unified Arab force composed of all Arab armies could corner Israel's small army and destroy her. But, owing to the rivalries and conflicting political aims among the Arab rulers, the scheme did not materialize. The Arab States enterd the war carefully watching each other's moves. The Syrians opposed King Abdullah's aspirations to conquer the land allocated to the Arab State of Palestine, which would also give him an outlet to the Mediterranean. Ibn Saud feared this for his own reasons, while Faruq was also troubled by Jordan's intentions and reluctantly joined the war against the advice of his officers.

To give Abdullah an advantage, the departing British permitted Jordanian troops to remain in Palestine, to ensure that hostile forces, whether Jewish or Arab, would not jeopardise the King's interests. The British, for their own strategic reasons, wanted him to seize territories outside the area allocated to the Arab State according to the Partition. But the King was fearful of going beyond the secret understanding he had reached with the Jews. Sober and shrewd, Abdullah always knew that the Arab leaders were deluded and dazzled by their own statements about the "40 million Arabs who will throw the Jews into the sea". He had a quite different appreciation of the Jews' determination and military ability, and was determined not to follow the Arab plan. He feared that not only would his forces be unable to prove a match for the Israelis beyond the areas in which they "consented" to his presence, but that such extensive military involvement could also endanger his grasp on the whole of Arab Palestine and Jerusalem. For he was aware of the limitations of his small army which could not be extended across a vast territory and still be expected to maintain law and order in the controlled areas of Palestine. With the consent of the Jewish leadership, the King was determined to occupy the area assigned to the new Arab State, prevent its coming into being, and make it part of his kingdom. He and the Jews both feared the possibility of having between them a state headed by the Mufti and this fear paved the way to their reciprocal understanding. Abdullah's contacts with representatives of the Jewish Agency, and his readiness for the attainment of a peaceful solution to the Palestinian Problem at the expense of the Palestinians, only intensified the fears of the competing Arab leaders. Hence the Arab armies' movements were dictated by their understanding of Abdullah's real aims, knowing that he had never really abandoned the Greater Syria scheme.

The renewed fighting after the first UN Truce from 10 June to 9 July brough about an Israeli occupation of areas outside the planned Jewish State of 1947, such as Lydda, Ramleh and Nazareth, thereby creating more refugees—many of whom were expelled. Whether through the fault of the Legion's British Commanders—Abdullah's version—or out of fear of weakening the Latrun garrisons and being defeated by the Israeli army with further losses—Glubb's version—Ramleh and Lydda were deserted by the Arab Legion. The Palestinians certainly felt that they were "sold out" by the

Hashimites and Great Britain, and Glubb has been a particular target for their hatred ever since.

Abdullah tried as far as possible to avoid fighting the Israeli forces in places where he knew they would have the upper hand. He decided to pay more attention to his left flank, where an Egyptian force was making some headway into the southern part of Palestine accompanied by the Muslim Brotherhood's troops (who generally supported the Mufti). The relations between the two countries had been poisoned just before the war, by Egypt's confiscation of a British consignment of ammunition intended for Jordan. The two armies tried to hamper each other's advance into Palestine. Abdullah decided to weaken the Egyptian forces by exposing them to the Israeli army. Rather than holding Israeli forces in static defence to allow further Egyptian advance, the King was more concerned with consolidating his own territorial gains. Abdullah later refused to help the besieged Egyptians in the Faluja pocket, thereby enabling the Israelis to obtain more land in the Negev.[9] Yet on the whole, and despite severe criticism, the Jordanian Legion emerged from the 1948 war as the only capable Arab army. However, the Palestinians themselves derived no consolation from comparisons with other Arab armies' achievements. On the contrary, Palestinians tended in interviews to minimize the Legion's success in battle, stressing that it was a political instrument in Abdullah's betrayal of them.

This bitter memory has coloured the attitude of the helpless Palestinians, and especially of the refugees, towards the Arab League in general and the Hashimites in particular. The Palestinians blamed both their old leadership and the Arab armies. The A.H.C. strongly criticised the Arab League and was also criticized by it[10]. Everyone accused everyone else, though a few called for self-criticism.[11]

The Communists were the most vociferous critics of the outcome of the 1948 war. Their illegal underground publications contained many articles which gave what they saw as the reasons for the weakness of the Arabs in general, and of the Palestinians in particular. Their newspaper al-Muqawamah al-Sha'biyyah, was published by the National Liberation League in Palestine[12] in the second half of 1949 and directed its attack against the old feudal leadership. They claimed it was guided by Britain and had "escaped the country with the sound of the first shot", taking the people's money and influencing others to leave Palestine "for a while" to return later. The articles criticized the Arab reactionaries who prevented any form of Arab unity and worked against the establishment of a Palestinian Independent State in accordance with the Partition Scheme. Thus, intrigues, personal rivalries and mutual distrust even undermined the unity which might have grown out of the Arab States' unanimous and unmitigated contempt for the Jews.

The 1948 war ended with a series of agreements between the two sides. Whilst the Armistice Agreements signed with Egypt, Syria and Lebanon were made more or less on the basis of their armies' existing positions, the border with Jordan was altered to Israel's advantage. Abdullah knew he could not extend his forces beyond their present positions to defend the area left by the withdrawing Iraqis, who refused to sign the agreements. He feared renewed fighting with the Israelis, and in order to secure his territorial and other achievements he was ready to sacrifice large areas of land at the expense of the Palestinians, fulfilling Israel's demands. Hence some villages formerly under the Iraqi army's protection in the "Triangle", as well as roads in the south, fell into Israeli hands.

During the negotiations which were held simultaneously in Amman and Rhodes, each side demanded and promised what it knew it would not be prepared to give or likely to get.[13] On signing the Agreement of April 1949, Israel gained vital eastern strategic points and vast areas beyond the proposed boundaries of 1947. Abdullah could now rule eastern Palestine, which was renamed as the "West Bank" of his kingdom, and the Palestinians there became his subjects.

Palestine was shattered and divided. The scattered Palestinians were left with nothing of their own. Most of them were to become dependent for their very survival on international relief, and their political future was in the hands of those Arab rulers whom they blamed for their disaster. The majority of refugees and non-refugees living in "partitioned" Palestine became either "Jordanian Citizens", "Israeli Arabs", or "Stateless Palestinians" in the Egyptian controlled Gaza Strip. Those living outside Palestine on Arab land other than Jordan, acquired the exclusive, naked status of "Palestinian Refugees". Regardless of their geographical position and political status, most of them became the responsibility of the international community. And the Palestinian Question became better known, in the vocabulary of the Arab-Israeli conflict propaganda, as the "Arab Refugee Problem".

B. THE GOVERNMENT OF ALL-PALESTINE

After the defeat there was little to unite the Arab countries. The fear that Abdullah might fulfil his objectives forced his Arab opponents to take measures against him. The only practical steps for them, at that stage, were to try to discredit him over the Palestinian issue. So they arranged for the formation of the All Palestine Government (A.P.G.) in the Egyptian-controlled Gaza Strip, and granted it immediate recognition. This brought the division between the Arabs into the open. Abdullah rejected the creation of this new body, which challenged his authority over the territories held by his army, and declared he would bar it there. He called for its dissolution, claiming it "was not democratically elected". He argued that its very existence implied a recognition by the Arab League and the Palestinians of the Partition Plan, and thereby of the Jewish State.[14] Such open recognition was unthinkable as it contravened the declared aims of the Arab nation.

The creation of the A.P.G. was announced by the Arab League on 22 September 1948. Based on the A.H.C., its members replaced the Administrative Council for Palestine set up in July. The new Cabinet, which had its seat in Gaza and declared Jerusalem as its capital,[15] included prominent Palestinians, some of whom had previously sided with Abdullah. It declared itself the sole representative of Palestine and all Palestinians. The Lebanese-born Ahmad Hilmi Pasha was its chairman, and Hajj Amin al-Husayni, returning to Palestine after eleven years absence, was elected as the President of the 86 member Constituent Assembly.[16] It was a dependent protegé of the Egyptian Government and, although they did not see eye-to-eye, both were determined to prevent the annexation of the Palestinian territories by Abdullah.

This Egyptian-sponsored government, whose "jurisdiction" encompassed a tiny enclave around the town of Gaza, had, in practice, no budget or army. The puppet government had no "country" to govern and existed only on paper. The whole attempt proved to be a farce as it could only function with the consent of the occupying Egyptian forces. Its importance lay, however, in maintaining the Palestinians' legitimate claims to a homeland. The Egyptians, whilst paying lip-service to its independence, held the A.P.G. on a short leash, manipulating and exploiting it against the Jordanian regime. For example, the sole reason for inviting the A.P.G. to the Arab League's meetings was to negate Jordan's claim to represent all Palestine. In this way, Egypt retained the confidence of the refugees under her control. The Gaza inhabitants appealed to be incorporated into Egypt.[17] But these desperate pleas of a population suffering from unemployment, economic hardship and numerous political social restrictions went unheard. Egypt conveniently regarded this area as part of Palestine.[18] Incorporating the Strip and its refugee population would, apart from harming the Palestinian cause, legitimize Abdullah's unrecognized annexation. And apart from not wanting the burden of the refugees, Egypt did not need to annex the Strip to run its affairs.

Yet the new government was gradually falling apart. The defeat of the Egyptians in the Negev caused some of the elected Ministers to desert Gaza and move to safer Arab capitals like Damascus, Beirut and Cairo. Some returned to Jordan,[19] hoping to be forgiven by the King. Even Hilmi was granted permission but feared the consequences of this move.[20] Using bribery to hire the support of those willing to transfer their loyalties, the Jordanian regime neutralized the political influence of the already insecure A.P.G. In order to further alienate the Mufti from those under his jurisdiction, the King appointed Shaykh Husam al-Din Jarallah as the Mufti of Jerusalem, and offered posts to some members of the A.P.G. Council who gradually changed sides. The A.P.G. was still losing support especially from the Palestinians both inside and outside[21] Jordan. Gradually more of its members moved to Amman, taking up the generous Jordanian propositions and accepting gestures of mercy.[22] Such counter measures proved an irreparable blow to the A.P.G. In fact it was inevitable that Abdullah would undermine the "high sounding but illusory 'All Palestine' Government",[23] since his army controlled most of Palestine and most Palestinians. Nevertheless, the Mufti represented an ominous background threat to his plans and prospects. The Jordanian authorities feared his intentions and influence, especially before the first elections[24] and after the King's assassination in 1951. They kept a careful watch on all former Mufti supporters during this period, both within and outside Jordan, using informers who had been closely connected with the A.H.C.[25] Abdallah al-Tall, who became a political exile, was tailed by the Egyptians as well as the Jordanians. The Jordanians were troubled by his reported connections with the Mufti in Cairo.[26] They were also concerned with the effect of the rumoured distribution of A.P.G.-printed money,[27] particularly since reports from Syria revealed that this clandestine body intended "to cause fright, sabotage, and harassment in Jordan and to distribute propaganda amongst the refugees stressing the British-Jordan connection". This action was to be assisted by Syrian Officers of the former Army of Deliverance and supported by Saudi Arabia.[28] But until Abdullah's murder, the A.H.C. had little success.

The Mufti hoped to turn his weakness into strength by winning Arab attention and respect for the Palestinian plight. He refused to play the expected role of manipulable ruler, or to comply with Egyptian restrictions on his freedom of movement, as he feared his position would be undermined. Despite his dependence on Egypt, he quarrelled with her and sought to create an alternative base elsewhere (at one time in Lebanon), from where he tried to operate against the Hashimites. However, the sending of petitions and cables became the main *modus operandi* of the A.P.G., a fact which further exposed its weakening position. The lack of response it received from the Palestinians demonstrated its loose hold on them. Without the support of either the Palestinians or the Arab States, it soon became a meaningless body. Its impotence helped Abdullah establish himself amongst the Palestinians. Four years after its creation the A.P.G. became a "department" in the Arab League. Theoretically it continued to exist,[29] but even its publications and cables appeared under the name of the A.H.C.

On the whole, the refugees were not attracted by the A.P.G.[30] because of its weakness and as it was led by those whom many held responsible for their tragedy. The refugees were more concerned with immediate problems of survival than with independence. They soon realized that "their" new government could offer no practical relief to alleviate their misery, nor could it decide their political future. Moreover, refugees were appalled by the high standard of living enjoyed by some of the A.P.G. members.

Abdullah took advantage of the A.P.G.'s dwindling impact in order to demonstrate his own strength both to the other Arab States as well as to all Palestinians. His personal victory was proof of his strength and skill as a leader: the Palestinians had to conform to his attitude and not he to theirs.

Chapter I

"Creeping Annexation" — The Policy and the Response

> "The Palestinians Arabs have at present no will of their own. Neither have they ever developed any specifically Palestinian nationalism. The demand for a separate Arab State in Palestine is consequently relatively weak. It would seem as though in existing circumstances most of the Palestinian Arabs would be quite content to be incorporated in Trans-Jordan".
>
> (Folke Bernadotte, *To Jerusalem*, p.113)

A. THE PALESTINIANS—WHAT CHOICE?

Abdullah neither trusted nor respected the Palestinians, but he knew he could not further his interests without establishing some base amidst them. His contacts with the Palestinian Arabs were intensified in the years leading up to the war.[1] They included overt and covert talks with members of the Nashashibi "opposition", local mayors, *mukhars*, with those who were disenchanted with the Husaynis and who had vested economic interests to protect, as well as with members of the A.H.C. Some showed support quite openly; others feared the consequences of doing this. Abdullah knew that if he could transform his influence into political power, which could only be achieved by the presence of his army in Palestine, he would enjoy more support from passive, conservative Palestinians. He was cautious in preparing the ground for his ambitions in Palestine, and preferred his supporters to come to him without invitation. This did not stop him from openly giving donations to anti-Mufti organs such as Muhammad Nimr al-Hawari's[2] para-military *al-Najjadah*, or small contributions to the Negev bedouin who suffered from the drought.[3] Furthermore he rejected the A.H.C.'s policy of issuing "Departure Permits" only to the old, the women and the children of the Palestinian population,[4] hoping thus to be more popular with the helpless refugees. Before the war, refugees enjoyed a warm welcome, including some relief, in the Jordanian-controlled territories. Yusuf Haykal and

Edmond Rok, prominent Jaffa refugees, were nominated to head a short-lived "Palestine Office" in Amman for the "recruitment of refugees and information", which in fact concentrated mainly on organizing limited immediate relief. And the King's personal donations to the refugees in April 1948,[5] were given wide publicity by the media.

Details were also given of the growing numbers of refugees and local delegations visiting him in Amman to express their fears, and request his intervention and aid. The rumours of enforced conscription and hard treatment of refugees in the other Arab countries only highlighted Abdullah's different attitude towards them. But, doubting their loyalty, he refused to arm them and even confiscated all weapons after announcing the dismissal of Qauqji's army. Abdullah also feared that the Mufti's forces, known as "The Sacred Struggle" (al-Jihad al-Muqaddas), would run subversive operations behind the advancing Legion and endanger his domination. So he ordered and forcibly secured their disbandment.[6] After the Jordanian "invasion" an administration was set up to maintain law and order and to neutralize as far as possible any local initiative which supported the establishment of an autonomous Palestine.

B. THE PALESTINIAN CONGRESSES

In September 1948 Shaykh Sulayman Taji al-Faruqi stated "on behalf of the refugees in Jordan" that they "opposed any Palestinian Government created by leaders who (had) deserted them and escaped to safe places", and called upon King Abdullah to ensure their rights under him.[7] A week later the "First Palestinian National Congress" convened in Amman to repudiate the A.P.G. and express loyalty to Abdullah. Many took part in the Congress because they were either ordered or expected to do so.[8] It received wide publicity on Ramallah Radio, which deliberately omitted certain items concerning the A.P.G.'s activities,[9] and exaggerated the number of participants in order to give an impression of strong support for the King.

Ajaj Nuwayhid, a Druze, acted as the Congress's Secretary and was its driving force. He stated that the A.P.G. was formed against the wishes and interests of all Arabs, and that a Palestinian Government, providing it was chosen by all Palestinians, should be formed only after the country had been completely liberated by the Arab States.[10] The Congress protested against the Egyptian Prime Minister's recognition of the A.P.G., requested recognition from the Lebanese Government,[11] and notified the UN that Abdullah was the only one allowed by the Palestinians to speak and act on their behalf.[12] The fact that people such as Yusuf Haykal, the Mayor of occupied Jaffa, Ahmad al-Khalil and Sulayman Tuqan (who had refused the post of Minister in the A.P.G.) actively took part in the Amman Congress gave weight to its impact.

Similar views were expressed by inhabitants of Jerusalem, al-Bira and Jenin, when they were visited by the Jordanian Governor General of

Palestine. There were votes of thanks to the "redeeming" King on the radio, which also reported on the many delegations of both refugees and non-refugees, who came to the King to pay their respects and express support. The Hashimite Propaganda Association, headed by Ali Khalaf and composed of local mayors and notables from the Ramallah area, also came to see Abdullah. They called him "Saviour of Palestine" and trusted that he would solve the Palestinian Problem by peace or war, and regard the inhabitants of Jordan and Palestine as one nation to be led by one leader.[13] A similar declaration came from Abd al-Karim al-Alami, "the Ramleh Lydda representative". The Jaffa refugees in Ramallah also told the military Governor there that they gave the King full authority to represent them.[14] Delegates from Jerusalem, Ramallah, Dayr Ghassanah, Amwas, Hebron, Bethlehem and Bayt Jala followed suit.[15] Most of these statements, like many others which followed, were organized and encouraged by the new administration. Furthermore, some of the representatives were self-appointed and concerned only to represent themselves, even if they also honestly supported the King. Many people were indifferent or did not make up their minds, not wanting "to commit themselves"; but they were left with little choice. Nonetheless, contrary to the widely-held belief outside Jordan, these various representatives did reflect the feelings of a large segment of the population.

The authorities vacillated over the next move.[16] Abdullah was also troubled as to how Great Britain and the U.S.A. regarded annexation. He hoped Great Britain would extend its Defence Agreement with Jordan to include the West Bank[17] and that the U.S.A. would grant Jordan recognition.[18]

The King therefore decided to prepare a large demonstration in support of himself. Since his direct involvement aroused the inhabitants' suspicion, he used the services of his loyalists, Nuwayhid and the mayor of Hebron, Shaykh Muhammad Ali al-Ja'bari, who had decided to join him after participating in the Gaza meeting. The Congress's setting and procedure were carefully calculated. Abdullah had to prove he was not imposing his will on the Palestinians and that they did not recognize him merely because they were under occupation.

The Second Palestinian Arab Congress, known as "The Jericho Congress" or "Ja'bari's Conference", was called by the Executive of the First Palestinian Arab Congress to assemble on December 1, 1948. It encompassed "delegations from all parts of Palestine, true representatives of all the Arabs living in her, and the refugees who were present owing to the existing conditions".[19]

The preceding preparations were designed to ensure a high attendance and to make clear the manner and purpose of the gathering. Government officials went to villages and refugee concentrations and assembled *mukhtars* and notables. Some of them had to be persuaded to give their much-needed support; a few others joined the small but prominent group of

Communist and Ba'th supporters, who made their position clear by remaining absent. To avoid that kind of protest, more dubious forms of pressure were exerted.[20] Transport was arranged and the Press attended. In the end there were hundreds of delegates—sufficient to emphasize the wide support for the policy.

The resolutions were to provide the juridical base for the Union. All Jordanian sources naturally stress that the King was requested by the Palestinians to unite the two parts into a single state, and that he decided to respond to this request. Since the terms "democracy" and "representative", in the form widely accepted and understood in the West, do not really exist in the Arab countries, it seems perhaps pointless to ask the oft-raised question: Was the Jericho Congress a "democratic" one and did the participants "represent" the Palestinians and their position? However, such gatherings were in fact the accepted way in which these communities were represented. In all events the Congress did include some of the regimes' opponents. Abdullah wanted them there to give the "accepted" resolutions a "democratic" flavour which would weaken his rivals in Gaza. A conference without opposition would not have had the same desired legitimacy. For this reason the King wanted representatives of all areas and interests to be there—bedouin, villagers and town-dwellers, Christians and Muslims, property-owners as well as the poor, Nashashibi and Husaynis, refugees and non-refugees.

The resolutions reflected both the monarch's policy and the Palestinians' inability to come up with any viable alternative. Only in this sense could it be said to represent the view of most Palestinians. The debate around the resolutions was far from dull or one-sided. Ja'bari's speech argued for the union of Palestine and Jordan as part of Southern Syria and stressed that Abdullah was the master of the Palestinians' destiny. This was opposed by some delegates, mainly from Ramallah and Jerusalem, who would only recognize him as their supreme ruler on condition that he "liberated the whole of Palestine"[21]. However, since the Congress had to present an image of unity, disagreements had to be avoided and the delegates' reservations were only vaguely embodied in the resolutions[22] to satisfy the parties concerned.

The original text of the resolutions ends with a declaration of allegiance *(bay'ah)* and calls for the immediate implementation of all decisions. Yet these were not the resolutions which had already been broadcast on Ramallah Radio. The text was again changed when it received wide publicity in December. This last text emphasized the idea that "Palestine was part of Natural Syria[23] which was divided up by the Mandate, which ended on 15.5.48, when a chance was given for either the establishment of an independent State or the merger with one of the Arab Countries". The new resolution said that the Congress wanted a united kingdom under Abdullah in the spirit of the historical connections between the two areas.[24] Additional changes were injected when the new text was broadcast, also expressing no-confidence in the A.H.C. and the A.P.G., and giving the King full authority to solve the Palestinian Problem.[25] These changes aggravated several prominent participants. A letter of formal complaint was sent to the Prime Minister on December 9 by Musa Husayni, whose unauthorised signature remained on the new text. He protested at the difference between the versions published in the Press and those sent to the Arab countries. Being a member of the Drafting Committee, he went on to emphasize that the agreed resolutions could not be changed and that "the subject of Greater Syria or Natural Syria is not contained in the real Congress's resolutions".[26] However, the inconsistency of the three versions was proof of the King's absolute control and exposed the virtual impotence of any opposition.

The Congress completely upset the already strained relations between Jordan and the Arab League. Apart from their uneasiness about Abdullah's Palestinian solution, the League members were naturally sensitive to his oft-repeated and widely publicized desire to annex Syria.[27] Egypt tried to get the al-Azhar *ulama* to impose religious sanctions against his steps,[28] but to counter this Abdullah managed to receive the support of the Supreme Muslim Council of Palestine for the union.[29] In order to strengthen Jordan's position against the growing discontent among the League's members, a third Conference was convened in Nablus on December 28, 1948, following the Parliament's and the Cabinet's approval of the Jericho Conference Resolutions. The gathering, chaired by Sulayman Tuqan, upheld the previous conferences' calls for unity with Jordan. In October 1949, Abdullah visited the West Bank and was greeted by many refugee delegations. After the visit Tawfiq Tuqan, "the refugees' representative in Jordan", cabled the King and asked him on behalf of the refugees to be their ruler, and to do his utmost in the forthcoming UN General Assembly to enable them to return to their homes.[30]

Despite these manifestations of public support, it should be remembered that a few prominent Communists and Ba'thists (who formed the core of any opposition) were arrested; and that, as newspapers were shut down when they contained anti-regime criticism, there was little chance of any discontent with the idea of annexation being openly expressed. The Communists, nevertheless, managed to publish a number of handouts denouncing Abdullah's creeping annexation.

Another kind of resentment came from those who were uprooted from their villages because of the Armistice Agreement, particularly in the "Triangle".[31] They protested bitterly against the Agreement's implementation and the fact that they had not been consulted.[32] Following some bitter denunciations and expressions of fierce opposition to the Hashimite regime's Agreement, those whose vast lands were trapped behind the newly established Armistice Line in the Tulkarm and Jenin areas, set up a committee to challenge the King's decision. In April 1949, when a delegation of northern West Bank mayors met with King Abdullah they urged him to arrange for free passage for the land owners, and questioned the accuracy of the maps because each map, supposedly "agreed upon", showed different borders. Every change in the map could decide the destiny both of hundreds of thousands of *dunam* and of many people.[33] The Executive Committee of the Arab Land Owners, Farmers and Citrus Grove Growers' Congress convened in Nablus. Their President, Radi al-Nabulsi, and Secretary, Mustafa Irshayd, presented the District Governor (D.G.) with their emphatic demands.[34]

Another such attempt at collaboration between land-owners and proprietors occurred in Jerusalem[35] but, like those in Nablus, they could do very little to reverse the situation. They continued to do the only thing they could, that is to send petitions to the UN and the Press. They had to be very careful about the way these were phrased, since they had to take into account the new regime's sensitivity to any open anti-Government criticism. They hoped to be assisted somehow by the other Arab countries which rejected the annexation.[36]

The Arab League tried to belittle the importance of the Congresses and maintained that the resolutions did not reflect the will of most Palestinians. But further expressions of support were cabled and broadcast to contradict these claims.[37]

So the annexation became more of a problem between Jordan and the other Arab countries, than between Abdullah and the Palestinians. When the merger was almost finalized, Egypt organized the other Arab States and tried to expel Jordan from the Arab League. Jordan was charged with annexing Arab Palestine against the League's declared policy, and holding secret talks with Israel.[38] Such indictments were intended to discredit Abdullah in the eyes of his new subjects, who would hopefully turn against him. However, he was not deterred by the League's resolutions and threats, and ignored all protests. The League realized it was too weak to impose anything on him which would prevent these final steps. The Iraqi P.M., Nuri Sa'id, therefore engineered a kind of compromise, reached without Jordan, which was contingent upon a declaration that Jordan would not undertake separate peace negotiations with Israel, and that its actions would not prejudice the final settlement of the Palestine issue. The League's declaration regarded the West Bank as a pledge in the hands of Abdullah "until the liberation of Palestine". It did not compel Jordan to ratify or reverse any of its administrative measures.

However, protests and compromises were to no avail. Annexation, or "the Union", was already a *fait accompli,* and the regime pursued its policy while continuing to assure its new citizens that their rights in Palestine were safeguarded.[39] To counter the impact of any bitterness or unrest, a large meeting of refugee property-owners was organized in Hebron on March 11, 1950 under Ja'bari's auspices. It included many who had suffered great losses as a result of the Armistice Agreement, and who announced their rejection of any organization of refugees which did not accord with the Jericho conference resolutions. They further requested King Abdullah to continue to represent them.[40] Such calls were followed by declarations from the Jaffa Refugee Committee in Nablus, which, reminding the League of the refugees' expulsion from their homes, stated:

> And now we prefer to be the masters of our fate and decide ourselves on our destiny . . . and we want our beloved King Abdullah . . . and want you to accept our acceptance and if not we shall withdraw our confidence in you.[41]

There were also a few articles in the Press supporting the merger.[42] Similar declarations, whether initially proposed by the regime[43] or motivated by personal interests, fear, respect or genuine support, reflected, more than anything else, the perplexed and ineffectual position of the Palestinians as a group. This was even more true of the Palestinian refugees.

C. THE REFUGEES, THEIR LEADERS AND THEIR COMMITTEES

Some 450,000 refugees arrived in Jordan, joining a similar number of indigenous Palestinians and some 400,000 Trans-Jordanians. They came from a mixture of backgrounds: some were bedouin (nomadic or semi-nomadic), some villagers, some town-dwellers. The urban refugees generally moved into towns after they had fled. They constituted some 30 per cent of the refugee population. These were the educated professional classes, merchants, landowners, artisans and shopkeepers, who, like the Christian refugees, never lived in the camps. The rest were either dispersed in the villages or lived in nearby concentrations. About one third, almost all of them villagers, ended up in organised camps. These, the more conservative, unskilled, illiterate and poor segment of the refugees, regarded everyone outside the camp with suspicion.

On the whole, up to the official annexation in April, 1950, the various refugee organisations and regroupings showed little solidarity or cohesion. A major reason for this was the fact that the refugees in the various concentrations had come from many different places[44] and were now living together through force of circumstances. Hence, deep-rooted suspicion, mistrust and envy soon developed among the refugees. This inevitably led to friction between town-dwellers and peasants, villagers and bedouin, refugees in the camps and those outside them, the poor and the rich, Christians and Muslims. There was also conflict between Government-nominated and refugee-elected representatives. Each group worked for their own personal or sectarian interests, which could only produce a general pattern of internal division among the refugees.

It was a number of years before a Palestinian leadership came into prominence which was young, vocal, vindictive, intelligent, westernized and contemptuous of their elders' policies and personalities. But they were also sharply divided. However, until the mid-1950s, when the UNRWA teachers emerged as new leaders who opposed the elderly, the old, recognized leaders generally retained their influence and position, and competed amongst themselves with little challenge from others.

Before the war, the structure of village society was strongly patriarchal. The clan *(hamulah)* was the highest unit and commanded great loyalty. Villages were run by a council of elders which included the most important and respected members of each clan. Depending on its size, each village had one to three *mukhtars*. They were by no means leaders, yet held positions of authority and were entrusted with certain administrative duties by the mandatory Administration concerning local village affairs. When the village scattered, nothing remained of these institutions, and the shattered peasant refugees regrouped to form new composite communities.

The ordinary refugee, shocked by the disaster, had no real say in his political future. Basically, he was not particularly interested in the political developments going on around him, preoccupied as he was with his struggle for survival. He did not trust the politicians, fatalistically believed that God would relieve his plight, and continued to yearn for the time when things would improve and he could return home. He trusted that until then the Jordanian authorities would see to it that he would not be deserted by the UN and other relief Agencies. Hence any attempt to organize these refugees or represent them was greeted with suspicion.

Essentially, there were two quite different considerations which motivated the refugees to organize themselves: the one was mainly concerned with daily needs and, directed at the Red Cross and the UN, aimed at securing the continuation and expansion of the relief operation; the other tried to secure or regain lost property and assets left on the other side of the border, and was directed chiefly at the West, Israel and the Jordanian Government through expressions of political separatism. In the camps they were more concerned with the former, outside them with the latter.

1. Camp Committees

For the first few months following the War, the refugees tried to organize themselves wherever they were, to ensure a continuous flow of food and relief. They formed *ad hoc* "committees", composed of notables and *mukhtars* chosen to represent their places of origin. Their purpose was to protect the interests of each former village in the distribution of essential relief items, and to serve as a channel through which complaints and requests to the authorities and the Red Cross could be made. These bodies did not seek, at this stage, to engage in politics *per se,* but rather in, what might be termed, "the politics of relief".

To cope with the disorganized and chaotic situation, the Red Cross[45] set up more highly centralized Area Refugee Relief Committees, with local branches. These were composed mainly of local town-dwellers and prominent educated refugees, assisted by the *ad hoc* committees and other groupings organized according to their places of origin. The latter were established to deal solely with their scattered relatives: the Jaffa Refugee Committee in Ramallah was of this kind, as were the Jaffa Committees in Jerusalem and Nablus. The Area Relief Committees survived for about a year, and disappeared as the local population became tired of serving on them, or, as more often happened, the Government terminated their mandate. The first to be set up, as well as to be disbanded, was the Jericho Committee.[46]

Dissatisfied with the Area Committees' services, the camp refugees insisted that only their own representatives should be assigned to handle the relief operation. The Jordanian files contain numerous such petitions.[47] However, many of the refugee committees nominated in response to such appeals soon dissolved. Their members resigned[48] or were dispersed by the authorities after accusations of corruption and favouritism.[49] New ones emerged.

The fact that the committees were composed of people from different socio-economic backgrounds, whether elected by refugees or selected by the authorities, was sufficient reason for new and old rivalries to be sharpened. The representatives did not trust one another, neither were they trusted by the refugees, nor by the authorities, nor, for that matter, by the relief Agencies. Many quarrels centred around "payoffs" in the rapidly growing black market. Hence mutual suspicion amongst the different refugee concentrations and conflicts over the composition of the committees (which consisted mainly of the old) prevented agreement on refugee representation to deal with basic relief problems, let alone any other concerns.

For their part, the camp inhabitants were aware that these committees in practice played a limited role in their communities. Some committees, however, maintained a measure of importance and spoke on behalf of the refugees when the camps were visited by the authorities or the Press.[50] More particularly, the committees survived if they showed support for the authorities, and did not cause the Red Cross any real problems.

The composition of these camp committees varied from place to place. If their members were elected, the committees represented the various interests of groups existing in a given concentration. If nominated, they were the government's "yes" men who were very carefully chosen[51] and were used to weaken other influential figures.

The old *mukhtars* and the other influential elders feared any rival authority and therefore sought to represent refugees in all affairs by nominating themselves. Some of them were renominated by the authorities as *mukhtars*. The refugees' sensitivity as to who became a *mukhtar* was due to the fact that this post gave its occupant considerable power[52] over his brothers, who then became dependent on him in many ways. Those *mukhtars* cut off from their old constituencies or simply not favoured by the regime, anxiously clung to the title as a symbol of their past influential status.

When approaching the Government, they attempted to appear as the sole representative of their villages, and similarly, tried to persuade the villagers that they were the only channel to the government. This soon became another source of friction between former and newly-selected *mukhtars,* each of whom tried to harm the other's position. In the early days this occurred when a refugee village's inhabitants arrived at an established camp. In Jalazun Camp, for example, a *mukhtar* of a small village which was among the first to form that camp, was renominated,[53] while other larger groups who had come later were not necessarily or immediately represented amongst new *mukhtars* or even on the committees.[54] So the nomination of *mukhtars* and committees always caused jealousy.

The committees were meant to provide for the representation of conflicting interests. The permanent refugee camp committees grew out of the *ad hoc* committees, and included all *mukhtars* and a few notables. In order to encompass all the competing groups, the committees sometimes became large and unwieldy. Even then, they faced criticism from dissatisfied parties. For example the Fawar Camp Committee, which had 55 representatives and published its own constitution,[55] soon confronted opposition within the camp from another group claiming to be the true representatives of the refugees there.[56] Under these conditions, and with endless disputes over representation, it was difficult to function effectively. The Government grew impatient and dispersed some of the committees; others were nominated in their place, however,[57] since they remained essential for the relief operation right through the 1950s.

Over and above the village and clan-orientated organizations, two other, more political types of organizations deserve attention: the regroupings of the old power structures and organizations which had existed in the refugees' places of origin; and the Area Refugee Committees which tried to represent the refugees' immediate and wider interests, and sought political recognition for this purpose. Although they also dealt with relief issues, the latter should be distinguished from the combined I.C.R.C. and Government-sponsored Area Committees which dealt solely with relief.

2. Regroupings of old frameworks

These included attempts to revive older bodies such as the Palestinian Arab Villagers League, the Haifa Cultural Association in Nablus[58] and the Jaffa-Muslim Sport Club in Ramallah.[59] The authorities, wanting to eradicate any exclusive Palestinian movement, regarded them with great suspicion. It seems that the administration, which carefully examined every licence application, was aware that such bodies were attempting gradually to acquire the position of sole legitimate representatives on broader issues, which had little to do with sport or culture. Refugees who initiated such regroupings felt it safer to revive well-respected recognized bodies. They hoped these would gain recognition from the government which was eager to win support. As it turned out, these bodies were not allowed to engage in politics and soon disintegrated. Furthermore, the authorities did not allow the formation of new bodies, both because they triggered off opposition from existing organizations which felt their positions threatened, and because they encouraged similar requests. As a result, the D.G. was even reluctant to license a refugee social club in Hebron,[60] and reviewed any application for similar clubs in the camps with great caution.[61]

3. Area Committees

These fall into two general categories: those primarily interested in defending their property rights in Israel; and those which concentrated more on relief matters. Both kinds sought official recognition as refugee representatives in order to emphasise their refugee status and secure their political rights. They therefore avoided any activity which could be interpreted as hostile to the regime and provoke their dispersal. However, they did not intend to allow their new Government to represent them in all spheres of action. The property-owners, who did not trust the authorities, did their utmost to preserve their autonomy even after the official annexation.

The first centralized committee to get involved in politics and express separatist notions was established in February 1949 in Ramallah and was mainly composed of property-owning refugees. For the first few months it was busy organizing relief. It intensified its activity during the period before the Lausanne Conference, which provided a catalyst for the property-owning refugees to organize their own representation. The first General Refugee Congress (G.R.C.), attended by some 500 delegates, was held in Ramallah on 17 March, Muhammad Nimr al-Hawari was elected President, and Yahya Hamudah and Aziz Shihadah as his deputies. The executive was empowered by the delegates to represent and negotiate on behalf of the refugees in all matters concerning them.[62] But it seems that other area refugee committees were disenchanted with this kind of initiative, for it weakened their own political position as refugee spokesmen. Consequently the next meeting extended an open invitation to all the refugee committees in Jordan, and called for the incorporation of refugee representatives from all other Arab Countries. This would make the G.R.C., whose status was declining, able to represent all refugees wherever they were. Its hopes were that, if this were achieved, its negotiating power would be considerably strengthened.

The fact that the Ramallah Refugee Congress was empowered to negotiate with Israel in Lausanne, independently of the occupying Jordanian regime, demonstrates that the representation of refugees was still a moot point. In the view of the Congress, accepting the Jordanian representative meant accepting annexation with all that it entailed and losing the right to a separate refugee body. Prior to the Lausanne talks, the G.R.C. sent delegates to Lebanon and Syria. But they failed to organize a united refugee delegation or to consolidate their position as a focal organization.

The conference which followed the Rhodes Agreement seemed at first to raise hopes for a peaceful solution between the Arab States and Israel. The Palestinians as such were not invited. Yet some three independent refugee delegations came,[63] and, regardless of their status, held talks with all parties. But they were soon ignored and mistreated by the Arab delegations which had their own advisory refugee contingent.[64] The Israeli Mission held talks with them merely "unofficially", as Israel maintained it wanted to discuss the refugee question, like all others, with sovereign Arab States only. Granting an official position to the Palestinians would be counter-productive for any State wanting to do away with the 1947 Partition Plan. Moreover, Israel felt there was no real basis for any agreement with the G.R.C., since it would have neither the support of the mass of poor refugees, nor of the Jordanian regime[65] — which Israel wanted to strengthen.

The Jordanians threatened to leave the talks if the refugees took part.[66] A separate refugee delegation from the West Bank could only undermine their pretensions to represent *all* Palestinians. At first the Jordanian authorities had refused to let the G.R.C. delegates join in the Conference. Later they granted permission, but soon realized the potential damage, both within and outside Jordan, which could be caused by the G.R.C.'s openly hinted acceptance of the Partition. Each declared that they alone were authorized to represent the refugees in Palestine and Jordan. Owing to these repeated and widely publicized challenges, and Hawari's claim that he was granted permission to speak by the Egyptian Government, the Jordanian authorities quickly tried to cut the G.R.C. off from its Ramallah base. Its office was closed down for a while and its contents confiscated. Rumours were spread that the G.R.C. members were about to "sell out" to defend the property interests and frozen assets of rich refugees,[67] and they were labelled as traitors and "Israeli agents". The underground Communist paper *al-Muqawamah al-Sha'biyyah* viciously attacked them in an article entitled "Who does the Refugee Congress Serve?"[68] And Kamal Nasir, in his article "Don't Go", scorned the refugee representatives, saying that the refugee problem was an Arab problem and therefore a solution could only be reached by the Arab States.[69] Deprived of public support and official standing, the refugee delegations were forced to desert the international arena. The refugee problem was left to be discussed between those held responsible for its creation.[70]

The implications of the Lausanne affair for the refugees were threefold: first, it again proved their dwindling and helpless political position as partners to the conflict, since the Arab countries as well as Israel refused to recognize them as a separate delegation; second, it showed that many refugees, particularly the large property owners who had great vested interests in the outcome of such talks, refused to accept the Arab Governments' control of their affairs (especially Jordan); and last, that even the common pragmatic interests of the refugee delegations were insufficient to overcome their inner differences.

In order to strengthen its ties with the Arab countries, the G.R.C. decided to send a delegation to the next Arab League meeting; it hoped to become a member of the Council and press their demand for the return of all refugees. This emphasis was to show the poor refugees—who regarded them with great suspicion—that the G.R.C. intended to represent their plight and not betray them once an agreement for compensation was achieved. Further-more, the G.R.C. condemned all the resettlement plans—which as would be shown, the Jordanians tacitly supported—thus once more indirectly criticizing the Jordanian regime.[71] It also rejected the Israeli position on the refugee question, perhaps to acquire more credibility amongst the refugees. In September the Congress was expanded to include delegates from the Nablus area and other prominent refugees. In October it published a detailed statement of its aims and policy,[72] which clearly indicated that it did not intend to surrender to the pressures exerted on it.

It seems the Government at that stage preferred a strong body operating inside Jordan which would weaken the A.H.C.'s position. They therefore allowed the G.R.C. to function within certain limits. The G.R.C. was aware of these limitations, and therefore softened its indirect criticism of Jordanian policy in order to survive. Yet it continued to challenge the regime's right to represent the refugees internationally. The G.R.C. also called for an alteration of the Armistice Lines to conform with the Partition Plan and to facilitate the return of refugees to the areas reinstated.[73]

As the 1950 elections approached, the G.R.C. realised that such declarations did little to increase its dwindling support among the mass of refugees who were preoccupied with the relief issues it had neglected. In the hope of improving its bargaining position with the Government, the G.R.C. again sent messengers to the camps to re-establish its grass-roots support. But after their abortive international experience it was difficult to claim representative status, for other camp and area committees were now firmly established. Even if such committees came to the G.R.C. meetings, they did not intend amalgamating with the G.R.C. as was hoped. Its image was further damaged by Hawari's desertion, the news of its contacts with Israel and the members' eagerness to protect their property. By now, successful Government policy had restricted its activity and further weakened the organization.

And so, until the annexation, the Congress's main activity consisted of sending petitions and speaking on behalf of a particular group of property-owners. But even in this they were not alone. A different and far more complicated situation obtained in Hebron. In contrast to the G.R.C., in which the most prominent people were educated town-dwelling property-owners, those trying to form committees in Hebron were village property-owners, who had been powerful leaders in the places they had left. They split into two groups: the very large property-owners and the rest. The first group stipulated a property qualification of some 200 *dunam* as a condition of membership, and this led to protests from other refugees. The authorities, after failing to unite the two groups, authorised[74] the second group to set up The Refugee Congress in Hebron (R.C.H.), which stressed its intention to assist the refugees with their return and compensation.[75] On 8 July 1949 a meeting of 600 delegates accepted a constitution.[76] It was made clear that all the local committees were to be affiliated to this umbrella organisation, and that the R.C.H. would represent them "before any official and unofficial bodies".

Following this congress, the authorities confronted protests from other refugee notables from the Hebron who opposed the R.C.H. This was another reason why the R.C.H. failed to receive the regime's official recognition although it expressed full support for Abdullah. This upset the relations between the R.C.H. and the authorities, and each side feared the other's intentions. Following a long correspondence between them, the R.C.H. changed tactics and demanded the formation of a Relief Committee which would be composed of their members. This was accepted, as the authorities feared strong reactions from the refugees if they thwarted a body such as the R.C.H., concerned with helping them. Nonetheless, this new grouping never received official recognition. The R.C.H. continued to assemble and send petitions on behalf of the refugees, complaining about the Red Cross relief machinery. They soon became more militant and tried to organize a demonstration against the I.C.R.C., but this was discouraged by the authorities. The refugee leaders, for their part, were displeased with Government attempts to control their actions and undermine their already weakening position. Nevertheless, the support of the ordinary conservative refugees allowed them to operate more cohesively than committees in many other areas. But the fact remained that, despite its consistent attention to relief matters, the R.C.H. was gradually losing its influence. This was because of the disputes between the affiliated committees, and because only a few of its executive members lived in the area's camps.

A different rivalry existed in the town of Nablus between the vociferous refugee committees. As elsewhere, it was not long before there was strife between the refugee leaders and the local notables who initially handled the relief operation. The refugee representatives felt ignored and made accusations of corruption and favouritism in an attempt to establish themselves as the only refugee spokesmen. Unlike other places, Nablus had a large contingent of local people amongst the refugees (who returned from Haifa and other coastal towns where they were employed). In addition, capable leaders from Jaffa and Haifa tried to organize themselves on the basis of their places of origin. Hence different refugee committees were set up: The Lydda Displaced Committee (L.D.C.), the Haifa and Galilee Areas Refugee General Committee,[77] and another two committees representing Dar al-Hijrah and Askar Camps. Attempts to reconcile their differences and set up a united body were fruitless.[78]

The L.D.C. was affiliated to a political grouping called the Palestine Arab Workers Association (P.A.W.A.) led by Husni al-Khufash, who tried to set up an all-refugee committee. The P.A.W.A. was trying to recruit support and enlarge its own membership amongst the refugees in Nablus by intervening on their behalf. It caused the authorities as well as the other refugee committees many problems. The committees feared that Khufash's strengthening position would weaken their own, and the Government was worried that if the more conservative elements were pushed aside, he would manipulate the refugees for his own purposes. (Eventually he was arrested along with some of his friends—the fate of many "trouble-makers".)

The Haifa and Galilee Refugee Committee's (H.G.R.C.) articles of association stipulated that those who co-operated with the Jews or were members of political parties were to be barred from becoming representatives (which excluded mainly the Communists). The Committee called for active support and said it would exist for as long as the refugee question remained unsolved.[79] Yet its constant interference in refugee problems, especially concerning the census, relief distribution and housing, led to an unsettling of its relations with the authorities, who were becoming more and more exasperated with the various area refugee committees.

Another different kind of area committee, organized by local non-refugees, was the East Jerusalem Villages Executive. This most persistent and vociferous committee aspired to recognition as a *refugee* body in order to acquire relief for the Frontier Villages and the bedouin in the Jerusalem area. In general, the bedouin tended to hold their own gatherings, meeting *en masse* only a few times during the period.

In the East Bank there were no attempts to organize area refugee committees. The only exceptions were the occasional calls[80] from refugees there to allow the convening of an East Bank Congress which could represent them in front of the international Agencies.[81] To complicate the whole pattern further, there were refugee committees in practically every village, most of which died away after a year or two.[82] Some bodies collapsed after they were initially convened, or after a particular purpose was completed. The refugee congress in Bayt Jala, which convened only once on 8 September 1949 to protest against the Red Cross,[83] is an example of the first type, and the Jericho Area Refugee Committee, of the second.

The Jericho refugees tried to organize themselves just for the Parliament Elections. Again they were divided. In this area, where camps included refugees from 40 to 50 different villages, it was practically impossible to set up a unified recognized committee accepted by all the refugees. However, on February 16, 1950 a big gathering took place and a large committee representing the refugees was elected.[84] The publicity for that meeting elicited protests from unrepresented groups, as well as from people who said their names were given as supporters or members of the committee without their prior consent.[85] It also led to a counter-meeting, headed by a local leader, Kamil Ariqat, who gathered 6,000 refugees three days later in the Ayn al-Sultan Camp.[86] As a result of this meeting, the refugees were temporarily unified. But owing to their conflicting interests and personalities, it was totally impracticable for the supporters of the two groups to abandon their differences and permanently unite their efforts after the elections were over.

Apart from their inability to overcome old and new disputes, the loosely-composed area committees were simply too big and ungainly. And they soon became no more than frameworks for preserving lost prestige and organizing pay-offs. Attempts to create central organizations failed to overcome the refugees' tendency to organize themselves according to their places of origin or their present sites. Moreover all area committees were considerably weakened by the strengthening of the camp committees in the period up to the annexation.

The political pronouncements by the leaders of the area committees clearly show that most were mainly concerned with their lost property. For this reason, they lost the support of the camp refugees who feared these policies and expected the committees to be more active in the sphere of relief. They regarded compensation for losses as treason, especially when it could damage their demand for Return.

On the whole the refugee area committees showed little solidarity. One rare exception involved the Nablus refugees who joined those in Hebron and in Bethlehem to oppose the attempted immunization against tuberculosis by the I.C.R.C. They demanded that the vaccinations should be given only by local staff in order to conceal the exact number of refugees.[87]

The call for refugees to unite became more pronounced as disillusion with the Arab Governments intensified.[88] But the refugees were soon disappointed with their own local leaders who failed to represent and defend their interests. An article in *Sawt al-Laj'in* (Voice of the Refugees) entitled "God will save us from your Deeds", reflects the contempt felt by refugees for these self-appointed "representatives". The paper exposed the ugly relations between refugee leaders who genuinely worked for the refugees and those who, unable to unite, sought instead to nurture their own interests.[89] In the light of this, there is an element of naive optimism in the Communist appeals to the refugees to:

> get up and select by yourself your own committees which would defend and represent your daily interests . . . and expel the *mukhtars* and notables and false committees which collaborate with the regime and the Red Cross clerks in cheating the refugees and making money at their expense . . . fight through those new committees to better your lot . . . organize yourselves in the struggle and the demand to return.[90]

But there was little response to such appeals, and the Communists soon lost confidence in the mass of ordinary refugees in the camps.

With such a diverse composition and fragmented leadership, there was little hope of a refugee group working together as a unit. Even their common plight and shared disaster were insufficient to overcome private interests. In fact, there was a growing disharmony amongst the refugees. Briefly, the refugees' inner divisions and rivalries, old feuds, conflicting interests and different geographical and social backgrounds, all conspired against their ever producing a common "Refugee position". The authorities sought to discourage large, exclusively refugee gatherings, since they might have emphasized the refugees' common ground. Experience showed that resolutions agreed upon at the meetings could somewhat weaken the monarch's claim to represent the refugees as "the citizens of the Hashimite Kingdom of Jordan". Hence such meetings lost favour, and instead the regime managed to obtain the support of the local refugee committees.

D. THE OPTION OF "NO OPTIONS"?

Abdullah was supported, at least on religious grounds, by a large section of the ordinary Palestinian population. In their wretched and powerless state, they trusted him to change their bitter fate, and feared a withdrawal of the Jordanian army. It was obvious that Israel was there to stay and that the Egyptians would control the Gaza Strip, but not that the Legion would remain in the West Bank. Many influential figures feared the alternatives: a Mufti-controlled Palestine or Jewish occupation — both of which meant a lowered status and the end of their political careers. In that respect, annexation was synonymous with security.

Moreover, many respected personalities knew that, if they gave their consent and were "counted in", they might reap benefits and enjoy the privileges of favourites. They could become M.P.s or Government Ministers and defend their own economic interests. They had little choice but in any case intended to make the most of the situation. All things considered, people grew accustomed to the idea of annexation.

Thus annexation was quite popular amongst large numbers of Palestinians, although it was opposed by the radical intelligentsia who in reality had little influence. In all events, Abdullah was not going to take "no" for an answer, and he made it clear that a political stalemate was unacceptable. All his moves clearly indicated his intentions. Time was running short. Even pro-Husayni veterans, who originally took a hesitant stand to acquire a bargaining position, now joined in, whether or not their expectations of gaining influential posts had been satisfied. Rather than remain idle in the face of Abdullah's growing influence, traditional leaders tried either to strengthen their ties with him by giving ardent support, or quietly resign themselves to the new era, regarding this option as the lesser of two evils. They sweetened the bitter pill by suggesting that the merger coincided with the idea of Arab unity, and that it would help remove the artificial differences between the Arabs created by imperialism.

The King was in a quandary over the refugees. He wanted to be accepted as their hero and leader, but if he openly encouraged them to resettle, he would be going against their declared will and interests. That was tantamount to an admission that he could not or did not want to liberate Palestine and that the

Palestinians had permanently lost their homes—something they were never prepared to accept. It was a dilemma which constantly faced Abdullah and his successors in the years to come. The King therefore encouraged refugees to take advantage of any work they could find, and any land given, until Palestine was liberated and they could choose whether or not to return. Consequently many refugees trusted Abdullah, and hoped he would keep his promise to allow the refugees to return to their homes before beginning any peace negotiations. The indisputable demand for the return was shared by all refugees regardless of their status, inclination or intention to actually exercise their rights. It was supported alike by large property-owners and refugees who had never had any property.

The refugees, like the non-refugees, fell into three groups: those who supported the monarch's solution, those who opposed it, and the larger group who were indifferent. None of these elements could be regarded as marginal. As with the indigenous population, many refugees refrained from indicating to which group they belonged. Most of their leaders and *mukhtars*, however, took sides. But unlike the local Palestinians, those opposed to the annexation feared, above all, losing their right to return. Therefore the Mufti did not win over this element who were mainly large property-owners. They felt that recognition of the merger might prevent their return and certainly any compensation (which they might have preferred). Other opponents were the Communists,[91] and poor people who feared it might mean the end of the relief upon which they depended. Many of the poor, and certainly many of the rich, secretly even wanted to come under a Jewish State. Others were either unable or did not want to define exactly what practical alternative they would settle for, beyond the mere demand to return. Egypt's maltreatment of the refugees in the Gaza Strip,[92] even when compared with the modest attention they received in Jordan, must also have influenced the refugees' opinions.

Appointing well-known refugees to ministerial and other important posts,[93] could only help Abdullah strengthen his position. Some felt he nominated certain Ministers from the refugees because these particular men were loyal and capable, thus managing to gain prestige and pacify the refugees at the same time. It was claimed they were selected not because they were refugees but because their personalities and individual merits served the monarch.[94] Not everyone shared this view.[95] Some wanted a refugee like themselves inside the Government, since they felt that he would understand their problems and guarantee the Government's active interest in their future. They wanted someone known and trusted whom they could approach directly. But the post of Minister for Refugee Affairs and that of the Minister of Development and Reconstruction (M.D.R.) which replaced it, were not necessarily given to the nominated refugee ministers.[96] This was perhaps because of Abdullah's desire to play down the political differences between the two parts of the Palestinian community, in order to ease their total incorporation into the kingdom. Nominating a refugee for this post could be counter-productive. The King wanted several refugee leaders near him to attract refugee support and to neutralize his opponents abroad. Once inside the Government, it was difficult to oppose his view, and the refugee Ministers' assent was used to show the refugees that their representatives approved of certain questionable policies. But not all those selected for the various posts had strong support among the refugees, and others became publicly known only after taking office.

There were news items in the local Press about the Government's official visits to refugee concentrations and also about the way Palestinians selected from amongst the refugees were taking care of their interests. This helped to alleviate the atmosphere of deep-rooted apathy and frustration among the refugees. However, any gratitude should not be interpreted as signifying an identification with the Hashimite rule, although it did make it easier to accept the idea that Abdullah would be King "until the Day of Return".

The various reactions to the policy of annexation and all that it implied thus have little to do with ideology. Rather, they are a reflection of the hopes and fears of the helpless, confused Palestinians who had no option but to rely on Abdullah's regime. Despite all the congresses, articles, support, arguments and protests, the simple question remains: Did the refugees, or other Palestinians for that matter, in practice have any other choice? Faced with their own internal divisions and weak position, the helplessness of the A.P.G. and the Arab League on the one hand, and Abdullah's firm intentions and policies on the other, the answer is clearly that they did not.[97]

Chapter II

Merger or Absorption?

Following the Jericho Congress, military rule was replaced by Jordanian civil administration. Official annexation became simply a matter of time. After some hesitation and delay—mainly because of pressure from Great Britain, which feared the Arab League's response, and preferred a gradual merger—the expected final steps took place to achieve "the fusion of equals" as the annexation was called by the Jordanians. To reinforce the impression of change, the name of the State was said to be altered. The newly elected Parliament, composed of both local inhabitants and refugees, ratified the union at its first meeting on 24 April, 1950.[1] A new Senate was nominated, half of it made up of Palestinians;[2] and a new Government, which included Palestinian refugees and non-refugees, was selected. With annexation completed, consolidation and integration could continue.

A. THE "STICK AND CARROT" POLICY

Abdullah, assisted by the privileged classes (both Palestinian and Trans-Jordanian), tried to cement his position by erasing any sense of separate Palestinian identity. Palestinian separatism was regarded by the King as a "blow to the meaning of the sacred unity in the conscience of every Arab", and he worked to thwart it regarding it as a threat to his own regime. Abdullah's sense of insecurity led him to believe that his best defence was offence on all fronts. Rather than waiting for events to work to his advantage, he initiated a series of moves aimed at antagonizing his foes and cultivating his sympathizers.

The centralized civil law[3] gave the monarch the power required to govern, leaving him completely unaccountable and allowing little scope for an effective opposition. Accordingly, any parliamentary amendment which proposed to reduce his absolute power by constitutional means was doomed to fail. Abdullah believed he was the sole source of sovereignty. He could not tolerate the democratic rights implied by the Jordanian constitution.

Western terms such as "reforms", "elementary civil rights", "freedom of the Press", "authority of the Parliament" and "democracy", often used in opposition speeches, were foreign to him, and he feared their popular impact. Any opposition which exceeded his idea of tolerable political activity was considered high treason and was suppressed. Rigid laws, arbitrarily interpreted, were used to eliminate such opposition.

The King could dissolve Parliament at will and authorize the holding of new elections regardless of all reforms and protests. He set up temporary, controlled "political parties" to offset those which were considered illegal and in an attempt to show that "positive" political regrouping was allowed. Censorship ensured control of the Press. By tempering autocratic severity with subsequent self-restraint and clemency, the regime succeeded in weakening, neutralizing and even winning over some of its opponents. So most of the serious opposition from the King's point of view was out-manoeuvred.

The executive apparatus for enforcing his policies consisted of the armed forces, the security services and the higher echelons of the central administration, over which he kept tight control through appointments, transfers and dismissals. The secret police investigation section (*mabahith*) of the Public Security service (*amn al-am*) worked hard and fairly effectively to control underground political activity both inside and outside Jordan.[4] The vacuum created by the destruction of effective organized opposition was filled by a system of close control and observation, touching on every sphere of life. Uncertainty and insecurity dominated the affairs of those who did not support the status quo.

Wishing to appear a popular leader, Abdullah did not want to quarrel with the local leaders. On the contrary, he tried to allay their fears by promising to preserve their highly-respected positions providing they sided with him. They in turn should adapt themselves to the new circumstances. They both needed and depended on one another. This system of "divide and rule" was effective owing to factionalism among the Palestinians. Up to the mid 1950s the small emerging group of "intelligentsia" maintained its limited influence only amongst the younger generation. In the face of a system adept at preventing any drastic change which might weaken the old leadership, there was little they could change from "inside" without active support from a large segment of the population. But the involvement of the highly-respected white-collar Palestinians in the politics of this period should not be considered marginal. Indeed, they were the ones to lead all opposition groups. They generally failed however to gain the backing of the ordinary population beyond the usual support for protests, meetings and petitions. One reason, perhaps, was that it was difficult for these professional men to acquire a decisive position in daily politics[5] when most of the population felt that the real influence and power remained with the recognized local leaders, who were still widely trusted and provided the traditional path for pressing personal and political interests. And although the period following the war marked the beginning of decline in the influence of many large property owners, some retained the support and respect of villagers who depended on their lands.

Under the highly centralized administration, local leaders and other influentials had the opportunity of serving as intermediaries between the local population and the authorities. The *"wastah"* upon which many depended could enhance their prestige and consequently their political influence. Such a position could only be undermined by the central administration.[6] Well-established pro-Hashimite elements striving to protect their status were assisted by the regime against those who tried to challenge them. The merchants, for example, depended for their livelihood on the Government's trade licences, since the West Bank had no outlets except through the East Bank. Pro-regime supporters could obtain permits far more easily and arrange employment in certain government departments for their relatives who could then assist them in promoting their interests.

However, any attempt to understand the composition of Palestinian society in terms of "classes" in the generally accepted sense, without qualifications,[7] would be somewhat misleading, owing to its vertical and horizontal stratification and various regional fragmentations.

It seems that, in the case of the Palestinians, political developments accounted for social change rather than the reverse.[8] Throughout this century politics in general and anti-Zionism in particular have been the paramount factors in moulding and shaping the characteristics of Palestinian society and its leadership. Many of those who emerged as influential "leaders" were originally traditional notables who became government officials serving as links between the ruler and his subjects. Removed from the mundane concerns of their "constituency" and yet powerless beyond matters concerning their everyday life, these figures were viewed by many primarily as intermediaries. This function in itself gave them tremendous power but it did not necessarily amount to leadership. The King knew that economic control was a potent source of power. He therefore protected privileged positions and rejected any demands for an equal say by groups outside this clique, whom he considered "agitators". In doing so he forced these groups to abandon "constitutional methods" and to resort to more violent means, tacitly approved of by many. This in turn provoked stringent control measures, including at times imprisonment of "the opposition's" leadership. By using economic penalties and rewards the regime promoted "moderate" figures who refused to adopt any "liberal" or "progressive" attitudes to the Palestinian—Trans-Jordanian relationship, or to develop any association which might be regarded with suspicion by the Government. The regime tried to encourage people to adopt a pragmatic self-interested approach to their new situation, facing up to the political and social realities of annexation. It demonstrated that material advantages and rewards were gained by acceptance of integration in the manner encouraged or dictated by the regime. The policy of the iron fist in the velvet glove employed by the

"Giver of Gifts" led many people to acquiesce in the situation though not necessarily to accept or endorse it.

B. WEST BANK VERSUS EAST BANK OR PALESTINIANS VERSUS TRANS-JORDANIANS?

The "Unity of Contrasts", as it may be called, had to embrace both a relatively highly "developed" and "advanced" population with a rather more "primitive" and "backward" society,[9] to use Western terms of comparison. The differing political and social experiences which each component had undergone during the three decades before their enforced partnership left their mark on their mutual perceptions and attitudes.

The Palestinians, through their contacts with the Jews and the British under the Mandate, were generally more economically capable and more politically conscious, though far from being more advanced in administrative experience. This resulted in a tremendous discrepancy between the two elements: Jordan was completely dependent on Great Britian, whom the Palestinians took to be one of their enemies; and she had sought a *modus vivendi* with Israel, whom the Palestinians regarded as the source of their catastrophe and with whom they could contemplate no contact. Furthermore, each side attributed to the other responsibility for the defeat and looked on each other with derision and contempt.

Although local "public opinion" was tenuously organized and was neither powerful nor important in the first years following the war, the Palestinians soon demonstrated their increasing discontent with the role they were being allowed to play. The division within the population developed, with the embittered Palestinians, being persistently discriminated against as a group, considering themselves as the underdog. Regarding themselves infinitely superior, they thought it inconceivable "to be governed by bedouin". Even though large numbers of Palestinians were absorbed into the constantly expanding administration—by virtue of their higher qualifications—this did not alleviate their dissatisfaction as they soon realized the purpose this machinery was serving. Moreover, forming the kingdom's majority and having enormous potential, they disliked the emphasis on competition between themselves and the Trans-Jordanians in all walks of life. They felt they deserved a far better role than the secondary one they were allowed to play, for the decisive high adminstrative posts remained the prerogative of the East Bankers.

Nevertheless, many Palestinians made a fortune, taking advantage of the possibilities presented by annexation. On the other hand many Trans-Jordanians felt they were being deprived by the Palestinians of their status and rights as masters of the country. The basic social differences were difficult to bridge. Political and economic competition and conflict of interests were to characterize the process of co-existence. Mutual adaptation, from which the Trans-Jordanians probably gained the most, took place through the modernization of the backward kingdom. The Press and other media, largely owned and staffed by Palestinians, were to play an important part in that change.[10]

Since very few Trans-Jordanians apart from Government officials resided in the West Bank, and as many Palestinian refugees and non-refugees moved to the East Bank, an examination of the mutual relations between the two segments of the population is best looked at in the East Bank. By contrast, the sense of being discriminated against by government economic policy can only properly be understood from the perspective of the West side.

1. Mutual Relations in the East Bank

To begin with, it is necessary to establish briefly which Palestinians resided in the East Bank, when they arrived there and where they went. The first category is that of Palestinians who migrated to Amman throughout the 1920s and 1930s. Being educated and capable people, they became senior civil servants and Ministers. A few of them engaged in trade and smuggling, together with some of thousands of emigrants from Damascus who actually controlled the commerce there. Most of them came from Safad, Acre and Haifa and, altogether, there were some 10,000 Palestinians who settled in Amman prior to the 1948 war. Irbid, Salt and Zarqa' also absorbed a number of Palestinians who came during this period. These townlets had a majority of Trans-Jordanians including a contingent of unskilled local villagers, unlike Amman, where Palestinians formed the majority of the inhabitants.

The second category was that of the 1948 refugees. Following the clashes between Jews and Arabs in 1947 waves of refugees arrived in Jordan. In the period until the end of the war they were joined by more refugees seeking shelter. Some of those who arrived in Irbid, for example, came there because they had good family connections and friends.[11] Others were brought there by army trucks after the evacuation of Tiberias and Samah and, more generally, many refugees from the Baysan area, Tirah and eastern Galilee came to that part of Jordan. A large segment of town-dwelling refugees arrived in the East Bank townlets. Refugees from Lydda, Ramleh and Jaffa could be found in Zarqa' and Amman since these places could offer better employment facilities and accommodation: living in tents was alien to urban refugees. The rich and the owners of vehicles and buses (used for transferring relatives, friends and moveable property) were the first to reach these places. Christian refugees went to Salt, Madaba and Amman,[12] and were joined by a group of Armenian Jerusalemites.

This initial movement was followed by the arrival of large numbers of villagers who scattered all over the East Bank especially in the areas north of Amman. Others had their cattle and flocks with them and found it difficult to encroach on the cultivated land in the West Bank. They therefore concentrated in the valleys east and west of the river, where water could be found. The constant movement of refugees was to bring even more of them to the East Bank through their search for relatives and employment.[13]

This tendency was accelerated later in the 1950's by the development of the East Bank, forming a separate category. More Hebronites for example moved to Amman and Karak, joining relatives.[14] Much of this movement paralleled the process of urbanization. With the growth of towns came competition amongst the Palestinians, as well as between them and the local population.

The Jordanian Government realized that if it wanted to speak and act on behalf of the Palestinians there had to be no restriction of movement. It also knew that the country would gain economically from their presence as many of them brought with them considerable assets and skills. The penniless were looked after by the international Agencies, which set up various employment projects from which it was hoped the local population would also benefit.

But how did the local population view this influx of newcomers? The more educated Trans-Jordanian town-dwellers generally co-existed quite well with the Palestinian group. However, the peasants, and especially the bedouin, were far more reserved in their attitude towards them. They could benefit from the experience and knowledge of the refugees but no longer wanted their presence once they had learned all they needed. Consequently a number of UNRWA agricultural projects opened in the East Bank were closed down when the local folk became tired of the Palestinians' presence.[15] They were also envious because UNRWA employed only Palestinians, preferably refugees. The Agency had hoped to supply refugees with some work and felt that, given the limited employment possibilities and the relations between the two sections of the population, the refugees would feel aggrieved if UNRWA were to hire Trans-Jordanians.[16]

On the whole, the Trans-Jordanians looked down on the refugees with massive contempt. This was especially true in the south where the local population was more conservative, and where there were even fewer employment opportunities to attract refugees. Kirkbride recalled that in Karak and Tafyla "they would not have them and very few refugees stopped in the south. They were almost thrown out".[17] The Trans-Jordanians were also displeased with the general Palestinian attitude towards the monarch and regarded their behaviour as implying an ingratitude unbecoming of guests. There was perhaps a more relaxed attitude towards the bedouin refugees, although they were also looked down upon, deprived as they were of their *dirah* and some of their livestock. But even this toleration changed, at least for a while, after the King's assassination in 1951. In spite of their sharing a common way of life, the East Bank bedouin considered the bedouin refugees to be Palestinians,[18] even if such a notion had little meaning for the latter at the time.

In the north of the East Bank many Trans-Jordanians shared the Palestinians' dislike of the Hashimites, for they had been antagonized by the development of Amman on the one hand and their closeness to Syria on the other.

But, generally speaking, Trans-Jordanians resented the Palestinians' superior education and felt that they had come to take their livelihood. Amman remained a special case. Eventually the economic life of Amman was to be controlled by the Palestinians most of whom were refugees. Many of them even acquired the local dialect in order to please the natives. This is true of Palestinians scattered throughout the Arab world and might be seen as part of a natural process of integration without any political connotation. Yet even those in Amman were constantly reminded that they were Palestinians, much as they tried to conceal the differences between the two "Jordanian" elements. This was especially true during the troubles of the mid-1950s in which the Palestinians in Amman were prominent.

In addition, every Israeli military action in Jordan induced mutual accusations between the two parties: the Palestinians, fearing for the safety of their families left behind, accused the monarch of not sending military help or arming the Palestinians themselves; the Trans-Jordanians reminded them that "they ran away from their country in the face of the Jews", and that anything done for them was undeserved since they were outsiders and foreigners. For these reasons the Trans-Jordanians also rejected recruitment, let alone conscription, of the untrusted Palestinians who were considered to be trouble-makers and to be primarily interested in changing the basic characteristics of the host country.

Therefore, despite the Government's attempts to integrate the refugees, there was a degree of antagonism which did not permit a smooth process of political and social absorption. This antagonism certainly sharpened the Palestinian identity even among those who tried wholeheartedly to integrate into a new environment by aiming to make the most of it. They were constantly reminded in various ways that they did not really belong there. The local Trans-Jordanians were generally loyal to the King and tended to regard with great unease any Palestinian demonstration against the monarch and his policies. Being bedouin in origin, many of them tended to take such expressions of non-confidence personally. Even the displays of opposition amongst East Bankers were viewed with more tolerance by traditional elements in Trans-Jordan than those carried out by Palestinians. Furthermore, such activities, regardless of their motivation, were seen as inspired by "politically minded" Palestinians. This had some basis: eager to secure for themselves a full measure of real participation in the running of Jordan, the Palestinians sought greater political and economic power and vigorously demanded wider political and economic rights. Only when political stability persisted did contact between the two elements induce—without erasing prejudice—a slightly more relaxed mutual attitude. This adoption of a more pragmatic approach through the need to face domestic and world realities occurred throughout the rapid economic developments from the mid-1950s onwards, and somewhat softened the competition between the two groups.

But it did not reorientate the Palestinians' political attitudes, mainly because they remained the inferior partner. Convinced they were treated as second-class citizens, they maintained that the failure to set up industrial schemes in the West Bank was the result of deliberate policy rather than mere negligence on the part of the regime, which wished to develop the East Bank at the West Bank's expense.

2. Economic Considerations — Jordan's West Bank Policy

Because of its poverty, limited natural resources and primitive agriculture, Trans-Jordan depended for its very existence on British aid. Predominantly agricultural, the newly incorporated West Bank had little light industry of its own. The Palestinians believed that their skills acquired throughout the British Mandate should be utilized to develop the West Bank.[19] But the government on the other hand wished to direct all its efforts towards the economic development of the area where the potential assets for economic development were claimed to lie, that is, the East Bank.[20] West Bankers saw proof of the justice of their complaints when the potash contained in the Dead Sea remained unutilized and the King refused to allow the opening of a university on the West Bank. "Since they could not transfer Jerusalem", one person commented, "the only thing they allowed was the development of the tourist industry". Other interviewed businessmen said they were pressurized to invest in the East Bank and, since the West Bank was unsafe owing to border tension, they readily acquiesced. Furthermore, heavy industry would need large quantities of water which were not available there. West Bank politicians understood this, but they wanted a balance of light industry, although they also realized this could not provide employment for more than a few skilled people. So the criticism and protest was more an expression of helplessness and anger against a regime that did not allow even for the development of small businesses. It also actively prevented the local population from improving their services by refusing to give the town councils their full budgets. Any *ad hoc* West Bank body set up to express this sense of bitterness was doomed to fail as the Palestinians themselves had conflicting notions of their priorities, every town seeing itself as the one most entitled to any development scheme. In any event, the government would not allow the attempted establishment of an all-West Bank organization.

Under the guise of promoting integration, the monarch did his utmost to "balance " the small, dense and relatively progressive West Bank with the vast, poor, backwards, sparsely populated East Bank. Cut off from its traditional markets, damaged by the war, saturated with unemployed refugees and with many of its inhabitants destitute, the West Bank faced severe difficulties. Most economic activity and building was concentrated on the East side, to which the government directed most allocations[21] and investments, together with agricultural and industrial projects. The development of the East Bank was carried out mainly by Palestinians who, having little option, put their knowledge, skill and talents at the disposal of the regime. Amman, the kingdom's backward capital, was to become a flourishing town thus shifting the centre of economic gravity.

The logic behind this policy was far from being exclusively economic. The constant flow of migration eastwards reflected the arbitrary discrimination of this one-sided development. Ironically enough, however, most Jordanians, East or West Bankers, gained financially. The refugees participated in this movement to a greater degree than the local inhabitants and succeeded in competing for work. The government used the fact that many refugees were living there in order to pressurize UNRWA to establish projects in the East Bank. Many arguments between the Agency and the Government centred around this issue.

Despite all the protests from Nablus over the Jordanian policy of denying the West Bank its economic potential, this town was at times favoured by the regime. This was to weaken Jerusalem and Hebron and to encourage economic competition thus accentuating political rivalry between them. It deepened internal divisions within the West Bank, making it more difficult for the area to act as a political unit. A valid question therefore is: did the regime's policy towards Jerusalem conform in this respect with its general approach to the Palestinian question?

3. The Status of Jerusalem

For the first couple of years after the 1948 war Jerusalem's special dual status became a centre of controversy: as an international city, with immense religious and symbolic importance, it became a bone of contention between Jordan and the Arab World; as one of the centres of pre-1948 Arab Palestine, and as the obvious rival now to Amman, it was the focus of some unease between Abdullah and the Palestinians. This unease sheds some light on the emerging pattern of political and economic relationships between the regime and its new subjects, and on the complex process of integration and development. The regime's general policy was to prevent Jerusalem from either gaining special status or becoming a symbolic focus for divisive West Bank–East Bank antagonisms.

(a) Abdullah and the Internationalization of Jerusalem

Although included in the 1947 Partition Plan, the internationalization of Jerusalem was in some ways still considered a separate issue. At the end of the 1948 war some refugee and non-refugee Jerusalemites, primarily Christians,[22] together with several Bethlehemites and Hebronites, called for the internationalization of Jerusalem under the UN plan. By this they hoped to reclaim their assets—now on the other side of the border.

In response, Abdullah, whose views were shared by Israel, made it clear that he would ignore the UN resolutions. Disregarding Jerusalem's importance to the outside world, he had no intention of relinquishing one of his major territorial gains, the city where his father was buried. Furthermore he feared the political consequences of yielding to his new subjects' requests and granting the city special status. So in a series of speeches he disassociated himself from such steps[23] and encouraged West Bankers, some of whom quickly took the hint,[24] to express views similar to his own. Abdullah also contacted the Muslim Heads of State of Turkey, Afghanistan, India and Pakistan, and asked for their support in the UN. He stated that acceptance of the UN's plan would harm the town's Arab population, separating them from their brothers and leaving them defenceless.[25] As the other Arab countries generally favoured Jerusalem's internationalization, if only to weaken Abdullah's position, such persuasion proved difficult; but as always the passage of time played an important part in realizing the King's dream. Opposition from outside Jordan again proved ineffectual.

(b) The Palestinians and Jerusalem

Yet the political future of Jerusalem soon became an issue between the regime and the Palestinians, reflecting the incompatibility of their desires. The question of the centrality of Jerusalem was frequently raised since the Palestinians were eager to see the city gain the economic and political prominence they felt it deserved. But despite its religious importance, Jerusalem was never the centre of the Palestinian movement even though the Husaynis had a stronghold there. Some Palestinians sought after the war to turn the city into a kind of capital for the Palestinian part of the kingdom.[26] These calls received little attention amongst most Palestinians. But the motives behind these calls led the King to refuse to grant the town this status, even though becoming King of Jerusalem was one of his goals.[27] In any event such calls died away with Abdullah's assassination in Jerusalem,[28] although the city continued to harbour many opposition elements.

With the city deprived of the special status it hoped for, a number of Palestinians continued to protest against the regime's policy, and occasionally tried to raise the issue in the hope of obtaining at least symbolic redress. The internationalization of Jerusalem was also raised once in an attempt to attract Western support for an overall settlement of the refugee question[29] — thereby indirectly challenging the regime.

A somewhat different and louder protest was voiced by both West Bankers and Jerusalemites against the overall policy of gradually weakening the city's administrative and economic position, in order to strengthen Amman. The transfer of all important offices from Jerusalem was a source of grievance both to the local population and to the refugees, as well as to the Town Council. The Council protested obstinately against the Government's refusal to allow even UNRWA's Jordanian Headquarters to be situated there, so as to serve the West Bank where most refugees were living. The Government's aim was twofold: first, it wanted tight control over all UNRWA affairs and, second, it sought to develop the capital. UNRWA represented a substantial economic contribution to a country which aimed at developing its relatively poor areas.

The Jerusalem Municipality and Government files on UNRWA are also full of demands that it transfer its Middle East Headquarters from Beirut to Jerusalem.[30] The Palestinians realized the potential economic advantages of UNRWA's activities which could offer vast employment opportunities for refugees and non-refugees, help develop the town and the West Bank and slow down the process of migration and emigration. The term in'ash, which in essence meant the revival and restoration of Jerusalem, was prominent in all correspondence to that effect. Jerusalemites wanted the government to regard the town as a front line settlement and to do its utmost to strengthen it. In fact, they faced a consistent policy to the reverse.[31] Amman was the seat of the centralized administration and anything which threatened the further entrenchment of its position was regarded as opposition to the regime.[32] As a result of this policy and the absence of a united and influential local leadership, Jerusalem lost its seniority. To further cripple the town's position, the Government even considered moving part of the Muslim Law Courts to Amman, against the helpless protests of the Town Council.[33]

This treatment was an insult to the Palestinians and was further proof of their secondary position in a country which supposedly offered them full and equal rights. Nonetheless, the West Bankers' protests against the regime's discriminatory policy throughout the 1950s did not call for separation from the East Bank, but rather for a change in policy. Eliezer Be'eri found that during 1952–9 such grievances, if aired, were not followed by any attempted separatist regroupings. This attitude changed somewhat in 1959 with the renewed talk of the Palestinian Entity's "revival".[34]

Moreover it would be something of a distortion to assert that there were constant political clashes between the inhabitants of the two Banks, or between the monarch and the Palestinians. One reason why this was not the case was the lack of leadership among the Palestinians.

The underground opposition "parties", which aimed at changing the regime's policy on certain issues rather than working against its very existence, could not fill that vacuum. Even though they had a certain appeal, these pockets of resistance were too small or weak to operate effectively, since Palestinian public opinion was divided and the Government held all the cards. The parties, moreover, never sought to operate as exclusively Palestinian bodies.

But to understand fully how this situation developed, it must be placed in the context of the whole nature and structure of the Jordanian regime (or the "image of Jordan", as it has been defined by Uriel Dann)[35] and its style of political influence, which remains, Dann argues, the same today as it was in the 1920's and 1930's.[36] One of the fundamental features of political life in

Jordan was a perpetual fear of foreign-inspired attempts to disrupt the "distribution" of power in Jordan and the delicate balances within the Kingdom. The regime relied for support on all those who had vested interests in preserving its essential character, be they members of the King's extended family, the *Sharifs,* his entourage and friends or his Trans-Jordanian and Palestinian advisors. And, in general, according to Dann

> those in Jordan who supported the Jordanian "entity" have shown an incomparably greater degree of consistency, intransigence and readiness for sacrifice than have those who opposed it.[37]

In other words, the regime enjoyed considerable support and successfully confronted opposition from Trans-Jordanians and Palestinians in both parts of the kingdom, regardless of its policy of strengthening and developing the East Bank at the expense of the West Bank. The question in the 1950s was not, therefore, that of Palestinian versus Trans-Jordanian, or of West Bank as opposed to East Bank, but rather that of Palestinian rights within the context of Jordan. The regime offered rights to Palestinians individually, but refused to regard them collectively, doing its utmost to suppress and dissolve any sense of separate identity. It maintained its semblance of support for the refugees' plight alongside a tacit checking and curbing of any exclusively "Palestinian" manifestations. And while Jordan did not solve the complex problem of its own legitimacy in the eyes of its adopted subjects, it certainly won some measure of acceptance, even respectability. Strange as it might seem, considerations of expediency went hand in hand with a growing sense of identification with the State. Hence it can be said that up to the 1960's the Palestinians could not and did not try to organize themselves as a distinct group, concentrating rather on their integration into the Hashimite Kingdom of Jordan.

Chapter III

Jordanization of the Palestinian Refugees

Beyond the practical steps and measures taken by the authorities to consolidate their position in the West Bank, the Government tried to gain the sympathy and support of the refugees by presenting itself as their spokesman. In this chapter the Government's policy towards its new subjects will be examined along with the refugees' response.

A. GOVERNMENT ASSISTANCE TO THE REFUGEES

Faced with hundreds of thousands of hungry and destitute refugees forced to live under extreme hardship, the authorities extended meagre aid to alleviate some of the suffering caused by the severe winters of the first few years. Refugee morale was deteriorating. Enforced idleness and gloomy employment prospects, coupled with uncertainty over the future and the duration of local assistance, made for increasing uneasiness and growing resentment towards the outside world which had "betrayed" them. Angry and frustrated, they hoped for extensive Government aid. But the Government, being poor, could not continue to supply the huge numbers of refugees with the required quantities of bread or other items. The small sums sent in 1948 by the Arab League and Saudi Arabia, together with the money collected from merchants that year, were soon exhausted.

Without substantial and constant aid from abroad, Abdullah faced considerable dangers in his struggle to consolidate his hegemony over the West Bank. A politically volatile situation could hardly serve the interests of those who sought stability in the area. Motivated by both humanitarian and political considerations, the West responded positively to the cry for assistance for the unfortunate refugees; so the Jordanian Government considered its main task at this stage to be one of ensuring the flow of relief items from abroad and the continuation of the international relief operation.

In the first few months after the war the local population was moved to compassion by the plight of their brother refugees and responded warmly to the authorities' appeals for assistance. During that year the government had to allow the squatting of refugees in vacant dwellings,[1] schools, mosques and churches. For a few refugees this secured the basic needs of drinking water and a roof over their heads. The local Refugee Affairs Committees were distributing all relief commodities that arrived. With waves of more refugees flooding the area and inadequate amounts of relief received, disorder and tension developed. At this stage, the occupying army tried not to get involved in the distribution operation, being neither capable nor equipped to do so, and having to attend to other problems. But it was not long before they realized that they would at least have to supervise the operation.

Fearing even stronger protests from the destitute refugees, the local Governors began to play a more decisive role in relief affairs after the Armistice Agreement. New arrangements were made for relatively more efficient distribution. Although this in itself did not alter the situation, it gave many refugees a feeling that the Government was attending more seriously to their plight. The authorities also tried to soothe the refugees by promising them better employment opportunities in Jordan,[2] assurances they had to repeat throughout the first few years.[3]

Government assistance continued throughout the winter storms, alongside constant intervention urging the UN to do more on behalf of thousands of complaining refugees. This "mediating" position became perhaps the most important function the Government fulfilled, since it was in no position to assist the refugees by itself even if it wanted to. Now and again the Government would remind the refugees of its achievements, in an attempt to convince them that it was doing its utmost for them in the political and economic spheres. The Ministers detailed at length the direct and indirect Government aid to the refugees, declaring their opposition to the Census and Resettlement projects, and stressing the "Jordanizing" of the Agency's senior posts—a step which it was hoped would reduce the many protests made by refugees, continuously demanding the UNRWA's employment of local persons instead of Western workers.

The Health and Welfare Minister promised the refugees during his occasional tours of the camps, that the Government was constantly watching their affairs and trying to respond positively to their demands. He assured them that "the refugees were not strangers" and would be included in all reforms and development projects the people in Jordan were going to enjoy, quite apart from the special international aid. This message was repeated time and again, being widely supported by all government members regardless of their political inclination, making it easier to be firm in the implementation of such schemes.

The annual (unpublished) D.G.'s reports, prepared for regularization of the UNRWA-Government balance of payments, reveal the nature and extent of direct and indirect assistance channelled through the government to the refugees, but paid for by UNRWA. The 1951 reports summarized the period from 1948 up to the establishment of ICRC, the Red Cross phase, and the first half year following the establishment of UNRWA. Although broadly similar for all districts, a strictly unified pattern of operation was missing. The main government functions were: assisting the Agencies to set up their own machinery, nominating relief workers, aiding the census operations,[4] transferring refugees, choosing the sites for the camps,[5] compensating the land owners of the camp sites, providing water and helping in the basic establishment of the camp, allocating beds in certain hospitals and covering some medical treatment and expenses. The reports also mention the distribution of bread and aid to unsupported refugees, provision of tents, nomination of *mukhtars,* examination of refugee complaints, regular visits[6] and the provision of small governmental allocations as token payments.[7]

Later, the expenditure on the police posts which were set up in the camps was included in every report. These stations gave the refugees a feeling of protection, and gave the government a clear picture of the developments in each refugee concentration, as well as a means to control minor demonstrations. Their duties included reporting visits made to the camp by all outsiders including UNRWA officials, local or international, and voluntary agency workers. In August 1952 the police also had to prevent refugees from leaving the camps,[8] the government fearing that the decline in numbers would result in a reduction in UNRWA's assistance. Throughout these years they guarded the camps and its installations and maintained law and order, watching over the distributions, defending UNRWA workers,[9] and reporting student demonstrations and other political activities.[10] The Nablus D.G. report stressed the yearly checking of tents in each camp—a project common to UNRWA and the Government of which the refugees were highly suspicious. This report also mentioned the land given for housing refugees, such as Nur Shams or the small refugee settlement project in Bayt Qad. It noted that about a third of the 34,946 pupils studying in the area's government and private schools were refugees subsidized by the Agency, which also paid their medical expenses.

The reports enabled the government to calculate and formulate its yearly budget for refugee affairs, to be covered mostly by UNRWA. Occasionally the reports were exaggerated to get a larger subsidy from UNRWA. For example, the Hebron D.G. demanded a far more modest sum than did his Nablus counterpart, though he added 10 per cent onto the expenses per refugee claimed by the Regional Officer (R.O.) who reported to him.[11] But UNRWA's already inflated statistics showed that there were less than the reported number in the three towns. The expenses for leasing land also seem to have been slightly exaggerated since al-Azzah and Ayda Camps were situated on relatively small plots of land, and Dahaysha and Qalandya Camps were situated partly on former Jewish-owned land. The Bethlehem D.G. further suggested that additional sums should be received from the Agency for the refugee clerks and teachers. These were classified as 'unneedy' and thus did not receive the aid to which they were entitled, saving UNRWA some J.D. 1,000. He also pointed out the high sums spent on refugees outside the camps on education, health and welfare matters.[12] The 1958 Hebron Area report included the assistance given to the Agency in building asbestos shelters in the area's camps and facilitating distribution in the Frontier Villages.[13] It can be seen, then, that the government manipulated the situation to its economic advantage by making the Agency responsible for any expenditure on the refugees even in spheres originally outside the actual agreement between them.[14]

B. JORDANIAN CITIZENSHIP,THE REFUGEE STATUS AND REFUGEE SEPARATISM

The Government pursued a two-sided policy with regard to the refugees' political status. It wanted to effect the political integration of the refugees, doing away with any notions of Palestinian separatism. The main instrument here was the granting of citizenship and all its rights. On the other hand, in order to ensure the permanent economic and general responsibility of the international community for the refugees, it had to preserve the refugees' exclusive status in the eyes of the outside world. As with annexation, it feared the other Arab countries labelling them as traitors, which would hamper the process of the refugees' integration. This was also a prerequisite for bargaining with Israel. The preservation of this special status was also used to pacify the refugees at the same time as pursuing the integration policy, as if there were no contradiction between the two. Furthermore, it tried to gain the trust of the refugee "citizens" by helping them to take advantage of the UN's willingness to provide, yet without forcing the refugees to commit themselves to all the implications of citizenship.

The refugees' special political status was also maintained for the enormous economic benefits it offered though this was an essentially tacit aspect of a policy which required that the Government constantly reiterate its commitment to refugee rights and the Return, with all their political connotations. The two policies inevitably had close bearings on each other, and clashes between them were likely. The question of just how far the Jordanian Government could contravene the wishes of her refugee subjects, and of how far the refugees could push the Government, is the story of their mutual relationship as well as of that between both and the Agency.

Jordan's proclaimed readiness to absorb the Palestinians and represent their case was followed by practical measures which the Palestinians saw as an indication of the regime's future aims. But, as previously indicated, neither declarations of policies nor constituted law could bridge the mutual suspicion and abuse between different segments of the population, or between the annexing regime and its annexed subjects. Yet these practical steps were prerequisites for any further consolidation. Jordan demonstrated its intention in this respect by being the only country to offer citizenship to its refugee subjects—which it had to do anyway to continue claiming to speak for most Palestinians.

The Additional Law No. 56 of 20 December, 1949 stipulated the citizenship rights, duties and obligations of all Jordanians. The new law provided for the refugees' participation in the special Parliamentary Elections that were about to follow, granting them equal political rights with other Palestinians or Trans-Jordanians. It also allowed them to acquire a Jordanian passport, thus enabling them to travel between the Arab countries in search of employment. Hence economic benefits were coupled with political rights to provide for the refugees' potential absorption within the new framework. The decree also abolished the short-lived Ministry for Refugee Affairs, as the refugees had now become an integral part of the Jordanian Community.[15] The carefully worded decree announcing the establishment of the Ministry of Development and Reconstruction (M.D.R.) states the principles of the Jordanian policy concerning resettlement while simultaneously emphasizing the right of the refugee to his former home. The new law gave every refugee the right to be employed, and to acquire land and a home "until the final settlement in Palestine". This formulation was a continuation of the Jordanian policy adopted since the creation of the problem: that is, to make practical provision for the refugees' full integration into the H.K.J. at the same time as issuing declarations concerning their rights to return to their former places. Such a policy would antagonize neither the influential former landlords and rich refugees, nor all those insisting on return to Palestine as the only immediate solution. The policy was designed neither to contradict nor to endanger this right, if and when implemented. The emphasis on the temporary duration of the refugees' presence made the law more appealing and easier to digest for the new and suspicious Jordanian citizens. It thereby eased their practical settlement into the enlarged kingdom in which both Trans-Jordanians and Palestinians became officially known as Jordanians. In 1950 a whole series of declarations made by the Prime Minister aimed at calming the refugees by announcing their official equality with all other citizens.[16] Jordanian citizenship, was designed to dissolve the differentiation between Palestinians, whether refugee or non-refugee, and Trans-Jordanians by taking the sting out of the political aspect of the confrontation. In view of the restrictions imposed by all other Arab Countries on the entry of refugees, their freedom of circulation and right of employment, the Jordanian Passport became a valuable asset enabling them to by-pass many of these difficulties. Although a certain stigma was attached to a Palestinian passport holder[17] and many had mixed feelings about the situation in which they were trapped, virtually all refugees grabbed the opportunity of a passport if only for the economic benefits it conferred.

UNRWA's placement and vocational training schemes made the Jordanian Palestinians the most important manpower reservoir for the developing Arab oil countries. This suited the poor Jordanian Government, with little to offer economically, since it was an indirect way of providing employment. In consequence of the scarcity of cultivable land, most of it owned by a few local inhabitants, and the surplus of largely destitute population, the young, skilled manpower went to work outside the West Bank. The regime was to gain from this process of emigration both politically and economically. Weakening the West Bank's economic potential had an impact on political activity there. It removed the bitter, unemployed young, perpetuating somewhat the influence of the idle more conservative elderly who remained behind.[18] The younger people who did not leave could hardly dedicate themselves to "politics" since they were the sole supporters of their families. This situation also had its economic rewards for the West Bank families who received large sums in monthly remittances. These payments, in addition to helping the Palestinians raise their standard of living, became an important economic input for the country as a whole.

By granting citizenship to the refugees, Jordan sought to legitimize its claim to be the only viable country for Palestinians. Still it ensured that the refugees retained their special status and continued to qualify for international aid. The UN was solidly behind these provisions, naturally preferring a situation where most refugees were granted citizenship as a precondition for possible future integration. It assured the Government's responsible co-operation with UNRWA and its identification with the mutually agreed schemes. But such a step raised considerable opposition from outside Jordan.

1. *Jordanian Citizenship and Inter-Arab Relations*

The differing policies of each Arab country towards the refugees rested on several factors. Apart from reflecting their basic positions in the Arab-Israeli conflict, they were the product of political rivalries within the Arab world, together with social and economic problems obtaining within each Arab State.

In the early 1950's there were rumours of a possible resettlement of some qualified, skilled refugees in Iraq to help remedy the shortages in the professions consequent to the departure of Jews from Iraq. These rumours caused additional unrest in some Arab quarters, but also created a more conducive atmosphere for those intending to settle down in Jordan. The fact that the regimes in Jordan and Iraq continued to declare that there was no real contradiction between the final solution of Return and enabling the refugees to live as dignified human beings until that day, when, as Abdullah put it, "they would return as masters and not as slaves", appealed to many refugees, especially those with little, if any, previous national awareness.

The other Arab countries argued that any step which provided for the refugees' absorption in their new places would endanger the claim to a right to return. Although they did not all reject projects for the integration of refugees, no Government could publicly announce its readiness to embark on such schemes under the prevailing circumstances, least of all Jordan which was in such a distinctive position regarding the Palestinians. Jordan's policy was therefore attacked on the grounds that it disregarded its holy duty of keeping "the spirit of revenge" alive in the Palestinians' hearts, and that, by granting citizenship, it might kill their desire to return to their homeland and thus help Israel "to liquidate" the Palestinian cause.

In view of the growing number of refugees in other Arab countries requesting Jordan's legations to grant them Jordanian citizenship, the Arab League tried to institute a certificate which would be accepted in all Arab countries and would serve as a recognized Arab passport. But again the basic differences between the Arab countries combined with their internal economic problems to prevent the implementation of any agreed resolution. Jordan would not accept such a document, claiming that her refugee citizens already had a passport. Later, some Arab countries hesitated to admit as many Palestinians as they had previously, owing to fear and mistrust of their more acute political awareness. Lebanon feared a further disturbance of the delicate Christian-Muslim balance and the potential effects of large scale unemployment on the political dominance of the ruling Christian sect.[19]

Iraq followed Saudi Arabia's action of 1951 by granting civil rights to the 6,000 refugees living there in 1953. They thereby gained official equality with other Iraqis in most respects with the exception of the right to vote.

With the Arab League's failure to provide an accepted *laissez-passer* or common Palestinian identity card, there were further calls for the expansion of the Jordanian citizenship law. The short-lived *al-Awdah* (The Return) newspaper, which was later banned by the Jordanian Government, called upon the new Government to review the Nationality law and make the necessary provisions to include refugees wherever they were if they so desired. The paper said that the unification of the two Banks should be viewed as a step towards Arab unity, and advocated concentrating the refugees in Jordan—"their first country"—since the continuing Palestinian dispersal served imperialism's interests.[20] Such a statement essentially conformed to those made by Jordanian Ministers who promised the refugees equal rights with other citizens. As Finance Minister Musa Nasir put it, "there are no refugees in Jordan, as all the Palestinians enjoy Jordanian citizenship".[21] The Minister of Health, Dr Khalifah, said that:

> Jordan was not a "host country" as refugees enjoyed nearly all rights and were found in the bureaucracy with their impact on the Jordanian economy.[22]

Eventually in February 1954, Jordan widened its Nationality Law to include:

> Any Arab person born in the Hashimite Kingdom of Jordan or in the occupied part of Palestine and emigrated from the country or left—including the children of this emigrant wherever they were born—who would submit a written application and renounce their former nationality[23].

This decree was followed by more applications, and the Arab League once again proved to be no more than a forum for debate with little, if any, practical power. Scattered refugees who were not allowed to join their relatives in other Arab countries became even more angry and bitter.[24] The League continued in its attempts to debate and establish an alternative arrangement for use by all other refugees. But under the circumstances it could do very little to enact an agreed plan or to implement accepted decisions which called for the transfer of refugees from heavily populated Arab countries like Iraq or Syria.[25] Its special department set up to handle refugee affairs concentrated more on "co-ordination" and assisting Palestinian students than on anything else.[26]

The agreement between Iraq and Jordan, which cancelled the need for visas between the two countries as from August 1953, enabled a stream of Jordanians to flow into Iraq in search of employment. With the burgeoning of this emigration the Iraqis decided to revise their policy.[27] A similar arrangement with Kuwait was later requested by Palestinians in Jordan after news arrived concerning the death of a number of illegal Palestinian immigrants who had tried to make their way there.[28]

The Jordanian passport also enabled Orthodox Muslims to visit Mecca, something most refugees outside Jordan were unable to do unless they carried another Arab passport.[29] Yet al-Jihad newspaper complained in an article of the sectarian and geographic discrimination between a Palestinian and an East Banker in issuing travel permits.[30] The government denied such allegations and even disallowed the use of the term "refugee" in official reports. But such cosmetic changes could not eradicate the differentiation that existed in Jordan between the two or rather three parts of its population. These feelings were accentuated by the growing popularity of Egypt's leader, Colonel Gamal Abd al-Nasser (Nasir) among all Palestinians. Speeches about the solidarity between Jordanians and Palestinians could not alter the latter's growing awareness of their inferior position. The Government reacted by pointing out the importance of Jordanian citizenship, and from 1957 withdrew it from a number of those engaged in subversive opposition who had escaped to Syria and Lebanon. Others were expelled, and entry into the country by suspected disloyal elements was prevented. The potential withdrawal of citizenship threatened those who could not manage to acquire any other Arab nationality.

And yet additional amendments made later in the Nationality Law,[31] reflected in the words of Hazza' al-Majali, the Jordanian P.M. at the time, that all refugees could come to Jordan which regarded them as her citizens,[32] proved to have little or any impact. It did not therefore help the regime to neutralize opposition from outside Jordan, when from 1959 onwards it was constrained to face the renewed idea of an independent Palestinian Entity.

For their part, the refugees faced a serious dilemma and therefore their reactions were divided. Most were uneasy that Jordanian citizenship would contradict and replace their right to Return. However even before the annexation, in the hope of gaining immediate economic benefits, some refugees tried to take advantage of the King's aim to consolidate his position, and presented requests for the declaration of a five-year moratorium in favour of Palestinian debtors, who had incurred losses through the war and were unable to meet their commitments. Three years later, in October 1952, the second Jordanian Chamber of Commerce even called upon the Government to grant Jordanian citizenship to Palestinians living in exile.[33] While such steps could be regarded as acquiescence in the new changes and a wish to benefit from them, the Ramallah Refugee Congress on the other hand tended to ignore the Jordanian option and insisted on an all-Arab-States united policy in relation to the refugees. As ration cards were issued only to needy refugees, these 'better-off' refugees repeated their demand to receive "Refugee Cards" from UNRWA, which they argued should be issued to all refugees regardless of their need for relief,[34] for they were a symbol of separatism. The suggested "Refugee Card" would serve as a special Identity Card, manifesting unique status. It would thus ensure the UN's continued efforts to bring about the Return, and imply their temporary status in Jordan. Many refugees justified such demands on the grounds that Palestinian refugee status could not be regarded simply in economic terms, owing to the political nature of their problem. The government feared that this idea would gain wide support amongst the rest of the refugees and hence regarded this request as an indirect challenge by the G.R.C. to its authority. But perhaps this demand should be regarded as a sign of the refugees' anxiety and lack of security, rather than of any feeling directed against the Jordanian Government, which they did not hesitate to criticize on numerous other occasions. The G.R.C.'s occasional representations were directed mainly towards Israel and the West in an attempt to regain their frozen assets in Israel since they did not trust the Jordanian Government to achieve this. This should not be taken as evidence of an internal separatist move; after all, their leaders were involved in local and parliamentary politics. Towards the mid-fifties when their aims were mainly achieved, they virtually ceased to function.

Another way in which the refugees showed their discontent with the Government's policy was by sending petitions and memoranda to the Arab League. Much as they were disenchanted with such expressions, the authorities could not prohibit this in view of the explicit and implicit connections with the idea of Arab unity. However these petitions were rare. One such case was when the Jordanian Government refused to allow her refugee subjects to file applications for recovery of their blocked bank accounts in Israel.[35] It seems that this refusal was designed to make political capital out of the protests of poor refugees against these applications.[36] On another occasion the Nablus refugees sent a detailed petition to the League's Secretariat sharply criticizing amongst other matters, the League's conduct of the 1948 war, their treatment of the Palestinian Question, their alliance with the West and their attempts to make peace with Israel. Many of these protests appeared, within the context of the refugees' suffering and despair, as criticisms of the Arab League for not really doing anything to better their condition and for failing to turn back the wheels of history as had been promised. They were also a way of provoking the Jordanian regime.[37]

The Government was understandably angered by this, and by the cables sent by some refugees to the Turkish and Iraqi legations condemning the Baghdad Pact which Jordan wanted to join. It was further disenchanted with the Nablus refugees' distinctly separatist memorandum of 1955 demanding a refugee delegation at the UN's next General Assembly, a special Arab League passport in the name of the Palestinian Refugees and the establishment of Jerusalem as the country's second capital.[38] In response the Government refrained from taking any action against these refugee leaders but tried to allay their fears by publicizing its attempts to launch a campaign in the UN on their behalf.

Whenever they faced such growing suspicion amongst the refugees, Government officials and Ministers, and occasionally even the King, would visit the refugee concentrations and make reassuring speeches. The Government was adept at using such techniques to damp down excessive political activity.

2. The Regime and Refugee Political Activity

As already noted, there were inherent difficulties in the Government's dual policy. In particular, the difficulty of assessing the political intent or import of refugee activity was encountered at almost every turn, since any refugee body, conference, meeting, petition or demonstration, whatever its real purpose, tended to concern itself with several issues. Thus a petition might include mention of a sensitive political question amongst more mundane affairs, a meeting on refugee affairs might turn "political", a demonstration on relief issues could be used by the political parties. So although a rough classification of these political manifestations will be employed, it is somewhat spurious in the context of an overall picture in which all the issues were interrelated and might arise at almost any time. The manifestations too were interconnected: a conference led to a petition, or vice versa; a committee sent petitions or organized gatherings; gatherings led to the formation of new bodies, and so on. Equally, a petition might come out of the blue, or a committee become active again for no apparent reason and set off a chain of reactions from other committees.

While some of these activities were actually Government-initiated, the complexity and volatility of the whole situation meant that the Government maintained constant vigilance over all refugee petitions, applications to license meetings and conferences, the meetings themselves, the activities of committees, and especially demonstrations. Demonstrations, since they were often unpredictable, could flare up suddenly, and were more ambivalent and open to opportunist manipulation, were a special case.[39] They could not be watched, controlled and woven into the delicate fabric of the dual policy so easily, although they had their uses. However, a distinction should be drawn between these demonstrations, which related to the refugees' own practical demands, and demonstrations concerned with wider political issues such as opposition to Israel and British influence, support for Arab unity, and other manifestations where separatism was always waiting in the wings.

(a) Petitions

Petitions originated from all quarters; from individuals, *mukhtars,* to contingents of a particular village in a camp, camp committees, area committees, central committees or any refugee organ. They were directed at UNRWA, and at the Government, which was expected to support them and pressurize UNRWA. The Government was inundated with petitions from the very first, dealing with endless relief complaints, demands and other problems. This incessant stream included cases of genuine grievance, together with others motivated by sheer greed and self-interest on the part of profiteers. Some resulted from misunderstanding, others from the vicissitudes of weather and geography. Some complaints were made in order that the protesting person or body, for example a refugee committee, should not lose influence relative to a rival.

But the political content of petitions, especially in relation to the position of the relief agencies, varied over the years and served different purposes.

To begin with, only a few political representations were made against the UN immediately after the establishment of UNRPR. One such incident was when the Arrub Camp and the Bethlehem refugees threatened to begin a hunger strike at the coming General Assembly of the UN if it would not deal with the return of the refugees to their homes. Their petition stressed their view that the UN should determine their fate.[40] The *Voice of the Refugees* published an article which accused the UN of being the primary cause of the expulsion of the refugees[41] and thereby responsible for their plight. It was also therefore responsible for the solution of the problem which, together with imperialism,[42] it had created.

But generally speaking, the numerous petitions presented in 1949 included few political demands and concentrated on appeals for aid. Even with regard to the sensitive question of eligibility for relief, very little reference was made to the Red Cross "wanting to bring an end to the refugee problem by diminishing their numbers" as was done later. An article did so in August 1949[43] when the Red Cross struck off from the relief lists the names of certain people who claimed they were refugees. The newspaper called for a committee of enquiry to examine actions like this which weakened the political impact of the refugee issue by reducing the number of official refugees and accordingly the magnitude of the problem. This was the exception rather than the rule.

The Red Cross at this stage was very seldom the target for political criticism.[44] Most political demands and accusations were channelled through the C.C.P. to the UN Secretariat. In 1949, these came mainly from property-owning refugees who had organized themselves in the hope of at least regaining their savings deposited in banks in Israel, and receiving compensation for their abandoned property. Alternatively, they hoped for the setting up of an international Custodian. This lack of criticism did not result from the refugees' knowledge that the Red Cross was not a UN body. On the contrary, the differentiation between the Red Cross and the UN was not their concern and was never understood by the refugees, although the Red Cross tried, with little success, to clarify this point. But it seems that, at this time, the refugees were still recovering from the trauma of the war's outcome and cared only about their subsistence needs.

The establishment of UNRWA in mid 1950 clearly showed that no immediate solution was about to materialize. It concentrated on relief and work projects and aimed at resettling the refugees away from their former homes. The refugees were upset by the fact that the UN did not solve the problem in the way they had hoped and expected. They began making political and, at times, vicious attacks on the body upon which they depended, ignoring the fact that UNRWA's mandate did not initially stipulate any handling of the political side of the question.

By this stage political demands and protests were incorporated into most petitions, whether as a mere expression of frustration, or as a means of giving their requests for assistance more validity and vigour. At first these political expressions called for facilitating their immediate return to their former places, and in some instances demanded the implementation of the 1947 Partition Resolution. More rarely they included criticism of political affairs relating specifically to Jordan. But the inclusion of political issues also demonstrated the refugees' growing consciousness of political developments and realities around them. So in a memorandum of 1952 presented by the Jericho refugees and demanding better health care—doctors, hygiene, blankets, tent-replacement—there were also demands for allowing free political parties and the release of prisoners.[45]

A whole list of demands was incorporated into most petitions in addition to the principal claim. The refugees had many justifiable claims: living under miserable conditions many did not receive the items to which they were entitled. The petitions were therefore a mixture of demands: any request for additional blankets or other items was followed by an expression of yearning to go back to their homes. The notion of "The Return" was an integral part of any demand for improving the relief services and their situation. But the authorities were wary of there being other reasons, whether personal or political, for drawing up a petition. They therefore looked into each one to see if this was the case and to show that they, rather than the committees, were the source of effective redress and contact with UNRWA.

Refugees in towns or from nearby camps presented far more demands and petitions than those in remote places who were relatively poorer and in greater need. The latter were often disorganized, illiterate refugees, unable to pressurize the Red Cross and UNRWA. The Government in Amman was naturally more sensitive to the plight of the thousands of refugees living there. But although they enjoyed better employment possibilities than refugees elsewhere, by comparison with refugees living in Jerusalem for example, they received much less attention from the international charity organizations and voluntary agencies. To placate the resulting bitter feelings the Government, which was relatively easily approached by refugees living in Amman, tended to intervene more firmly on their behalf. Government intervention, control and manipulation of the petitions addressed both to itself and to UNRWA was absolutely necessary because of the overall refugee attitude to the Agency. As one local UNRWA employee put it:

> They said UNRWA doesn't work for refugee interests and are U.S.A. agents. The Agency, which they needed, was not acceptable to the people who considered UNRWA a drug to keep them quiet. They regarded it as an obstacle . . . up to 1960 they considered the Agency functioned against them, and were against the idea of UNRWA as it would keep them as refugees. They were eager for a radical change and the Agency could not help them in the Return but only help make them stay longer.[46]

In general, the Government was successful in using the petitions to balance the two sides of its policy, finding UNRWA amenable to pressure and persuasion, and the refugees ever ready to protest and demand more.

(b) Refugee Gatherings, Regroupings and Committees

The authorities viewed with great anxiety and caution any attempt by the refugees to form themselves into political bodies that would emphasize their separate status, thereby making it more difficult for the Government to act on their behalf. It was assumed that during this period of unemployment in the early 1950s the refugees, especially the youth, would live in an atmosphere of political tension and disorder congenial to the development of feelings of hostility to the regime. Alert to any activity amongst the refugees, the authorities looked with great suspicion on any application for licensing committees and conferences. It was their claim that "the Government and the M.D.R. took upon themselves all refugee affairs and their interests".[47] Therefore the Government pursued a policy of expedient allowance and containment in an attempt to balance "the triangle of forces"—Government/UNRWA/Refugees.

These committees were a mixed blessing: they enabled refugees to air their demands and criticisms and to channel them to the Government; they were also an instrument by which the authorities could easily mould "public opinion" in the camp and learn a lot about the prevailing views there. After consolidating its position and becoming tired of the frequent quarrels between these committees, the Government decided it no longer needed them and tried to make it easier for individual refugees to approach the authorities.

But it was not Government policy, especially in the early 1950s, to ban all meetings outright. Much as they feared them, there were occasions and reasons for authorizing some. Thus the authorities allowed a gathering each year on 29 November, the anniversary of the UN Partition resolution, and on 15 May, the day Israel was formed. These symbolized the refugees' disaster and their continued plight. Other occasions were external events such as debates in the UN on the refugee question, visits of foreign personalities, or major events in the Arab world.

The reasons for allowing meetings were to give vent to the pressure of criticism; to show the refugees that the regime was on their side; and to indicate to the West that unrest existed in Jordan. This would ensure continued pressure on Israel and most important, the indefinite continuation and expansion of the UN and other Western relief and rehabilitation operations. The meetings also enabled the Government to keep a close eye on the discontented elements and to bring into the open feelings of unease.

Hence it was inconceivable to turn down some applications, while others served Jordanian interests. But the tone of the meetings had to be carefully judged by the Palestinians, since they were closely observed by the authorities. In most cases the resolutions were checked prior to the gatherings. A tacit understanding of the rules of the game was achieved: the Palestinians usually not going too far and making sure criticism was indirect; the Government clamping down only when its limits of tolerance were exceeded. This cat-and-mouse game went on right through the fifties.

Thus the Government discovered quite early on that the annual meeting on 29 November could be used by Communists, who at this stage advocated a Palestinian State alongside Israel and opposed Jordan's presence in the West Bank. The gathering of the H.G.R.C. in Nablus on 29.11.51[48] was outlawed because the authorities felt it was "communist-inspired". The banned body tried to re-register and obtain a licence as a Charitable Association. The Government was not fooled and refused this too. Despite being prohibited, however, the body still sent innumerable petitions throughout the 1950s and continued to appeal for a licence.

On the other hand, support for the 1947 Partition from non-communists, mostly property-owning refugees or those whose villages fell within the Arab part of the Partition area, was not considered hostile to the regime. Such meetings were still being held as late as 1953[49] by which time the Communists had abandoned open support for the Partition. A secret report reveals that some of the non-communists confidentially informed King Tallal that, no matter what agreement might be reached between Jordan and Israel, they would remain in Jordan.[50] That is, they did not oppose him by supporting Partition, and hoped to receive his support by promising that any assets regained would be invested in Jordan. The applications which the authorities most favoured and encouraged were those from refugees who wished openly to support the Hashimites as representatives of all the Palestinians. For example, in 1951 the government warmly greeted an initiative by some refugees who tried to replace the many committees and organs in each country by forming a united body of refugees for all Arab countries under Abdullah's chairmanship. The proposed resolution for the conference[51] called on the government to expand its economic plans for the refugees, to reject the A.P.G. and demand the inclusion of Gaza in the Kingdom of Jordan. However, a delegation of self-appointed "representatives from Syria, Lebanon and Jordan", some of them recognized spokesmen, gained little response from the refugees. This was mainly because of who they were and what they stood for. Unrepresented elements feared being undermined and strongly protested. The government therefore cancelled the plan in order to prevent any dangerous snowballing of political debate. Appeals for licences for meetings often resulted in similar demands from other committees, or in protests from groups who felt that a rival was contesting their influence.

Visits of distinguished guests like the American Secretary of State John Foster Dulles, of Western Parliamentary Commissions or UN Delegations stirred up immense unease amongst the refugees, who felt they should emphasise their separateness and exclusiveness so that their political rights would be safeguarded in the event of a renewed attempt to solve their plight.[52] On such occasions formerly dispersed committees would revive their activity for a while, and the government, which had a direct interest in proving that a Refugee Problem was far from being solved, would allow these protests while attempting to control them.

(c) The Refugees, Relief and Separatism

(i) Up to the Brief Period of Relaxation

The major sphere of public affairs in which the Government allowed popular activity was the relief operation. Refusal to allow meetings on this issue could be damaging. It might alienate the refugees and weaken its negotiating position with UNRWA, whose continued work was growing ever more essential. When committees went too far in attacking UNRWA, the government stepped in and took measures to protect UNRWA's personnel and dispersed or even arrested the committee members. Such measures were occasionally taken against the heads of various refugee committees following their action against UNRWA's census operation. This census issue, like the cancellation of ration cards, placed the government in a difficult position. Government defence of UNRWA over these issues — although the regime itself had an interest in an inflated list — aggravated relations with the refugees, sometimes quite dangerously. The agitation and unrest following attempts by UNRWA to take a census, for example, gave committees a chance to reassert themselves and served as a stimulus to exclusive refugee consciousness.[53] Still, the Government decided not to ban all refugee gatherings and carefully considered every application on its merits. But the Government found that at all levels, from local initiatives

and UNRWA-Refugee congresses to tripartite Refugee/UNRWA/
Government and inter-Arab Conferences, the same problems kept recur-
ring. It was never possible to establish regular meetings or stable consultative bodies to ease the implementation of its policies.

In February 1953 the Hebron D.G. was asked by the Deputy Minister of
Interior for his opinion on an application from a group of refugees to
convene a general refugee congress. He answered that it would serve the
government's interests if a general refugee organization was established
which included carefully selected refugees from all areas, so that this unifying body would have decisive power on refugee affairs and be attached to the
appropriate Government authorities.[54] This experienced official was aware
of the refugees' concern for the continuation of these committees to ensure
their rights. He also knew that the existence of various groups, though it
undermined the possibility of a united refugee reaction to political events,
only complicated the Government's position. He therefore sought to create
machinery which would give the refugees a feeling that their view was taken
into account and their unique position preserved, while at the same time
terminating the numerous committees. It would make life easier for the
authorities if the refugee representatives were the regime's supporters.

One month earlier the Government had called a common meeting in the
form of a congress at which refugee delegates together with UNRWA
expressed their views. An article in *Filastin*[55] stated that until now, in Jordan,
as in the other Arab countries, the refugees were given relief and decisions
were taken without their having the chance to voice their opinions even
though they were the focus of all the activity. Now the refugees would have
their voices heard and would not remain mere signatures on petitions and
protests. But the response of the refugees both before and after the Congress showed the Government that it was impractical to hope for the establishment of a unified, amenable committee of "Yes men" without having to
confront unsatisfied demands from other unrepresented interests. The
Government, deterred by the mild criticism directed against it, feared that
allowing such gatherings would encourage counter-regroupings and stir up
the issue of representation, thereby highlighting the existence of potential
separatist political bodies. The existence of a number of competing refugee
organizations and committees only complicated the question of representation. Their fundamental personal and factional differences, mutual accusations and suspicions, coupled with the Government's fears that meetings
would get out of hand and engage in "politics", only hastened the authorities' decision to try to do away with them in the name of "unity" and
"security".

On the strength of the January Congress, the Nablus refugees held a
meeting a few weeks later where they called on the Government to
convene another all-refugee congress in Jordan.[56] The Government in turn
decided to gather its supporters from amongst the refugees at the end of
March to neutralize this demand. However, owing to the sharp reaction this

idea received from refugees all over Jordan, it abandoned the project. It, nonetheless, refused to licence either the Nablus or the Hebron applications. Similarly, in Hebron in 1954, the Government cancelled permission for a Refugee Congress following protests from other refugees there.[57] In such cases a position of stalemate had been reached.

All these proposed meetings were also opposed by the members of the Parliamentary Committee on Refugee Affairs—some of them refugees themselves—who feared that they would lose their unique position. This Committee strove but failed to represent all refugee committees. Refugee committees did not want to lose their influence and function, especially the camp committees which survived longer and did not trust the Parliament members.

Sensing the pragmatic nature of Jordanian policy and fearing its impact on their relief rights, many refugee committees called for their inclusion in a tripartite committee with the Government and Agency's representatives. This was a direct vote of no-confidence in the way the Government was conducting its policy towards the refugees. The refugees felt that the Government let UNRWA carry out all the projects they had made a point of rejecting, and insisted that the Government should control and supervise more closely UNRWA's activities. They regarded their inclusion in all common working committees as the only way to ensure and facilitate that demand. Tired of the refugees' constant requests, the Government diverted them by suggesting the establishment of a consultative committee.[58] But owing to the conflicting responses, the Government again abandoned its own proposal, fearing that this suggestion would become a divisive issue, and because it was very difficult to set up a committee which would represent all refugee factions.

It further hesitated to allow the 1955 UNRWA-Refugee Congress, restricting it to a-political subjects[59] and limiting its duration to one day. The Government was hardly enamoured of this assembly and did not share the Western view of "participation in the process of decision making". The Congress was urged by the American heads of UNRWA who thought that it would benefit everyone if claims were aired and answered and if, more generally, the refugees were given a feeling that their views were being taken into account. The Minutes of the meeting[60] prove that it was extremely difficult to ensure this, as it was impossible in such a delicate situation to make a distinction between relief and politics, especially when every subject involved interpretations by the refugees of the Agency's policy. Questions such as the Census, eligibility, housing etc. had immediate political connotations. Practically every problem was in essence "political" and, although the Government was involved in the selection of the refugee representatives[61] and its clerks were present, the authorities could not prevent the natural course of such a gathering. Following the Congress the Government was faced with a request by refugees to set up a "Refugee Office" in Amman.[62] In order to appease them the Government permitted the office to be set up. However, it was not allowed to function until the beginning of the brief period of Government concessions.

But committees, gatherings, congresses and meetings were regarded by the refugees as essential, being the only way they could keep alight the flame of refugee separatism, debate their own future and have a say in their fate. They were a way of ensuring their political rights and the expansion of UNRWA's schemes "until the Day of Return"—the ever-present proviso. Their growing insistence on these committees and meetings arose out of a disillusionment with the Arab countries on the one hand and an antagonism towards the aims of UNRWA on the other, rather than out of criticism of the Jordanian regime as such. But there remained a powerful yearning for the achievement of real Arab unity, without which they felt victory over Israel was impossible. The latter was given impetus by the Egyptian President Nasser's immense and growing popularity amongst the Palestinians in general and those in Jordan in particular. He was seen as their leader and Messiah who would take them back to their homes. He was the incarnation of Arab unity and the British were the obstacle to the realization of this dream. Accordingly many refugees, like others in Jordan, opposed the Baghdad Pact, rejoiced at Glubb's expulsion in 1956 and were filled with hope when the first National Government was set up thereafter headed by the Trans-Jordanian member of the opposition Sulayman al-Nabulsi. Even Egypt's defeat in Sinai that year did not alter this kind of feeling. The nationalization of the Suez Canal was viewed as Nasser's personal triumph, and as the victory of all Arabs over Western Imperialism. They became far more proud and confident. The Day of Return seemed finally within their reach.

(ii) Months of relaxation

All political activity was now co-ordinated on a wider level, the refugee committee showing little sign of action. The refugees enthusiastically participated in the common gatherings which demanded the democratization and liberalization of life in Jordan, though their voice in these general meetings was kept to a minimum by the far more prominent local leaders. The issues were different, and there was no room for their petty quarrels.[63]

Since many complaints from refugees were directed against the Arab League, the Arab countries sought to demonstrate their good intentions by convening the Arab States Conference on Refugee Affairs in Jerusalem in September 1956. This helped to strengthen Jordan's position amongst the refugees. The Government was anxious to host the meeting, knowing that speeches delivered in Jordan by the Arab Countries' representatives would not be directed against Jordanian policies. It could point out that its aims coincided and were co-ordinated with those of all other Arab countries. A meeting held elsewhere would probably have different results. By publicizing its aims widely before the conference the Government tried to indicate to the refugees its important role not only within Jordan but outside it, in the Arab arena. The Conference received a number of petitions calling for an all-Arab countries' refugee body to be set up to represent the refugees, protests against the failure to include refugees in the debates, and demands for a higher standard of living similar to their brother Arab citizens and for the removal of employment restrictions.

The Conference only proved to the refugees and to all host Governments that, beyond such meetings, very little could be done in terms of a unified Arab policy. Once again the Jordanian Government could not but gain from this inability, claiming to continue to perform its duties to the refugees in the name of Arab unity. The participants decided that the conference would convene annually. The refugees were pleased that the new Government consulted them on their problems. Thus in December 1956 it asked the Refugee Office to review the proposed new UNRWA/Government agreement to replace that of 1951.[64] The Refugee Office opposed the new version and suggested amendments. This was supported strongly by the new Committee for National Guidance, set up in Nablus and by a special refugee conference which convened in Jerusalem on 11 January 1957. This Congress was convened by the Government as a show of solidarity with Egypt and in order to condemn Britain, France and Israel, who were still occupying Suez and Sinai. It included refugees from all over Jordan. They congratulated the Government since, as one of the speakers put it,

> previous Governments in Jordan opposed any convening of gatherings and congresses of refugees, especially during the period of the tyrant Glubb. But now our Government is from the people, to the people and gave us this freedom.[65]

The Congress's resolutions supported the Government's policy and praised the King for his new role as a liberal monarch and for his promise that Jordan would reject any solution of the Palestinian Question unless the Palestinians had been consulted. This conference was followed by a call for a General Refugee Congress in Jericho to be convened on 25 January 1957. And it seems that this kind of mutual respect continued for a few months until April 1957, when the attempted coup by Nabulsi's supporters within the army took place.

(iii) Following the Clampdown

After Husayn's success in putting down the coup all forms of political activity were banned—from camp committees and newspapers to political parties and sports clubs. Petitions of course continued, but without political content, and gained a new prominence as the Government showed its care for the refugees. The planned yearly meetings of the Arab States Conference on Refugee Affairs were now shelved. Given the rising hopes of Arab unity and the repolarization of the Arab World, Jordan felt that additional meetings would not serve her position amongst the refugees, particularly in view of the now tense Egyptian-Jordanian relationship. The Jordanian files show that even before this, there is little evidence that the refugees as such ever "revolted" against the monarch or even played any prominent part in the mid-fifties disturbances as claimed by outside sources.[66] Being aware of attempted Egyptian subversion, the authorities took measures to ensure that it was not the refugees they had to fear during the final three years of the decade. Government officials met refugee *mukhtars* and ordered them to warn the refugees. Army forces were stationed in certain areas ready to move in "to restore law and order". Furthermore, the regime organized its loyal supporters throughout the kingdom, especially in the West Bank, arranging "spontaneous" delegations which came to the Palace to express their support for the King and to condemn Nasser's policy. This was now the only form of licensed refugee committee. Some of their members believed wholeheartedly in the King, others felt compelled to join in as they were expected to. At that crucial period the regime considered abstention to be siding with the opposition. Many of those who, emotionally or otherwise, supported the opposition suppressed expression of their feelings, fearing the consequences for themselves and their families.[67] They knew that if they failed to pay their respects they might be "asked" to do so, and might be classified in a political category which would hardly serve their immediate interests. Communism was anathema. Any opposition elements were likely to be regarded as such even if they were orthodox Muslims.

The disturbances of 1957 and 1958 which were widely publicized in the Egyptian and Syrian Press, were described in the propaganda warfare as "The Refugee Rebellion" *(thawrat al-laji'in)*. The Jordanians responded not only by defending their position but also by publishing resolutions of refugee gatherings in support of the King, and in condemnation of Nasser and his administration in the Gaza Strip. A "congress" held in Amman renewed the refugees' *bay'ah* and invited the Egyptians to visit them in their camps and see for themselves their calm, secure life as equal citizens.[68] The Prime Minister also met various refugee groups which came to the Palace to express their support, assuring them of the government's intentions concerning their Return to Palestine.[69] Amongst the cables and letters of support received by the King those from the young were given specially wide publicity to demonstrate the regime's "considerable popularity" amongst them.[70]

Government officials travelled around the camps and villages to encourage support, making promises of improved conditions, listening to complaints and demands, and handling immediate problems to prove Government efficiency and concern. During such visits refugees were warned both against joining subversive activity, and failure to report it,[71] which was dealt with.

The Government took similar measures in response to the protests triggered by the UN Secretary-General Dag Hammarskjöld's report on the Refugee question in mid-1959. Once again the Prime Minister assured all the delegations that there was no contradiction between their being full Jordanian citizens and their natural right to Return[72] and the army commanders went around the camps to clarify this policy.[73] Much the same happened following the Iraqi President Qasim's declarations on the independent Palestinian Entity.[74]

There has been a tendency to categorize these cables of support or solidarity gatherings as instigated solely by the authorities. It should be pointed out, however, that the reviewed Jordanian files and top secret records revealed only one gathering where this was definitely the case. It might be claimed that the orders were issued to the officers by telephone, or conveyed orally to local politicians by army officers whether or not they had received orders to do so. However, the suggestion that they were always oral seems somewhat strange in the light of the content of some classified reports in these files. In any event people joined gatherings whether they were the King's known supporters or were ordered to.

In general, refugees' political reactions and visible responses to problems relating to their immediate living conditions were far more consistent, and their timing was frequently quite independent of political developments inside Jordan or concerning Arab rivalries as well as of events connected with the Palestinian Question. In that respect, refugee separatism was a constant feature in the political life of Jordan and the authorities had rapidly become adept at watching for its manifestations, and allowing its controlled release, especially when this coincided with the regime's own interest. This was particularly true of relief issues, provided refugees did not seek a position apart from the Government. This pattern of initiative and response was similar throughout the 1950s, with slacker or more active periods reflecting the prevailing political atmosphere. Once again, the refugees' difficulty lay in their diversity of motives and lack of cohesion, which made it all the easier for the Government.

C. RELATING TO THE INTEGRATION SCHEMES

The Press and the Parliamentary Papers contained many declarations by the Heads of State and Ministers ruling against any possible resettlement of the refugees in Jordan as a solution to their problem, or even as an intermediary step "until the Day of Return". In that respect the official Jordanian policy was quite clear, though Jordan still claimed to be a homeland for all Palestinians and the Government emphasized its support for the various economic schemes, saying that these assisted the country's development from which all citizens were benefiting. Jordan was attacked by Israel for preventing the refugees' resettlement and for preserving their status in the camps; she was attacked by the Arab countries for supporting the West's aim by accepting the principle of their absorption outside their homes and ignoring the refugees' wishes. Hence Jordan, which could resettle only a limited number of refugees in the various proposed agricultural projects, was faced with constant criticism of its Government from within and without whenever it opted for a project relating to refugees.

An examination of attitudes, policies and actions with respect to refugee integration must therefore centre around the regime's manoeuvres in its attempts to cope with the problem. One must ask whether the steps initiated by the Government conformed to its official policy, and whether the refugees' response truly reflected the predominant attitude common amongst them. Could the Government advance any economic schemes without the approval and participation of at least some refugees; and how did their reaction to the Government's steps influence its policy?

The immediate meaning of integration to the refugees was the denial of any possibility of the Return or of receiving compensation. Hence the refugees were deeply troubled about the Government's position on the subject. The regime could not afford such popular resentment when trying to consolidate its position. It therefore tried to gain political capital by publicly ruling against all the proposed large resettlement projects—which in practice ignored the monarch's political and economic handicaps—and turned quietly to support any small so-called "rehabilitation" schemes, which in essence meant the same. The large programmes were not feasible as they became a major issue arousing political activity which was not only undesirable, but hampered any relief work amongst the refugees.

For the first few years following the war even the small projects were not successful. For example, Musa al-Alami's project[75] received some support from the Government which allocated a certain area in the Jordan Valley. But this help was far from what Alami expected to receive. The Development Council which served as its Executive was composed of prominent Palestinian figures including refugees.[76] The Government thought that this array of personalities would calm the refugees, whose opposition to bettering their situation was crumbling away in the face of the severe conditions of the first two winters. More than anything else in fact, these winters led the refugees to start building more permanent shelters, and thus initiate new patterns of life-style within the camps, as the only way of protecting their families.[77]

The Government urged the refugees to consider all possibilities for helping themselves for the sake of their loved ones. It pleaded for trust to be placed in its policy of supporting the Return while bettering their lot "until that Day". Wide publicity was given to Palestinian statements supporting the refugees' participation in such schemes.[78]

At times pressure was exerted on refugees who refused to enrol in UNRWA's Work Projects which, like all of its schemes, regardless of their names or titles, were intended to accelerate the refugees' integration into Jordan or elsewhere. In November 1950 the Nablus D.G. notified all *mukhtars* that according to the Supreme Council for Relief of the Refugees, refugees could face cancellation of their ration cards if they refused to be employed in the Agency's work schemes.[79] This firm approach was aimed at those who incited the refugees to reject the projects. In many cases such people were themselves living more comfortably than the refugees, or holding more ration cards than they were entitled to.

The Government also began allocating plots of land for "cultivation by refugees"[80] who received seeds, equipment and guidance from the UNRWA. From 1951 small agricultural projects made modest progress resulting in an increased number of refugees wanting to join in. This was by no means a large proportion, but these pilot schemes were meant to pave the way for larger ones. The Government, together with UNRWA, examined the economic absorption capacity in areas where there were State-owned lands. It did not want to provoke more resistance from local Palestinians by having to expropriate their land for such purposes. Apart from such State-owned land, the authorities allocated former Jewish-owned land[81] for these projects. The Press reported the utilization of some 22,000 *dunam*[82] of land in this category in Qalunya and Bir Nabala, for example, in the Jerusalem area and Hubaylah[83] (formerly Gush Etzyon lands) in the Hebron Area. Artesian wells were dug and land was acquired in the Jordan Valley from local *Shaykhs*. One of the arrangements agreed upon in 1951 between the Agency and the Government concerning the integration of refugees was that UNRWA would:

undertake works of public utility such as water supplies, schools, dispensaries etc. in villages in Jordan on condition that the village benefiting from such works shall provide reintegration facilities for one refugee per JD1,000 spent . . . placing at the disposal of named refugee families:
a) either a house or sufficient land on which to build a house, and
b) sufficient cultivable land to enable him to grow crops for his maintenance . . . 40 *dunam* of land . . . in the case of non-farming craft . . . no land is needed . . . but the village must undertake to allow the man to establish himself in the village . . .
But there must be a clear link between money spent on village utilities and refugees rendered self supporting. Apart from the money spent on the former, UNRWA will also assist the refugee in providing their housing and in preparation of the land allotted to them . . . (or) provide the capital to enable them to obtain tools and the raw materials to set themselves up.[84]

It was also agreed that the land should be provided by the Government and that a formal transfer of the land to the refugee would be necessary. Needless to say, such an arrangement entailed far-reaching economic implications since it gave the widest interpretation to the Agency's terms of reference.

Meanwhile the Government encouraged UNRWA's policy for the

establishment of huts instead of tents in the camps. This programme met
with vicious rejection from the camps' inhabitants, who saw it as the first step
towards their resettlement. But by then refugees had begun building shacks
and making "extensions" to their tents, though more so in some camps than
in others. Other refugees followed suit, the weather and fear for their
children's health encouraging them more than anything else, even if most
refugees continued openly to oppose the scheme, remaining adamant in
their official position.

UNRWA gave roofing materials to anyone who would build the walls. In
some places it provided the necessary wood, stones, materials and tools.
More refugees took advantage of this opportunity towards the winter of
1952,[85] especially after UNRWA's Press communiqué telling anxious
refugees that the Korean War meant a world shortage of tents, that the
Agency could not replace the tents and that they would therefore be well-
advised to take advantage of the offered building facilities.[86] UNRWA
further calculated that the huts could be built at the cost of the worn tents,
which had to be replaced often. Owing to a sudden shortage in building
materials and the "disappearance" of large quantities from the stores, a
proposal for providing each family with a JD15 "Building Grant" was
discussed by the authorities.[87] The Jordanian documents on this subject
reported vocal rejection amongst the camp refugees alongside their actual
enrolment in the scheme — which was purposely left unnamed.[88]

The small resettlement schemes under the more acceptable name of
"Rehabilitation Projects" were well on their way. The construction of
houses upon which UNRWA hesitated to embark owing to its fear of the
refugees' fierce reaction, began in Ghur Nimrin[89] in the Jordan Valley, and
Jabal al-Nazif in Amman, along with two other programmes in Ghur al-
Far'a, Bayt Qad[90] near Jenin and Burma in the East Bank. The Development Bank established for that purpose with UNRWA's money was examining any proposal from refugees, who were encouraged to work together on a
co-operative basis. UNRWA emphasized that its mandate was for handling
the relief problem and that these projects were not replacing a political
solution but merely helping the refugees to help themselves "until the Day".
Suspicious refugees were reluctant to accept this and feared that gradual
integration would jeopardize their entitlement to Return. But many viewed
with growing interest the various projects where enrolment was conditional
on cancellation of the ration cards. Still, even those who held more cards
than they were entitled to hesitated to take the risk of making a new start in
life.

The stipulation concerning the surrender of cards made it difficult for the
refugees to join in, since it was generally interpreted as giving up the right to
Palestine. The cards were seen by poor refugees as their only asset, guaranteeing
the continuation of the relief operation, serving as an "insurance policy" for
the UN attendance to their plight. It was their "Passport to Palestine". In
view of Israel's propaganda campaign on this subject, the ration cards

gained even more importance in the eyes of the suspicious refugees, who could not understand the conditional surrender unless there were other hidden implications in the UNRWA schemes. It was as if handing in the card would cancel the refugees' status and diminish the size of the Palestinian Question. And this view has continued ever since.[91] Owing to this kind of feeling, the Government withdrew proposals in both 1949 and 1953 to replace the ration card with an outright payment from UNRPR and UNRWA.

For the Agency, pressurized as it was by the U.S.A. it was essential to strike off the names of project participants from the list. Yet such deletions had neither economic logic—as the rations given to the refugees did not cost that much— nor political logic, as there was no way the various projects could either at that stage, or in the foreseeable future, absorb large numbers of refugees, even if UNRWA was to be saturated with applications. Since the lists were already inflated and the numbers distorted, cancelling small quantities of cards could do nothing for an international organization eager to make progress and attract more refugees to its projects.

In its effort to recruit more refugees to the project the Government attempted to clarify its policy and pacify the unease. And the UNRWA-subsidized M.D.R. gave the usual reassurances, namely that the right to Return was not affected, and that the projects were for all Jordanians' benefit.[92] But owing to political agitation the number of refugees applying was still lower than expected. Even in Amman the number of applications did not exceed 140 by October 1952.[93] The instructions given to the tenants of the Jabal al-Nazif Housing Project in Amman reveal the scheme's regulations: the Government leased units of 50 sq.m. at a rent of JD1 per month for 3 years, to each refugee in exchange for his ration card, while item No. 7 clarified that such acceptance did not contradict his Right to Return.[94]

Now that it was clear that ration cards were the 'passport' to inclusion in the projects, those refugees whose savings were by then exhausted and who held no card, naturally tried to obtain one. Further friction resulted when they were rejected by UNRWA, leading to pressure against the projects from the disappointed and making it more difficult for others to join.

The refugees became increasingly restless with the growing number of UNRWA official visits to the camps, frequently conducted in the company of the foreign Press. One report on such a visit to Dahaysha Camp said the refugees regarded it with great suspicion, seeing it as an UNRWA attempt to spy on them and to discover their attitude to the projects. They were even more sensitive owing to the absence of Government officials on such occasions.[95] On the other hand, UNRWA became increasingly perturbed by the continuing Jordanian declarations of opposition to resettlement which, the Agency felt, affected their work and hampered the agreed schemes.[96] UNRWA claimed that the Government was playing off the refugees against the Agency in a manner that served no-one's interest. It wanted full Government co-operation, insisting that this would better UNRWA's image and enable it to function far more effectively. UNRWA therefore rejected the

Government's ambivalent policy of working for resettlement in practice yet denying that it was doing so. Paradoxically, it was precisely for that reason that the various political parties[97] attacked the Jordanian Government.

The parties, the Press and the regime, each for different reasons, gave wide publicity to Israeli declarations of intent not to allow refugees to return to their former homes, many of which had been taken over and redeveloped: the first two, whose influence could not be ignored, in an attempt to strengthen the refugees' yearning for the Return; the Government in order to urge refugees to turn to more practical efforts such as joining the various Resettlement and Rehabilitation Projects. News about the waves of Jewish immigrants and establishment of new settlements and the development of Israel, was spread by the Western media and more especially by the various local radio stations. The Israeli Arab Christians, who were allowed to cross the border into Jordan through the Mandelbaum Gate for Christmas and the New Year, gave personal accounts of these developments which further perplexed the refugees and induced an ambivalent attitude. Growing bitterness and awareness of the new reality went hand in hand. More declarations came from the refugees as well as from the Government on the proximity of the Day of Return, even as practical steps were being taken at odds with the supposedly interim nature of their presence.

Owing to the high cost involved in the maintenance and yearly replacement of tents, the Agency and the Government both felt by the mid-fifties that building permanent, more decent dwellings would serve everyone's purposes. But replacing the tents and the huts built by refugees in 1949 with proper asbestos shelters was for a while a somewhat sensitive operation. The refugees regarded it, like most projects, as a further measure to tie them down in Jordan—some claiming, perhaps rightly, that it was an indirect form of resettlement. The term "shelter" (malja') was used to emphasise its temporary nature so that it would appeal to refugees as just another form of protection "for the time being". The basic aim was the establishment of the "shelter" in place of the shack, hut or tent. In the Jericho camps refugees refused the offer, justifying this supposedly on political grounds, but in reality because they were inappropriate for the hot weather of the Jordan Valley, where the only way to survive the heat was by living in baked-mud straw huts. In fact they were the first to build huts as early as 1949/50. A different situation occurred in Hebron where the D.G. said that many refugees rejected the idea of a stone hut as it would hinder their moving in search of employment.[98] In the harvest season, for example, they took their tents to the East Bank. This induced the Government to postpone the execution of this project[99], which it whole-heartedly supported, out of the hope that better living conditions for the miserable refugees would accelerate the process of practical integration. Before long, building started in most camps, and the Press was full of details giving the number of units in each camp and the dates of proposed erection. The project was to include 10,000 units to be established in two phases.[100]

Once the process of building shelters was underway, it reversed the trend for refugees to move gradually out of their tents into the neighbouring town or village. The camps in or near towns, with their rent-free shelters and attendant amenities, began to be more attractive. This led to three groups of people moving into the camps: those who had left the camps previously; refugees living in surrounding villages and towns[101] (where rents were often high); and, later, poor non-refugee villagers who envied refugees these facilities. This movement ran counter to the Agency's intention, which was to improve conditions for the remaining camp refugees and help their integration, while keeping down the size of the camps. Now the Agency faced growing concentrations of refugees, and had reluctantly to assist a few poor people who, by any definition, were non-refugees. The Agency was troubled by this latter development, because they found their way into the camps by two means. Most of them rented dwellings or rooms from refugees whose sons had emigrated to Arab oil countries. A few bought or rented shelters from refugees who had built their own houses close to the camps, using money sent from their sons working abroad. As emigration expanded, so did this whole process up to 1967. On the few occasions when UNRWA tried to evacuate these people, it found itself legally powerless and opposed by the Government.

So the camps gradually turned into "a temporary form of resettlement", as one interviewed UNRWA official put it. By 1958 they became self-contained villages,[102] changing the refugees' pattern of life.[103] UNRWA promoted sports competitions between camps in the hope that they would foster some kind of new "local patriotism" amongst the youth who had been born outside their fathers' place of origin or who were too young to remember. In 1959 refugees even began planting trees, which in the Middle East signifies a deep attachment to a place. For this reason they had vehemently opposed such planting in the mid-fifties, destroying the nursery in Dayr Ammar Camp.

On the whole, refugees inhabiting camps in or near towns were pleased with the building scheme, regardless of what they might say in public, because it offered reasonable rent-free housing close to work. But the scheme confronted indigenous opposition from landowners, who feared that once such permanent dwellings were erected their land would become irretrievable, resulting in financial loss. This loss became considerable since land prices were rising as refugees themselves were starting to buy and build houses. The landowners feared that once the refugees were living in stone houses they would remain there regardless of any political arrangement, and that the camps would become proper suburbs of the town, with some refugees eventually living in better conditions than the native poor. So they criticized the refugees for "agreeing to be resettled", hoping to stimulate them to reject the scheme, and protested to the Government and the Agency.[104] The annual rent of JD1 per *dunam* per year they received could hardly compensate or placate them.

The Town Councils (T.C.s) tended to include these landowners and therefore often objected to these schemes. Hence the Jerusalem T.C. was relieved by the Government-UNRWA decision to transfer the Mu'askar Camp in the Jewish Quarter of the Old City[105] to another site in Anata, a few kilometres away. The site chosen for their resettlement was mostly formerly Jewish-owned land; hence the transfer would not be at the expense of the natives, nor would it raise problems of confiscated land. Furthermore, showing the refugees that they still occupied Jewish land would perhaps give them some satisfaction and a kind of tangible security, while naming the new camp Shu'fat attracted refugees, it being in a salubrious neighbourhood where many villas were built. Nevertheless, most refugees refused to move as they feared losing both their source of income—the market and the tourists— and the opportunity to pray in the second most holy place for Muslim believers. Consequently the army had to transfer them by force to their new camp as late as 1965.

Another UNRWA-Government scheme was in the Ramallah area where eight concentrations of refugees[106] were to be broken up and given land of their own. The Government wanted to resettle them near the Broadcasting Station away from the town's entrance. UNRWA refused to carry out the project as it knew it was bound to encounter problems. It was also not its policy to build new camps or to take over unofficial ones since it wanted to dilute refugee concentrations.

However the T.C. was anxious to move the refugees and promised it would provide and be responsible for sanitation facilities and would cover the land's rental for the first year, after which the Government would pay. UNRWA agreed.[107] The old houses which disfigured the town were to be demolished and the many non-refugees were to be evacuated by the Police to their respective villages.[108]

Throughout the period occasional rumours from outside of Jordan's intention to resettle the refugees, either in Jordan or in other remote countries, made it more difficult for refugees to join the schemes and for the Government to give them its blessing. But the fact that in 1953 Egypt agreed in principle to the Sinai Resettlement Project[109] could always be used against her. In mid-1955 the Jericho refugees attacked Egypt and Syria for their "spreading of false rumours", reminding Egypt of the severe restrictions imposed in the Gaza Strip:

> Did Egypt forget she was the first State to accept the projects of resettlement for the refugees in the Sinai Desert in return for $200 million for its execution? . . . you promised the Sinai Desert would be a graveyard for the Jews and it is turning into a graveyard for the Arabs.[110]

The publicity given to the fact that even Syria set up agricultural and rehabilitation projects[111] and to the tentative moves to join Jordan in the

Yarmuk Project helped validate the Jordanian Government's efforts to obtain the refugees' participation.

A special Government booklet entitled *The Eastern Ghur Project* detailed the scheme and its aims at length in the form of questions and answers, and provided data as to the rights and duties involved in it. The booklet emphasized that any farmer, not only a refugee, could be resettled in the project and later purchase the land he cultivated.[112] Like all rehabilitation projects, it aimed at offering the refugees something tangible in the hope that they would work harder once they owned it. As the Johnston Scheme (which had proposed the division of the waters of the river Jordan between Israel and the countries bordering it) had become a disturbing issue, the publication stressed that the new project had nothing to do with it. It emphasized that the army would defend the project in the face of an Israeli attack. It thereby hoped to give the impression that Israel rejected the project and to dissuade the refugees from categorizing and rejecting it as an "imperialistic" scheme. It also emphasized that this project had nothing to do with UNRWA, ration cards or any other refugee resettlement project.[113]

Overall, Jordan gained tremendously from the vast economic input provided by UNRWA, which did far more than simply relieve it of handling the relief of refugees. The backward State was modernized not only by the making of roads, the afforestation and the subsidizing of the education and health frameworks, but also by all the benefits accruing from the fact that an "international" organization of such magnitude, 98 per cent composed of refugees, functioned within a poor country. Naturally, almost everyone tried to exploit this situation and a great deal of corruption was involved. The rumours that high officials tried to arrange interest-free loans for themselves or relatives, and profited from land transactions needed for UNRWA schemes in the Jordan Valley were not without basis.[114]

UNRWA for its part had to justify its existence and aims, and the schemes had to start with anyone who would agree to the conditions stipulated. UNRWA's eagerness to find "ice breakers", as one interviewed UNRWA Representative put it, turned out even in the short term to be the projects' handicap: if the Agency wanted to make headway and bring in as many refugees as possible, it was forced to accept anyone. "We wanted some to begin and others to become envious and imitate". But they often attracted people who manipulated the system for short-term gain, selling the livestock and tools which they had been given to start their own small-holdings. They knew that UNRWA could not prosecute them and that they would eventually be readmitted to the ration lists. Only towards the end of the 1950's did most UNRWA projects pick up. Thus while some refugees managed to make a real success of their projects, others, impatient as they were, would not wait for their scheme to develop and deserted it to return to the camps.

The Agency, unable to plan for the long term since its mandate "could expire'', put vast sums into programmes whose output was not on the whole impressive by comparison with the expectations. Several factors militated against the successful accomplishment of the programmes: the kind of refugees joining the various projects, the bad soil in some places, insufficient water in the rain-fed project, never mind the right of refugees to return to the relief lists once they left a scheme. Furthermore, pressures against the various schemes from the educated and skilled refugees, from those who had assets and from the political leaders made it difficult for others to join. Those who could not get anything out of the projects feared that, given a chance, most penniless refugees, having practically nothing in the places they came from, would gladly opt for any project. This would diminish the size of the problem and allow settlement of the refugee question in a way that might destroy the possibility of receiving compensation or returning to their property. The ordinary refugees did nothing as a group to challenge these widely accepted dictums since they believed in these leaders and their explanations.

Yet the contribution and importance of these schemes lay perhaps in the foundations put down for the subsequent consolidation of projects from which the refugees, and especially the Government, could only gain. The precedents created facilitated the expansion of all the other rehabilitation projects in which the refugees began to participate more eagerly after the Sinai campaign of 1956. The defeat of Egypt shattered many refugees, to whom the Return began to seem even more remote. Although their belief in Nasser persisted they increasingly did what they could to improve their lot. Many of the older refugees opted for these projects of self-help while the younger generation generally went for vocational training, temporarily emigrating or migrating, with only a few engaging in their fathers' professions.

Since education was the path to re-establishing oneself, UNRWA, disillusioned with the agricultural projects, began towards the mid-1950s to concentrate on the second generation's integration through various education schemes. But the Agency's involvement in vocational training and education more generally brought forth complaints from the refugees of discrimination against them by the Government authorities, although UNRWA subsidized both Government and private schools which absorbed refugee students at elementary, preparatory and secondary levels.[115]

So the field of education was another area in which UNRWA gradually succumbed to insistent claims and demands that it originally had no intention of fulfilling. This pattern was followed in practically all its spheres of action. Eventually, this led to the creation of a "state" in itself which functioned alongside the kingdom's own machinery.[116] The Agency's international workers somewhat cynically named it "The Blue State" after the emblematic UN blue. Accordingly, the Agency's allocations grew, and its share of responsibility for refugees living outside the camps increased, thereby enlarging both the Government's economic reliance on it and UNRWA's dependence on the Government for facilitating its continued relief operation.

The Government even managed to relinquish responsibility for a section of the local population, the inhabitants of the Frontier Villages, which UNRWA judged not to be refugees. The 111 Frontier Villages (F.V.), towns and hamlets[117] had been largely disregarded and faced many problems.[118] The border cut them off from their lands and water supplies and from markets and employment further west towards the coast. Their communications were poor, both along the border where their road was broken up by the winding frontier, and with the West Bank towns, on whose markets they now depended. The economic stagnation that was steadily setting in was exacerbated by the processes of migration eastwards and of emigration by the young. (Only later did the residents begin to benefit from money sent home by migrant sons.) Furthermore, the Government neglected them not only on account of its lack of funds, but also because the migration aided its policy of "thinning out" the border areas to reduce infiltration activities. These villages became increasingly isolated and their inhabitants completely dependent.

Through petitions, protests, committees and lobbying, and with the help of the Government's intervention,[119] they tried to have themselves considered refugees under that part of the UNRWA definition which stressed loss of "means of livelihood". The Frontier villagers generally received half-rations, which were extended in 1955 to some previously excluded.[120] But the Government continued to refuse to subsidise the F.V. So it was left to UNICEF, UNESCO and many other international voluntary agencies to step in,[121] with assistance, providing for health, rations, relief items, education, small pilot projects, rehabilitation loans and self-help schemes. This aid was considerable and should not be underestimated, but it could not alter the fundamental problems.

Thus a complex pattern of interdependence between the Government, UNRWA and the refugees developed and became firmly established. UNRWA, which needed to justify its continued operation to its subsidisers, had to work through the Government. Only in that way would the refugees consider joining the various projects. Under the prevailing circumstances it was inconceivable for the Government to take over or to participate actively in the control of these projects. First, had they done so the UN could conveniently have stepped out, leaving the burden of running refugee affairs to them. Second, apart from the friction that would be caused by the UN's leaving, the Government would be in the impossible situation of itself working for direct resettlement—quite unthinkable in the Arab World. Such a situation could easily lead to a direct clash between the refugees and the Government, nourishing the animosity between Jordan and her Arab foes. Strengthening the Government's mediating position in the eyes of the Palestinian refugees helped promote their belief in the regime and consolidated the process of integration. Outside Jordan this was not the case. Reflecting in retrospect on the development of the Palestinian awareness, and comparing the refugee communities of Lebanon and Jordan, a senior international UNRWA worker remarked in an interview:

Despite all the refugees' vicious criticism directed against UNRWA, this American subsidised Agency did more than anyone in the world to preserve the refugee spirit and separateness and in actual fact fostered the development of the Palestinian Entity especially outside Jordan.

Chapter IV

Border Activity—Infiltration and Retaliation

The story of the years following the 1948 war is one of violations and counter-violations of the Israeli-Jordanian Armistice Agreement and of frequent escalations of tension.[1] The first attempts by the refugees to return to their homes and rejoin their families and retrieve deserted moveable property and assets that had been hidden[2] demanded courage and determination to overcome the numerous dangers. As a result of the activity of the unskilled "infiltrator" tension grew along the border. Border incidents also arose from the unwary attempts to occupy houses in demilitarized zones; from shots fired for no particular reason, and from the explosion of mines. The predominant form of infiltration reached its peak in the harvest season with peasants being tempted to pick their crops, fruit or olives from the other side. Malnutrition, attachment to their land and a burning sense of injustice moved peasants to face the risks involved. Even the various pilot projects which aimed at breaking this attachment did not lessen the peasants' determination to benefit from what they considered their own but was denied them by an artificial line they did not recognize.

Infiltrators also engaged in thieving and smuggling, though these were usually carried out by professional groups. Of course the local population, especially the Frontier Villagers, were also engaged in infiltration, much of it carried out by the bedouin. Additional problems were caused by the large scale infiltration from Gaza to Hebron, through Israeli territory, which began towards the end of 1950.[3]

Some infiltration occurred for the purpose of revenge. In these instances the nature of operations varied: sabotage of telephone and railway lines and water pipes, bombing houses, laying mines—all entailed clashes between the Israeli army and the various armed Palestinian groups, whether professionals or "Freedom Fighters". Most border incidents involved loss of life and heavy property damage. The number of casualties claimed by each side up until the Sinai campaign ran into the hundreds, most of which were caused by "regular and irregular terrorist and armed bands" in Israeli terminology, or "*fida'iyyin*" in the Arab Lexicon. Hence the Jordanians like the Israelis had a common interest in trying to prevent these "squads" functioning.

The literature of the time romanticized the reality to a certain extent.[4] Some Arab writers described all infiltration activities as part of a planned, organized struggle against Israel and as an expression of the yearning to Return. Consequently, they condemned the Arab Governments for seeking to limit it.[5] Such descriptions sometimes magnified and glorified the various operations. They put the simple smuggling in one category together with the later 1955 Fedayyin activities.

Smuggling was widely condemned by West Bank Palestinians. Two Refugee Conferences which gathered in Nablus on 29.11.51 called among other things for the condemnation of all smugglers as traitors and for severe measures to be taken.[6] Apart from lowering the prices of commodities in the West Bank markets, these activities were seen as an indirect form of Arab help to the Israeli economy and the local traders and merchants therefore felt justified in their protest. The Ba'thist Abdallah Rimawi, also regarded smugglers as traitors, but called for the money spent by the Government on preventing smuggling to be invested in the Frontier Villages themselves from where the incidents were launched, arguing that most infiltration sprang from the villagers' destitution.[7]

To the Israeli and Jordanian authorities acts of infiltration, whatever their motive, came under the umbrella of "outlaw intruders". Both armies were worried that, if they did not block the physically unsealable border, further successful infiltration would occur. They both became very rigid in their attitude to such operations, fearing the disruption of the status quo between their Governments. Glubb knew that every border incident was potentially the cause of a clash between the two armies. Unlike the politicians who demanded Jordanian military action, he felt that in open battle Jordan stood to lose more than just its army; border clashes had therefore to be prevented at all costs.

Israel claimed that easing border tension was basically dependent on the strict[8] implementation of the 1949 Armistice Agreement. Jordan argued that Israel took advantage of the incidents to demonstrate her powers. Both sides sent numerous memoranda to the UN and publicized what they called "the atrocities" and "aggressions" committed by the other. The Israelis felt that the Jordanians and the Egyptians should be able to control operations launched from their territories whether they be smuggling or, as later on, the activities of the Fedayyin. As far as the Jordanians were concerned, they were incapable of doing this even if they wanted to.

Bearing in mind the various coercions under which the Jordanian authorities functioned, it seems that they did their utmost to check clandestine crossings of the long, winding boundary. Still the Armistice Line was constantly crossed by different groups with varying degrees of difficulty.

A. CONFRONTING AND CONTROLLING INFILTRATION

There were three main ways of doing this: First, Israel and Jordan could reach agreements, make compromises or set up liaison bodies, at either national or local level; second, stringent controls could be imposed using the armed forces and the security services; and third, there were attempts at "thinning out" the populace of the border areas to lower the general level of violations.

Fear of Israeli retaliation prompted the various ways of dealing with infiltration, and was itself a possibility that had to be provided for by the Jordanians.

The Local Commanders' Agreement between the two armies, signed in Jerusalem between Moshe Dayan and Abdallah al-Tall in 1949, aimed amongst other things, at creating a forum where problems could be discussed and some agreement hopefully reached on arrangements to curb marauding, resolve disputes and discourage border clashes. It functioned under the auspices of the U.N. and sometimes proved quite useful but was later disbanded. The frequent meetings of the Mixed Armistice Agreement Commission also did little to help resolve border disputes.

At the local level only Battir Village reached an agreement with Israel. According to this agreement anything likely to harm the Israeli railway, which passed through that village and Bayt Safafa on its way to Jerusalem, would result in the villagers' being prevented from crossing the border daily to work their lands on the Israeli side. This kind of understanding entailed the fulfilment of all conditions of the arrangement to the benefit of both sides. Battir Village wanted to gain as much as possible within existing limitations and so sought to prevent any infiltration activity from its territory. It came to learn that infiltration, whether by refugees or F.V. people, could endanger the whole delicate basis upon which the arrangement rested.

As for the Jordanian authorities, one of the first steps taken was a widely publicized emergency measure against crossings of the border.[9] With many outlaws in the area, and arms being held by those who used to belong to one Arab force or another, the authorities ordered the confiscation of all arms. This was to prevent robberies or attempts to murder officials out of bitterness against the Trans-Jordanians, and to restrain any vengeful Palestinians from taking the law into their own hands and threatening the delicate agreement between Israel and Jordan. The Jordanian files are full of details concerning the various measures taken against infiltration and smuggling from the West Bank.[10] Many who took part in such activities were severely punished. Yet it seems that in some cases where pay-offs were made the activities were ignored. Jordanian officers were sometimes themselves involved in such operations or else overlooked activities which benefited the loyal bedouin. The punishments administered to infiltrators were widely publicized[11] to deter others. The Press gave prominence to the prohibition of infiltration and arms transactions[12] and to the fact that some people were killed or jailed after trying to cross the lines.[13] *Mukhtars* who failed to provide names and report such activities either through complicity or incompetence, were fired. They were replaced by new ones whom the authorities trusted but who were not necessarily more efficient.

Palestinians who infiltrated from Gaza generally requested their transfer to Zarqa'. The authorities, suspecting their loyalty, put them under surveillance[14] before granting permission. All new arrivals, who expected better treatment than in Gaza,[15] were questioned by army officers. By 1954 the Jordanian Government, having to a certain extent consolidated itself in the West Bank, approached the Egyptian Government to prevent this constant migration of refugees to Jordan. In order to deter this movement the Jordanian authorities announced that any refugee leaving the Gaza Strip and arriving without a permit would have no right to receive UNRWA assistance and would be subject to expulsion.[16]

Another measure against infiltrators was the occasional reinforcement of troops stationed near the borders. However this could not stop the Israeli army from striking at the local National Guard and the villages whence it was claimed they operated.

The Jordanian regime feared that the inferior Legion would be dragged into a clash with the Israeli army. The Legion was therefore ordered not to initiate any action, or even to respond to provocative Israeli operations, so as to prevent the Israelis from exploiting the situation and hitting the Jordanian forces.[17] The trigger-happy were punished and removed, and later Ahmad Sidqi al-Jundi, the Jordanian deputy Chief of Staff, ordered the armed forces not to shoot at any Jewish civilians unless they entered Jordanian territory and then only with special permission.[18] The local Press also called for action against infiltration which, they claimed, enabled Israel to take advantage and retaliate.[19] Since many incidents occurred through mistakes by shepherds grazing their flocks near the border, a special decree was issued prohibiting their presence close to the Armistice Line.[20]

Tougher measures tended to ensue after a series of particularly bad instances of violation or retaliation. Following the Israeli raid in Qalqilya, the Jordanians declared a curfew in the region six miles east of the border.[21] Ramallah Radio later rejected the Israeli allegations of Fedayyin activity launched from Jordanian territory.[22] The authorities, fearing that the arms distributed to the frontier inhabitants would start a new wave of border incidents, ordered the registration of any weapons and ammunition held by these people[23] with the intention of confiscating them.

B. REMOVAL OF REFUGEES FORM BORDER AREAS

To prevent the growing movement of Palestinians to and from Israel, the Jordanians decided to "thin out" the border areas, and to transfer the concentration of refugees who lived in the ICRC Refugee Camps close to the border to new camps further east. The regime had to decide whether to set up large camps, which ICRC could run more efficiently, or smaller scattered ones which it preferred for political reasons. The Government tried to establish eleven new smaller camps but only four were built and these grew to be relatively big. It also took advantage of the bad winter weather conditions of the first few years to encourage refugees to move into the warmer eastern Jordan Valley. But this mass movement was reversed in the summer when the valley became unbearably hot. The refugees moved back to the cooler border hills where they again became a problem to the authorities.

So in June 1950 the Jordanian Defence Minister ordered the removal of all refugees to a position 20 km east of the border lines.[24] This coincided with UNRWA's policies, the border camps being difficult and unsafe to reach. There was no main road access, besides which large central camps were easier to maintain and administer than small dispersed camps.[25] Still the Government faced severe security problems because of the high concentration of refugees along the border.[26] However by 1951 the bulk of those prepared to move had entered the camps. Apart from Tulkarm, no official camps were left for those scattered along the border. The reason for the camp remaining at Tulkarm was mainly fortuitous. The refugees initially occupied homes deserted by local inhabitants who had sought refuge in eastern regions. As more refugees poured into the area, the Military Governor was forced to commandeer temporary accommodation for them.[27] ICRC provided tents and necessary facilities and the camp established itself. The lack of available camp space elsewhere combined with the Government's concentration on the movement of the many refugees scattered around the area, were to ensure that it remained as it was. But the stream of refugees in 1951 from the evacuated, rain-flooded Janzur Camp situated further east, to the new Nur Shams Camp—specially set up for them near the town—troubled the A.C. as it inflated the border refugee population there. He therefore recommended their transfer to the more easterly Far'a Camp or to the East Bank. But this was not accepted.

Two large concentrations of refugees however still existed. There was an unofficial camp at Bayt Aula[28] which was dismantled in 1954; and the other at Qalqilya[29] which managed to achieve some recognition as late as 1965.

The Press hinted at the Government's policy of transferring refugees from the border camps[30] possibly out of a desire to discredit the regime. It certainly aimed to warn the refugees of the Government's intentions which were never publicly announced.

For their part, the refugees had mixed feelings.[31] Some were pleased to move and even requested transfer to the East Bank[32] anticipating more help and better care. Others viewed the move with suspicion;[33] they wished to remain in sight of their occupied homes, always hoping to return. A transfer to another camp in the east signified for them that their absence from their homes was not temporary. They felt betrayed by the Government and became suspicious of its actions after they were told that they could either join other camps or stay where they were, and expect little help from the Agency.

The Government certainly did not want to set up any development projects near the front line which might encourage these people to stay. The policy of transference contradicted the rumours of Jordan's intention to set up "model villages" there to be populated by refugees "until the Day of Return". This was said by some to be the best means of safeguarding the refugees' rights, since they would be settled close to their places of origin. *al-Urdunn* newspaper, which reported this scheme in December 1952, reflected the belief of Anwar al-Khatib[34] and of Defence Minister Anwar Nusayba in this kind of scheme.[35]

Nor did transferring refugees eastwards conform with the views and opinions of those outside Jordan. Prominent Arab writers called for the fortification of the border area. Muhammad Taqi al-Din al-Nabhani, in his book published in Damascus in 1950, called for the settling of all refugees in the remaining part of Palestine. He felt that all refugees along the borders of Arab countries with Israel should be housed in special temporary camps that would serve as army bases and not mere refugee camps.[36] Some Arabs further urged that these temporary settlements should be run by the refugees and serve as a departure point and preparation for the revenge, rather than as a means to stability *(istiqrar)* and reconciliation *(sulh)* as the West envisaged.[37] The Arab League's calls to establish tightly knit refugee settlements along the borders promised an active role for the refugees until the "next round". Acting as the League's spokesman, Ahmad Shuqayri, a refugee from Acre, visited the West Bank in July 1952 and put forward plans along these lines. He stressed that this kind of consolidation should not be seen as either direct or indirect settlement. On the contrary, it would create a firm base as a jumping off point for the "Second Round".[38] Nonetheless, refugees were hostile to all such plans,[39] regarding them plainly and simply as resettlement. The most vociferous opponents of these plans were on the one hand, former property owning refugees and on the other, the Communists. In reaction to Shuqayri's statements most of the Hebron refugee leaders declared they would accept nothing less than the implementation of the 1947 Partition Scheme and rejected settlement outside their homes. On the other hand, Qalqilya refugees protested bitterly in 1954 at what they considered UNRWA's intention to remove them from the front line. They argued that this plan contradicted the Arab League's proposal to settle the refugees near the Armistice Lines.[40]

However by then the escalating rate of migrants to Amman, resulting from the exclusive economic development of the East Bank, began to trouble the Government. It not only caused health, hygiene and economic problems, but posed a direct political threat to the vulnerable regime in the unstable days of 1954 onwards. The capital of the kingdom was already crowded with bitter, hungry people without these additional disillusioned refugees.

The first years: *A Refugee camp at South Shunah, Trans-Jordan, 1949. Situated in the Jordan Valley, the camp's population reached some 15,000 Palestinian refugees, who crowded into tents supplied by the LRCS — an arm of the UNRPR. (Courtesy of the League of Red Cross Societies Archives)*

Second Phase: *Soon the tents were replaced by different types of shacks. In the Jordan Valley the refugees erected mud-built shelters as shown by this photo of Ayn al-Sultan camp (near Jericho).* **(Courtesy of UNRWA)**

A new era: The Camps — a temporary form of resettlement: By the end of the 1950s, these shacks, in turn, were replaced by UNRWA-supplied asbestos and concrete shelters. A general view of Fawwar camp, one of the twenty camps in the West Bank, which housed some 5,000 refugees. Unlike most other

In other parts of the West Bank, the camps were generally situated along the main roads and near or in towns of which the camps gradually became proper suburbs. Compare photo taken of Dahaysha camp in 1949.........

.........to one taken twenty years later. (UNRWA photo by Odd Uhrbom)

View of Jabal Husayn camp, which became an integral part of Amman. According to UNRWA, the camp sheltered 14,527 refugees in 1961. (UN photo)

Distribution of Relief Items: UNRWA distributed flour to the refugees. This monthly event occasionally generated tension between the recipients and UNRWA's staff. (Courtesy of Mr. William Clark)

Concentrating on Education: More than half of the registered refugees were under 20 years of age. Although UNRWA always gave high priority to her health services and to the supplementary feeding programme, most of the Agency's budget went to education. The education system has grown to 623 overcrowded elementary and junior secondary schools as well as eight highly-equipped vocational training centres in and around the 57 camps UNRWA

Reversing previous policy, the Minister of Interior ordered the Agency not to transfer refugees' ration cards to Amman on health grounds.[41] The Deputy Minister for Welfare announced that only refugees who could prove they could support themselves and have a place to live could migrate to the capital.[42] The two agreed to remove refugees from over-crowded urban centres to the refugee camps, as the towns did not have adequate sanitary facilities.[43] Refugees outside the politically sensitive towns were better cared for and, from a security point of view, easier to control.

However it seems that such steps did not stop thousands of youngsters from moving into Amman and other East Bank towns.[44] Moreover, stopping this migration would have meant confronting the fierce resistance of the refugees, who depended on these urban centres for their living, and who might feel discriminated against by such a plan. As UNRWA refused to establish any additional camps and rarely granted recognition to the "unofficial camps", which were the Government's responsibility (although they assisted them), the Government had to implement tighter security control in the town camps, especially those in Amman which became an integral part of the developing city. Following the 1957 outburst of disturbances and demonstrations there, in which thousands of refugees and inhabitants took part, persistent rumours of the town camps' transfer to isolated areas appeared in the media. These were followed by widely publicized denials by the M.D.R.[45]

Attacked by the Syrian and Egyptian media, Jordan paid lip-service once again to the old "model village" plan advocated and principally supported by the Arab League. Having failed to receive the requisite funds to establish new refugee border settlements, the authorities quickly took the opportunity to blame the Arab countries which, as Jordan put it, did not want to make the project feasible. Not that Jordan ever really wanted to embark on such a project, fearing the consequences of housing a large, poor, frustrated population close to its lost homeland.

C. THE REFUGEE TRIBES' MOVEMENT EASTWARDS

1. In the West Bank

The bedouin refugees moved into the West Bank or straight on into the East Bank immediately after the war, leaving behind them several tribes.[46] The dispossessed Bir Saba' (Be'er Sheva) tribes[47] were by far the largest group arriving in Jordan. Their sheer numbers, their conservative outlook and their limited experience of agriculture meant that they soon became a burden to the local villages, to the already sedentarized tribes[48] and to the Government.

The first wave of refugees pitched their tents on the outskirts of villages, or lived in caves and holes in the ground. The UNRPR gave relief priority to refugees living in camps or large concentrations and was unable to help those scattered in remote areas, who received only a few extended services. But in contrast to the bedouin coming from central and nothern Palestine, the southern Negev bedouin could not adapt to the pattern of life in camps. Instead they preferred to continue their only life-style, living in their tents in the cooler zones in summer, finding protected places in winter. Some camped on the outskirts of the refugee camps, especially in Jericho, grazing what remained of their flocks nearby. Their priority was to find sufficient water and to use the camp as a market place for their dairy produce and meat. The years of drought severely reduced their small flocks, causing many of the semi-nomads extreme hardships or even starvation. Their former pasture land (*dirah*) was on the Israeli side of the Demarcation Line and the prospects of acquiring land for grazing and cultivation on the West Bank were limited.

The majority of the Negev bedouin were unemployed and during the first years after the war made little effort to improve their lot. Those who lived close to the extensive border retained close connections with their families in Israel, making a relatively good income through smuggling. Some bedouin made their way back to Israel under the Unification of Families Scheme, (through which a number of relatives were allowed to return to their families still in Israel).[49] Others crossed the border secretly, joining their families or other tribes on their old land or at a new site. A unique example is that of the Jawarish[50] people. This tribe originally came from Libya towards the end of the nineteenth century. They settled in Gadera where they lived in shacks, working as guards hired by the Jewish settlers rather than engaging in husbandry. In 1948 they fled to Hebron where they were unpopular because of their good relations with the Jews. With the help of Israeli friends they later infiltrated back and were settled in Ramleh[51] together with refugees from southern coastal villages, Negev *fellahin* of Sudanese origin[52] and bedouin from the Negev and Sinai.

In the West Bank most southern bedouin were forced to turn to intensive work in agriculture which they detested. Generally speaking they lacked the inclination, experience or know-how to be capable of engaging in hard labour. Many of them ended up as tenants, tilling the poor quality soil under hard conditions alongside other *fellahin,* whom they always looked down upon. They were unwilling partners in the tremendous agricultural development of the Hebron Hills achieved since 1950 with the cheap refugee labour saturating the area. Life for these bedouin became increasingly difficult. The area became overcrowded with little land available or suitable for cultivation or grazing. Nor was employment a feasible option, especially with thousands of better trained, more eager villager refugees competing anxiously for available work.

Consequently these bedouin could not survive in their large traditional social frameworks for any extended period of time. In the past the *qabilah,* the Federation of Bedouin tribes, had been a prestigious unit and a unifying force. Within the *qabilah* each clan measured its strength in terms of physical capability. But lack of economic viability and of the space to live together as a tribe led to the disintegration of this framework, dispersing the tribes over a wide area. (However the scattered units continued to identify themselves as part of their federation as a matter of prestige; the solidarity of the tribes, which rested on blood connections, still remained a social asset with regard to such matters as blood-money and marriage conflicts.) The increasing migration of youngsters in search of employment further loosened the clan (*hamulah*) and larger groups were forced to split unless they moved eastwards to southern Jordan. And so, facing grim economic prospects in the West Bank, many bedouin were tempted to move eastwards with or without Government assistance, anticipating their re-establishment in agriculture or other activity. The Jordanian files contain petitions requesting such a transfer,[53] though some of them later claimed they were forced by the Government to leave the area. Other petitions enquired about joining UNRWA's rehabilitation projects[54] under which the Development Bank of Jordan would provide funds to buy land and equipment for an agricultural co-operative. Most of these projects failed either through misappropriation of the money or because bedouin interest in them faded very quickly. This made the poor, unemployed bedouin more ready to move to the East Bank.

At first the number of those who moved eastwards was very low. The authorities, troubled by the movement of bedouin in and out of Israel, thus aimed at removing the bedouin refugees from the Armistice Lines. Fearing the border tension caused by their large scale smuggling and infiltration operations, which they continued in part as a matter of honour, Glubb sought to transfer them to remote eastern areas where they could re-establish themselves.[55] He called a meeting with the *shaykhs,* warned them against "collaborating with Jews against the Jordanian interests", and made tempting offers to those who would move to the East Bank with their people. Shaykh Atiyyah Id Abu Rabia (Zarabah-Azazmah) claimed:

> Glubb approached me in 1955 and offered me personally money, land and a tractor if I would convince the tribe to go to Azraq . . . He (Glubb) exerted direct pressure on me and instructed the army commanders here to neglect the bedouin refugee demands, making them thereby accept the plan.

This was his explanation for the departure of the Sawahnah sub-tribe which, he claimed, was threatened by Glubb and left the area for the East Bank.[56] The *Shaykh* of each sub-tribe decided whether or not the Government's suggestion was acceptable. For many clans like the Jarawin, Alamat, Iqdirat and Diqs, the Hebron area turned out to be a temporary station on their journey eastwards. Members of some tribes remained.[57] Individual families joined other tribes or settled in villages; thus very little remained of the distinctive sub-tribe characteristics.

But not all bedouin refugees were pleased with this Jordanian policy. The Press reported on April 24, 1954 that a government order had been issued to a tribe to move to the East Bank and that its leaders had approached the

Arab League to intervene on its behalf. Yet the Jordanian Government's policy, apart from suiting its security interests, was very much in line with that of the Arab League, which after an intensive study of the nomads' problems, demanded that settlement of the bedouin be fostered and developed.[58]

Such settled concentrations were found along the Ghur Valley where UNRWA self-help schemes operated. Some of these groups built mud huts, engaged in husbandry and moved eastwards in the harvest season in search of work. Others settled in Auja, which also absorbed bedouin from central and north Palestine. A few entered the camps or settled near them. The Amarin settled in Nu'yma and in Ayn al-Sultan camps, and in 1956 began, like a few other bedouins there, to construct houses. Another example is provided by the Wuhaydah who settled in Arrub Camp after squatting near it for a long while, living in a special quarter of the camp in which they began to build dwellings. They managed to establish themselves economically but, unlike other tribes, they retained the bedouin traditions, refusing to mix with the villagers and even demanding a separate camp. This process of entering the camps was common among the smaller groups of semi-sedentary bedouin who came from central and northern Palestine. As they brought few, if any, livestock and had experience of farming, camp life was not as inimical to them as to some. Nevertheless, they kept themselves separate in the camps. Most moved to camps in Jenin, Tulkarm, Balata Askar, Far'a and Karamah; a few to nearby villages like the Arab al-Sidrah living near Abu Shkhaydim, which was an unofficial camp, and in Dayr-Ammar Camp, both in the Ramallah area, as did the Saturiyyah tribe. Dayr-Ammar Camp was set up near the village of that name which was the nearest safe place with a water supply, essential for the cattle. After a few years, members of the Saturiyyah tribe began moving from Dayr-Ammar to the Amman region; and by the mid-1960s half the members had left the small camp which had been established on their behalf and for villagers from the Lydda region.[59]

Some bedouin moved into frontier townlets. For example the Arab Abu Kishk people, who came from the fertile region near the River Yarkon, moved together with the Qur'an bedouin into Qalqilya. Bringing their herds with them enabled them to establish themselves economically in a relatively short time.[60] The Qur'an built makeshift huts in the town, and have produced an educated and highly skilled second generation. This they achieved through the hard work of all the families which resulted in their providing the town's dairy produce. The Qalqilya residents, who had little respect for the Qur'an, were forced to sell them land in the early 1950s, as the town had suffered a serious economic set-back in consequence of the war.[61]

A rather different example is that of the Wadi Hawarith bedouin who until the war lived near and co-operated with the new Jewish settlements. When hostilities broke out 1948 they came to Tulkarm which was their traditional market place and where they had established contacts.[62] Those amongst them who had cattle, and did not settle in the camps situated in the town, moved to the region of the Damaya Bridge as it was the only area available for them and for others who had flocks. At a later stage some of them joined their relatives when shelter building began in the camp. Until the 1967 war there were some 150 families scattered within the camp's shelter; many of their offspring have emigrated to study in Spain and West Germany or to work in Arab oil countries.

Another concentration of 2,500 refugees, of whom a quarter were bedouin, lived further north near the Frontier Village of Rummana. In 1963 the Jordanian Government urged them to leave the village lands because of their proximity to the border. Even before this order was made, many of them moved to the vast agricultural lands of Irbid.[63] The bedouin refugees who remained in Rummana lived in tents and caves and only few imitated the village refugees who rented and later built stone houses.[64]

As we have seen, only a few bedouin established themselves in the Hebron region. Even those like the Shalalin, who did try, were forced to move northwards being pushed around by the local *fellahin*. One tribe that did settle, the Bili (Abu Mas'ad) sub-tribe (Tayyaha) remained in the West Bank only until 1954 when the Government transferred them to the Azraq region in the East Bank. Until then they lived near Khirbat Karmah in Abdah (which belonged to Dura) around the school built by UNRWA in 1953. This kind of attempt to resettle bedouin by building a school for their children succeeded only in the case of the Ramadin (Tayyaha). This tribe, one of the richest on the West Bank, retained part of its land, some 9,500 *dunam*;[65] currently the tribe is practically settled and concentrates primarily on agriculture although it raises some livestock. In 1953, UNRWA built them a stone school at their request to accelerate their settling.[66] The tribe erected stone houses around it and later rejected both UNRWA's intention to transfer the school and the Government's attempts to transfer them to Azraq in the East Bank. The Ramadin seem to be more advanced than other refugee tribes, having relatively more university graduates and teachers, most of whom have emigrated to Saudi Arabia.[67] They preferred to remain as a "Frontier Village" living within sight of their lands.

Hence by the mid-1950s most tribes were found on the East side of the river.

2. In the East Bank

The indigenous tribes were joined by a further three groups: a contingent of bedouin expelled from Israel on the grounds that they were Egyptian-paid agents engaged in espionage and terrorism; bedouin leaving Israel voluntarily to join their brothers in the East Bank; and those forced out of the Sinai desert by extreme hardship, infiltrating Jordan via the Israeli Negev. The latter were attracted by rumours that they could get jobs and aid there.

The invasion into East Jordan territory upset the delicate balance between the local disenchanted Jordanian tribes, and caused additional problems for the authorities who even tried in some cases "to push them back".[68] In the East Bank the refugee tribes had no territory of their own and found it very difficult to form large concentrations or to raise their camels and other livestock on land that was not theirs. A Government plan to regroup the Azazmah near al-Jafr 15 km from Ma'an did not materialize[69] owing to local opposition from the southern Trans-Jordanian bedouin. With the lack of land available for pasture or cultivation, the local bedouin became very uneasy about the presence of the refugee tribes especially in years of drought. They envied them the relief care they received. Indeed some of the tribes which had relatively meagre possessions, managed over the years to better their economic situation with the assistance of the international Agencies[70] which from the mid 1950s were persuaded to become involved. Tents and animals were donated in a project named Azazmah Mobile Villages — including the provision of feeding centres, new schools and other amenities. This was designed for 1,025 families in the Karak area not far from the Dead Sea Coast.[71] Besides direct relief, a number of bedouin refugees received grants of livestock to facilitate their rehabilitation under UNRWA's Bedouin Livestock Project. This was partly realized by the Jordanian Government's gift of state domain land in the Bardala region. From its inception until mid 1958, 287[72] selected families from the Turkemen, Abu Kishk and Suqr tribes were given about 22,000 head of sheep and 287 camels. Thus some 1,500 refugees recovered their traditional means of self-support, many more applying for this aid in 1958/9[73] when UNRWA managed to withdraw from some of them the rations it had been providing over the years. Still *Filastin* claimed on 21.11.58 that there were some 8,000 bedouin refugees who received no form of assistance from the UNRWA, the Voluntary Agencies,[74] or from any Jordanian institution. Many arguments between UNRWA and the refugees centred around the question of the entitlement of the bedouin to relief services. It was decided to grant them half rations since the tents they brought with them were regarded as "homes". The exaggerated figures given in the local Press of those without relief were used to pressurize UNRWA to provide even more assistance. These various Agency schemes served as a further inducement to move eastwards.

However the Government did not succeed in preventing the bedouin refugees from engaging in smuggling, or from causing border clashes with Israel, which was the main reason for this policy of transfer. This was because these operations were not launched solely from the Hebron area, but also across the Negev between the Wadi Araba and the Sinai.

D. THE FRONTIER VILLAGES

The Frontier Villages (FV), neglected by the Government and with severe economic problems, gradually lost most of their young people, who drifted eastwards in search of employment. This virtually carried out the Government's policy of "thinning out" for it, leaving the defenceless elderly exposed to Israeli attacks. As the National Guard (N.G.) could not protect them, the local villagers became discontented with the presence of refugees on their soil, fearing the consequences of their infiltration.[75] The villagers complained that the government officials seldom toured the FV and that most such visits dealt with security problems, infiltration and smuggling.[76] This, they claimed, reflected the Government's attitude to their problems. They held it against the Government that it did not build roads until the late 1950s. Such roads would not only have made it easier to market their few products, send their children to school and find employment, but above all would have enabled the army to patrol the area and hasten to defend them when the Israeli attacks occurred.[77] As one of them put it:

The Frontier Villages were forgotten and neglected. The government did not assist us and did not even pave security roads to protect the soft underbelly all along the borders. They had here one or two small army camps and they established this mockery of a National Guard to protect us.[78]

In addition to the calls for setting up refugee concentrations along the border, demands for the fortification of the FVs themselves were expressed. Stressing the fact that the Frontier Villages were not only Jordan's first battle line but that of the whole Arab World, a new charitable society set up in Jerusalem decided to concentrate on FV affairs by assisting the younger generation to gain employment in their villages. This was to avert their emigration elsewhere which would have weakened the front line.[79]

However a few years later the Jordanian Government became troubled by the size of the mass departure and ordered an end to it. The considerations here were different from those concerning the large migration of refugees. The M.D.R., in a letter to the Ministry of Defence, suggested that the FV had become more exposed to the enemy's threats. This stemmed from the fact that the youngsters departed to seek employment, leaving behind the vulnerable and weak, the old and the very young, with little protection. Hence the Jordanian authorities decided to embark on measures to prevent this migration. The Government ordered UNRWA not to allow the transfer of ration cards from FV to the East Bank.[80] This was in line with the Agency's policy of stipulating that Frontier Villagers would only be entitled to relief if they stayed in the villages.[81] Despite such changes of policy this drift away continued, because these people who graduated from vocational training courses sought employment elsewhere, leaving the FV exposed — which was not quite what the Government intended.

E. SMUGGLING

The years after 1948 saw a decline in the frequency and size of smuggling convoys, although the network between Trans-Jordan and the Sinai was still used to transfer the hashish growing in Persia, Turkey and Syria to Egypt. The smaller groups operating also smuggled expensive merchandise, relief items and food. Tubas village, for example, was a smuggling centre in the north, but the main smuggling was in the south. Illegal activities from Wadi Araba, an area between the Dead Sea and Eilat, were carried out by bedouin who employed their expert knowledge of the arid area, and their vast family network to smuggle contraband, only certain items finding their way to Israeli markets. The refugee tribes proved indispensable to these operations.

The local Trans-Jordanian tribes situated in the middle of the routes between Egypt and Arabia gained immensely from their position. Their *shaykhs* became rich, influential people who could expand their smuggling network. In doing so the Bani Sakhr bedouin enjoyed the support of their leaders whether they were politicians or senior army personnel. According to Egyptian secret reports, the southern Huwytat tribe network was known to be run by the *Sharif* Nasir Bin Jamil, King Husayn's uncle, and one of the central figures in the army, together with one of the most influential notables in the Hebron district.[82]

Prominent among the refugee tribes involved were the western Sa'idiyyin, who had close relations with the authorities, unlike the Azazmah whose sons were generally mistrusted and excluded from the Jordanian armed forces because of their long established connection with the Egyptian authorities. The Ahyiwat did not find army connections so necessary. Living on both sides of the narrow, most southern strip of the Israeli border facilitated their smuggling activities using the camels raised by the tribe.

Another kind of movement across the Jordanian border was that of wandering bedouin who crossed because of the sudden but temporary overcrowding in the Araba area and the relatively small amount of grazing land available in winter. Some of them used water sources west of the line. Conflicts between tribes inside Jordan led to crossings of the border into Israel, at times with cattle stolen from another tribe. These activities caused border incidents and clashes between the armed bedouin and the Israeli army.

Thefts were also quite common, mostly among the poorer bedouin who utilized the opportunity to steal valuable property and machinery used by the Israeli Government in developing the southern part of the country. The shooting of these bedouin by Israelis incited blood feuds and resulted in vendettas which caused chain reactions, culminating in additional killings. Many such incidents occurred in the Negev and might be explained as bedouin actions of blood revenge. The massacre of the bus passengers in Ma'aleh ha-Akrabim (The Scorpion Pass) on the way to Eilat was possibly one of them. The bedouin infiltrators also tried to deter the Israelis from any further action against them under the pretext of "live and let live". In response, Israel sometimes opted to hit Jordan in places where it was particularly vulnerable. The Israeli Government also acted against those tribes situated in the south east and, as mentioned above, expelled bedouins from Israel suspected of assisting their relatives.

A different type of smuggling was that carried out by individuals either for personal profit or for political purposes. UNRWA's car fleet was used for smuggling into Jordan in the hope that there would be no searches owing to immunity privileges. In 1952 the Jordanian Government complained to the Agency "that more drivers were using UNRWA vehicles for smuggling goods and Israeli currency". The Agency's Field Supply and Transport Officer notified all his workers that "any driver who is found to be impli- cated or who deliberately infringes any of the laws or security arrangements of this country will be instantly dismissed."[83] Yet it seems that the offers made to the Agency drivers were too tempting to resist for it was alleged a few months later, that an Agency car brought rifles from Syria hidden among rations.[84] After opium was found in an UNRWA car arriving from Syria, new orders to search the UNRWA's vehicles were issued.[85] Border police were then anticipating the smuggling of political leaflets and handouts in these cars[86] and searched any vehicle crossing the border.[87] The regime became increasingly troubled by the continued subversive activity of the Mufti[88] and Syrian agents[89] and by material smuggled in by opposition movements.[90]

With the growth of arms smuggling into Jordan by the Egyptians, carried out for them by some of the tribes, the Israelis became increasingly anxious as they feared that the incipient Fedayyin groups would succeed in imple- menting at least part of their plans. Guided and inspired by Egypt, such activities only increased tension. Israel also feared that the arms consign- ments might be used against the Jordanian monarch to overthrow the regime — a situation which Israel calculated would not serve her interests.

F. EGYPT, JORDAN, THE "FEDAYYIN" AND "RETALIATION"—THE VICIOUS CIRCLE

The refugees' growing expectations forced the Arab League to make a number of resolutions on its forthcoming action for recovering Palestine. These were designed to "defuse" Arab demands by proving that appropriate "action" was being taken.

The Arab governments were forced to display their readiness to accept the idea "that something had to be done" about revenge, and the refugees expected to be included. A negative response to this natural demand would only cause suspicion, which in itself could cause the internal unrest feared by the Arab rulers. Repeated declarations did little to quell the refugees' growing impatience. Each Government had to decide for itself whether or not to include refugees in its army, or at least to give them some basic training. Conditions were different in each country. In Lebanon, the idea was totally unacceptable. Syria was the first country to recruit refugees and Egypt felt relatively untroubled by the prospect since the refugee concentrations were isolated from Cairo; the establishment of Fedayyin units could serve Egypt's external political needs but only if their military action was controlled, so as to avoid a full-scale war for which the Egyptian Government was unready. Countries which did not follow suit were discredited, whilst immense popular support was gained amongst the Palestinians by those who did. The Palestinians generally felt that Egypt was contributing to the idea of Arab unity by preserving the "Refugee Entity", thereby preventing the blurring of the separate Palestinian identity—regarded as instrumental for the struggle for the Return and the delegitimization of Israel.

The Egyptians had a twofold aim: to hit targets in Israel, and to try to strengthen subversive elements in Jordan which would press for greater participation in such activities, thereby bringing Israeli retaliation. This would weaken the regime and consequently undermine the British position, so as to facilitate changes within Jordan.

The Fedayyin were organized towards the mid 1950s in the Gaza strip and later in other Arab countries. They functioned under the supervision of the Egyptian Army which trained, organized and equipped them. But it seems Egypt itself feared the consequences of Israeli raids in retaliation to un-controlled infiltration.[91]

Only in 1955 was the Palestinian National Guard in the Gaza Strip used as part of the army, and even then in a limited capacity. Egypt's operations were then expanded to the West Bank[92] with the Jordanians trying to stop them. On returning from their missions, the Fedayyin were received in the Hebron Hills with great enthusiasm. Although many Hebronites still felt the bitter taste of the days of 1948–49 when the Egyptians were present, they directed their support towards Nasser—the emerging new all-Arab leader. The Egyptians enjoyed a tremendous growth in popularity and support in Jordan. The cornered Jordanian regime had little to offer.

During the Sinai Campaign, Jordan was forced to house some 3,000 refugees from Gaza, including many Fedayyin who had escaped out of fear of possible Israeli reaction. The Hebron D.G., who notified the Minister of Interior, reported their immediate transfer to Zarqa',[93] whence they were moved to Ghur Nimrin.[94] Until their return they were cared for and assisted by the Hebronites, UNRWA workers, the Jordanian Government, as well as by local philanthropic agencies set up in Jordan for that purpose.[95]

UNRWA refused to assist those who could not provide their name and ration card number as proof that they were genuine refugees on the relief lists in the Gaza Strip. The Gaza people refused to do so on the grounds that they suspected that the names would finally reach the Israeli authorities. They feared that the latter would punish their vulnerable relatives in Gaza for reporting their death during the Israeli occupation when in fact they had escaped and were living in Jordan. Following the Israeli withdrawal from the Sinai, most of the Gaza refugees demanded that they should be allowed to return to their old camps. Discussions between the two Governments took place through the Indonesian Embassy, which represented Egyptian interests in Jordan,[96] after the two Governments had broken off diplomatic relations. Yet many preferred to stay in Jordan because they had found employment and wanted to be with relatives or friends whom they had met after years of separation. Others feared Egyptian action against them on their return. They anticipated accusations of collaboration with the Jordanian authorities, who had in fact received valuable information concerning the Egyptian-controlled Fedayyin activities from some of them. The Jordanians distrusted them politically and regarded their presence as an economic burden.[97] It was difficult at this stage for the Government to trace their whereabouts,[98] as they had scattered and were being assisted by their friends to conceal any information which would result in their deportation. A few of them still took part in subsidized Fedayyin activities.

The Jordanians managed to seize arms and to arrest those who received them from the Egyptian or Syrian agents operating within the kingdom.[99] By 1957 most political parties and movements, whether outlawed or licensed, had smuggled arms at their disposal.[100] The Muslim Brotherhood in the Hebron area engaged in some sort of training,[101] and took part in some of the Fedayyin activities organized from Jordan by the Egyptian Intelligence. It was later claimed, however, that they were armed by the Jordanian army to assist the monarch in the suppression of attempted revolution.[102]

The Egyptians operated mainly through their Consulate in Jerusalem until it was shut down in 1957. A secret Jordanian report gave details of twelve people from the Hebron area who were paid by the Consulate for infiltrating into the Gaza Strip, and bringing arms supplied by the Army there, back to the West Bank.[103] The Egyptians used their airline offices and Qalandya airport as a place for meetings. A government agent reported that the Consulate gave arms to the National Socialists and Ba'thists through a local worker who served as a go-between.[104] According to another report, the Consul also provided one of the prominent Ba'th leaders, who at their time was a senior government official, with money to supply the families of those who had escaped from Jordan.[105]

The Jordanian Secret Police carefully followed the movements of Palestinians employed by the Governments of Egypt and Syria. Although their position was weakened somewhat following the killing of the Egyptian attaché in Jordan, Colonel Salah al-Din Mustafa, as well as by the Sinai Campaign, they still posed a threat to the monarch. Additional Syrian support in the form of money and arms only made them more dangerous. By the end of 1958 they were outmanoeuvred by the King's uncle, who was in charge of internal security at the time, and many of them ended up in jail. Others compromised with the new situation and became the King's supporters.

There is little evidence to suggest that these measures, the growing risk of casualties or the fierce Israeli reactions deterred those who, for one reason or another, were determined to continue their operations. Border activity continued spasmodically and in different ways. It is difficult to establish a pattern since the situation varied from year to year. However, infiltration in this period was an acute problem for Israel, whose Government warned the Jordanian regime against allowing the Fedayyin to continue their operations from Jordanian territory. It accused Jordan of failing to take all the necessary precautions and to arrest those whose names had been supplied by Israel.

The few Arab youngsters who left Israel illegally for economic and political reasons further complicated the delicate relationship between the two countries.[106]

The Jordanian Government for its part, knew that the policy of repressing marauding was understandably unpopular, and could lead to threats to its existence from within—especially in the context of the growing sympathy for Nasser and the Fedayyin in the mid-1950s.[107] The arrest of hundreds of infiltrators in accordance with Jordanian policy was naturally considered by the Palestinians as collaboration with the Israelis.

To a certain extent Israel overlooked Jordan's handicaps and did not appreciate the elements of truth in her explanations.[108] Mutual condemnation and accusations only aggravated the delicate relationship between the two States. The mounting tension brought the two Governments under severe internal pressure. As far as the Israeli Government was concerned, pressure from army officers and citizens in favour of retaliation—following the killing of Israeli citizens by premeditated acts of sabotage—proved virtually irresistible.[109] Jordan was regarded as directly responsible. The angry Israeli border patrols acted at times with no official authorization. The Israeli frontier settlements would ask for protection and Jordan would send her army to control its side of the border: hence both armies confronted one another. When so potentially massive an explosion was imminent, both parties opted to defuse the situation. The West feared that such confrontations would eventually become uncontrollable and tried to arrange for a settlement which would ensure the observance of the Armistice Agreement by the two countries. But increasing numbers of civilians were being killed on both sides. Normalization was far from being reached and this cyclical pattern recurred.

Israel was anxious to have a moderate, stable eastern neighbour. Yet it would seem that the frequency and manner of Israel's so-called "retaliation actions", far from achieving their aim of preventing such activities and stimulating tighter control of law and order along the common border by the Jordanian Legion, were counter-productive in that they harmed a Jordanian regime which itself had a direct interest in a quiet border. Furthermore, these retaliatory actions and especially that against Qibya on 14 October 1953 in which many of the village's defenceless inhabitants were killed, exposed the Jordanian Government to violent demonstrations and protests against any Western or UNRWA scheme for the resettlement projects, which the Israelis wholeheartedly supported. This only added to the pressures on those refugees wanting to integrate, and hindered UNRWA's work. And the Jordanian Government was forced to reiterate its rejection of these schemes, some of which had to be temporarily postponed.

The Arab Legion, though trained and armed by G.B. and very capable, was too small to maintain a constant observation of all borders. It was simply not established or equipped for such a task. Its main preoccupation was defending the monarch in Amman and not the West Bank Palestinians. Israeli action against Jordan only undermined the Legion's position as well as that of Great Britain, and ironically helped the Jordanian opposition elements, thereby facilitating the growing influence of Nasser in Jordan. The cornered King was bitterly criticized for his unwillingness to enlarge his army. This of course would have forced him to recruit a growing number of Palestinians whom he generally feared. The Palestinians attacked Glubb and the monarch for purposely neglecting the West Bank, for not properly training them, and for failing to provide modern equipment for the N.G.[110] The regime feared that if the N.G. was provided with such equipment, the eventual result would be further clashes, precipitated by trigger-happy Palestinians, which would bring about an Israeli invasion. The King wanted a weak N.G. which would realize its limitations and which, having seen the fate of FVs hit by Israeli action, would be reluctant, if not unable, to start the chain reaction feared by both. P. J. Vatikiotis has described this vicious circle:

> If these Israeli raids inflict extensive damage to life and property they can result in popular political agitation against the regime. The political demonstration against the regime is directly against the inability of the state to give Arabs on the frontiers adequate protection against Israeli raids. This, in turn, often carries the political charge that the state is not interested in restoring the forfeited rights of its Palestinian subjects.[111]

Chapter V

Recruitment of Refugees into the Armed Forces

The Jordanian armed forces were made up of the Arab Legion (al-Jaysh al-Arabi—the "Arab Army") and the National Guard (al-Haras al-Watani). The latter was a part-time militia based on the 1950 National Guard Act conscripting every able-bodied Jordanian between the age of 18 and 40 years to a one-month annual training and service period. The Legion consisted of the regular army and up to 1958 of the *amn al-am* (in fact the Secret Police). Naturally, many Palestinians were secretly recruited into, or were in the pay of the Secret Police, which could not have functioned as efficiently as it did without the help of Palestinians, whether voluntary or otherwise. While the National Guard (N.G.) was mainly Palestinian, the Arab Legion remained, in the 1950s, almost exclusively Trans-Jordanian.

In this instance the Government's policy was not geared to the process of integration itself, but was rather intended to forge the armed forces into an instrument for the implementation of the overall policy of Jordanization.

A. THE NATIONAL GUARD

"Jordan needs to protect 650,000 refugees and 650 km of
border line."[1]

Glubb sought in mid-1949 to establish a defensive force which would give the West Bankers some sense of security and participation in the kingdom. He wished to relieve the Arab Legion of border duty without restricting its effectiveness. Its presence there had been a deterrent to Israel and a reminder to the West Bankers of the new authority. Yet it gave the inhabitants some feeling of security, for despite their constant criticism, they knew their fate in 1948 would have been different but for the Legion.

"Glubb's Doctrine" had been to keep the Arab Legion in modest reserves behind the frontier, at points with reasonable lines of communication to the villages, while using poorly armed villagers aided by Legion N.C.O.'s on the actual border. It was impossible for Jordan's own forces to defend every point along the rugged line if they were in static defence positions which would tie them down.

The N.G. appealed to some Palestinians, and especially to those living in the frontier areas with little if any defence. It was to function as a separate but controlled force which, it was hoped, would delay and repulse Israeli attacks. Perhaps its most important function, however, was to stop any local incidents which might cause retaliation. The N.G.'s real task, in fact, was to control border "infiltration" by its members' own brothers.

Until its amalgamation with the Arab Legion in 1965, the N.G. was comprised of groups of villagers garrisoned in their own Frontier Villages, the assumption being that the villagers would stoutly defend their own homes. Organized in loose, local units, the N.G. served as Jordan's "regional defence system". Although seen as a valuable addition to the regular forces in case of attack, there is little evidence to suggest that the army intended the N.G. to fulfil its assigned tasks. The N.G. was neither equipped, trained nor designed to carry out these duties. With twenty bullets,[2] a few rifles, little training and hardly any co-ordination or transport, very little could be done in the face of an attack. This was because the regime feared mobile troops of this type.

Responding to local pressure, the Government decided in February 1950 to expand service in the N.G. to include more training hours. Villagers in border areas received training first; for others it followed later. Refugees in the FV's were at times placed in the same category as the people amongst whom they were living.[3] To further satisfy such demands and boost the prestige of the N.G., a decree amending the 1950 National Guard Law announced that its members could be used for army purposes at certain periods when they would have to obey all the Arab Legion regulations.[4] This was ostensibly to indicate an intention to amalgamate the two, although it was to be several years before this took place. In an attempt to refute allegations implying that the Government not only barred Palestinians from the Legion, but also refused to accept refugees into the N.G., the Government announced on 15 November 1952 its decision to train groups of refugees, in accordance with its belief that "military training was the best means of preparing good citizens". All Palestinian refugees of the required age were to be called up for training. The first would be refugees from the largest concentration in Jordan, Aqbat Jabr Camp, and the training was to be concentrated and not too demanding so that "it would not harm their chances of employment". The training of inhabitants of this camp, remote from the border and the main towns, could not threaten the regime's interests. Its main purpose was to help pacify the refugees by indicating to them the Government's future policy; not that the monarch ever intended to extend this training to all other camps. The reason for not embarking on such a programme earlier was given by the Prime Minister as "owing to the tight schedule which the frontier villagers' training demanded and the absence of proper additional facilities".[5]

The Press was full of details in the following months, of the increased salaries in the N.G., its expansion, the training programme[6] and donations made by the local population.[7] In response to the demand of a number of M.P.s that the army and not the N.G. should handle the defence of the border lines,[8] the Government ordered additional budget allocations to the N.G.[9] It also gave wide publicity to the training in progress of refugee students from secondary schools[10] and to a new law which enabled wounded N.G. soldiers to receive compensation similar to that paid to the Arab Legion's soldiers.[11]

It was by such virtually meaningless and anodyne measures, or by pacificatory statements, that the regime dealt with each wave of criticism and demands for involvement. The use of this technique was intensified following every Israeli retaliation action. By then, training had already been received by those residing in the eastern part of the West bank and by the town dwellers. Like everyone else, these people urged the expansion of the N.G. to cover the West Bank, although they personally were not interested in serving. As Glubb put it:

> you are asking, did the Palestinians want to join the National Guard—in general townspeople didn't but villagers did, particularly villagers who could see the Israelis just across the road . . . I can well remember that when we started the National Guard and there was a meeting in Nablus, and I said we'd like a contingent for the National Guard from the young men in Nablus, they said "Oh, I don't know" and somebody said "Oh, no, the Nablusis will make the speeches and the *fellahin* will do the fighting". And that's about right, their sort of turbulent political speeches and so on, but they weren't anxious to be soldiers.[12]

The Israeli attack on Qibya was a turning point, however. It clearly demonstrated the inefficiency and ineffectiveness of the entire defence system. The whole situation became more dangerous and explosive and the regime had to react with extreme caution. Both the civil and military authorities were blamed and criticized. The British-guided Arab Legion bore the brunt of these complaints.

There were fierce demonstrations, Western emissaries were stoned, and the cry for revenge was widespread. So the Government tried to appease the Palestinians with a long statement which reiterated a commitment to the Return within the terms of the UN and Arab League resolutions. It rejected the idea of peace with Israel and of any schemes for resettlement, and claimed that "any further aggression will be repulsed by force".[13]

The Government had also to cope with pressure from the Political Committee of the Arab League which announced its boycott of any international project for the Jordan Valley involving co-operation with Israel. The League declared its intention to quadruple its aid to the N.G., replacing the British aid and thus facilitating their expulsion. This manifest readiness for a firm line popular with the Palestinians and the Press made Jordan's position even worse.

Very soon afterwards, however, it became obvious that the Arab countries did not intend to fulfil all these promises. Once again they halted their financial support, possibly out of reluctance to continue subsidizing a body over which they had no control. They also suspected that some of the aid went not to the N.G. but to the Arab Legion which they were hardly keen to support in its existing form. Political capital could be made among the Palestinians by declarations which entailed no practical steps. When the Arabs failed to pay up, a few articles criticized Egypt and Syria. Nevertheless, despite this equivocation over financial support, Egypt's exclusively Palestinian fedayyin units and her calls for a refugee army were a constant thorn in Jordan's side, and were a major reason for the Palestinians' support of Nasser.

The Jordanian Government announced its continued financial responsibility for the N.G.[14] hoping thereby to gain politically from the Arab League's refusal. It further promised to unify the budget of the army and the N.G.,[15] indicating the lines of its supposedly future policy in the face of this internal pressure. Again one can observe the pattern which typically followed nearly every retaliatory incident—demonstrations, empty promises, evasions, minor concessions. Thus, in 1955, the Government replied to a demand for a refugee army by saying that refugees in Jordan were "Jordanian citizens" and that their refugee status should be preserved only from an international point of view so as to protect their rights.[16]

Faced with the growing bitterness and apathy of the frontier villagers, inevitable given the N.G.'s worn and inappropriate equipment, low salaries, and the heavy burden of feeding the guards, the Jordanian authorities decided towards the mid 1950s to effect a number of changes; but these required a substantial financial allocation. Britain was reluctant to make dramatic improvements in Jordan's military power. It did not consider that a more capable N.G. would be able to prevent infiltration, and feared that a strong N.G. would bring more military clashes with Israel. The Arab League, when called upon by Jordan and the Palestinians to contribute, again conditioned allocations on having some control, since it considered the Palestinian Question a common Arab issue—an approach which the Jordanian regime felt it necessary to reject.

With the British no longer present to take the blame following Glubb's dismissal, the "purged" army continued up to 1967 to follow the same basic principles, the general situation in Jordan remaining very similar. The protesters realized, if they came to be decision-makers, that the Arab Legion and the N.G. were no match for the Israeli army.

For the FVs, the N.G. proved to be virtually their only defence: hence their sensitivity to its composition. From 1952 onwards they became more efficient in checking infiltration from their own side. They watched out for action from places to their east as well as from their own villages. Being generally loyal to the King, they were not enthusiastic about the Fedayyin operations of the mid 1950s launched from their areas. They also feared the consequences from both the Israeli and the Jordanian authorities, although some did extend help either for payment or because of their natural emotional inclination.

Generally speaking the N.G. could not be viewed as a real military force. The people themselves did not have much regard for an organization which was styled by local cynics as "The Protectors of Israel". It seems that the N.G. served as an outlet for the accumulating pressure in the F.V. rather than as a viable military unit. Through it the villagers became, in a sense, masters of their own fate. They felt better protected holding old rifles than if they had none. It gave them some sense of security, and their small achievements, much magnified, boosted their morale. While not terribly keen on serving in the N.G., the frontier villagers wanted its continued protection. Since training took up valuable time, especially for the young employed, it was not long before the N.G. was mostly manned by the virtually incapable elders. Once compulsory training was introduced, more people began evading it[17] and giving bribes to gain exemption, since for those who worked away from home the cost of travel made it too expensive to be a member. The frontier villagers increasingly wanted to be relieved of the duty of guarding their villages and claimed that the country already had an army for this purpose. The modest salaries it offered could not turn the N.G. into a real source of income. So the first reaction of enthusiasm was soon replaced by a growing awareness of its real position and role. And given its exclusively local formation, it seems the N.G. could scarcely contribute to the Jordanization of the Palestinians.

B. THE ARAB LEGION

Jordan's army was the foundation of the monarch's strength throughout his reign, serving as his solid power base and reliable protector. Loyalty was understood in personal terms by its main and most important component — the Trans-Jordanian bedouin. Whether illiterate or educated in the Arab Legion Schools,[18] they displayed in the period under review, a definite apathy to politics. Arab nationalism meant little to them, as they, like the King, feared any political change within Jordan which might affect their dominant position. This feeling was shared by other minorities represented in the army. Their strong identification with their legitimate traditional ruler was also based on tribal and religious allegiance. The bedouin, regarding the warrior role as the most respectable source of income, developed their own personal notion of "patriotism", although this never bridged the differences between the north and the conservative south, or the bedouin and the more politically-minded *hadari* East Bank elements.[19]

Joining the army promised enormous prestige and status, and provided for many a better standard of living than they had enjoyed in their places of origin. As the army was seen as a stepping stone to influence and power, the regime always had plenty of applicants from which to choose and carefully selected its recruits, preserving a *corps d'élite*, and preventing it from turning into a conscripted "National Army" open to all citizens. Conscription would mean no salaries—something which would be unthinkable so far as the bedouin were concerned.

A gradual, limited development of the army did not lead to any immediate need for technically skilled soldiers. The latter's requirement was prompted mainly by the border situation, which called for a better equipped army. The additional arms required suitable recruits in the developing Infantry, Artillery, Armour and Engineer units. The new, more technical posts could not be manned from the traditional reservoirs of the bedouin tribes, and called for the recruitment of Palestinians.

Some of them were drawn from the refugees living in Zarqa', many of whom were skilled villagers who had acquired their experience and migrated to towns under the British Mandate. Glubb set out to recruit only those he felt would be loyal and trustworthy, and therefore restricted as far as possible the number of educated, town-dwelling Palestinians whose influence he feared.

On the whole, very few Palestinians who had previous experience in war were recruited.[20] Tight control and extensive scrutiny characterized the process of accepting Palestinians.

As far as the Trans-Jordanian elements were concerned, the few Palestinian[21] newcomers had little effect on the striving for promotion which prevailed in the army. Unlike the civilian bureaucracy where the Palestinians played a prominent role, the Palestinian element in the army of the 1950s—though irreplaceable—was an inferior part of the Arab Legion with very few high ranking officers.[22] They were greeted with little enthusiasm by the Trans-Jordanians, especially those from the South. The latter constantly reminded the Palestinians of their defeat in 1948 and of the role of the Arab Legion in that war. The refugees were regarded as deserters and the Palestinians' capability as warriors was generally abused, not that they were ever given a chance within the Legion to prove otherwise. Moreover they were always regarded both inside and outside the Legion as untrustworthy "strangers".[23] Hence even the few Palestinians who became soldiers experienced alienation.

The King had to decide how far he could allow the process of the army's "Palestinianization". He chose to slow down this process as far as possible because of the danger it entailed, yet by not utilizing its potential he risked defeat at the hands of the Israeli army. He preferred to perpetuate the traditional composition of the army although it now faced additional tasks. Rapid inclusion of Palestinians, the monarch felt, was too much of a threat to his own interests and would probably further antagonize the loyal elements of which he was in constant need. The King perhaps overestimated the threat entailed in large scale recruitment of Palestinians as such. But he already confronted opposition from Trans-Jordanian elements[24] within the

Arab Legion and feared the gathering momentum of internal opposition once such a step was taken.

Overestimating the Legion's power, dazzled by its parades, and impressed by the way it maintained law and order in the streets, many Palestinians felt that their recruitment would finalize the last preparations for the "D-Day". In their view, it was Britain and the U.S.A. who, in their common interests, held back the King and prevented such action.

C. THE REFUGEES' ATTITUDES TOWARDS MILITARY TRAINING AND RECRUITMENT

Whereas the Government pursued a single basic policy with regard to the armed forces, the Palestinians as usual displayed a variety of responses which altered with changes in the political climate and with external events.

Immediately after the 1948 war, many refugees wanted to be protected against the possibility of renewed hostilities in their new locations. There were different suggestions as to how this should be achieved, all of them tentative but insistent. West Bank politicians made appeals[25] to the Jordanian authorities for arms and training, to be paid for by local taxes. At this stage they expected to have autonomous local forces, as before the war. A pro-Hashimite meeting in the Ramallah area, including representatives from 60 villages, asked for the establishment of a Local Defence Council. This would control small Palestinian "Border Forces" under the aegis of the Arab Legion. Criticism of the Arab armies' conduct of the war accompanied these proposals. But suspicion that the Mufti had a hand in the proposals was enough to deter the Government from acting on them, quite apart from its desire to disarm rather than re-arm the Palestinians.

The first training course for the N.G. in mid-1949 raised the hopes of the Palestinians, who expected it to form the core of a future army of liberation. This was apparent from the speeches made at the opening of the course in Dayr Tarif. Kazim Badawi, the chief exponent of the idea, praised Jordan for what it was now doing, but called for a further widening of the scheme to include every town and village in readiness for the "Second Round".[26] Such views[27] illustrated the divergence between the Government's and the Palestinians' perceptions of the situation.

The refugees' attitudes on this issue were unclear. For example, recruitment merited only a subsidiary mention at a meeting held in Bayt Jala,[28] which was concerned mainly with relief problems. In Nablus, on the other hand, refugee teachers asked for military training like other Palestinian teachers[29] (they were excluded by the Government) and the incorporation of refugee boy scouts into the N.G.[30]

Nevertheless, the spiritual need of the Palestinians to serve their country and people is apparent from the articles which appeared in *Voice of the Refugees*. This paper expressed the growing belief that Jordan was not going to commit herself in practice to military involvement or to embark on the promised "revenge". The fact that refugees were not being recruited was taken as proof of this while the bitter memory of the Ramleh-Lydda affair was still alive.[31] Generally refugees really believed that their enthusiasm, will and courage could strengthen the Arab ranks. The harshly critical articles reflected the increasing disapproval, distress and frustration felt by many refugees, as well as their yearning that the Arab regimes should put aside all past rivalries and set up a unified Arab force with a prominent position for the refugee fighters. They saw such participation as a guarantee of the sincerity of Arab rulers' promises. For the moment they could not but feel a deep and bitter disappointment with the regime. The notions of restoring *sharaf* (honour) and *karamah* (dignity) were repeatedly sounded in these angry articles hastening the closedown of this newspaper a few weeks later. Those refugees who were offered military training soon realized, as had the frontier villagers, that the time it took up prevented them from working or finding employment.[32] Enrolment was therefore low, and even a special locally-organized office set up in Jerusalem[33] failed to increase it. Articles appeared expressing disappointment with the refugees' response.[34] The Jordanian regime, which now saw that the Legion might have to fulfil the undermanned N.G.'s role, used a form of mild coercion in an attempt to improve the situation. Orders were issued to Government offices not to accept new employees unless they had finished their training in the N.G., this to be proved by the presentation of a special certificate.[35] There were refugee protests against this certificate, which when withheld prevented them finding employment.[36]

Hence the refugees found it difficult to comply with the Government's policy, even though this sought to demonstrate solidarity by providing training. As intended, the Government's insistence on occasional intensive courses, which prevented refugees from holding down jobs, tended to quieten down the demands for training.

For their part the Palestinians justified their reluctance to join the N.G. on the grounds of the pitifully inadequate equipment provided. It seems that refugees were strongly attracted to the Arab Legion, not only for its steady salary,[37] status and perks, but because it was a serious, professional fighting force. So there were calls for the refugees to be recruited into the army, and also for the N.G. to be incorporated into it. These refugees expected Jordan to follow the example of Syria which had recruited quite a large number of refugees. Cables from refugee committees in Jordan to Syria praised her policy and requested recruitment into the Syrian army.[38] The implied indictment of Jordan was obvious. After Egypt announced her intention to set up a refugee force in Gaza, an Egyptian Committee visited Hebron and found the locals warmly in favour of this step.[39] There was a similar response from the Nablus refugees when the Lebanese President visited Jordan. As on previous occasions there were calls for the formation of "an Arab army from the Refugees".[40]

Another demand, this time from the A.H.C. in Cairo in 1952, called for the recruitment of the Palestinians into all Arab armies. In a letter sent to the heads of state of Egypt and Syria, the Nablus Refugee Committee urged the gathering of all refugees in the Arab part of Palestine for military training so that they could bring about the return to their villages.[41] The Heads of state were further reminded of the "Secret Baludan Resolutions".

This kaleidoscope of differing formulas for Palestinian military involvement reflects both the desire to participate and the variety of ways in which this could be conceived of as happening. It has already been shown how the Government responded, although no one accepted their explanations at face value. For example, the Parliamentary Committee on Refugee Affairs[42] criticized the Government for its policy towards the recruitment and training of the refugees. Articles along these lines appeared in the Press.[43] The Arab League leaders were approached in the hope that a positive response from them would induce Jordan to act. Sa'id al-Azzah sent a cable to that effect to the Conference of the Arab Chief of Staff in the name of the Hebron refugees. But, generally speaking, during the period up to the Qibya massacre, requests for the recruitment of refugees into the Arab Legion, and for their military training were neither frequent nor very firmly expressed. Following incidents by contrast, demands became extremely vigorous for a while, though they mainly came from the constantly threatened Frontier Villages.

After Qibya, demands for the recruitment of Palestinians, for open conscription and for the strengthening of the N.G. became more pronounced.[44] The notions of *tajnid* (recruitment), *tadrib* (training) and *tathir* (purge) were voiced more strongly than ever before. The Government was petitioned to expel the British army commanders inside Jordan. These calls were supplemented by articles and manifestoes initiated by political activists.[45] The Muslim Brotherhood organized demonstrations in Aqbat Jabr. There were demonstrations of solidarity with Qibya by the people of other places. The Ba'th party became more vociferous and persistent in its demand for the inclusion of refugees in the Arab Legion, which it felt would strengthen the army and weaken the position of royal supporters within it. Hopefully, the Legion would eventually become "Palestinianized".[46] The Ba'th leaders also made it clear that their support for the strengthening of the N.G. was conditional upon its being an additional means of defence—supplementing the army which they regarded as the force responsible for the West Bank's protection.[47]

Above all, the Palestinians wanted some sort of appropriate action rather than the repetitive words and promises, which were the only things the regime was willing to give them. The Karamah Camp refugees appealed to the Islamic Conference convened in Jerusalem in December 1953 to declare a *jihad* in all the Muslim countries, and to work for the recruitment of refugees and their arming. More criticism of this kind followed the Israeli retaliation on Nahhalin village for the killing of Israeli bus passengers in the

Scorpion Pass. Calls for the dismissal of Glubb and Patrick Coghill (the Director of General Investigations Department in the army) and for "Arabizing" the Arab Legion[48] became more vociferous.[49] This was also true of calls for withdrawal from the treaty with Britain; and a more independent note began to characterize refugee demands of the Arab League. A memorandum from the Nablus refugees pointed out that it was the Arab countries' duty to train the able amongst the refugees, and to supply them with the necessary arms to enable them to form a spearhead in the fight for the return of their country.[50] Outside Jordan, the A.H.C., in its book published in Cairo in 1956, added that it would be even cheaper for the Arab Governments to turn the refugees into fighters than to give them relief[51]— neither of which they did.

The Press outside Jordan published news items on the growing awareness, enthusiasm and interest of the Palestinians, both refugees and non-refugees, in the Fedayyin activities, and talked of their desire to participate. However, such items need to be read with great caution as the Jordanian security forces' "black lists" of suspects for this period do not reveal much actual involvement beyond the verbal expression of support. Many Palestinians, sympathetic as they were, knew also that the Secret Police might well catch them. Functioning as part of the Fedayyin meant challenging the Hashimite authority, a position generally intolerable in Jordan.

The response to Glubb's dismissal was as overwhelming as the King expected. It was seen as signifying the end of British imperialism's control over Jordan, and therefore aroused great hopes. The popular support received by the King reflected the people's deep hatred of Glubb. He symbolized a major barrier to Arab unity.[52] His departure meant that there was now nothing to stop Jordan joining her Arab sisters.

The subject of recruitment arose in the election campaign that ensued.[53] However, once the excitement of the dismissal had died down it became clear that there had been little substantial change. How far Palestinian thinking had progressed by this time and how exasperated they had become can be seen from two developments. Politicians now sank their differences, and the gist of the statements they issued was "We want arms, not words".[54] The Press responded similarly. An article by the Trans-Jordanian Shafiq Rashidat took a particularly extreme view. In more explicit manner than earlier writers he drew up a blueprint for an incessant war of nerves with Israel, using guerilla tactics, in which Jordanian refugees would figure prominently because they knew the Israeli terrain and people. The refugees, he said, should also form the vanguard of the United Arab armies:

> As of 1948 our policy was to prevent the refugees from crossing the Armistice Lines by naming those of them who did so "infiltraitors", trying them and punishing them in order to respect the terms of the Armistice

and to protect the security of Israel. But today we should change this policy and form an army from the refugees who would operate every night from every camp and village from every road and valley along the border drawn by the imperialism, in all the areas which it named Israel, killing burning and destroying in revenge of our innocent martyrs.[55]

This extremism is the second indicative factor; and such articles reflected the beliefs and feelings of many Palestinians influenced by the rising wave of Arab nationalism. At this time refugees also condemned the Government's inconsistency in preventing their recruitment into the N.G. and the army, even though it had given them Jordanian citizenship, and officially regarded them as equal citizens.[56] They claimed that "Glubb's policy" continued to prevail.[57] The Government's rhetoric was becoming more transparent to many of them. Following the clampdown a year after Glubb's dismissal, public debate on the matter came to an end.

In short, it seems that there was no clear-cut pattern in the refugees' attitude on the issue of their recruitment into the Jordanian armed forces or on the question of what such service might mean for them. It should be noted that, relative to other demands centring around the problem of relief, resettlement and rehabilitation, the requests of the refugees to be included in the armed forces were neither frequent nor especially prominent. This demand generally received emphasis in specific response to the Israeli raids and to Jordan's proven inability to protect them. It might be considered a form of criticism and an expression of expectation rather than anything more. Demands for military training were directed against the Government and the army as criticism for their failure to extend appropriate protection or to enable them to defend themselves. Refugees did not trust the Government and thought they could effectively remind it of its duty to work for their Return only once they were part of the armed forces. Demands for a separate "Palestinian Army" or a "Refugee Army" came more from outside the kingdom than from within it. Appeals for equal recruitment, especially when not differentiating between the National Guard and the Arab Legion, can only be understood in this light; that is, the desire to transform the army into both a vehicle for change in Jordan itself and thereafter as a central force in the struggle for the retrieval of Palestine. The strong will to participate instead of being on the sidelines reflected the Palestinians' feeling of isolation and their burning desire to seek revenge. They did not want to be considered "different". Military training was synonymous with equality. But when protests were met with the extension of military training, limited as it was, many tried to evade the service. Nevertheless, they wanted the right to choose whether or not they joined the army.

While recruitment signified for the Palestinians, or rather for the refugees, becoming an integral part of the Arab nation via Jordan, what was the significance and level of refugee involvement in Jordanian politics?

Political life in Jordan was carried on at two levels: the open, Government-sanctioned "democratic" processes, and the underground political activity. These were in reality inextricably linked. The Government was sensitive to both kinds and kept up constant surveillance and control to maintain its position. The following chapters concentrate on the way the political parties related to the refugees' plight in publications and election campaigns; the refugees' actual participation as voters and candidates in Parliamentary and Municipal elections; and their response to attempts to recruit them into these parties in the context of constant Government interference and confrontation.

Chapter VI

The Participation of the Refugees in the Parliamentary and Municipal Elections

A. PARLIAMENTARY ELECTIONS [1]

1. To vote or not to vote?

One political dilemma confronting the Palestinians after the official annexation was whether or not to take part in the first Parliamentary elections following the establishment of the Union in 1950. Doing so could mean not only acquiescence but full voluntary acceptance of the fact that Jordan was their new country. For the refugees the problem was even more complicated. Voting, let alone candidacy, indicated a measure of support which could affect their political rights over the homes they had abandoned. They realized that they could not participate in elections and at the same time maintain non-acceptance of annexation.

Did the refugees, therefore, perceive any conflict between taking advantage of the political rights granted to them as citizens of Jordan and their declared aim of Return? Did they not fear that participation would tend to undermine their rights as refugees? Did they see a contradiction in electing and being elected to a Parliament which many of them claimed was not "theirs"? In the light of their demands would not it have been appropriate for those who emphasized their political separateness to abstain from taking part in this process of political integration?

Although granted citizenship, very few refugees thought that Jordan was politically the best place for them to live. It was only the refugees who moved from other Arab countries into Jordan who appreciated, in relative terms, the situation there.[2] The refugees were neither thankful nor were they satisfied with the regime. A majority of them in fact were rather passive and initially showed little interest in the country. They certainly did not want to take over from the locals as this could create annoyance, while some feared it might be assumed that they wanted to remain.

On the other hand, many Palestinians were discontented that they did not receive proportional representation[3] since they formed the majority of the population. Refugees were disappointed at not being allowed to elect their members as delegates from the places from where they came,[4] hoping to retain their exclusive uniqueness in the Parliament and perhaps secure a channel of influence which would preserve their interests. The Negev bedouin even complained they were discriminated against compared with the East Bank bedouin whose seats in Parliament were secured. But the regime did not want to reserve special seats for refugees. It wanted to blunt the edge of their separatism, preferring to grant them the right to vote and to be elected like all other citizens. The Government wanted them to see the elections as a way of ensuring, not losing, their right to Return.[5]

However, the Government did not need to encourage people to become candidates.[6] Many refugees tried to be elected despite various pressures against this. These came from the A.P.G., the Communists, large property owners and those who for one reason or another supported the internationalization of the Holy City. From abroad, the Mufti continued to attack the idea of holding elections and tried to influence his followers to refrain from voting.[7]

The G.R.C., however, was the first body to show some sense of *Realpolitik*. At its meeting in October 1949 the Congress decided it would not enter the election campaign, but would allow its members to participate individually if they so desired.[8] It was felt that if the G.R.C. entered the campaign on behalf of the refugees, it would give indirect recognition to the annexation and full endorsement of their citizenship, which would contradict their claim to appear as an exclusive separatist refugee body. The P.A.W.A. and the H.G.R.C. in Nablus followed suit.[9] Soon afterwards, the former Mufti supporters, Kamil Ariqat and Anwar Nusayba, became prominent in the election campaign, competing in the Jerusalem-Jericho area.

The Ba'th supporters, who regarded the Parliament as a most important instrument in their prolonged and stubborn struggle for basic social and political reforms,[10] formed an *ad hoc* list "the Constitutional National Front" which included Yahya Hamudah, Dr Musa Husayni, Abdallah Rimawi and Abdallah Na'was. They also used their newspapers *al-Ba'th* and *al-Hadaf* in their propaganda campaign. The P.A.W.A. put forward Anwar al-Nashashibi and Shafiq Nabil as its candidates. Other old Palestinian bodies also tried to win seats by recruiting support from villagers. Among these were the Village Council, the Arab Village Reform Association, the Executive of the Arab Villages Union and the Hebron Village Reform Association. Most candidates, however, were "independent", including Ministers whom the law did not force to resign if they stood, and who therefore enjoyed a distinct advantage.

Only the Communists continued to attack participation, and they distributed leaflets[11] and sent threatening letters to candidates.[12] But demonstrations in Nablus protesting against the elections only exposed their weakness in the face of the regime's strength and obstinacy. Moreover, the punishments received by the leaders of this protest (they were ordered to walk barefoot from Nablus to Salt) deterred anyone from supporting a boycott.

In view of the extent of the Palestinians' participation in the first elections, the Communists and other groups which boycotted them had to change their position. They faced the dangerous possibility of losing what was viewed as an important channel of political influence.[13] In subsequent elections they were vociferously involved.

For their part, the refugees were generally great believers in Pan Arabism, and did not see any contradiction between participating in this process of "decision making" and maintaining their rights in Palestine. They argued that to be the vanguard for Arab unity was the only way to bring back their lost rights. It seems they were unconcerned about the regime's intention to integrate them as Jordanians rather than as Palestinians and there is little evidence to indicate they were troubled by this "dilemma". On the contrary, some of them were even attracted by the fact that they could, for the first time, take part in "democratic" political machinery, believing the legislature itself could bring about the hoped-for changes. They felt they could influence its decisions and bring their Trans-Jordanian partners to view things their way. Others were responding to a certain sense of belonging that participation gave them. They also knew that elections would take place anyway and feared being represented by the Trans-Jordanians or by other Palestinians whom they neither trusted nor respected. And, of course, many refugees were simply pleased that they had had the opportunity of becoming citizens, unlike their brothers in the other Arab countries. So participation in the first elections, especially in view of the lack of a tangible alternative, meant practically the same thing for different refugees: becoming a respected Arab citizen able to voice his "rights", though these were not necessarily in line with the regime's interpretation.

It seems the refugees wanted simultaneously to vote, to be equal citizens, and to be returned to their homes. Aziz Shihadah, a refugee candidate in the Ramallah area, reflected the view of many others when he said:

> I thought, I will be able to voice the feelings and wishes of refugees. We could not organise ourselves independently, so by going into government we could try and influence our interests from within.[14]

Anwar Nusayba, who stressed that he felt no internal conflict after talking to Abdullah following his return to Jordan, said:

> The elections were never boycotted. They were very hotly contended. The refugees were very much a part of them and never was it regarded that if you take part you are betraying the cause. On the contrary, you felt you are placing yourself in a position to influence, working for justice for your own people through the instrumentality of Jordan.[15]

2. Refugee Candidates

In the first election in 1950 there were 125 candidates, 65 of them in the West Bank.[16] Eighteen of the total regarded themselves as "refugee representatives",[17] though not all were "true" refugees. In the event, only 3 refugees became M.Ps. In the 1951 elections, which came about after the King ordered the House's prorogation, there were 15 refugee candidates, some of whom were persuaded to withdraw their candidacy in the course of the campaign. This happened in Bethlehem when Abd al-Majid al-Azzah dropped out to enable Abd al-Fattah Darwish to represent all the area's Muslims and to be selected with the Christian Qatan, thereby avoiding elections under the *tazkiyyah* arrangement.[18] In the Hebron region, where Fawar Camp had been recently built and which had absorbed many refugees, there were 4 refugee candidates. The refugee voice was quite an important factor there and made the campaign more active and intense. This campaign saw the new "political parties" playing a more active role and refugee and non-refugee candidates coming together in common lists.[19] There is little evidence that refugees tried to organize themselves as refugees, or worked for a separatist refugee vote. In Nablus the two refugee committees met separately to discuss their support of candidates, but did not nominate a candidate of their own as they knew he stood no chance, would only split the votes and might upset the delicate balance among the contending lists. They therefore expressed no overtly partisan support for any list. Becoming entangled in local politics could undermine their position as refugee spokesmen and aggravate their relations with local leaders by what was considered unwarranted interference. In the end they decided to appeal to the refugees in Jericho to vote for the non-refugee Anastas Hananiya, the former Minister.[20] On the other hand a new, little-known body called "The Refugee Camps Youth" published an advertisement (paid for by the candidates) calling on the refugees in the Nablus area to vote for the Constitutional Front which included Masri, Salih, Tuqan and Qadumi.[21] The election results showed that only former refugee deputies were re-elected.

In the 1954 elections only two of the 9 refugees who stood were voted in from amongst 116 candidates. No refugee candidates appeared in Nablus and, for the first time, Hebron was represented only by local M.Ps.

In the 1956 so-called "free elections" there were 144 candidates including 12 refugees, three of whom stood in Amman where 23 candidates competed for 5 places. Seven refugees stood among the 71 candidates in the West Bank and only Sa'id al-Azzah from the National Socialist list was elected.

In brief, if one can regard the participation of the refugees in the Parliamentary elections as providing some indication of their striking roots in the political life of Jordan, it seems that, with the passage of time, this process coincided with the *decline* both in the number of refugee candidates as well as in the emphasis put on their refugee origin. Apart from a single occasion when in Ramallah in 1952, Ahmad Raghib al-Dajani advocated a party for the defence of refugee rights to be named "The Voice of Palestine"[22] (which received no response), there were no attempts by refugees to join together on a common list to try to appear as a separatist body.

3. The Weight of the Refugee Vote

When considering a refugee candidate's chances of being elected or the potential impact of the refugee electorate in a given area, one has to go beyond the actual number of refugees and the candidate's personality and political affiliations to consider a whole set of related factors. These include the social, economic and ethnic characteristics of the local community, the number of seats accordingly allocated to the area, the relative qualities of the local and refugee leadership there, and the social structure of the refugee concentration in each area—their religion, place of origin, blood relations, connections within the area, and their mode of living. It is therefore difficult to generalize about the political behaviour and effect of the refugees in the various areas in which they were concentrated. Since the above factors interacted in different ways, it is necessary to examine each area separately. For example, the refugees who arrived in Nablus, being generally Nablusis or villagers in origin, had very little political impact on the town's long established leadership or on its economy.[23] They generally voted in accordance with the local pattern, and even the more capable and influential among them remained economically dependent on the established local system.

In Ramallah by contrast, the arrival of Christian and Muslim educated, town-dwelling refugees upset the religious, economic, social and political balance of the predominantly Christian town. The refugees eventually became the dominant element in the town's economy and politics. The *ghuraba'* ('strangers') outnumbered the locals by two to one. Many brought substantial assets with them, smoothing their absorption into the life of the town. The Christians among them could integrate far more easily, becoming allies, with the local population which tried to preserve its position. Political instability and competition in the parliamentary elections between refugee and non-refugee, Christian and Muslim, was largely avoided since the Christians there were granted sectarian representation, each religious community being allocated one seat. This allowed the urban Muslim refugees to secure parliamentary representation at no expense to the town's Christian community.

Bethlehem, the other predominantly Christian town in the West Bank, was a different case. The town absorbed the relatively few Christian refugees who tried to integrate there and who remained politically passive. The local Christians were more intensely competitive and remained in control. The rest of the refugees were Muslim villagers who mostly settled outside the town in neighbouring camps and townlets. Those Muslims already in the town had arrived from neighbouring villages or Hebron during the process of urbanization, or were Ta'amirah bedouin. As a seat was reserved for the Muslim population in the area, the "locals versus strangers" conflict was absorbed into the existing pattern of divisions between the town-dwellers and the villagers, the educated and the illiterate, the employers and the employees and between the skilled and the unskilled. The representation of local town Christians was not endangered.[24]

In places which suffered deleterious economic effects from the war, the resulting political changes took place amongst the local families with little influence exerted by the refugees. In Tulkarm, for example, the refugees played no part in the politics of the town with its complicated system of social stratification.[25] But the area candidates badly needed their votes since the tough competition in the area elections produced a relatively high number of contenders.

However, contrary to the general belief,[26] the refugees were not a decisive factor in determining a candidate's success, certainly not in the eastern part of the kingdom. Apart from the fact that refugee opinion and groups were split left, right and centre, their numbers compared with the local population were far smaller than those published by the relief agencies. The Jordanian authorities knew roughly the numbers of the refugees in each area and produced two sets of figures: an inaccurate higher one for the relief agencies and a far lower, more accurate one for the ballots. In Jerusalem, for example, there were 7,261 electors to which the Jewish Quarter Refugee Camp contributed only 430. Jericho area had a large concentration of refugees but their potential weight was diluted since it was part of the whole Jerusalem area which included another 30 surrounding villages. In Hebron area the Arrub Camp had 1,326 electors out of the total of 30,096.[27] Nablus had three small camps within the town while Ramallah had none.[28] Most refugees were outside the camps scattered all over the kingdom in small villages.

Moreover, refugees who migrated from the West Bank during the 1950s could not, according to Jordanian law, vote in the east side. Hence this movement, along with emigration, only weakened the refugees as an electoral force.[29] Furthermore, while the refugees actively participated in elections it seems they never sought to be regarded as a separate group of voters. From the 1954 elections onwards there is no trace of any substantial difference in the electoral behaviour of the two parts of the Palestinian community. Refugees did not, therefore, automatically see any refugee candidates as "their representative" simply because he was a refugee. Local candidates were generally more popular with the refugees; and since the refugee electorate was divided no refugee candidate could really usurp the local representative or capture his votes. In Muslim areas any such attempt was viewed by both sides as unhealthy to their delicate mutual relationship. This was even more the case with the accelerated assimilation of refugees from the mid-1950s onwards. Wherever there were refugee candidates they stood like any other citizen on their own merits. In fact they paid even *less*

attention to the refugees' plight, fearing the label of refugee spokesmen—
which would deprive them of much-needed local support.

As for the indigenous population's voting behaviour, it is evident from the
result that they did vote for a refugee when the candidate retained his
wealth, prestige and reputation from "the good old days" or when his
religious affiliation would not harm the local candidates' chances.

4. Failure and Success

It is difficult to establish whether old loyalties left over from the Nashashibi-
Husayni friction had any bearing on the electorate's behaviour, at least in
the first elections. Although this prolonged and deadly conflict began to
disappear in the 1940s,[30] it left its mark on people on both sides especially
amongst the ordinary villagers. Kirkbride said he found some vague traces
of the division in the Jericho area to which many Husayni refugees had
come.[31] However, since the conflict was partly transformed, for at least a
while, into Husayni versus Hashimite (the weak Nashashibi playing no real
role in this confrontation), the enmity dissolved, leaving few traces apart
perhaps from influencing some votes in the Jerusalem[32] and Ramallah[33]
areas in the 1950 elections.

Since Parliamentary elections were previously unknown in the country
and Government had been centralized under the British Mandate, with the
A.H.C. as the focus of all political activity, very few of the people living in
Jordan were known outside the boundaries of their home district. This was
certainly true as regards the refugees. Their traditional leaders proved
indispensable in gaining publicity as they still retained extensive influence,
and candidates had to receive their approval as a precondition for wide
support in the leader's constituencies. For this reason the *mukhtars,* notables,
shaykhs and of course the local leaders were courted by candidates. Some of
them paid large sums of money in return for promises that they would
actively back them by bringing their people to the ballots to vote for them.
With little money and means at their disposal either to gain more publicity or
to acquire votes,[34] refugees found it very difficult to match the more respected
and better known locals. Against this background, some of those who had
aspirations were deterred from even trying, fearing the shame of defeat and
the loss of the deposits all candidates were required to leave.

For example, it proved impossible for a refugee living in one of the Jericho
camps to win in any elections. Candidates were disabled once again by
rivalries and conflicts among the refugees. They could not unite behind one
representative from amongst them and, even if they did, it was practically
impossible for such a candidate to stand a chance against the local Ariqat in
the villages or a Jerusalem townsman. The same went for Nablus, Tulkarm
and certainly in the East Bank, where it was considered discourteous to
become a candidate. They could never gain much support from a local
population who were protecting their own interests by solidly backing their

own candidates. In addition, the more numerous the candidates who ran in each area the tougher it was for the refugee candidates. Consequently the refugee vote tended to be dissipated among the numerous choices. Only rarely did the refugees support a single candidate as with Abd al-Fattah Darwish in Bethlehem. He was well known amongst the area's population being the leader of the Bani Hasan association of villages which included Christian Bayt Jala. So in the Bethlehem area, where fewer refugees were living, a member of the Darwish family could almost guarantee them a seat. The rivalry of Bayt Jala and Bayt Sahur with Bethlehem helped Darwish to gain favour with the two townlets, thereby making the refugee vote a decisive factor even for the Christian candidate.[35] However not all refugees supported Darwish because many of them did not like him. With no other refugee leader in the area, those who opposed him supported local Muslim candidates. This was quite common in al-Azzah and Dahaysha Camps. Although Hasan Mustafa from Battir village failed against Abd al-Fattah Darwish, his brother Ribhi succeeded later against Hasan Darwish.[36]

Another example was Sa'id al-Azzah who was elected in the Hebron area because he was a powerful leader in Bayt Jibrin. He was later elected in Hebron, where the fact that he had relatives through his father's marriage helps to explain his local support. He was trusted by the refugees, who knew of his vocal attempts to represent their plight and of his demands for further action from the relief agencies and the Government, both of which he criticized strongly. Being a gifted speaker, educated and highly respected locally, his candidacy appealed to the refugees who wanted someone forceful to serve their interests. There were other strong refugee figures in the region but they knew their influence did not exceed the camp boundaries. Whether or not they accepted Azzah's hegemony, they knew they could not defeat him, and that the only result of opposing him would be the loss of a direct refugee link with the House. That was indeed what happened in 1954. Outspoken as he was, Azzah reached his peak of popularity in the 1956 elections, heading the National Socialists and becoming the party's secretary. But his views were incompatible with those of the regime and he soon realized the only safe place for him was outside Jordan. He escaped the country following the attempted *coup d'état* of 1957.[37]

To excuse their failure most candidates alleged the elections were "rigged".[38] Although this was true in some cases—as the regime intervened in various ways for the election of those it wanted in Parliament (not necessarily its supporters)—this does not explain the success of other candidates. Clearly, some people were favoured by the regime and so were elected. However, Sa'id Ala' al-Din, for example, was nominated for Minister a number of times even after he had failed in all his attempts to be elected to Parliament. Although he was a University of Liverpool graduate, the nephew of the former Ramleh Mayor and the cousin of the former Lydda Mayor in the Ramallah area where most Ramleh-Lydda people were living, he confronted the combined influence of the far more respected families of Khayri and

Taji. He was unknown and considered an ally of Britain, which ruined his image in the 1950/1 election campaign against Khayri (who strangely enough escaped this stigma) and the more popular Ba'th leaders of village origin. Although nominated for Minister, he still maintained that his failure was due to the regime's hostile interference. He also suggested that the King, fearing the influence of the Ba'thists Rimawi and Na'was, wanted them near him under his eye. So he released them from jail knowing they would win seats since they were popular because of their protests against the regime. By doing so, he said, the King hoped to appease the Syrians as well.[39] But perhaps Sa'id Ala' al-Din's failure should be attributed to the fact that he was simply unpopular with the refugees, owing to his elevated position and his lack of attention to the refugee plight, which made him doubly remote from the camp refugees.[40]

This was a reason why people tended to ignore some M.P.s who requested re-election, saying "we only saw and heard them when election time came. After that they forgot we existed . . . people who live in misery remember who comes to visit them and who speaks for them". It was said that "refugee representatives were only interested in their own benefits and interests and didn't care for the refugees".

On the other hand even refugee activists failed to receive the support of their brothers. Hamudah and Shihadah both failed because the majority of refugees did not trust them as they concentrated on defending the rights of the property-owning refugees.

Even ICRC relief workers who resigned from the Red Cross in the hope that they would receive large support from the refugees who knew and trusted them, were not voted in by the refugees. This happened to Nihad Abu Gharbiyyah, ICRC Jericho Area Officer, to Abd al-Karim al-Alami, who was the Camp Leader of Mu'askar Camp in Jerusalem, and to Uthman Muhammadiyyah. Daud al-Isa, whose "refugee" newspaper, *Filastin,* supported the refugee plight and was very active in trying to voice their feelings, was not elected. Even the support he received from the Jaffa community in Jerusalem and other Christians, and from the *Khalylah* (the Hebronites living in Jerusalem) whom Ja'bari, the Hebron Mayor, asked to vote for Isa,[41] was not sufficient for him to win elections. A candidate always needed the support of the area villagers. An example here is the local Kamil Ariqat who managed to win the support of most of the Jerusalem area villagers, the Jericho Camp refugees and the bedouin.[42] He was the only one who succeeded in setting up special refugee bodies to ensure himself massive cohesive support. In 1950 he amalgamated the two rival Jericho refugee committees, persuaded some candidates to withdraw to prevent a split in the votes and out-manoeuvred all the other five refugee candidates and a number of locals. Ariqat enjoyed the support of most area villages because of his reputation for courage and his former association with the Mufti,[43] even though he became the King's staunch follower. Above all, the refugees believed that this highly respected local figure would be a better spokesman for them than any town-dweller or camp refugee who was neither known nor respected, and whom they generally did not trust. As their new spokesman rather than leader, he indeed impressed them with his attempts to speak for them in Parliament. He used his influence with the authorities and the relief Agencies, and did far more than was even promised by others.

In short, the refugees favoured candidates who they believed had a powerful mediating position through contacts with government officials or who had a strong political bargaining status. They supported those who were more politically active and vociferous, regardless of their ideological affiliations, and also those who dedicated time to their miseries and helped them privately in one way or another. So the incohesive refugee vote was seldom behind one candidate. No refugees from the camps who stood as candidates ever succeeded. In all realism the refugee had to rely on the power of local leaders rather than on that of his fellow refugees.

However it was not too long before the Palestinians, especially the refugees, became disillusioned with their representatives. Despite all the hopes and expectations the Palestinians had of their deputies,[44] they soon bitterly realized that most deputies either did not try or were unable to implement their promises since all the economic changes they wanted were in the hands of the monarch and those who surrounded him. District Officers and Area Commanders proved to be far more effective than Ministers (who were viewed as senior clerks), while M.P.s were even less appreciated. Anxiously waiting for someone to take action for them, by 1956 the West Bankers were influenced at the polls more than ever before by their yearning for change. And while the new House of that year was not all that different, and most of its members were old faces now siding openly with one of the parties, new figures replaced those with whom the electorate was disappointed. Even Ariqat was not far from losing his seat to the Ba'thist Bahajat Abu Gharbiyyah.[45]

The various developments in the villages and camps during the mid-1950s such as the process of urbanization, the influence of the young teachers in the rapidly expanding education system, closer contacts with neighbouring towns, the rise of Nasserism and the effect of the radio transmissions, all contributed to the growing influence of the young at the expense of the old. This made political penetration into these places by the various leftist parties much easier.[46] Growing numbers of followers were recruited into these parties from sectors which they had previously neglected. In the 1956 elections therefore, disillusioned villagers began supporting candidates whom they learnt of through the Press as party representatives rather than as personalities. This was true both of candidates from the orthodox religious bodies on the political right, who generally maintained old village associations and loyalties, and of the "leftist" parties who became popular with the young. Little trace was left of "refugee solidarity".

5. The Refugee Issue in the Election Campaign

As candidates tried to appeal to a wide audience it was expected that some heed would be paid in their published platforms and "manifestos" to the refugees' plight. After all, the platforms, being "packages" of programmes and commitments, were not all-important and usually included many items solely to please voters and gain their support. The electorate, like the candidates, knew there was not and could not be any real commitment to these statements. Nevertheless, people loved listening to promises, speeches and even reading the parties' platforms. Naturally speeches were made to excite the listeners, and their content reveals both the intensity and variety of criticism made by candidates of the Jordanian regime and its refugee policies.

Overall, in the four propaganda campaigns the refugee issue received little attention from the various political parties even as a vote-winning subject. This was because the candidates realized there was no such thing as a "united" refugee vote and that platforms meant little to the villagers. So mentioning the refugee plight in one's platform did not convey a real concern, while omission of it simply reflected the lack of interest in this subject. There were other more immediate and painful issues on which to focus.

Even in the first elections the topics which received attention from the candidates were essentially social and economic,[47] though they also gave some space to the refugee question since they were a heavy burden on the country's economy. Needless to say, in the East Bank the subject was hardly ever mentioned, and even Shafiq Rashidat's platform for the National Front published in 1950 related only to social and economic problems without even mentioning the plight of the refugees.[48] Those who wanted to be popular with the refugees claimed they would fight the cancellation of ration cards. They accused the Red Cross of starving the refugees, demanding and achieving ICRC's surrender to their pressure owing to its fear of the refugees' angry response.[49] Nevertheless, they failed to be elected and received very few refugee votes.

The second campaign in 1951 proved very much the same. The salient features, hotly debated, especially in Ramallah where the Communists and Ba'thists[50] were very active, were the rights of Jordanian citizens and the change of the Constitution. Again the refugee issue received little attention whilst each candidate promised to work for the welfare of his constituency, fighting for more citizens' rights and against unemployment.[51] Nonetheless, reports and news items show that candidates spent more time electioneering in the camps. As always the authorities followed all their appearances with great concern.[52]

This trend increased in 1954 and even more in 1956 owing to the tough competition and the proliferation of political activity. More visits were paid to the camps than ever before and the different speakers felt they had to relate to the refugees' misery before touching upon the more popular issues[53] of purging the army, Anglo-American imperialism and the need for Arab unity. Each one reminded his listeners that he opposed resettlement and had always worked to ameliorate their condition far more than others. As one interviewed candidate put it: "Even if you have little regard for the refugee you still needed their votes."

Ironically those who did highlight the issue did not do well, getting support from neither the refugees[54] nor the locals. It is not suggested that their failure stemmed from taking up the issue, but simply that support from the refugees did not necessarily accrue through focusing on their problems. The latter voted more or less along the lines of the rest of the population, attracted more by a candidate's personality than his written promises. Moreover, it seems that the refugees were not troubled by their plight receiving little attention and did not call upon candidates to express their stand on this issue. No evidence was found that the refugees, who were very much involved in the elections, insisted that their problem should receive more coverage compared with other issues. Their main interests were similar to the rest of the population, that is, they were concerned with the developments in Jordan and its policies, which they naturally felt had an impact on both their position in Jordan and their rights in Palestine. The more educated urban refugees who gradually integrated into their new communities were pleased with the development of the idea of Arab unity which promised them an equal role.

Whatever their political affiliations, however, candidates employed the technique of referring to grievances. And obviously all candidates showed concern with the Refugee Problem when actually appearing before them. All those who went to the camps had to discuss two main subjects. One was the Future, which involved the vision of the Return of the refugees to their places, and the redressing of the injustice done to them, meanwhile safe-guarding their rights in Palestine and rejecting the resettlement pro-grammes. The other was the Present, which entailed commitment to do their utmost to better the conditions in the camp until the Return.

Like the refugees themselves, the candidates never stipulated exactly what they meant by 'the Return' or how it could be achieved. Did it mean they were to become citizens of Israel, or part of an independent Palestine State side by side with Israel, or owners of the whole area from the sea to the river? In fact there was no need for any clarification as its nebulous nature was taken for granted. An open recognition of the State of Israel, implicit in the first two possibilities, was inconceivable. The Communists, who preached for Partition, ceased doing so when they ran for the third election as they feared being discredited in the eyes of the electorate. Surprisingly, it was the Trans-Jordanian Amman-based group of Dr Mustafa Khalifah, Salim al-Bakhit, Wasfi Mirza and others on the winning Popular List whose 1954 election manifesto (appealing to the large Palestinian electorate) pro-claimed their support for the principles laid down by the 1947 Partition Plan as the only way of solving the Palestinian question. They were quickly supported by the H.G.R.C. in Nablus which cabled the refugees in Amman to vote for this list. It is not suggested here that they were elected on the strength of their platform but rather that, being influential figures—all of them Trans-Jordanians, Muslims, Christians and Circassians—they attracted some Palestinian votes despite the fact that the result of the 1954 elections could hardly be taken seriously.

Khalifah and some of his friends were voted in again in 1956, receiving more or less the same support when they ran as candidates of the 'Constitutional Party' which hardly mentioned refugee affairs in its published programme.[55] Like other Deputies, Khalifah succeeded not on his platform but because he was known and respected in his constituency. The refugees there recalled that as Minister of Health he was one of the only members of the Cabinet who ever came to visit them, listened to their grievances and actually did something about them. Apart from Hasan Mustafa, who failed, only Ariqat dedicated a whole part of his detailed platform to the Refugee Problem in 1956. This alone could not attract votes, and space was given to many other pressing issues. Nevertheless, it is interesting to compare his four-page leaflet with those of Shaykh As'ad al-Imam al-Husayni, Yusuf Niqula Abda and Daud al-Husayni against whom he competed, since they hardly mentioned the refugee cause in their brief and condensed platforms. Counting on receiving their support, Daud al-Husayni gained nearly twice as many refugee votes as Ariqat, their traditional representative, who narrowly escaped losing his place. The National Socialist Party, which did not even mention the refugee plight,[56] emerged as the real champion of the 1956 elections. It included amongst its candidates many of the most prominent figures of the time—hence its success. Mufti supporters appeared under the name of the New Arab Party. In 1956 their local candidates were elected in Nablus[57] and Jerusalem though their refugee candidate Mahmud Ala' al-Din failed in Ramallah.

In the third and fourth elections the various political parties played a much greater role, while the whole population pinned more hopes on them and were more interested than before. This growing refugee support for the political parties was not due to their dedicating more time or attention to the refugees' plight. The issue raised by the parties in the 1954 election centred around the question of Arab unity. This became more salient in the 1956 elections when it superseded all other problems. It was viewed as a necessary stage whose implementation would enable all other subsequent changes. For the refugees, whose plight was hardly mentioned, there was no contradiction. Their goals remained very much the same; only the manner of achieving them was somewhat different. The fact that by the mid-fifties most refugees did not feel like, and were not regarded as, a separate and different class did not counteract this shift but rather supplemented it. The reports of the government intelligence agents following the various candidates, especially in the camps, show that even the refugees themselves, when questioning the candidates, did not relate to the Refugee Problem as such, but expressed growing interest in topics such as strengthening the army, conscription, Arab unity and, of course, Nasser. Siding with the "radical" parties was regarded as a reaffirmation of their goals. This was certainly reflected in the outcome of the 1956 elections.

B. ELECTIONS TO THE TOWN COUNCILS

Participation in municipal elections was also seen in the perspective of the major issues of refugee rights, ultimate goals and necessary compromise. But obviously it was also much more closely bound up with particular local situations.

1. The Municipalities and the Refugees

On the whole the Town Councils (TCs) became displeased with the presence of refugees in the towns. The feelings of duty and pity behind the work of some of the TCs in the first few months when they did their utmost to assist the refugees, trying to meet their needs and requirements, gave way to mutual discontent. The tremendous problems they had to face with their inadequate facilities and funds were insurmountable and could only result in chaos.[58] The locals could not cope with this huge pressure and became fed up with the endless demands of the refugees who streamed into the towns. Trespassing, thefts and deteriorating hygiene conditions accompanied their arrival.

The refugees occupied the schools, mosques and churches in the first few years and accused the local authorities of taking advantage of them by not distributing all the relief items sent by the Red Cross and friendly countries. Abuse of the relief system, which was only natural under such conditions and committed by both sides, only aggravated their relationship. Refugees were called gipsies or worse in some places, and were reminded that according to local customs, a guest was only welcome for three days and three nights. Gradually many refugees left the towns for places where water and care could be found. Those remaining became part of an official camp within the town or managed to rent places. The latter group complained bitterly that the natives took advantage of the situation by making rents very expensive[59] and by taxing the few refugees who managed to open a stall or small shop.[60] Because refugees were willing to limit their profit and accept a small return for their work, there was tension between them and the poor non-refugees as well as between the towns' shop owners and those who quickly opened shops in the camps. Shoppers found it much cheaper to buy food items in refugee shops, and employers to hire refugee labour.

At first refugees looked to some of the TCs to receive relief, assistance and letters certifying they were refugees, as some had nothing on them to prove their status.[61] Generally they felt the TCs should do far more for them, especially the villager refugees who often regarded the TCs' approach as discriminatory. Though there were many exaggerations, not all such accusations were groundless.

As to the refugees not in the camps but living within the municipal boundaries, the municipalities played an important role in providing them with essential services. The councils were therefore anxious to receive support from UNRWA in exchange for these activities, often getting far more than their real expenditure.[62] Some municipalities also tried to take advantage of the refugee presence. For example, the Jerusalem TC taxed the American School of Oriental Research as a hotel since it housed shelterless refugees for a year following the war which prevented it from continuing its work.[63] Other TCs demanded from UNRWA that employment projects for refugees should take place within the municipal boundaries[64] so that allocations would be ear-marked for the benefit of the towns' water supplies and sewerage systems, public markets, roads, afforestation, hospital facilities etc.[65] Of course such programmes, if executed, would satisfy all parties concerned and relieve the local authorities as well as the Government of the cost of such essential development schemes, unloading the responsibility for the whole development onto the U.N's shoulders.[66]

The municipalities refused to accept any responsibility as such for the refugees; so much so that the Jerusalem TC refused to accept Ja'bari's idea of a West Bank Mayors' meeting to discuss refugee questions,[67] saying that the refugees were the responsibility of the Government and UNRWA alone,[68] and did not fall within the TC's terms of reference. The period during which they extended what meagre help they could soon ended (to their relief) when UNRWA took over. With UNRWA's increasing involvement and the attempts to resettle the refugees and better their conditions through erecting asbestos shelters, the question of requisitioned privately-owned land and the problem of refugees squatting in the towns became important political issues for the local people.

Another issue concerned sanitary conditions. After the Armistice Agreement was signed, the Jerusalem TC appealed to the authorities to allow the evacuated frontier villagers to return to their homes as their presence caused sanitary nuisances.[69] For this reason they also wanted refugees moved to the camps outside the towns.[70] The Jerusalem TC also had its problems with Mu'askar, the only untented camp in the Jewish Quarter, half of which was populated by poor non-refugees. The place became unsafe for habitation owing to the lack of maintenance and sanitation and the collapse of the old houses' foundations. There were also problems of sewerage, floodings, hygiene and unsightliness. The TC was troubled by the beggars who populated this part of the town and were a nuisance to tourists.

Other troublesome issues were those of supplying the camps with water,[71] and the limited space for the burying of dead refugees.[72] In some places the TCs refused to allow refugees to be buried in the town's cemetery owing to limited space and the fear that in view of constantly rising prices, they would soon have to allocate or purchase more expensive land.

Thus owing to a whole range of issues relating to their immediate everyday problems, the refugees had an interest in the composition of the TCs even if they did not participate in them, hoping that people more sympathetic to them would be elected.

2. The Refugee Electorate

If refugee participation in parliamentary elections was tacitly approved by most Palestinians and justified on the grounds that it would enable them to play a more active role in matters relating to their plight, the question of refugees taking part in the municipal elections received a cooler and even somewhat hostile response from the local Palestinians. It was to turn into a tense question in some towns, clouding the relations between the two parts of the Palestinian community. The natives were displeased that "strangers" could have a say in the running of their town affairs. It was suggested to the refugees that this kind of involvement would have far reaching implications on their political rights outside Jordan. They could not simultaneously claim direct involvement in local affairs while declaring that they did not want to integrate into their new places of abode. Camp refugees feared that participation by their refugee brothers would jeopardize their cause.

The Jordanian law did not provide directly for refugee participation in local elections. To be a voter one had to pay urban property taxes. However, as many refugees came with their assets and quickly opened businesses in some places, they could legally vote and be elected once they paid taxes. Whilst some locals accepted this with good grace so long as these refugees paid their share, most people, including other refugees, bitterly rejected the idea that a refugee should try to be elected as a member of the local council. Many refugees believed that contesting these seats in the first elections of 1951 would be likely to engender social disharmony.

However the refugees never wished to be regarded as a group aspiring to separate representation. Some were simply not interested; others felt no desire to take part in the politics of a town to which they did not truly belong. The minority who did pay taxes were afraid of antagonising the natives, who would regard their interest in local affairs as an expression of ingratitude. The urban refugees knew that running for office would upset the anxiously preserved traditional balance between the local clans, and that any seat gained would be at the expense of the clan's representation, thereby creating more discord. They were aware that social and economic integration could not come about through any kind of competition which deprived the locals of their say. Not wanting to emphasize their inferior status and "difference", knowing that only harm would result, many refrained from getting involved.

In the first election they felt that they would be going back home soon and that participation could only count against them. Some saw little wrong in the way things were and knew they were powerless to change things even if they so desired.

When they realized that the Return was not imminent, some townsmen decided that, given a chance, they would opt for remaining and got more involved locally, becoming better known and in some ways accepted. But only in the twin towns[73] of Ramallah and al-Bira, the former with its numerous well-off, town-dwelling refugees, was there a need for a redistribution or rather reallocation of seats. Thus the passage of time saw a change of view among some refugees and local town-dwellers. However, despite the special position of Ramallah, it was in Nablus[74] and Hebron where the refugees first demanded municipal participation. Petitions to that effect were presented in Hebron in January 1951, suggesting that allowing refugees to vote would make them feel like local inhabitants *(muqimin)* and not refugees. These letters were also signed by a group of poor locals who, like the refugees, protested against the voting qualification being a monied prerogative. They maintained that the houseowners paid their taxes from rent received, thus depriving the tenants of the voting of a tax payer.[75]

The authorities modified the local election law for the second municipal elections of 1955 to make participation conditional on payment of any municipal tax exceeding JD1 for those resident at least a full year prior to the elections.[76] This enabled many refugees to have a say in local affairs. The new law empowered the authorities to appoint the Mayor as well as nominate two additional members, if they so desired, to protect unrepresented interests.[77] This was aimed also at making integration easier for refugees, especially the more capable amongst them. They would then feel less alienated in their new places and be assimilated more quickly.

The elections concentrated on local issues but at times radical parties would try to sway the electorate on subjects that had little to do with, say, refuse collection, and endeavoured overtly to politicize the campaign. But TC elections were regarded as essentially non-political. The pliant moderate traditional leaders, drawn mainly from local families of long established wealth and influence, dominated the life of the TC and were content to stick to local economic problems.

So these elections changed the situation very little, which was just what the Jordanian authorities intended. They kept things well under control, and every candidate's political affiliations were examined.[78] Moreover the regime was not keen to have election campaigns in which delicate political questions were bound to arise when rival candidates attempted to discredit each other.

But in most places local elections were by no means a minor event. Although they involved only a few voters, they were hotly contested since the composition of the municipality would affect people's interests.

In the first election the refugees' plight was referred to in an attempt to win the votes of the tax payers amongst them. In Jerusalem in 1951 one of the lists included a refugee in an attempt to defend their interests and attract their votes. In Ramallah the contenders were very active amongst the refugees[79] who were reluctant to take sides openly. However this was soon to change. The clearly conflicting economic interests of the locals and refugees, and the latent strains in the existing social structures led to the formation of a variety of alliances within the two communities.

As for the local community, the conflict was not over specific gains or losses but centred around their overall hegemony. Their relatively small number of qualified electors were forced to stick together more than ever before[80] so as not to lose their say. The interests at stake were considerable, hence the importance attributed to TC elections there. The Christian refugees were recruited to join a coalition against their brother Muslim refugees. The latter composed over 50 per cent of the town's population but were a mere 25 per cent of the electorate. During the 1950s the Christian refugees enabled the local Christian alliance to retain its control over the Council without the former receiving proportional representation in the TC (Christians comprised 27 per cent of the total population and 33 per cent of the voting population).[81] Those Christian refugees eventually elected were educated middle-class politicians who were linked to the leftist parties, which became deeply involved in the local elections there. This coalition of local and refugee Christians, relying on religious affiliation, superseded the alignment of refugees on the basis of place of origin or "status" and helped the Christian refugees' integration there. Their endeavour to assimilate into these communities was regarded as serving the interests of both sides and therefore ruled out an alliance with Muslim elements whose aim was to shift the balance of power in their favour. The Christian refugees in Ramallah were the first to whom local land was sold[82] and some of them had even married locals by the mid-1950s—much earlier than elsewhere. Such economic and social changes and such active participation in elections blurred the sense of alienation and strangeness felt by refugees in most places.[83]

The Muslim refugees in Ramallah gradually took over the trade in town, managing to displace the locals' economic influence. Deprived of real representation on the TC, they eventually[84] came to control the Chamber of Commerce. This turned out to be an important factor in the Muslim refugees' integration and later fomented conflict with the municipality. As was indicated previously, the process of emigration from Ramallah only accelerated this refugee takeover. Before and during elections there, the animosity and antagonism between refugee and non-refugee intensified. The original inhabitants, envious of Christian Bethlehem where the question never arose, considered the refugees as intruders trying to impose themselves. The consciousness of "we" and "they" crystallized again and refugees were "reminded" that they did not belong there. The second[85] and third councils each included a nominated Muslim refugee. The first refugee to be elected was the Christian Alfred Kishk in 1960. The gradual takeover by the refugees of Ramallah's affairs, partly government-assisted, continued in the 1960s and was complete by the 1970s.

Al-Bira had a considerably higher proportion of refugees of mainly village origin and all the refugees were Muslim. In 1951 a refugee tried to get elected though he did not raise the refugee issue.[86] Unlike other towns, the differences between the two communities were not sharp and the TC was not, on the whole, that important there. The refugees gradually occupied prominent positions in the town's economic development and whereas no refugee had participated in the 1955 elections, they easily took half of the Council seats in 1962. Most of them were affiliated to the Tahrir party.[87] The Government feared these developments and nominated two more members to the Council to ensure that the Mayor's successor would be as loyal as the former had been.

In Nablus, in 1960, ten years after their first appeal, the refugees presented a demand that they should have a seat on the TC, especially since the camps were inside the municipal boundaries.[88] They protested against the municipalities' harsh treatment of them[89] and emphasized that no refugee worked in any of the TC departments although many paid taxes. However, such protests were futile. There, perhaps more than in other places, the question of the Council's composition, like that of the area's parliamentary representation, was always considered a local matter with the refugees having no real say in it.

In Bethlehem the situation was different as the local community managed quite easily to defend its position in all elections. This forced the Government to use its power to nominate a Muslim refugee to the Council from 1963, together with one Muslim from the Ta'amirah. These two joined the traditionally elected local Muslim. As strife between the old Bethlehemites and the "strangers" was not a serious problem in the 1950s, the local community did not have to organize against the latter although it suffered itself from internal divisions. The local politicians tended to stick to local affairs, keeping a low profile, not wishing to antagonize the predominantly Muslim neighbourhood or the regime. In Jericho the TC was eventually to be headed by a refugee.

In all other places the question of refugee representation never really arose: the refugees were either a marginal poor element, or were content with the situation as it was, or else were powerless to change it even if they so desired.

Chapter VII

The Political Parties and the Refugees

The nature of political life in Jordan changed dramatically following annexation. The new era brought about new groupings across the River and the beginning of a crystallization of "parties" in the form of "a man and his hangers-on", to use P. J. Vatikiotis's definition. Yet they were quite effective. The regime was forced either to stunt their growth and limit their "institutionalization" and potential impact, or to ban them outright when they became intolerable to the monarch, who regarded their action as "illegal" and "destructive". Nevertheless, the whole range of party political activities, whether overt or clandestine, between or during elections, rapidly gathered momentum until the clampdown of 1957. All parties were of course intent on gaining influence and power through either a "democratic" or subversive foothold in Jordan's hierarchic, autocratic political structure.

A. THE PARTIES: PATTERNS OF SIMILARITY

While most activity was in the West Bank, it should be noted that all parties were composed of both Palestinians and Trans-Jordanians although the former were more prominent and had a higher rate of party membership. So there was no trace of separatism in their make-up. Each party strove to maintain its own membership and following, to reinforce solidarity and increase their supporters' readiness for mobilization, and to break down the barriers of suspicion and rejection among the populace. They sought to rally support by discrediting the regime and the other parties, and through identifying themselves with the popular forces existing outside Jordan. Thus all quarrels over particular policies immediately raised the fundamental issue of the whole system's survival. And in fact people did increasingly identify the parties in terms of their representing powers outside Jordan rather than on their own merits. So any support for the parties was less a sign of acceptance of their ideologies than of support for the forces outside

Jordan, of a yearning for Arab unity and a desire to change the Government's policy towards achieving the goal—the recovery of Palestine.

Since opposition parties were either banned or at least restricted in their scope for open activity, they opted for a system of local organization based on small cells. Thus their ability to spread their ideas and programmes was hindered but not prevented. In fact their underground operations added a touch of mystique to their image.

Not all parties were interested in large membership. They all distinguished between trying to rally rank and file support and recruiting members as such, the two being quite different operations. Of course they did try to enlarge their membership; but among refugees, for whom they had little regard or trust, membership remained low. In order to arouse the mob, the J.C.P. did no more than establish one cell in a given place. Similarly, all political parties tried at times to take advantage of refugee demonstrations and gatherings which, as will be shown later, in most cases started for non-political reasons. They tried to make them appear their own achievement and an expression of support for their ideas.

Although they differed in their ideological beliefs and affiliations, the parties' published manifestos were surprisingly similar, certainly on the refugee issue. But even those who cultivated refugee support had no particular intention of exacerbating the differences between refugees and non-refugees. As of 1954, at least the Ba'th aimed at blurring this dividing line [1] (though without openly declaring so) through their idea of Arab unity. So by the mid-1950s, few substantial policy differences marked the published statements on national questions troubling the people in Jordan. All parties right across the political spectrum shifted their main focus to the more general problems of the Arab world. As Amnon Cohen put it:

> The different shades of opinion which had at first been distinguishable now began to disappear, giving way to a more or less uniform negativism. [2]

All called for the expulsion of the British forces, condemned Western imperialism and advocated Arab unity, with democratization to be followed by social reforms. The burning issues were naturally those relating to the Baghdad Pact and other "imperialist" intentions, aimed at strengthening the West's position in the Middle East by fortifying "reactionary" regimes. For the refugees, the shift of emphasis from narrow local issues to an all-Arab context went hand-in-hand with their own concerns and problems of identity. All such developments, it was claimed, had a direct bearing on the Refugee Problem and the Palestinian Question.

However, Palestinian refugees could not escape at least some confusion over their problematic identity since they fell within five concentric categories. [3] They were part of the Islamic World community, and part of the Arab World—better known as the Great Homeland which was the sphere of pan-Arabism. [4] They were citizens of the "small Homeland", Jordan. They were Palestinians with a common identity, regardless of all the inner complexities and geopolitical divisions[5] in this category. And they were refugees, with a weak, divided leadership which never sought to be specifically Palestinian.

In a highly controlled situation in which they were without means of legitimate political organization and protest, Palestinians willingly placed their faith in the power of pan-Arabism[6] and all forms of Arab Unity as preached by all political parties.

B. THE POLITICAL PARTIES' STANCE REGARDING THE REFUGEES AS INDICATED BY THEIR PUBLICATIONS

The clandestine operation of the parties meant that activity was concentrated on writing articles and distributing hand-outs with their message. These were directed mainly at the young intelligentsia. This section tries to examine the way the parties treated the Refugee Question in their publications and their attempts to appeal to the refugees through this medium, by approaching them directly or by raising their problems—which are of course separate but interrelated approaches. In other words, did the parties have a particular "refugee policy" and did they differ from one another, as regards their assiduousness in raising this subject and communicating their position?

It might be expected that any party which aimed at attracting the refugees beyond merely seeking their votes would attend to their problems and misery in its publications. It would impress on them that these subjects were close to the party's heart and try to appear as though it spoke on their behalf. Yet this was only partially the case. Up to 1953/4, only the Ba'thists and Communists paid attention to the refugee issue, although, compared to other topics, it still received relatively little space. After this, Arab unity tended to eclipse the refugee issue which now merely received occasional mention when a particular event gave the issue new impetus: for example, when there were visits by UN representatives or foreign missions, or when it was suggested that refugees' tents be replaced by more permanent shelters— a motif which was constantly cropping up during 1955-7. Nevertheless, because manifestos and publications contained every subject that concerned the people in Jordan, the refugee issue was never completely neglected.

Some party leaders explained that the lack of attention given to the refugee issue up to 1954 was because the refugees were largely illiterate and could not read the publications, and because they were too involved in their daily relief problems to pay attention to wider political issues. Certainly the circulation of the daily papers in the camps was low. And it seems that few party publications reached the camps during these years, while those that did, tended to be critical of the regime rather than appealing specifically to the camp refugees. However, the refugees were not as isolated at this might suggest. They would hear about the content of publications on their daily visits to the neighbouring towns' coffee houses, while, in the camps, the teachers often read aloud any paper or leaflet distributed. And, of course, everyone listened to the radio in the coffee houses.

By 1954 the parties were aware of a changed situation. The camp refugees were becoming more conscious of the wider issue of Arab unity. The parties discovered that relating to refugees' problems in the way they had done previously, whether motivated ideologically or as a strategy for gaining support, had little bearing on the refugees' response.

By this time, also the teachers had risen to prominence in the political life of the camps. Thus a situation developed whereby the refugees started supporting the political parties at a time when they were hardly mentioned in the parties' propaganda. This pattern of occasional and sporadic reference to the refugee problem continued until June 1959, when the UN Secretary's report on the refugees, following his visit to Jordan in January of that year, triggered off the debate anew.[7] This is not to suggest, however, that even within their limited treatment of refugee problems, the overall uniformity of attitude among the parties reflected either the sharing of specific policies or the absence of any policy at all. Examining the publications does shed some light on the way the parties approached the subject, which in each case, tended to be directed towards the more educated amongst the refugees. Their approach was inconsistent, sometimes taking for granted that refugee questions were included by implication in any discussion of Western imperialism, or sometimes detailing their policies and criticisms. Neither the refugees nor the parties saw any contradiction in this. Furthermore, the inconsistency reflects the mixture of reasons for relating to the refugees and of ways of doing so. Most of the parties used the subject as a weapon in their attack on the West and the Jordanian regime. But they also, at times, showed a genuine compassion. Occasionally the parties attempted to become the refugees' spokesmen, or to persuade them to accept their programme and possibly join their party. On the other hand, the failure to deal specifically with the refugees could show either sheer neglect, or lack of mutual trust, or be taken as a measure of how much they disregarded and looked down upon the refugees. The motives and intentions were various.

All the parties had similar stands on the Refugee Question. They all tried to establish the point that acceding to UNRWA's integration schemes and the resettlement principle was tantamount to giving up their rights in Palestine—whether of return or compensation—and should therefore be regarded as high treason by the Arab nations in general and by the Palestinians in particular. This is true for the whole period under study.

The refugees generally accepted this stand in principle, which made the authorities and UNRWA uneasy. But the rhetoric of the parties was no solution to their grinding, humiliating situation. The odd hand-out could not change the reality of years. Nevertheless, the refugees knew that the parties were the only people to keep their dream of Return politically alive, even if they did use them for their own ends as well. They were painfully torn between their hope—a return to their old homes—and reality—the concrete offer of slow integration and a bearable life. So, even while they joined in the condemnations of the Agency projects, many of them felt forced, or were even glad, to take what was offered by these schemes.

Witnessing this quiet, gradual process of integration, the parties soon became disillusioned with the refugees' response to their intransigent stand that the refugees stay in their tents. Taji al-Faruqi summed up the typical party position thus:

> We never wanted projects *outside* the camp but only *in* them. We opposed all resettlement and rehabilitation schemes as we knew once a refugee takes what you offer individually and establishes himself he will forget his country. If he leaves the camp he is no more a refugee. And then the camp was a unit and it was easy for us to spread propaganda there and affect people in miserable conditions. That is how we could cause UNRWA and the USA trouble.[8]

It seems the refugees did not go far beyond vocal rejection of any attempt to deny them the "Free Choice" of returning or remaining.

As for the Government and UNRWA, they were doing their utmost to integrate the refugees economically. In so far as the parties could get the refugees to equate approval of the rehabilitation and re-settlement schemes with betrayal of the pan-Arab cause, this attitude represented an obstacle and a threat to these plans for integration. Hence the Government's uneasiness about the content of all the parties' publications.

Within the pattern already outlined, the occurrence of references to the refugees and their problems in the publications can be roughly divided into two categories: the first dealing with a particular refugee problem in a certain place; the second dealing with a larger, more general refugee issue or situation. Beyond these were all the issues which the refugees seem to have understood as involving them. For example, between 1948 and 1950 the Communist publications dealt with issues[9] such as the question of the responsibility for the Palestine disaster; the role of the so-called reactionary monarch and his British imperialistic allies; the setting up of a Palestinian democratic state in accordance with the Partition Plan to enable the refugees to return; and the notion of the Palestinian People. Later on in the mid-fifties there was the kaleidoscope of issues and opinions based on the idea of Arab unity.

In the period up to 1954 when the Ba'th and J.C.P. often mentioned the refugees, there was a fairly wide range of particular localized issues. However, the Communist publications[10] were found to dedicate just under 10 per cent of their space to refugee affairs. These included items on corruption among ICRC workers,[11] the inability of the refugees to organize themselves,[12] condemnation of the UN Palestine Conciliation Commission plans, opposition to the nomination of a Minister for Refugee Affairs[13] and calls for the refugees to close ranks and oppose the King, "the traitor" Glubb and all others held responsible for their tragedy.[14] The Ba'thists also published and wrote articles on particular issues up to 1954. In 1949 they strongly protested against the rumoured mass cancellation of ration cards and the end of the Red Cross relief operation, relating these to fears that the UN would abandon their commitment to working for the Return. They urged the Arab Governments to allocate the appropriate resources to enable the refugees to live with dignity, strengthen themselves and ensure that the Arab States would have at their disposal the one thing that could enable the refugees' Return—military power.[15] Simultaneously, they demanded that the refugees be supplied with employment carrying a higher salary,[16] and education for their children in proper schools.[17] They opposed the idea of compensating the refugees if this waived their rights to their lost homes, saying that the refugees *preferred* to live in camps for years before relinquishing their rights. They demanded that the Arab Governments should champion those rights and attacked refugees who sought to be compensated, since by doing so, the Ba‘th claimed, they renounced their rights.[18] They attacked the Jordanian Government for failing to be firm with the Agency on the census operation. They said it was inconceivable in Syria and Egypt that UNRWA should enjoy such freedom of action as it had in the H.K.J., where most of its plans received the Government's blessing.[19] Such attacks became more intense just before and after John Foster Dulles' visit to Jordan.

The occasional debate on extending UNRWA's mandate and its terms of reference provided an opportunity for the A.H.C. to appear as the refugees' spokesman. It presented petitions and appeals demanding the prolongation of the Agency's mandate. It also sharply criticized the work of both the UN and the Arab Governments, and viciously attacked them for intending to abolish the Refugee Problem and thereby the Palestinian Question.[20]

The particular issue which cropped up more often than any others of course, was resettlement or rehabilitation. It was universally condemned by all the parties and the A.H.C. Actual schemes like the Yarmuk and Johnston Projects, the tent-replacement programmes, and the whole concept of resettlement were all the targets of many articles, leaflets and manifestos. They attacked it as part of Western imperialism's plan to get rid of the refugee question, seeing UNRWA as the agent of Imperialism. They criticized any Arab country (usually implying the Jordanian Government) that co-operated in or accepted the schemes, calling this treachery and defeatism. And they attacked any elements among the refugees who supported the programmes, as did some rich refugees, when it became clear that many poor refugees intended taking advantage of the various schemes. They urged non-cooperation with UNRWA and praised those refugees who refused to join in. Their approach was essentially that of claiming that resettlement was not a humane or economic issue but a political one; and they always linked it to the preservation of the refugee's right to Return and to the need to continue the struggle against Israel.[21] The only occasion on which this stance was not maintained was in 1949 when the Ba‘thists supported Musa Alami's Constructive Scheme for erecting "model" refugee villages on the Jericho Valley, possibly owing to the party's close connection with Alami.

However, by the mid-1950s the shift in emphasis as reflected in all parties' publications was clear. The little mention the various schemes received compared with the more acute political problems, indicated perhaps just how far the refugee aspect of major Arab unity issues was taken for granted. The N.S.P., whose short-lived newspapers published in 1956 and 1957 rarely dealt with refugee affairs, played an important role alongside all other political parties at the greatest display of opposition prior to the coup—the National Congress held in Nablus on 22 April 1957. But the manifesto published after the widely supported convention did not even mention their opposition to the resettlement schemes, although most of the manifesto dealt with the imperialists' attempts to tie Jordan to the Western inspired treaties.

The larger general issues and problems relating to the refugees in the publications concern their actual plight and conditions, as well as the Return. Discussion of these questions was also rare, with a mild resurgence of published material at the end of 1950s with the U.N. Secretary General's report and the surfacing of the idea of the Palestinian Entity.

Earlier, stirring articles like "J'accuse" by the Ba'thist Abdallah Rimawi[22] which was a vicious attack on the Arab regimes, certainly reflected the feelings of thousands, and caused much uneasiness to the regime which could not remain idle in the face of such indictments.[23] He attacked the Arab rulers for despising the refugees and for signing a series of agreements which gave up their rights one by one, whilst consolidating their personal interests at the expense of the Palestinians. He ended by strongly criticizing the Palestinian youth for doing nothing in response, proving themselves unworthy of the mission delegated to them by the history of the Arab Nation; their passivity would only bring further disasters.

In addition to such general appeals the Ba'th dedicated some articles to the refugees' miserable conditions, stress and confusion.[24] They asked the indigenous population to assist the refugees, "the victims of politics and natural calamities", more than the shamefully inadequate way in which they did.[25] Some J.C.P. publications also drew attention to the difficult conditions the refugees were living under in contrast to the high salaries paid by UNRWA to its international workers.[26]

Though active in charity work, the Muslim Brotherhood did not deal with the refugee plight in publications or Friday sermons. Just one *khutbah* in 1955 out of the hundreds delivered referred to the refugees waiting seven years, depending on the monthly ration and always seeing the wire fences preventing them from returning to their lost homeland.[27]

The issue of the Return was raised in different contexts in all publications. Up to 1954, the Ba'thists viewed the refugee "Return" as a way, or rather a strategy, for dismantling Israel from within,[28] preventing her from absorbing new Jewish immigrants and leaving a Trojan Horse in her midst.[29] Na'was argued that the West wanted to solve the refugee issue by the burial of the Palestinian Question at its present stage. "Absorbing the refugee meant creating the vacuum necessary for Israel to fill it with new immigrants that would strengthen the Jewish State and prevent the refugee's return."[30] Until the day of return, he demanded, the UN should set up a custodian over the refugee property left behind and arrange for its annual income to be transferred to its owners.[31] This was widely supported amongst the refugees. The Ba'th also attacked the Arab leaders for the way they conducted their Palestine Policy and for their empty declarations and unfulfilled promises to do their utmost for the refugees' Return.[32]

In 1951 the J.C.P. criticized the UN for preventing the Return, and, in a hand out of 1952, Glubb was accused of preventing the solution of the Refugee Problem. What the Communists conceived of as a "solution" changed over the years. Even as late as 1952 they called on the refugees to set up a "refugee congress" to preserve their rights and fight for the only solution—partition.[32a]

An L.P. manifesto published in 1955 related the Return to the aims of Israel and Western Imperialism, calling for a *jihad* against them and saying that Israel's existence would only become safe once the refugees gave up their right to Return. Two similar leaflets were distributed in 1957 both attacking the Arab Governments which acceded to the West's aims. These were in essence, they argued, apolitical and economic.[33] In 1958, in a leaflet dedicated to 15 May, the date of Israel's foundation, the Q.A.M. said:

> You the refugee in the camps, remember the Day of Disaster. Sense in your souls, the Day of Return is near. Remember your beautiful homes and your lands into which you poured all your strength. Its fruit belong to you and not to your sons. This land is not yours today but at the scattered Jews' disposal. Oh, the sons of Palestine, our homes were made into Jewish homes, from your lands they build a homeland and you are at the edge of the camps. Today one must individuate and think on the return to the homeland . . . you are the force to beat the ones who coverted and expel the thieves. You are the command, you are the soldiers, you are the force . . . the unity.[34]

By 1959 they became more aggressive in their declarations on the Refugee Question and like most parties reacted viciously to the UN Secretary General's report. Both the Q.S.P. and Q.A.M. publications up to this point had related very little to the refugees or their problems, but during this time they became fairly vocal. The Q.A.M.'s manifesto *Revenge is the only solution to our problem in Palestine,* published just before the visit, expressed their firm opposition to Israel's very existence:

> We assure Hammerskjöld that our problem in Palestine is not a problem of refugees living in tents and not a question of financial compensation and not a problem of changes in the Armistice Line but it is a problem of a

stolen Homeland, whose people are determined to recover it . . . we confirm that any attempt at peace would be destined to fail . . . and the very existence of the Jewish entity in our Homeland is a stab of betrayal for any peace . . . no peace and no Partition and no compromise and no negotiations and no half solutions, only one solution would bring about peace and that is the removal of the Jews from our Homeland.[35]

C. RECRUITMENT BY THE PARTIES AND THE REFUGEES' RESPONSE

Two basic questions are being asked here. First, how much did the parties try to recruit from amongst the refugees? Secondly, what was the pattern of the refugees' response, and was it different from that of the local population in each area?

Though numbers and statistics are not all-important and are even at times misleading, perhaps the only source[36] that can give some indication of the level and kind of participation by refugees in the various political parties are the Jordanian Secret Police's records. The Jordanian Government's so-called "black lists" were put into three categories A B and C according to the activity of the suspects and their reported position in each party. They were far from accurate, especially in categories of lesser importance B and C which, for example, occasionally mixed the Ba'th supporters with those of the Q.A.M. There are also numerical exaggerations, while someone taking part in a demonstration might be found in Category C or even B, according to which party the informer felt had organized it. Yet such participation should not be taken seriously as indicating political affiliation. Names of people were repeated even if they had not been involved for quite some time. Some informers were over-keen to supply information which often proved unsubstantiated. Owing to such potential inaccuracies, of which A.C.'s and Amman H.Q. were aware, instructions were issued occasionally to update all lists and re-register all suspects, with their new and old addresses, places of origin and occupations.[37]

But, having said this, one can learn a great deal from these records, on the one hand about the activity of each party, its recruitment and composition, and on the other, about the Government's efficiency.

It is difficult to define from the records any precise trend in the refugees' political affiliations. But it is evident that only a handful of camp refugees were members or loyal supporters of the parties, let alone part of their leadership. It is not suggested that when one party had more members than another in a certain place it was necessarily more successful in attracting refugees to its ranks, or that its activity there was more intense and efficient. The statistics provided below on each party, for all their inaccuracies, nevertheless demonstrate the generally low membership and refute the widely prevailing Western view that the camps as such were hotbeds of political hostility and Communism—a view also propagated by Glubb and other British officers in the Legion, even though they knew better.

The low rate of refugee participation reflects both the parties' attitudes toward them and their passive response, excluding of course the educated few who, as always, were split. Thus many reports are dedicated solely to UNRWA's staff, especially to the teachers' political affiliations and activity. An ordinary refugee was rarely on the lists although his son, probably a recruit via his teachers, might be found there. Furthermore, it is difficult to establish from the Jordanian files any deviation among the refugees from the local patterns of party affiliation.

1. The Jordanian Communist Party

The N.L.L's interest in international problems such as Korea, its firm support of the 1947 Partition Plan, and the fact that U.S.S.R. voted with the U.S.A. in recognition of the State of Israel, counted against it. Aware of its weakness, the J.C.P. tried to "water down" this "stain" taking advantage of the growing popularity of the U.S.S.R. following the Czech-Egyptian arms deal. However, the Jordanian Lists on the J.C.P. (the most elusive of the parties) clearly show that throughout the 1950s its membership[38] was relatively low, especially amongst the camp refugees, as was the number of its supporters there. The first West Bank list of suspects produced in 1950 shows that out of 226 reported names only 24 were refugees, most of them living in Nablus town.[39] Like many other lists it was incomplete but detailed the most important activists. Yet the J.C.P. managed shortly after this to set up small cells in many camps. More intensive was their activity amongst the refugees in 1953-4. A report from Tulkarm suggested that the Communists became very strong in the camp area amongst the teachers and pupils.[40] Government agents reported that the strikes in Balata, Far'a and Arrub Camps were motivated by the J.C.P. activists who were UNRWA Camp Leaders in the first two[41] and the teachers in the latter.[42] Moreover, the reports show they were still active in the places they were subsequently transferred to in response to their activities, and the authorities considered removing them to isolated teaching posts in the East Bank.[43] Accordingly one year later reports indicated that the Communist groups in the Hebron area were disintegrating. Similarly the authorities managed, though only temporarily, to weaken the strong cells functioning in Far'a and Aqbat Jabr by arresting a number of suspects and rounding up a pedlar who ran a shop in the camp (its merchandise and revenue belonged to the J.C.P.) which was used to pass on messages and instructions.[44]

However, much of their action was in the open. In 1954 the Communists tried to appear as refugee spokesmen when meeting the editors of a number of dailies to persuade them to publish a petition against UNRWA's loan scheme. This gained them little popularity with poor refugees who, without openly admitting it, would have liked to enrol in this project. It seems the youths generally did not share this attitude. A report of 1954 said that, owing to unemployment in the Jericho area, more people were responding to their propaganda, instigated by certain teachers. This tendency grew stronger with the growing popularity of the U.S.S.R. amongst the refugees. Even then their membership remained very small. It should be remembered however, that the J.C.P. was reluctant to admit villagers, whether refugees or non-refugees, as proper members. Generally they did not trust people unless they were educated and they were well aware of how successful Jordanian intelligence work was amongst the rural population. This is not to say that they did not try to recruit their support and sympathy as both were necessary for any effective popular demonstration of subversive action. Hence the authorities watched the Communists closely on the few occasions when they tried to incite the camp refugees to demonstrate against the Agency. The J.C.P. took advantage of the refugees' miserable conditions to create tension with the West and its ally, the Jordanian Government.[45] Naturally the J.C.P. did not share the regime's view that such action was "against the public interest" and tried to exploit any suitable situation. In 1956/7 they were attentive to the refugees' grievances and made promises to help them with their demands. Some Communist doctors gave free medical treatment in order to attract the miserable people to support the J.C.P. The records of 1956 provide details on a number of teachers and teenagers involved in Communist activity in Aqbat Jabr Camp.

One list, which named 113 recruits from different political parties, suggested that only 5 were refugees of whom 4 were from Jaffa.[46] A report which gives the names of 8 refugees out of 74 suspected Communists in the Ramallah area shows that the leading figures were: a tailor, a prominent lawyer, two unemployed, one journalist, one grocer and two pupils.[47] Another report listed similar categories though with more teachers, pupils and unemployed.[48] The largest list produced was in August 1957 when the authorities issued orders for detaining or watching some 389 people of whom 54 were refugees.[49] By then many were already arrested or detained, or had fled the country. Very few of the people named were camp refugees and most of those listed as living in camps were students or teachers. In a 1958 list of 99 names there was not one refugee;[50] and out of 60 suspects in a list in 1959 only 9 were refugees, indicating the same pattern. Most of them were Communists though there were two Ba'thists and one Tahriri.[51]

2. The Ba'th Arab Socialist Party

The Ba'th failed in all its attempts to be regarded as a fully legalized party. It tried to appear as a "watchman" doing its utmost to "tell the people the truth about what was taking place in Jordan", seeking the trust of the masses. Despite all its popularity, however, the Ba'th remained very much the party of its educated middle-class leadership[52] and did not have many grass-roots supporters amongst the refugees, certainly not in the camps.[53] Reports clearly indicate that the J.C.P. was far more popular amongst the teachers although Ba'th ideology attracted many students, especially those who returned from Syria. (These were always followed by the authorities). Organizing secret meetings in houses with lectures in the manner of the J.C.P., had its appeal for the youngsters. In Qalqilya for example, where most political activists sided with the local Liberation Party,[54] the Ba'th won over most of the teachers though only a few were refugees.[55] But in Nablus among the reported 37 names in Categories A, B and C in January 1955 there was not one refugee. A list a few months later showed they had some followers in the secondary schools and colleges in the area. A list from 1957 of 80 names contained one refugee from Far'a Camp.[56] In 1956 the Ba'th strengthened its influence in the camps especially in the Ramallah area. In 1957 in Ramallah and al-Bira town there were 11 refugees out of 54 suspects all living and working outside the camps, with only 2 of them UNRWA workers.[57] A list from the Jenin area in 1958 reported 25 suspects with 2 refugees.[58] The 1959 records pointed out that in Ramallah, the Ba'th stronghold, 18 out of the reported 76 suspects were refugees[59] compared with a list of 169 names in the Nablus area where 13 were refugees, mostly UNRWA teachers. In Bethlehem the party had some support among the teachers (including the Headmaster of Dahaysha Camp School) and the secondary school pupils in town. In Jericho they had a limited impact in Ayn al-Sultan and Aqbat Jabr Camps though this virtually ceased after the teachers were transferred or arrested.[60] The pattern was similar in Dayr Ammar Camp.

Because the party had several members in UNRWA's Education Department it had the upper hand over other parties. It easily transferred opponent teachers, sometimes managed to prevent the removal of its own[61] and even secured appointments in places where the party's interests needed preserving or its activity widening. But their vociferous campaign against the replacement of tents[62] with proper shelters did not attract many camp refugees.[63] The refugees were disgruntled that those who preached against the erection of huts themselves lived quite lavishly. In 1957-9 lists clearly show the ebbing of their support amongst the refugee population, as by then most of those who led the party were either jailed, in exile or had simply stopped their political activity.

3. The National Socialist Party

Up to 1957 the examined lists indicate that their membership included very few refugees.[64] A 1957 list of the Ramallah area activists listed 21 names of whom only one was a refugee. In Nablus the proportion was similar[65] as opposed to the Bethlehem,[66] Jericho[67] and Jerusalem areas where the lists showed 6 refugees out of 13 suspects. But one should bear in mind that it was a different type of "party" from the rest and that it dedicated less time and resources to recruitment of members than to rallying popular support.

4. The Arab Nationalist Movement

This movement was a "late-comer" to the political scene in Jordan. Most of its members were doctors, lawyers and other members of the intelligentsia who met as graduates of the A.U.B. at its annual meeting in Jerusalem in 1956. They declared their opposition to Communism as well as to Imperialism and regarded Arab unity as the only way the Arab Nation could achieve its goals. Their main stronghold was in Nablus. Some of their activity coincided and was even co-ordinated with that of the Ba'thists. Most of their reported activity took place after 1958, when they began calling for firmer action for the Return of Palestine. They appeared in the 1950s as a "centrist" group, but from 1960 onwards became a "leftist" body with a "socialist" platform.[68]

Generally the Jordanian files demonstrate that the authorities were unable to trace or track down even the few activists within this movement. However the 1958-9 report indicate that they had only a few refugee supporters:[69] 4 in Bethlehem and 4 in Karamah[70] and a few more individuals scattered in other places.

5. The Syrian Nationalist Party

The Q.S.P. advocated a Greater Syria to include Palestine. It was supported by many Palestinians living in Lebanon and Syria and also for a while in 1961/2 by King Husayn as an instrument to be used against the supporters of his enemy Abd al-Nasser, and against the Palestinian Entity followers. He sent the party money, and co-operated with Antun Sa'adah's people in Lebanon.[71] In Jordan its leaders were carefully followed but rarely harassed, as they were very weak during the 1950s, despite the arrival of certain members who had escaped from Damascus. Syria accused the monarch of employing the services of the Q.S.P. for subversive purposes there. The Q.S.P. had some support in Jenin, but its centres were in Beirut and Damascus. On the whole it was not very active in Jordan and certainly not amongst the refugees.

Up to 1958 very few of their members appeared on the black lists, and one list in that year which gave 112 names included only one refugee.[72] Their membership grew somewhat in 1961 and 1963 mainly in the Jenin and Nablus area, as the lists for those years show.

6. Muslim Brotherhood[73]

The Jordanian lists show that as far as active membership was concerned, the refugees did not play an important part in the leading group, nor did they constitute a large proportion of the Associations' supporters. Nonetheless, in Nablus for example, there were more refugees associated with the M.B. than with any other party. Three lists for 1954 and 1956/7 indicate that they composed 25 per cent of the 80-odd names listed, mostly town-dwellers in origin now living in Nablus town, and all of them labourers. A list of 1961 shows they were also fairly strong in Askar Camp and included a number of UNRWA workers. In Ramallah only two refugees of 28 reported names were in the 1959 lists compared with one refugee out of six Tahririn there.

As to the impact of the religious parties it can be confidently said that they had great influence among the more traditional elements of society. Their ideas appealed to, and were widely supported by, many of the uneducated, fatalistic, religious refugees, excluding in the main the younger generation. Many refugees remembered the Brotherhood's active role in the 1948 war, and were more inclined to support the M.B's orthodox religious ideas, especially regarding.charity which they needed badly. With the expansion of the M.B's activities, such as their donations and charity work, their frequent camp visits and firm position on problems relating to the refugee plight, they set up a number of branches in Aqbat Jabr, Karamah, Irbid, Arrub and Askar Camps. In Askar the request for a club licence was presented by younger elements in the camp[74] who were attracted by the M.B's free uniform, the sports activity and modest but organized "military" training.

However, most of their work continued to centre around charity. An important achievement was the establishment of a school in Aqbat Jabr Camp for the Sons of the Martyrdom.[75] In fact the M.B. was the only political body that actually did something practical for the refugees and the frontier villagers, maintaining a special committee for assisting them. This greatly enhanced its popularity. Even attempts to label the M.B. as "British agents" and to suggest they received money from Great Britain did not seriously undermine their support.[76] Yet some refugees were disturbed that the M.B. was helping to build and repair the old walls on the Jerusalem border. They were apprehensive that these defence lines would eventually become permanent border lines, indirectly recognizing the State of Israel.[77]

Many of the National Guard were members of the M.B., and the Brotherhood distributed blankets, uniforms and money to the families of those who were killed on guard duty. This was greatly appreciated especially since at times it was more than the Government ever gave them. Their early calls for arming the Palestinians and for preparing for the "Second Round" received growing attention in the West Bank especially in the aftermath of each of the Israeli attacks. At times they became more militant and organized a few turbulent demonstrations in Aqbat Jabr vociferously attacking Western imperialism. As early as November 1953, they called for the dismissal of Glubb.

They were also extremely active against all Leftist groups, especially the Ba'th. In their numerous public addresses made during every feast, festival or fast, they exhorted their listeners within and outside the mosques to fulfil their duties as Muslims, attacking the Communists and Ba'thists and especially these parties' supporters amongst the teachers. They also criticized the Government for neglecting its duty towards the Palestinians.

The process of migration and emigration assisted the M.B. leaders as they appealed more than the radical parties to the old who remained behind. This was less apparent in the camps situated in the towns, where this movement was not so marked and the camp dwellers were more aware of the local leaders' opinions and where they kept up with the political trends in the towns' coffee houses.

7. The Islamic Liberation Party

Whilst the M.B. refused to become a political party in the full sense, the Liberation Party, whose principles were quite similar, was far more politically orientated. The Tahririyyin, also known as the Nabhaniyyin after their leader Taqi al-Din al-Nabhani, declared themselves as a party in 1952 but failed to receive the regime's legal recognition. The party's pan-Islamic orientation called for the establishment of a State to be run solely according to the *Qur'an*. They believed that Islam as a concept as well as a system should determine the political fate of the Muslim world.[78] Furthermore the L.P. was an anti-Western body, and, unlike its sister the M.B., directed much of its criticism against the regime. It also later opposed the idea of a separate Palestinian Entity.

Up to 1958 the L.P. did not pay much attention to the refugees' plight although one of their founders, Daud Hamdan, was himself a refugee from Lydda. Undoubtedly this was an area in which they could have recruited quite easily owing to the conservatism of many refugees. This is not to say they did not try, and occasionally succeed, in setting up cells amongst this sector. After these were formed they enlisted support through teachers they had recruited in the Jericho Camps,[79] Qalandya, Nur Shams and elsewhere.[80] They even had some support in the army and the NG although after the Government's repressive measures in 1957 they were considerably weakened. In Qalqilya, for example, a few youths initially joined the party under the direct influence of one of the prominent leaders of the L.P. Ahmad Da'ur but later lost interest. Some turned to leftist groups out of dissatisfaction with the L.P's "American" stigma and religious approach to life. Others refrained entirely from any activity since they wanted to complete their studies and feared punishment or interference in their careers. In the northern West Bank, where the authorities found growing support for the L.P. by 1954, the number of refugee members was relatively low.[81] The 1957 lists of suspects fail to show any change in this proportion.[82] Still, reports of 1958/9 indicate that they were strong in Mu'askar and Nur Shams Camps where, it was suggested, the Camp Leader, a number of notables and the local *imam* were members. There is no indication that their membership amongst refugees grew with the upsurge of propaganda and activity in 1958 (which was motivated by the renewed international debate on the resettlement of refugees).

8. The Arab Higher Committee

It is evident from the Jordanian black lists of suspected anti-Hashimites that the Mufti had very little support among the Palestinians in Jordan and even less among the refugees either inside or outside the camps.[83]

It seems that the regime realized that the power of this movement had weakened considerably. In 1952 the Nablus A.C. rejected the lists compiled by Area Intelligence Officers who claimed that all in all, there were 200 A.H.C. supporters in Jordan and 50 outside it who came from Jordan.[84] He demanded that the lists be brought up to date.[85] Up to 1956 there are no details on the A.H.C. supporters in the files, apart from one incident of an infiltrator sent by the Mufti to organize terrorist activities.[86] A report of January 1956 noted signs of renewed activity amongst Mufti supporters[87] and that the A.H.C. intended to expand its operations amongst the refugees by sending money, men and materials through Ramtha.[88] Yet the black lists do not reflect this trend and out of 126 reported names (including some prominent people)[89] in the Nablus area, only one was a refugee.[90]

On the whole it seems that Hajj Amin was aware of his position in Jordan. His limited activities there demonstrate both his weakness and his soberly realistic attitude. He knew that any independent action against Jordan's monarch, especially if directed from outside the country, had precious little hope of success. Although watched by most Arab intelligence services and remaining dependent on money and good will from Egypt, Saudi Arabia or Syria, the Mufti sought in 1957 to strengthen his loose ties with the Egyptians who also had subversive intentions in Jordan. A report of that year clearly indicated Jordan's sensitivity in this development. Muhammad al-Suhaymat, the Intelligence Director, notified all A.C.s of the meetings held between the two sides at which methods for building up the A.H.C. element in Jordan were discussed. He ordered a close watch on the old Mufti supporters.[91] The lists clearly show that since the dangerous opposition elements were "leftist" there was no real reason to fear the A.H.C. groups.[92] Most of their supporters in Jerusalem, for instance, belonged to the Husayni family who had been passive for quite some time.[93] In 1958 the authorities prevented all A.H.C. supporters from leaving[94] or entering the kingdom.[95] New black lists were prepared, now singling out the refugees.[96] With the renewed inter-Arab debate on the "Palestinian Entity" gathering momentum in 1959, the Jordanian regime became very alert to any moves to obtain active Palestinian support in this campaign. The revived idea of a Palestinian Government was, of course, counter to Jordan's interests, especially when the propaganda promised that it would emerge under Egypt's wing.[97] The Mufti naturally tried to consolidate his position amongst the Palestinians. Reports indicated that A.H.C. agents were visiting refugee camps in Lebanon where the Mufti had moved again after Nasser tried to limit his activity,[98] and gave details of the smuggling of arms, money[99] and propaganda material into Jordan. Influential Palestinians involved in the

"Entity" movement[100] were known to the authorities, who became anxious about the U.A.R. radio transmissions. Camp inhabitants were warned not to show support for a Palestinian Government or Army, and speeches against these ideas were made.[101] The authorities kept track of the activities of UNRWA's Area Officer, Ishaq Duzdar, amongst the refugees: these included meetings with the Dahaysha and Fawar Camp Leaders, demands for the transfer of UNRWA clerks who supported the Mufti, and contacts with a senior woman UNRWA worker in Beirut through whom money and instructions were sent.[102]

A careful screening made in mid 1960 of 81 former Mufti followers who lived in the East Bank revealed that many had died, whilst others had emigrated or were no longer interested in him. With the development of the Entity idea, the authorities became troubled by the movements of Dr Daud Husayni[103] and his salaried team of 16 people from the Jericho area.[104] Yet some of those who supported the Entity were irritated that the A.H.C. members were merely trying to re-establish their own positions. A report of mid-1962 suggested that Ahmad Shuqayri, then in the service of the Saudi Government, was also regarded by refugees as an "American Agent", and the A.H.C. members were seen as reactionary traitors.[105] And as late as 1962 it seems that few refugees were directly involved in the Palestinian Entity movement,[106] although that was soon to change.

In short, there is no easily discernible pattern of support for the various parties among the camp refugees; each one was different. Even after the harsh measures of 1957 some activists remained in every camp. Each party had its old and young followers, and no camp was ever monolithic in its support. Jalazun was a stronghold of the Ba'th and Nur Shams of the Tahrir but in both camps the Muslim Brotherhood had some support according to the Jordanian records.

It should be noted that refugees who said in interview that they were associated with either the M.B. or the L.P. could not really explain the ideological differences between them and put their support down to personal grounds, apart from the obvious explanation of being orthodox Muslims. The same went for many refugees who were asked to explain their preference for one or other of the radical bodies.

Only after January 1959 did the authorities begin attaching more importance to political activity amongst the refugees and for the first time produced separate lists consisting solely of suspected refugees.[107] A list of refugee political activists from all parties, categorized according to camps and other refugee concentrations, proved beyond doubt that each camp had on average only between 5-15 political activists,[108] the bulk of them listed as being relatively passive.

Contrary to the widely accepted Western belief, therefore, the camps did not prove to be pockets of resistance, hostile to the regime in the 1950s, and certainly not in the early period when the refugees were starving. Apart from a few educated youngsters, most camp refugees feared and respected, even if they did not actively support, the Hashimite monarchy. Still some refugees believed that a Communist order established in the region would "send them back to their homes and land and would make them 'comrades', a status much preferred to their present state". Furthermore they voiced their growing support for the USSR to every foreign journalist and visitor. This was a reflection of their frustration and disappointment with the West, which they claimed was inspired by American Jewry. They hoped this kind of attitude would deter the Americans from supporting Israel[109] and induce them to exert pressure for the return of the refugees and the expansion of UNRWA's activities until such a day.

The various parties did not actively recruit amongst refugees. Manipulating the masses by exploiting their passions did not necessarily entail forming a movement within the populace. Apart from having little respect for the unsophisticated rank and file, the parties rightly appreciated that it was premature to preach ideologies which meant little to illiterate people. They realized that it was extremely difficult to operate safely in the easily controlled camps. Their foremost task therefore was to create a reliable clique and their main emphasis was on drawing support from the educated urban middle class. The camps, like the villages, were of secondary importance and only opportunist advantage was occasionally made of their general malaise.

Up to the mid-1950s, the frustrated refugees were not generally interested in vague promises. Their apathy to anything unrelated to their immediate problems was not easily overcome. They were reluctant to trust anyone. The opposition, which took credit for any public demonstrations, tried to become the channel through which support and criticism had to be expressed. The truth of the matter was that the masses did not share the parties' own perception of themselves. The various "stains" and stigmas attached to each party demonstrated the lack of respect they commanded amongst the refugees. Participation in demonstrations did not turn a person into a "Communist" or "Ba'thist". Nor was supporting the parties considered by refugees to be opposition to the regime's very existence. It was rather an expression of their longing for a change which would make the hoped-for and promised dream of Return come true.

D. UNDERGROUND POLITICAL ACTIVITY AND ITS CONFRONTATION

In the first few years following the war, the Government regarded Communist activity as a conspiracy against it, and not merely as representing the discontent of alienated elements in society. The monarch was troubled by the so-called "penetration" of Communism into the ranks of the idle and hungry refugees inciting them against the Government. But as was indicated, in spite of certain reports and Western Press stories, neither Communism nor other radical opposition groups made much headway with the mass of refugees in this period. The major reason for this was the effectiveness of the Government's various measures to control the operations of political activities. Through its use of informers, spies, information gatherers, bribery and pay-offs, the Jordanian regime was remarkably well-informed about most political activity and usually found it quite easy to control the refugee concentrations.

Before 1952 however, the regime did have some difficulty in actively combating opposition, especially the Communists, since its agents were inexperienced and untrained for this kind of work.[110] Yet these agents gradually developed skills which enabled them to monitor most underground political activity in its various forms and phases. Extensive security legislation was passed once the regime came to regard itself as being under attack both internally and internationally. Severe penalties became a political weapon. In response to public disorder the Government would proclaim a state of emergency, followed by tough measures. The penalties and measures ranged from execution, extended imprisonment,[111] indefinite detention without trial (for suspects accused of withholding information) with release only on high bail for a limited period, through to searches without warrants. These were all employed to prevent the continuation of underground activity and to deter any involvement in undesired political action. A system was also developed for controlling activity among the younger generation. The measures here included: threats to pupils and their families; expulsion from school—which could prove very costly to a student who was hoping to become a teacher or clerk or continue his studies; withholding permission to leave the country for external exams in the Arab universities; refusing permission to study abroad; and preventing the re-entry of students or teachers on their arrival at the borders. House arrest, banishment, and orders to report twice a day to the local police station, were all used to stop a suspect or politically active person being regularly employed. Any relaxation of these measures did not indicate a change of heart but was simply a sign of the policy's success.

The regime was sensitive to and intolerant of any signs of unrest within its bureaucracy. All the political parties tried to recruit UNRWA personnel, senior clerks, teachers and doctors,[112] since they appreciated the decisive and influential position of the professional classes. They felt that once they had an elite core it would be easier to operate and enlist more support. Recruitment of these people was done through secret meetings with them or by mailing political publications to their homes. Abdallah Hamdan, an UNRWA senior clerk, said he was approached by different parties and that Sa'id al-Azzah tried to make him join the N.S.P. Like many others, fearing the loss of his job should he be caught, he rejected all such approaches. Nonetheless, many senior and junior Agency workers were fully involved in politics. The teachers were expected by the Agency to act impartially and to refrain from any political activity during working hours. Although warnings to this effect were issued by UNRWA[113] and the Government, they were the largest group which engaged in politics. This emerging educated stratum which included many extremely capable people, was virtually the only group trusted by the various political parties. They were also the only ones to understand the parties' ideological differences. Most teachers who were party members came from outside the camps. Those teachers who were camp inhabitants faced greater obstacles than the former, owing to the refugees' suspicions, conservatism and patterns of loyalty, although the politically committed amongst them did not surrender to local threats or pressure. And whereas the teachers from outside left the camps in the early afternoon, those living there had the advantage of being able to spread their message after working hours. Of course the ability to propagandize and recruit varied from one individual to another.

The Government also countered the political activities of the senior UNRWA staff, both refugees and local employees, by seeking to veto the nomination of some new teachers[114] or by demanding their removal to more remote places. Although preferring the Government to put suspects on trial, UNRWA sometimes had to surrender to its demands to fire those engaged in politics[115] as well as to withhold nominations or transfer certain people. As a further deterrent wide publicity was given to these measures by the Government and UNRWA. Yet it seems that part of the rapidly growing militant young intelligentsia was not deterred by the threat of transfer far away from their families and friends, or of losing the jobs upon which their families depended. Nevertheless most of them did fear these strict measures since, once caught, it would be difficult to find employment.

Most politically active teachers were Communists[116] who brazenly tried to recruit their pupils. In fact, students were the prime target of all parties. Encouraged by their teachers, they would graduate in virtually no time from classroom politics to activity in the streets, where they were the leaflet distributors and messengers. Although the secondary schools were generally outside the camps, their pupils were active in the camps when they returned home and they maintained contact with teachers both within and outside the camps. Students were enthusiastic about their involvement, feeling not only that they were fulfilling a responsibility but also gaining satisfaction from a sense of participation.

Political rivalry between teachers in the schools became quite common. Some teachers were arrested on the strength of anonymous information supplied by pupils allied to rival parties. Students suggested that marks were given according to their political affiliation. In any event, between 1954 and 1956 the standard of education deteriorated. Most active students were Communist recruits. They managed, for example, to win most seats in the short-lived students' union when elections were held. Thus it was that of all UNRWA employees, the teachers in particular were very carefully watched, because during the 1950s the government felt them to be an especially dangerous element.[117] The moderate influence of the old traditional leaders was declining, whilst the teachers had been strengthening their influence over the younger generation since the mid-1950s. In remote places the traditional leader's influence was stronger than that of the teachers, and the Government tried hard to preserve this state of affairs.

Political activity in the little villages and remote camps was confined mainly to arguments amongst the more educated, again led by the teachers. As in the camps, there were only primary schools, so there was little point to propaganda in the classes. Nevertheless teachers still competed fiercely amongst themselves. Those headmasters who were not party members sometimes managed to control this rivalry, which had a bad effect both on studies and on their personal position.[118] They feared the loss of their own jobs if they were unable to prevent it. The parties also tried to enlist the headmasters, although, having little contact with the pupils, their value lay in recruiting teachers and limiting other parties' activists.

The importance of the Camp Leaders in reaching the older refugees should also be stressed. For example, the fact that the UNRWA Camp Leader (C.L.) of Balata was a Communist helped their members to function more easily.[119] He was also very active in fighting for refugee rights. The party was thus able to gain more support from the ordinary refugee who tended to respect the C.L., usually one of the camp's influential personalities.[120] Consequently the A.C. recommended his transfer.[121]

The Communists were particularly feared by the regime and always received heavier penalties than any of the other opposition parties. But the J.C.P. continued its struggle in spite of the pervading terror, persecution and wave of mass arrests. The local Press was full of these arrests, as the authorities tried to deter others from joining the party. In jail, most real Communists withstood torture and earned the respect of all their opponents. This could not be said of all the other parties' members. Of course some of those "arrested" were government agents. These would be released now and then, together with some other political prisoners, under a Royal Decree which gave occasional pardons, so that they could return to their work within the parties' ranks. Some who acted as undercover agents had little choice in the matter, being pressurized by the authorities through their families or other personal interests. The Communists could thus be watched even in jail, where they continued to be active and tried to recruit from amongst the embittered prisoners. Only rarely, when the jails were not overcrowded, were they separated from the rest of the prisoners.

The label "Communist" became synonymous with trouble-maker and was attached to anyone who appeared to oppose the Government, including religious people who themselves opposed Communism. The authorities encouraged people to become informers and gather information. Much of this information was mere slander motivated by attempted revenge. But the regime managed to create an atmosphere of insecurity for anyone who withheld information, making operations more difficult for the various parties. They also pressed detainees to write to the newspapers condemning their party's activities, and to declare in public their disassociation from the party.[122] Those who did so were pardoned.[123]

Suspicious of any kind of gathering, the Secret Police also watched the sports clubs which some of the parties tried to use as a cover for their meetings and activities. This was why the authorities refused to license a sports club in the Balata Camp in 1952 and again in 1956.[124] Similarly a sports club in Jerusalem was shut down in mid 1954, after the authorities had followed its Communist members for a while. However, knowing they could not completely prevent underground activity, they preferred it to be in the open where it was more easily controlled and their agents could infiltrate. Altogether, Communists made up about half of the political activists who manned the management of the different clubs and associations during the mid-1950s.[125] Other clubs were dominated by Ba'th, Q.A.M. or Q.S.P. supporters.[126]

The authorities also carefully watched the activities of any of the UNRWA Workers Unions and shut them down once it was apparent that they were used by various political parties.[127] Their records reveal that the Jerusalem branch, set up in 1954, and the Tulkarm branch were dominated by Ba'th supporters, while UNRWA's Teachers Trade Union in Hebron was composed mainly of N.S.P. followers.

One of the parties' main and most successful activities consisted in the distribution of their publications, which proved impossible to control completely. This activity was organized by small groups who tried to deceive the authorities and impress the inhabitants by creating the impression that it involved many people. All parties used children for the purpose of distributing leaflets, hanging posters or painting slogans on walls. Some of them were paid for these services, and old and poor people were hired to carry messages in the hope that no-one would suspect them.

Many leaflets were confiscated before they could be distributed. Police searches would find books, pamphlets and hand outs at the disposal of teachers and students, some of them in the camps. Often, nothing at all was found, proof to the authorities of both the efficiency of the underground opposition and of the difficulty of relying on informers. In sudden searches in buses and taxis, leaflets were sometimes found on people trying to arrange their distribution. Drivers as well as passengers were detained. People were arrested either before, during or after the distribution of hand outs, or else were tailed to discover their other contacts. The regime encouraged anti-Communist activity and itself published and distributed "underground" material condemning the J.C.P. and the Ba'th. The authorities also managed to close down a number of printing presses, confiscating typewriters and duplicating-machines. This meant that the Communists, for example, had to write out their leaflets in longhand in 1952-3. Rigid laws for licensing the Press made life more difficult for the various parties, but again the Communists were more efficient at secretly publishing the underground papers in different places under various names. The Government had good reason to fear the impact of these publications. They contained subversive information and much sharp anti-Government criticism which could provoke unrest. Although a great deal of printing equipment was confiscated, most opposition groups managed to get hold of additional machines from their friends abroad. Here the J.C.P. had an advantage over the others, as it was assisted by its sister party in Israel which sometimes supplied it with the printed material itself.[128]

The local Press was another medium used to spread the parties' views, enabling them to appeal to the public and annoy the Government. The fact that the two most prominent dailies, *Filastin* and *al-Difa'*, were "refugees" themselves, originally published in Jaffa, and that many of the journalists were also refugees, made it only natural that they devote a lot of space to the refugees' plight.[129] Problems arose because most newspapers could not survive solely on their low subscriptions. Advertising was not common in the 1950s and not all papers owned their printing equipment. They therefore depended on direct and indirect Government assistance such as large advertisements, the purchase of a large number of copies, or exemption from customs taxes for the paper used. In return the editors were expected to keep a low political profile and only modestly criticize the regime. If a newspaper exceeded these boundaries, it was shut down for a while to "cool down". It could be re-licensed again later. This sort of tacit "understanding" was supplemented by the offer of "suggestions" and instructions for the writing of certain articles. Threats or protests about particular items published which angered the authorities came either over the telephone or orally.[130] Despite these constraints, numerous vicious attacks on the Government's policy appeared. In fact, in the period under review, the Jordanian Press generally was quite reliable and gave wide publicity to the various parties and their policies.

But far more difficult for the Government was the handling of the propaganda warfare via broadcasts from abroad. By then the radio was probably the most important factor in shaping opinions and political ideas in the camps.[131] The radios given to each camp by the British in the early 1950s in the hope that listeners would tune to the Jordanian and Near East Radio Station, were tuned instead to Egyptian and Syrian broadcasts. These had special refugee transmissions of inflammatory and subversive content, the impact of which Jordanian programmes could not counterbalance. The generally illiterate camp refugees listened eagerly, especially to their Egyptian leader Nasser. Regardless of the jamming, Nasser's message got across. Warnings to radio owners, often coffee-shop proprietors, only to tune into Government stations[132] where Jordanian policy was expounded were secretly ignored.

The regime also watched the movements and affiliations of Jordanians working abroad.[133] They were known to be the source of additional money, ammunition and illegal political material smuggled into Jordan; and therefore they also tried to prevent political leaders from leaving the country to function from outside Jordan.[134] Part of the money from abroad went to the families of detainees or of those in exile.[135] The authorities often managed to discover which families received donations and from whom.

Keeping track of the expanding membership of each party, its composition and meetings was the main occupation of the Government agents in Jordan. Most parties were proud of their numerical strength, regarding it as a measure of their success and a prerequisite for further expansion. Yet this last assumption sometimes proved to be wrong. Unlike the J.C.P., the Ba'th first recruited people and then indoctrinated them. Zealous recruiting inevitably brought undesirable elements into their ranks, whether Government agents, opponents or people who would break down while being interrogated by the authorities, telling everything and incriminating friends. So the Ba'th party's peak of apparent success when its membership was at its largest, turned out to be the beginning of its deterioration.

Communist cells were far more difficult to track down, and this relatively small party proved very efficient. A special secret P.M. document sent to Intelligence officers, entitled "The Successful Ways and Means to Combat Communism", stressed that conventional methods were not effective. It explained some of the principles which guided the J.C.P. in its activity and described the party's composition.[136] Smaller than the Ba'th, the J.C.P. in 1952 had about 200 members in the West Bank and 100 in the East Bank, many of them Palestinians. It was organized into cells, in which a member knew only one or two others to whom he passed orders received from a third person. Orders were given orally and no documents were kept. False names were used as well as forged identity cards. So even if a member was forced to talk once he was arrested, he could not provide the important information required by his interrogators. The J.C.P. used book shops as a sort of secret post office, and became proficient in the use of codes and cyphers. It was very careful in the way it absorbed new members.

When monitoring the right-wing religious parties' activists the authorities faced a different set of problems. The M.B. and the Tahrir both tried to gain favour with their listeners in the Friday sermons (*Khutbah*), which led to a contest in political declarations. Each tried to persuade the people gathered that their party was the most active on essential issues. So the authorities were forced to control and censor the content of these speeches, which had to be vetted before delivery. A special decree in 1955 reinforced the use of these measures.[137] Agents followed all *imams* and *khatibs* but were more troubled by the addresses delivered in the towns' mosques (especially those in Nablus[138]) than those in the villages or even the camps. The regime itself also took advantage of these public addresses and used them to widen the monarch's popularity and emphasize his legitimacy as a ruler. Separatist views were condemned, and such ideas were pointed to as a threat to the unity of Islam, the kingdom and the people. As a further precautionary measure the authorities listed all army personnel who visited the mosques during a sermon delivered by an L.P. member. It was found to be much more difficult to observe all the meetings held in houses where L.P. leaders would teach and preach. These meetings grew considerably in 1955 when the L.P. reached its peak.

The attempt to combat unwanted political activity was working efficiently by the time of the heightened political tension of the mid-1950s. The King knew that he would be faced with a crisis unless he took stern measures in the near future and maintained control of events. He gained much-needed popularity through a series of liberal steps in 1956; and the next confrontation was made easier by the fact that the underground movements were operating openly before the 1956 so-called "free elections". The Jordanian records of 1956-7 are full of details regarding affiliations and party memberships. And the government was greatly aided after the clampdown by the fact that its agents, planted in the period of open activity, managed to continue operating from inside the parties when they went underground.

Rapid political developments sharpened the polarized choices. Husayn opted for the natural choice and fortified his own position. This position was strengthened following the Free Officers' attempted *coup d'état*, and the King sought to crush all political activity, which did not support his own regime. He eventually gained the upper hand. Most opposition leaders fled abroad and attempted to operate from there, leaving behind a political vacuum which prevented any real activity against the regime. As Dr Hamdi Taji al-Faruqi, the Ba'thist, put it:

> This movement of politicians out of Jordan weakened the opposition within the country. We failed because we ran out. The people will not fight without us. We repeated the Mufti's mistake.[139]

Once again the King had managed, though not without difficulty, to win over or neutralize oposition and eventually to consolidate his own position. He was able to renew his connections with the West, albeit in a different manner. Some of his enemies were pardoned and allowed to return to Jordan as long as they abandoned any further political activity. They attached their names to various Jordanian publications praising the regime and subtly discrediting the opposition abroad. Before returning, these figures had continued an active struggle against the monarch from the place of their enforced exile. They had put themselves completely at the disposal of Syrian or Egyptian Intelligence forces, and had appealed to their followers to continue the struggle. But these calls went unheard.

In summary, one might conclude that the competition between the parties only weakened them as serious opposition forces and made it easier for the regime to terminate or undermine their activities through its efficient secret police. The latter found it fairly easy to operate in the period under review, especially among the refugees who were not too politically active.

Chapter VIII

Refugee Demonstrations and Protests— Opposition to Whom?

Bitterly discontented with their situation, the refugees naturally expressed their sense of frustration and suspicion through numerous petitions and furious demonstrations.

The Press outside Jordan described many occasions on which furious refugees demonstrated against the regime. They put these protests down to their exasperation with the whole political entity of which they had become part, interpreting demonstrations as opposition to the monarch and his policy. Moreover, riots in the camps were seen by the West as proof of the success of Communist[1] and other extremist groups which wanted to subvert the monarch: by operating amongst the starving angry refugees and gaining their full support and co-operation, it was claimed that they easily incited them against the annexing regime. It was argued that the refugees could upset the Middle East's stability, forming a threat to the possibility of peace and becoming a strain on Arab internal security. The camps were seen as reservoirs of deep political bitterness. It was thought that the inmates, with nothing to lose and with all loyalties exhausted, would naturally be excited by the new left-wing stirrings. These were still in their infancy but it was feared they could easily gather force. Their increasingly impressive performance at the polls was treated as evidence that the J.C.P. ideology "infected" even the villagers.[2] The U.S.A. and Britain were worried that the camp inhabitants' blind hatred of the West and their contempt for the reactionary Arab rulers (the West's proteges) would make them "the best breeding grounds for Communism".

But is this an accurate picture of what happened? If not, against whom were the many demonstrations directed, and what were the main issues? Who started them, where did they begin and who took part? And what was the Government's reaction?

As far as the refugees were concerned, most demonstrations centred around the issue of relief. The protests were not only expressions of angry discontent but a way of agitating for and usually ensuring immediate changes in the relief situation. Most action was directed against the UN and its agencies and not against the Jordanian Government, whose help they successfully sought to force the relief Agencies to concede to their just demands. The refugees quickly learned the political weight of violent protests and marches. Although refugees were Jordanian citizens, none of the cases examined was a refugee protest against the Government as such, for not assisting them directly. This was because the refugees regarded the UN as responsible for their plight and therefore their care.

Generally speaking most activity against the monarch's policy on other, wider issues was initiated in urban centres by educated political figures and not within the refugee camps. The issues involved did not relate to the immediate needs of the camp refugees and so failed to appeal to them. They were harassed by the problems of everyday existence and sought any opportunity to improve their lot. They were worried about their uncertain future with little time for, or interest in, anything else.

The only real exceptions which did involve the refugees were the spontaneous demonstrations against the King in 1948 in Amman after the Ramleh-Lydda affair; those of the following year in Nablus by the "Triangle" inhabitants; the mid-1950s pro-Nasser demonstrations; and those against Glubb, Imperialism and the Israeli raids. Only seldom did refugee committees themselves organize demonstrations to express, for example, solidarity with Nasser.[3] Usually they just joined in with the local population.

Refugee demonstrations over relief arose in various ways. They might flare up suddenly, broadening out spontaneously to include other protests and demands, or they might develop out of an already established and connected series of protests on a particular issue.

The refugees' sense of what constituted a "real" grievance was conditioned by their whole perspective on the international relief operation. They felt quite justified in all their protests and demonstrations. They were well aware of the UN's enormous monetary resources and became impervious to the Agency's reply that it was limited by its budget. They considered comparisons with their conditions and facilities before the war, or with those in other places in the Middle East, to be irrelevant. The relief Agencies' sensitivity and vulnerability to criticism was exploited, and wherever something could be done immediately to improve or extend services more often than not it was. The whole situation was made more tense by the sensational and hostile reporting of the Press, which tended to inflame the refugees. UNRWA's attempts to "get the Press off their backs" through covert payments were to no avail.[4]

In the early years, the conditions in the camps were often squalid and unsanitary. Yet there was never a serious outbreak of any of the diseases that might have been expected, considering the ignorance about medical and hygienic precautions of many poor refugees. But there were many protests about the quality of the medical care. The refugees were terrified by the possibility of epidemics and were further unsettled by the sometimes groundless or exaggerated Press reports about them. The death of a baby, alleged by the Press to be from T.B. and whipped up by noisy refugee committees into a major issue, often led to a violent demonstration claiming that UNRWA was trying to solve the refugee problem by getting rid of the coming generation through medical neglect. But neither the UNRPR nor the World Health Organisation nor UNRWA experts shared the refugees' view of their health and nutritional standards. A YMCA report of January 1950 summed up the situation as follows:

> The conditions of the refugees physically is fair for the Near East, as most receive food, clothing, shelter and medical care. But the moral standards of these people after 20 months of poverty and what is more, inactivity, is very low.[5]

This is how an unpublished ICRC document described the situation that year:

> Whereas the standard of health of adult refugees was relatively satis-factory, the same thing was not true of infants and children under three years of age. Their condition was not due to the war, but is unfortunately chronic among all the poor classes in the Middle East.[6]

Early in 1950, F. W. Clements, Chief of the Nutrition Section W.H.O., surveyed a representative number of refugee camps. He examined many hundreds of refugee children and enquired about cooking practices amongst the housewives. He inspected the shops and bazaars as well as the contents of garbage bins. In his report[7] he stated that, contrary to common belief,

> The nutritional status of the refugee groups investigated was considerably better than one had expected to find amongst people who had known refugee status for approximately eighteen months. There was no case of starvation or even semi-starvation . . . and that in general the nutritional status of refugees who had come from towns and cities was considerably better than that of former villagers and farmers.

The following year another investigation was carried out on similar lines. The author of this 24-page report summarized his findings thus:

> In conclusion I believe the Palestinian refugees on the whole are in reasonable nutritional condition, having regard to their previous circum-stances and those of the population among whom they are at present living. In Trans-Jordan and the Gaza Strip, they appear to be in better nutritional state than the local population.[8]

However such reports were never given wide publicity, the UN fearing the refugees' fury when they were already so dissatisfied with what they were receiving.

There were various protests about the food distribution, including complaints about the overall calorific value of the ration and the proportion of fresh food. The different proportions allocated to the employed and unemployed were queried: should those working get more food because they used more energy or less because they were earning money? Claims were made that bad quality items caused undernourishment and disease; that mismanagement of fresh or tinned food in the extremes of summer or winter led to supplies being destroyed; that some items were adulterated, unfamiliar or unusable, and so on.[9] Flour, the staple food, was often the focus of protests. These were always directed at UNRWA or channelled to it by the Government, even though local suppliers were the source of much of the Agency flour found to be inferior. For example, in 1952 a distribution of unfamiliar foreign flour occurred in Hebron. Some refugees claimed that the flour was bad. This led angry demonstrators to demand the closure of the Census Office in Hebron and the return of Palestine according to the Partition Plan of 1947 and to condemn all the "imperialist" Agency's schemes. Finally, they demanded an immediate additional distribution of flour,[10] which was promptly carried out. Expert reports after the event revealed that there was nothing wrong with this imported flour except its unfamiliar properties in baking. But this was not always the case, especially when the millers in Amman tried to make larger profits by mixing different or inferior grades of flour.[11]

With regard to the relief workers, not only were there protests about corruption, but under the UNRPR and during the early days of UNRWA, the question of just *who* was hired by the agencies was at issue. Everyone wanted to become an Agency employee because of the benefits attached. Refugees resented local Palestinians being employed and were worried that too many educated Christians were taken on, whilst the bedouin wanted jobs as well. Refugees were also annoyed at the high wages and amenities enjoyed by the international staff. They complained that the Agency staff ill-treated or provoked many refugees. And whilst any reductions in staffing levels were strongly opposed, the dismissal of certain relief workers was often demanded, usually that of the distribution inspectors.

Attempts by the Agency to rationalize the refugee lists naturally led to some refugees having their ration cards cancelled or withdrawn.[12] Immediately after its establishment UNRWA was saturated with thousands of petitions and queries concerning such cancellations. It became increasingly difficult technically, let alone politically, to handle all these complaints. Investigations were followed by re-investigations. When the grounds for certain refugees holding ration cards were questioned and several cards then cancelled, appeals for reinstatement also started flooding in. Special committees to deal with this were created, composed of both Government and Agency representatives. Refugees' names were deleted either by reason of false or duplicate registration, or because they were no longer needy, or through absence or marriage to non-refugees.[13] These people all strongly condemned the Agency. The ones who succeeded in their appeal[14] praised the Government. Protests to the Agency and the committees took issue on various topics: it was asserted that the certificates used in evidence against refugees were forged; that decisions were made on the grounds of ill-founded guesswork, appearances, spitefully given misinformation or false documentation; and that the Agency deliberately obstructed the process of appeal. The refugees whose cards were confiscated in Nablus gathered there and decided to march in demonstration from the Haifa Refugee Committee Office to the Government House. They also made a point of meeting the King, who was due to arrive there, and appealing to him "to save them from UNRWA's wickedness".[15]

The idea of the "census" was strongly associated with "the reduction of the numbers of people receiving monthly allowances"[16] and was therefore opposed by all interested parties. UNRWA's director summarized the situation:

> The lack of co-operation from the Government in the past and the active opposition of the refugees for several years made it impossible to operate in Jordan any system to determine the bona fides of ration rolls and the names of persons not entitled to relief.[17]

During the first census, as with all those following, the Agency was confronted with fierce demonstrations. For example, in the "Winston Camp" UNRWA had to be assisted by the Police and the civil authorities to restore order and defend its workers who were refugees themselves.[18]

This pattern of protests and demonstrations continued right through the period, and the nature of demands shifted with the general relief situation and political climate. As late as 1961, when the census issue came up again, the Nablus D.G. suggested that the Government[19] disallow and publicly disassociate itself from the renewed operation as he felt it would trigger off the usual chain-reaction of bitter protests on politically sensitive issues. He argued that preventing the question of ration cards from arising would aid stability and even weaken the opposition of "independent Palestinian Entity" supporters by offering proof of the King's loyalty to the refugees.

Demonstrations which did have a political tenor were sometimes organized by interested elements outside the camps, though they were not necessarily affiliated to any political party. These were people who felt that their private economic interests were threatened by actions the Agency was proposing to take.[20] In a typical case from as late as 1961, UNRWA's Area Officer approached the Hebron D.G. requesting his assistance in taking "the preventative measures deemed necessary" because he had come

> to know that the undermentioned persons (eight names given) are spreading untrue rumours against the present UNRWA operation in Jordan and urging the refugees in this area to have a general strike during the next ration distribution. I also came to know that these persons are collecting contributions from merchants to enable them to fulfil their criminal aims. Such activities will undoubtedly disturb the general security of the area and cause the refugees and the Agency inconveniences.[21]

Edgar Chandler, the former Director of Refugee Services of the World Council of Churches, and President of the Standing Conference of Voluntary Agencies working for Refugees, described the refugees' attitude to the various donators as follows:

> Refugees are increasingly demanding, and they insist on getting, every possible form of donation without any regard to comparative need. Individual refugees seem to pride themselves on what they can get, rather than what they can do for themselves.[22]

The relief demonstrations were also used occasionally by the various political parties. In most instances, they did not organize the demonstrations but merely joined in, taking advantage of a non-political protest to raise their own banners. Thus the biggest wave of demonstrations in June 1952, for example, which spread all through the West Bank camps, and was regarded by the Western Press as leftist inspired, in fact started when an old man intentionally mixed sand with the distributed flour which he had spilled from his torn sack, and returned to the Distribution Centre accusing UNRWA of trying to poison the refugees.[23] The Area Commander who investigated this outburst assured the security services that it was not a well-organized and co-ordinated political campaign.

Even the idea of "The March of One Million Palestinians back to Palestine" (that is, Israel) which was put forward throughout the 1950s and was a source of worry to Israel and the Arab regimes, received far less response in Jordan than in Syria and Lebanon. It has been suggested that this was because the West Bank was, after all, part of Palestine. This is not altogether plausible since most refugees, regardless of their attempts to re-establish themselves, did not regard the West Bank as "their Palestine". As one refugee from Kafar Saba living in nearby Qalqilya put it, "My Palestine starts two kilometres to the west of here, and nothing in the world can change that".

Equally, the West's assumption that eradicating illiteracy and developing the educational system would lead to a moderate acquiescence and incline the second generation to political compromise proved fundamentally wrong. It was really only among the educated that the opposition parties had any real success. Political activity developed hand in hand with the expansion of the educational system towards the mid 1950s, by which time the camps' residents were far from going hungry.

At this time too, the refugees' resentment and hatred of "The West", including the international UNRWA staff, on occasions became even more acute. Israeli raids and inter-Arab political developments only increased the tensions. Mobs sometimes attacked UNRWA workers since they associated them with the West.

The authorities were worried by these different expressions and about the consequence of any political debate developing among the refugees. They therefore attended promptly to all refugee demands for additional assistance from UNRWA. As one official said:

Any demonstration is like a snowball. You may know where it starts but for sure you don't know where it ends. The refugees knew it, the Government knew it and certainly the Agency did, and that is why it surrendered sometimes to many of the refugees demands.

The Government exerted further severe pressure on UNRWA at times by exposing her completely to these protests—since it was forced to side officially with the refugees' claims despite the unpublicized agreements reached with the Agency. One interviewed UNRWA Area Officer described the situation as follows:

Refugees would enter the UNRWA office every day and shout and threaten, bringing some of their friends with them, hoping to reverse the previous decision against their appeal. They would also threaten the government officials that they would demonstrate against the Government too. The Government interest was that peace and order should prevail. They feared that any protest against UNRWA would turn and develop against the Government interest and that the political parties and other refugees would gladly use such accusations to move against the Government. Also, any person in the H.K.J. who received help from outside the country benefitted the Government and so the Government would ask UNRWA to accept their demands, in the interests of peace, which was a basic elementary condition for UNRWA's operating efficiently.

After all, the Government claimed, such demands cost so little and rejecting them could prove costly to the whole operation. Refusing to concede could endanger all UNRWA-Government achievements with regard to the refugees, and make it far more difficult for those who wanted to integrate or dissuade those still hesitating. In this way the Government could prove to the refugees that it protected their interests (while serving its own as well) by getting the Agency to change or transgress its relief criteria, which it had earlier agreed to abide by. But events could not always be controlled. At times the mob would turn against the UNRWA installations crying havoc and burning down warehouses containing items which were intended ultimately for them. UNRWA offices were often a target too.[24]

Such trouble naturally flared up sometimes among the idle, dejected and embittered inmates of the camps. In response, the Government was obliged to protect UNRWA personnel and installations, fearing that violent protests might give the UN reason enough to suspend its activities which could prove fatal to the regime. So in the event of demonstrations getting out of hand, the Government did not hesitate to employ harsh measures. Army units stepped in; shots were fired; people were killed and wounded. Thus the mere presence of the army was usually a deterrent in itself.

The silent majority vacillated and preferred to be left out of politics. In general, camp refugees did not want to be bothered with such delicate matters, either through lack of interest, apathy, illiteracy, inability to organize themselves politically, concern for their prospects of gaining relief and employment, or fear of the "hand that fed them". Glubb recalled that:

> During my time there was never any question of the refugees making trouble for the Jordan Government that I can remember, or any disciplinary troubles with the refugees; they were just miserable. They wanted to go home and so on. The fighting spirit came with the younger generation, born in the camps, not with the people who had lived in their own villages. And so in my time the refugees were just miserable people, and hadn't got any idea of retaliation or resistance or anything.[25]

However, one UNRWA Camp Leader compared Dahaysha Camp with others he had served in, saying that every camp differed in its response owing to its geographical position, the influence of the Camp Leader relative to that of the teachers, and the issues involved. He claimed that Jenin and Tulkarm were quiet like the towns in which they were situated. But Jalazun and Dahaysha were always active.[26] The remote camps were easier to control:

> In those camps it was difficult to organize a demonstration without the authorities prior knowledge and consent. In the town you just joined in.

With regard to the general political issues in which all Palestinians had an interest, neither the refugees in more isolated places nor those in urban camps resorted to any attempt to organize action. In the villages such protests seldom took place; while in the towns they were organized by the local, educated politicians and activists of a type who were certainly not found in the camps. One of the party organizers said:

> demonstrations started in towns. Very rarely in camps. Refugees would come to town. We would send for them. We contacted our members and others. Not the *mukhtars* except if they were our members.

Ibrahim Abu Rish, Aqbat Jabr's Camp Leader, described the situation as follows:

> The old did not take part in the political parties or in the demonstrations. They helped the UNRWA Camp Leader to crush down tension. They believed in other means, a logical approach. They didn't like to interfere in politics as they were fatalistic, and because they were Muslim orthodox and took everything as "God's will". Also the clannish spirit prevailed. The youngsters still feared and respected their fathers (but) they respected their teachers even more. They were forced by the teachers who frightened them. We were against the teachers. I used to join them and lead the demonstration as I feared for my life and so that UNRWA's installations would be protected. Then I ran back to the Camp. Also the old leaders had to join. They took their leaders out from the coffee shops. They had to join.[27]

So with the exception of Jericho and Amman, the "political" demonstrations did not normally start in the camps and did not always spread into them. The contention that political demonstrations and riots always began in the camps is, therefore, plainly inaccurate. The simple fact was that the camps were very easy to control and that everyone was aware of this. The police let demonstrations take place there so long as they did not exceed certain limits of violence and did not turn hostile to the regime. The Government sometimes regarded them as an essential pressure vent and their toleration could show the refugees that the Government was on the side of its citizens. They were useful to the regime when it wanted to pressurize the Agency to give up its demands or to change its original plans when these did not suit the Government.

The Western contention, common in the 1950s Press, that the refugee riots threatened to overthrow the King seems even odder if one bears in mind that most camp inhabitants usually worked outside the camps and that the younger generation was away seeking employment wherever it could. Nor were there any teenagers in the camps for most of the day since most of them attended secondary schools outside the camps in the nearby towns or townlets. Only the old, the idle and the elementary school children remained in the camps, neither of whom could really be a threat to the regime, let alone to any small police force that was sent to maintain the peace.

With the growth of Nasser's popularity the country passed through a very troubled phase. Nasser seemed to be the first Arab leader to challenge the big Powers and to stand up for Arab rights. He therefore exercised enormous influence, and the masses were eager to listen to his speeches. The people flocked into the streets and with the Templer visit the camps rose in demonstrations.[28] For many refugees their support of Nasser was not, as the Government saw it, a matter of preference for him over Husayn or of a final choice between the two. It was rather a reflection of their yearning for a drastic change in Jordanian policy and a movement to give backing to the one person who they believed could make their dream come true. They urged "their" Government to join in as a partner, which is how they wanted to see themselves.

Political party activists were aware of this attitude, although they did not necessarily share it. They knew that despite this enthusiasm for Nasser, the King still enjoyed a relatively high regard amongst the conservative camp refugees. But they also knew they could rely on their participation in acts of protest so long as they could point out the clear connection between the political issues involved and the refugee plight. This was quite easily achieved and refugees needed little persuasion to show their contempt for Britain, the U.S.A. and the UN. Sometimes this agitation was even encouraged, as one activist put it, by "expense fees to cover the loss of time of the camp refugee . . ." The political parties proved they were still capable of organizing demonstrations even when the authorities thought the hard core of Government resistance had disappeared.

To sum up, most refugee demonstrations up to the mid-1950s centred mainly around the problems arising from the immediate need for more relief and better care. This is not to deny that refugees joined other political demonstrations, either because it served their interests to do so or expressed their political belief, or both. Moreover, they often conveyed a militant political image, which helped to secure the satisfaction of at least part of their demands. The point here is, however, that *exclusively* refugee demonstrations and other acts of protest were generally centred around their intolerable situation and their Right to Return, rather than being part of any wider political move against the regime or its policy. Ten years after they had become refugees the issues were still the same, the arguments were similar, and the chain reactions followed the same old pattern—the difference being that refugees in Jordan were far better integrated into the country. And on the whole the refugees, in particular those living in the camps, played a rather passive role in the country's political affairs during the period under review.

Conclusion

Manoeuvred out of the picture during the late 1930s, with no effective recognized leadership to guide them and more internally divided than ever before, the scattered Palestinians were given no real choice as to their political fate after the 1948 war ended. Those who became part of the extended Hashimite Kingdom of Jordan, both refugees and non-refugees, were granted Jordanian citizenship by the monarch, who managed to neutralize any internal or external opposition he confronted. He annexed that part of Palestine his forces controlled with the acquiescence of his powerless new subjects who outnumbered the original Trans-Jordanians.

For their part, the East Bankers were unhappy at becoming a minority in their own country and were antagonized by the waves of refugees flooding the area. Hence they were reluctant to support the granting of citizenship to the Palestinians, and "Jordanization" became a process which meant that the country would not be "Palestinianized".

The attempt to integrate the Palestinians into an enlarged Jordan, without dislodging the monarchy in the process, was bound to face problems. The most important of these arose from the presence of a large segment of refugees whose separate entity had to be conserved both to ensure the continuing flow of massive support from UNRWA and to maintain the bargaining power *vis-à-vis* Israel and the UN let alone because of local and external Arab pressures.

The Government, for its part, pursued an ambivalent policy. It naturally favoured any scheme that would assist the refugees to improve their conditions, keep them busy and promote their economic integration, thereby helping Jordan in the process. But it was harassed by elements who advocated opposing policies and it often had to surrender to such pressure since siding with the Agency was dangerous to the monarch's image. Certainly Jordan did not intend to take over from or share UNRWA's responsibilities, as was hoped by the U.S.A., the main financial contributor to UNRWA. The U.S.A. was motivated primarily by its fear that "stability" in the Middle East would be upset by the refugees. Consequently the Agency's mandate was renewed time and again. UNRWA, which was created originally as a temporary body, gradually developed into a permanent element in the Middle East, its activities and terms of reference perpetuating its existence. Pumping in enormous sums of money, its contribution became a carefully calculated item in the Jordanian Government's budget. It served indirectly as a channel of subsidies whose continued existence was most convenient to all recipients—the country in general as well as the refugees.

It is often claimed that the Arab countries sought to keep the Palestinian Refugee Problem alive as part of their war against Israel, mainly by preventing any measures which could lead to constructive integration. It is further suggested that it was their policy to maintain the abnormal status of the refugees by using discriminatory practices which prevented or obstructed their absorption, confining them to the camps and compelling them to lead an unproductive life. The refugees, feeling unwanted and resentful, would provide a fruitful breeding ground for extreme nationalist sentiment and subversive adventurism. This study has suggested that in Jordan at least this was not the case.

On the contrary, such a policy and state of affairs would have served Jordan's interests neither politically, since it could cause dangerous unrest; nor economically, since it would have stopped all the large UNRWA schemes outside the camps which resulted in the creation of the "Blue State" with the financial burden carried by the UN; nor socially, as it could endanger the unified base on which the Throne wanted to establish itself. It seems that the Jordanian regime, quite apart from its desire to represent the Palestinians regardless of their status, was well aware that any policy discriminating against refugees would only make the Government's task much more difficult. This could nurture a large unstable element likely to imperil the viability of the whole framework. Therefore Jordan was reluctant to practise discrimination such as that exercised by Egypt in the Gaza Strip, and it carefully opened all avenues—apart from the armed forces—to the refugees.

In so far as discrimination existed, it was not a calculated policy but sprang mainly from the emotional reactions of two competing, clashing sections of the population, each fearing and looking down upon the other and wanting a larger say *within* the kingdom. Neither of the elements ever became fully unified or acted as a totally separate camp hostile to the other. Yet the granting of citizenship could ease, but not eradicate, the differences that continued to prevail in Jordan. Similarly, antagonisms could not entirely disappear since the two sections were not welded into a complete union. It was only on such a basis that a real sense of partnership could have been developed.

The regime had supporters and opponents amongst both segments of the population. Developing the East Bank at the expense of the West Bank led most Palestinians to obtain an economic stake in the former, while the latter was deprived of its young manpower which either migrated eastwards or emigrated abroad.

Any opposition to the monarch proved to be weak and, above all, fragmented. The political parties were not deeply concerned with the refugee plight or with the refugees, who were generally looked down upon and distrusted owing to the ease with which security forces could control the camps. The refugees in turn did not prove to be over-interested in politics as such, apart from the "politics of relief". In this they were very active, a phenomenon mistakenly viewed in the West as involving hostility towards the monarch.

Towards the mid-1950s they became more involved in the idea of Arab unity, which once again raised their hopes, regarding it as an answer to their painful problem of self-identity and an instrument for the recovery of Palestine. Nasser became their leader and they supported the various parties which advocated such ideas, though they never understood the real differences in their ideologies. This support was a reflection of their belief in Nasser, their gratitude to the U.S.S.R. and their bitterness against the West. It was coupled with an explicit hope that at some time in the near future they would be able to choose between returning to their homes or being equal citizens of the Arab World. Their political activity during the period was aimed not at the creation of a separate political framework but at a change of the monarch's policy.

Subversive activities were organized and subsidized by the king's deadly Syrian and Egyptian foes, who managed to discredit him in the eyes of many of his citizens but failed to achieve their goal—the fall of the Hashimite House. The Fedayyin activity from Jordan, organized by the Egyptians, involved only a few refugees. It succeeded only partly in its object of hurting Israel and undermining the Jordanian regime. The Arab Legion, whose task was to defend the monarch, tried anxiously to prevent such activities, which were answered by Israel's so-called "Retaliation Activities". These in turn weakened the Jordanian regime and forced it to surrender temporarily to some of the prevailing Arab expectations of the time, which proved counter-productive to Israel and to the monarch whose position she sought to bolster.

Palestinians, who were never really trusted, began manning the technical units of the slowly expanding army after a few years. But their wish to be an integral part of the Jordanian forces and to contribute their share was never fulfilled because the regime was reluctant to arm any Palestinians. Hence the National Guard, which generally excluded the refugees, always remained an ineffective, weak and untrained force. It might perhaps have given its members some satisfaction but could not, and was not expected to stop any hostile activity from Israel.

With his army firmly behind him, the monarch took advantage of the disunity of the opposition he confronted and, by employing harsh methods, successfully continued the process of consolidation. A new era began however, with the development once again of the idea of the Palestinian Entity. This was mainly initiated through inter-Arab rivalries, eventually gathering enough momentum to make re-emergence of this conflict between Palestinian and Trans-Jordanian inevitable. However, it is obvious from a study of the Jordanian secret lists of political activists that in this period, as in 1949-50, the refugees generally lagged behind the local Palestinians in their enthusiasm for the idea of a separate Entity.

Many refugees willingly took part in the offered process of integration, voting and being elected to Parliament, serving in the rapidly expanding Jordanian administration, and in effect carrying out the policy which aimed at thwarting any Palestinian, or for that matter, refugee political separateness. The regime, which encouraged this process of controlled participation, faced little if any opposition from the disunited, helpless refugees.

Most protests from the refugees, in the forms of petitions and demonstrations, did not seek to challenge the regime's authority but rather to ensure its care and responsibility for them by securing the continued work of the international relief machinery. Their greatest fear was that they would be deprived of such essential assistance: hence their uneasiness over any attempt to cut back their official "number" and change their status. The refugees viewed with great suspicion any scheme which they felt could endanger their rights. Hence they rejected the various widely publicized integration or self-help programmes which many of them wanted in practice but could not openly accept in principle. UNRWA made things more difficult for them when it made participation conditional on the cancellation of the symbol of their status—the ration card.

However, they gradually became part of numerous UNRWA projects whose common aim, regardless of their names, was to provide the refugee with the tools to start a new life away from his former home. Many refugees took advantage of the rehabilitation projects to establish themselves economically. But they never approved of nor really acquiesced in the basic idea behind these programmes, which was essentially complete resettlement and the surrender of what they regarded as their rights to their former lands. Nevertheless, with the passage of years most refugees realized that it would be a long time before they were granted the "free choice", if indeed ever at all, and began to strike firmer roots. The Egyptian defeat in the Sinai Campaign of 1956 accelerated this process. The tents in the camps were replaced with fixed shelters as part of a combined UNRWA-Government project aimed at stabilizing their life, turning the sites into permanent dwellings in the form of large villages and ensuring the UN's continued operation. The camps retained their "temporary" status although the way their inhabitants lived hardly coincided with this notion. Politically the camps were relatively more stable than other places and also offered many facilities which were envied by the native villagers adjacent to the camps. Consequently more refugees entered the camps, together with some non-refugees who rented places from those established outside the camps, and many willingly enrolled in one or other of UNRWA's rehabilitiation projects. Idleness and apathy amongst the refugees were replaced by the strong will of an industrious people who aimed at re-establishing themselves. Whatever their outward attitudes, they took advantage of all UNRWA facilities, under the "permitting" rubric of "Until the Day of Return".

Refugees outside the camps, who comprised 70 per cent of the refugee population, started integrating much earlier. Though they were regarded as strangers, and felt themselves to be such, even amidst their Palestinian brothers, they managed to re-establish themselves economically and socially towards the end of the 1950s. However, their successful competition with the natives, be they Palestinian or Trans-Jordanian, aroused some antagonism towards them.

In general, the Palestinians might be regarded as the "builders" of the Arab Oil States which were then backward countries. They developed Amman and turned it into a flourishing city. Those who stayed in Israel helped to build the Jewish State and, more generally, the Palestinians have built for everyone, everywhere, apart that is from the remaining parts of Palestine—the Gaza Strip and the West Bank. Relatively more prosperous than others in the Middle East, the refugees in Jordan conveniently tended to ignore the fact that many of their achievements came about through the citizenship and the passport that the Jordanian Government offered them, which allowed them to move around the Middle East.

Outside Jordan, especially in the oil-rich Arabian Peninsula, the refugees at first found a ready welcome for their skills, experience and know-how, acquired mostly in the British Mandate days or through UNRWA vocational training, as well as for their business acumen and industrious characteristics. They helped kindle the spark for those countries' economic boom. They took up important positions: they were the teachers, doctors, lawyers and manual workers. In economic terms it was a fair exchange, with each of the parties gaining tremendously: the oil countries were able to modernize; the refugees received large salaries, difficult to come by elsewhere in the Arab world, and their parents were sent money and could improve their social position; the Jordanian Government benefited from these indirect contributions of foreign currency which took a great burden off its shoulders. At the same time this emigration of the youngsters created local social and political patterns to which those returning would have to adjust. UNRWA and UNESCO succeeded in encouraging emigration to the places they had wanted refugees to go to originally, getting rid of potential trouble-makers who were likely to reject many of the integration schemes.

They became perhaps the most educated section in Arab society. But the new white-collar generation proved that education does not necessarily induce "compromise with the new reality and coping with it"—quite the contrary. In exile among their Arab brethren, to whom they were a reminder of the defeat, refugees felt neglected and estranged. In some way they were "different". Refugees were considered to be guests and not always welcome ones. Their skill and experience, which was exploited by their hosts, became another reason why they were disliked. Envy from the local unemployed was common and social tensions were therefore inevitable.

So, even if refugees wanted to be socially integrated into these countries, many of them were in practice prevented from doing so, being constantly reminded of their status by the local population or the bureaucracy. The term *gharib* was an expression of their alienation in those places and of the unsympathetic reaction of their neighbours. All this only strengthened the refugees' yearning for "The Return". The lip-service paid to the *awdah* (the

Return), and the insistence on calling the refugees *al-a'idun* ("The Returnees"), reflected also the desire of the local population to get rid of these strangers, economically successful and potential political trouble-makers. And the young generation born mostly outside Palestine was to develop its Palestinian orientation in a completely different and far more militant way than that of its parents.

Notes

Introduction

1. For further reading see Abdullah Ibn Husayn's views in the relevant chapters of his book *Mudhakkirat al-Malik Abdallah Bin al-Husayn* (Jerusalem 1946); Israel Gershuni's articles "The Arab Nation, The Hashimite Dynasty and Greater Syria in the Writings of Abdullah" in *ha-Mizrah he-Hadash* (The New East) (hereafter N.E.) (Hebrew), Vol. XXV, 1975, No. 1–2 (97–98), pp. 1–26 and No. 3 (99), pp. 161–83, and Anis Saigh *al-Hashimiyyun wa Qadiyyat Filastin* (The Hashimites and the Palestine Question) (Arabic) (Beirut 1966), pp. 292–4.
2. Abdullah's views are contained in *Suriya al-Kubra. Al-Kitab al-Urdunni al-Abyad* (Greater Syria: The Jordanian White Book) (Arabic) (Amman, 1947).
3. For an extensive account of Abdullah's intentions and manoeuvres in Palestine in the 1940s, see Yosef Nevo *Abdallah ve-Arviyey Eretz Israel* (Abdullah and the Palestinian Arabs) (Hebrew), The Shiloah Institute, Tel Aviv University, 1975. For Abdullah's version see his *al-Takmilah Min Mudhakkirat Sahib al-Jalalah al-Hashimiyyah al-Malik Abdallah Ibn al-Husayn.* (Supplement to his Hashimite Excellency King Abdullah's memoirs), pp. 107–17.
4. For the details of his 12 point plan see (English Text) in *al-Takmilah: My Memoirs Completed* (American Council of Learned Societies, Near East Translation Programme, Washington 1954), pp. 99–100 and in the original (Arabic), *op. cit.*, pp. 121–2.
5. Public Record Office, London, F.O. File E6956/15/31, p. 195, M (45), 30th Conclusion, Minute 7.11.1945.
6. Later the Communist National Liberation League (N.L.L.) distributed a hand out in August 1948 entitled "To the Masses of the Palestinian Arab People" calling for the immediate establishment of a National Front to work for the implementation of the Partition, the expulsion of all Arab armies which betrayed them and to express opposition to all the Arab rulers' attempts to exploit the Palestinians.
7. See Meir Pa'il's article "The Problem of Arab Sovereignty in Palestine 1947–49, Arab Governments Versus the Arabs of Palestine" in *Zionism,* Studies in the History of Zionist Movement and the Jews in Palestine (Hebrew), Vol. III, Tel Aviv University, The Institute for Zionist Research, pp. 439–89.
8. For an extensive analysis of the developments leading up to the Rebellion and a detailed account of it, see Yehoshua Porath, *The Palestinian-Arab National Movement 1929–1939: From Riots to Rebellion,* Frank Cass, London, 1977.
9. In his memoirs Abdallah al-Tall quotes King Abdullah as saying "I fear in Palestine a jealous relative more than a hostile enemy". In *Karithat Filastin Mudhakkirat Abdallah al-Tall Qa'id Ma'rakat al-Quds.* (The Calamity of Palestine, the memoirs of Abdallah al-Tall, the Commander of the battle over Jerusalem) (Arabic) (Cairo 1959), p. 432.
10. See Jam'iyyat Inqadh Filastin *Karithat Filastin* (The Palestine Disaster). (Arabic) (Baghdad 1949), p. 54.
11. The "Disaster Literature" as it is called began appearing shortly after 1948 and proliferated in the 1960s. More people began analysing the various reasons for the Arab failure whether military, political, social or economic. For example Musa al-Alami's *Ibrat Filastin* (The Lesson of Palestine) (Beirut 1949); Qadri Hafiz Tuqan *Ba'd al-Nakbah* (After the Disaster) (Beirut 1950); Qustantin

Zuraiq *Ma'na al-Nakbah* (The Meaning of the Disaster) English translation (Beirut 1956) and others. See Yehoshafat Harkabi's "The Palestinians in the Fifties and their awakening as reflected in their literature" in Moshe Ma'oz (ed), *Palestinian Arab Politics,* Truman Institute Studies (Jerusalem 1975), pp. 51–90.

12. For further reading on the Palestine Communist Party (P.C.P.) and the National Liberation League, see Yehoshua Porath's "Revolution and Terrorism and the Palestinian Communist Party 1929–1939" and "The Origins, Nature and Disintegration of the National Liberation League (Usbat al-Taharrur al-Watani) 1943–1948" in *N.E.*, Vol. 18 (1968) pp. 255–67 and Vol. 14 (1964) pp. 353–66.

13. Abdullah's demands for allowing the Ramleh and Lydda refugees to return, the free usage of the Haifa port, a secure road to the Gaza port, the opening of the road between Bethlehem and Jerusalem, the return of certain quarters of Jerusalem, the return of the Tulkarm lands he previously surrendered, and his strong claims on the southern Negev—were all rejected by Israel. Instead, Jordan was given territory near Zahiriyyah and was promised a refund for the paving of a new road to join Qalqilya and Tulkarm. Israel further agreed to allow the Frontier Villages to cultivate their lands on the Israeli side. Free access was assured but it never really materialized, since most items stipulated in article eight of the Agreement which were to the benefit of Israel were never implemented: for example, the use of the Bethlehem and Latrun-Jerusalem roads, free access to the Wailing Wall, the Jewish Cemetery on the Mount of Olives and Mount Scopus Institutions, whose regular functioning was also vouched for, and to water from the Latrun pumping station. Details on the negotiations between Israel and Jordan were released by the U.S.A. Department of State, Vol. 6, 1949 (Washington D.C.).

14. *Ramallah Radio,* 20.9.1949.

15. See Muhammad Nimr al-Hawari *Sir al-Nakbah* (The Secret of the Catastrophe) Arabic) (Nazareth 1955), pp. 269–87.

16. For the names of some 59 delegates see Nevo *Abdallah, op. cit.* pp. 126–7.

17. *al-Ahram,* daily Cairo, 27.11.50, 9.6.51; 28.10.52; *al-Difa',* daily, Jerusalem, 18.12.52. Following the establishment of the U.A.R. in 1958 more calls were made for that merger, both from inside and outside the Strip.

18. *al-Ahram,* 27.11.50; *al-Salam,* weekly, Gaza, 1.4.52; *Damascus Radio,* 25.1.53; *Filastin,* daily, Jerusalem, 23.4.55; *al-Ahram,* 23.5.55; *Cairo Radio,* 12.5.56.

19. In an answer to the Jordanian Chief of Staff (C.O.S.) who demanded information on all former Mufti supporters, whether passive or active, the names of those who, it was claimed, transferred loyalty or were very passive were indicated. From Jordanian Unpublished Records in the Israel State Archives, Jerusalem, Section 65 (hereafter S.A. JUPR) File entitled "The Arab Higher Committee", Order No. Q25/3/743 dated 25.2.50 and Ramallah's Area Commander (A.C.) report, MB/3/1–510, to Jerusalem A.C. dated 23.3.50. (Secret). Another report gave the names of prominent Palestinians who quarrelled with or deserted the Mufti, three of whom worked in the Jordanian intelligence in Tulkarm and Nablus *(Ibid),* File 0/297, report dated 29.3.50. (From summarized (unpublished) Jordanian Secret Records found in the Israeli State Archives (S.A. JUPR), part of an extensive project on the political parties in the West Bank done by the Hebrew University of Jerusalem, the Institute for Asian and African Studies, the Centre of Research of Eretz Israel Arabs, The Truman Research Centre (hereafter Truman Papers) (No. 17–19).)
Following the Jericho Conference more A.H.C. supporters were reported as joining Abdullah's camp or refraining from any political activity. Some of them were *mukhtars* who perhaps feared losing their jobs. Anwar Nusayba, the former Secretary of the A.P.G., said he rejected the offer he received while still in Cairo for the position of Jordanian Attorney General. His return to Jerusalem

was nevertheless, arranged by his brother Hazim, who served as the Jordanian Representative to the Mixed Armistice Commission. (Interview with Anwar Nusayba in Jerusalem on 14.1.75). Unpublished Personal Files found in the Israeli Foreign Office and those of the Truman Research Centre studied in the field research, reveal names of A.H.C. supporters who for personal reasons returned to the enlarged HKJ to take jobs with the Government and UNRWA because they were better off there. As one former A.H.C. supporter said: "We had to realize which side our bread is buttered on. The other option was too dangerous". (One of them, Khalid Husayni, the Mufti's nephew, was murdered in 1951 in revenge, whilst serving as UNRWA's Nablus Area Officer).

20. Hawari, *Sir, op. cit.,* p. 290 and interview with him held in Nazareth on 5.8.75.
21. S. A. JUPR Letter from Jerusalem Intelligence to C.O.S., MQM/3/2/12275 dated 12.8.51. The report mentioned two refugee students, Shafiq al-Hut and Muhammad al-Lisawi, who accused the Mufti of being the main reason for the refugees' expulsion, and claimed that one of the A.H.C. reported them to the Syrians, who arrested them and their friends as Communists.
22. Emil Ghuri became an M.P. and a Minister (1969) and a member of the Jordanian National Union Executive in 1972; Akram Zu'ytir became Jordan's Ambassador to Syria in 1962; in 1967 Hajj Amin was allowed to visit Jerusalem. For further reading see Na'if Hijazi and Mahmud Atallah (ed) *Shakhsiyyat Urdunniyyah* (Jordanian Personalities) (Amman 1973). For details on Palestinian Personalities under the British Mandate see Ahmad Khalil al-Aqad (ed) *Min Huwa Li Rijal Filastin 1945–6* (Who is Who) (Jaffa 1946), and eleven articles by Haviv Kena'an on "The Arab Dynasty 1969" in *ha-Aretz* daily (Hebrew) (Tel Aviv), November-December, 1969.
23. Edward Atiyah, *The Arabs,* (Edinburgh), 1955–58, p. 184.
24. The C.O.S., John Glubb, ordered all A.C.'s to put under surveillance those entering from Lebanon, Syria, Gaza and Egypt, until the elections were over, in particular the movements of Faysal al-Nabulsi in Nablus and Rafiq Raghib al-Husayni, the Mufti's messenger. (S.A. JUPR, Letter No. N/S/23/337 dated 6.4.50). Other reports reveal details of the Mufti's movements, his car, and the names of his guards.
25. Unpublished documents reveal details on a number of people granted permission to return to Jordan if they co-operated with the security forces, providing details of the movements and actions of their friends in the same category. One man, a member of the Jerusalem Chamber of Commerce handled imports, enabling him to move around the Arab Countries.
26. *Ibid,* File 0/297, report dated 29.3.50 in Truman Papers No. (16). Another report signed by the C.O.S. said Tall received from the Mufti in Damascus an enormous sum of money to stir up conflicts and create tension in the West Bank. Letter T8/19/5664 dated 10.5.50. Another report listed those in the West Bank with whom he was to make initial contact.
27. Bank notes (which carried the Mufti's picture in Christian and Muslim holy places in Jerusalem) were said to have appeared in Nablus and Talkarm. S.A. JUPR report MQM/26–9721 and 10127 dated 7.8.50 and Minister of Interior Order No. M/Gen/26/50/3474 of 14.9.50 saying that such money is illegal in Jordan and ordering its confiscation.
28. *Ibid,* letter from Glubb to all A.C.'s on the network in Damascus which was hostile to the Hashimites and which sent threatening letters to the Egyptian and Syrian members of the Armistice Commissions and to the C.C.P. delegates. The network was allegedly composed of Subhi Abu Ghanaymah, Darwazah, Rafiq al-Tammimi and Faris Sirhan. (Letter No. Q3/17/5/3850. JLN/136/N/110528 dated 4.10.50). File MQM/26, p. 26 dated 9.5.50, Truman Papers, No. (210). Hazim Mahmud al-Khalidi, a former Damascus UNRWA Area Officer, said

the Mufti was very active amongst the refugees in the camps in Syria which he often visited, trying to recruit their sympathy through his agents. (Interview in Jerusalem on 20.1.75). To strengthen its position as a recognized and representative body vis-a-vis the international community, the A.H.C. demanded, for example, that any YMCA club about to be opened in Syria or Lebanon would have to be authorized by it. Accordingly the YMCA, not wishing to face any problems, approached the A.H.C. for approval in 1950 (unpublished YMCA paper titled: *Report on the provision of YMCA clubs for the Palestinian Refugees* signed by E. Fraser Smith, January 26, 1950, Beirut, p. 13).

29. Asher Goren, *ha-Ligah ha-Aravit 1945–54* (The Arab League) (Hebrew) (Tel Aviv 1954), p. 202.
30. Even in Gaza Abdullah enjoyed some support from the prominent al-Shawwa family. A further division amongst the Palestinians was marked by a declaration which came in March 1949 from the "Galilee Refugees" in Lebanon expressing their desire that the Galilee should become part of Syria.

Chapter I

1. During the late 1930s Abdullah employed agents from among the Palestinians paid to propagandize for him and report back on developments and moods among the Palestinians. One was the editor of *Filastin* newspaper, Yusuf Hanna (see Nevo, *Abdallah, op. cit.,* pp. 21, 75). His main supporters were the mayors of Hebron and Nablus, Shaykh Muhammad Ali al-Ja'bari and Sulayman Tuqan, Farid Irshayd from Jenin, Hikmat Taji al-Faruqi from Jaffa, Sulayman Taji al-Faruqi from Ramleh, the Jerusalemite Raghib al-Nashashibi and Hashim al-Jayusi and Falah Hanun, both from Tulkarm.
2. To him the Mufti was "the incarnation of the devil—a corrupt demagogue who victimized those in whose name he spoke and whose plight he created, always safely away from the fighting in Palestine". (Interview, *op. cit.*) See also Muhammad al-Tabi'i in Cairo daily *Akhbar al-Yawm,* 12.10.63.
3. Nevo, *Ibid,* pp. 48–9, 76–7.
4. From Beirut the A.H.C. tried to stop the stream of people deserting Palestine as it feared the consequences of this, issuing in December 1947 three leaflets condemning those who fled, accusing them of treason. The local Press followed suit and demanded their return, urging them not to abandon their homes. Special visas were issued by the local Palestinian Arab National Committees and those who fled without authorization were threatened with their homes being burnt down, demolished or confiscated.
5. To weaken further the Mufti's influence in Gaza he appealed through his ambassador in Great Britain for aid for the refugees in Gaza—see *The Times,* 24.3.49.
6. See Sir Alec Kirkbride *From the Wings, Amman Memoirs 1947–51* (London 1976), p. 59 (hereafter Kirkbride, Amman); Ibrahim Sakik *Tarikh Filastin al-Hadith* (Palestine's modern history) (Gaza 1964), pp. 103–4; Saigh *al-Hashimiyyun, op. cit.,* pp. 258–9.
7. *Ramallah Radio,* 22.9.48, 09.00 hours.
8. Hawari said he was ordered to attend, refused to do so and escaped to Gaza that night. (Interview, *op. cit.*)
9. *Ramallah radio,* 13/14.10.48 speeches and official explanation of the different Arab Countries giving reasons for their support in and recognition of the new government.

10. *Ibid*, 1.10.48.
11. *Sharq al-Adna* (Near East Radio Station) (N.E.R.S.), 7.10.48.
12. *Ramallah Radio*, 16.11.48.
13. *Ramallah Radio*, 18.11.48.
14. *N.E.R.S.*, 23.11.48.
15. *Ramallah Radio*, 21/30.11.48.
16. Kirkbride, who met Tawfiq Abu al-Huda, the Jordanian Prime Minister of Palestinian origin, prior to the convening of the Congress, said he was unsure of the prospects of such a convention, but, like everyone, decided that it was the only thing to do. (Interview held in London on 3.12.73).
17. See A. Dearden, *Jordan* (London 1958), p. 84 and Kirkbride, *Amman, op. cit.*, p. 99. The annexation was, in due course, recognised *de jure* only by Great Britain and Pakistan and *de facto* by many other countries (including Israel). Kirkbride said he received instructions not to go to Jerusalem, and to avoid the West Bank and all the refugee camps. (Interview, *op. cit.*)
18. Jordan was recognised *de jure* by the U.S.A. on 31.1.49. See Uriel Dann "The United States and the Recognition of Trans-Jordan 1948–49", reprint from *Asian and African Studies*, Vol. II, No. 2, 1976, pp. 238–90.
19. S.A. JUPR, File 35/3, paper signed by the members of the Permanent Office of the Second Palestinian Arab Congress—preamble to the resolutions. Amongst them were: Ja'bari—the Congress's President; Fu'ad Atallah—Vice-President (a Christian refugee from Haifa); Ajaj Nuwayhid—Secretary; Musa al-Husayni; Hikmat al-Taji al-Faruqi; Uthman Muhammadiyah (Haifa); Dr Kamal Hanun (Judge from Tulkarm); Yahya Hamudah (a refugee from Lifta, lawyer)—who were all members of the executive of the Permanent Congress's Office and whose names were carried on the Congress's resolutions. For details on the participants see: Tall *Karithat, op. cit.*, p. 377; Nevo *Abdallah, op. cit.*, p. 128–9; Zvi Ne'eman, *Mamlehet Abdallah le-Ahar ha-Sipuah* (Abdullah's Kingdom following the annexation) (Hebrew) (Jerusalem 1950), pp. 27, 40.
20. Some among those interviewed said they were threatened by the Army officers and had to turn up in Jericho. Kirkbride put it: "The King exercised all his personal and other forms of influence to induce people to vote for their annexation, but there was no coercion". He said, "This is our policy, you ought to vote for it". (Interview, *op. cit.*)
21. Aziz Shihadah (interview held in Ramallah on 22.1.75) and Ibrahim Mustafa al-Ahmad, *mukhtar* of Rummana village (interview there 11.4.74). A point expressed later by Isa Aqil reads: "the mission of Jordan (is) the safeguarding of what is left of Palestine *until* the appropriate time for its re-capture arrives". (Courtesy of Isa Aqil, draft of a Parliamentary Speech).
22. For English text see Aqil Abidi, *Jordan: A Political Study 1948–1957* (N.Y. 1965) pp. 54–5.
23. Underlined in original text.
24. The text signed by the Congress selected Executive was distributed through the External Liaison Office in Jerusalem. (S.A. JUPR. File 35/3).
25. *N.E.R.S.*, 2.12.48, also J. Nevo, "Abdallah and the Arabs of Palestine", in *Wiener Library Bulletin* 1978, Vol. xxxi (No. 45/46) pp. 60–1.
26. File 35/3, *Ibid*.
27. *al-Nahdah* daily (Amman), 12.7.50. Kirkbride in *Amman Memoirs, op. cit.*, p. 36, wrote that the sore was opened once again with the coup taking place in Syria a year later, when Abdullah paid some Syrians bribes so that they would send him letters of support.
28. Nevo, *Abdallah*, p. 115.
29. *Ramallah Radio*, 7.12.48.
30. *Filastin*, 16.10.49.

31. See Arif al-Arif *al-Nakbah, Nakbat al-Maqdis wa al-Firdaws al-Mafqud 1947–1955* (The disaster, the calamity of the Holy Land and the lost paradise) (Beirut 1959?) pp. 897–901, 920–9, 1032–41, and Hazza' al-Majali in *Mudhakkirati* (Jerusalem 1960), pp. 90–2.

32. "The Triangle Disaster" as it was called by many is the subject of a vicious attack by Faysal Abd al-Latif al-Nabulsi in his book *al-Takattul al-Raj'i wa Awdat Filastin* (The Reactionary Grouping and the Return of Palestine), pp. 29–36. An interesting accusation against Fawzi al-Mulqi was made by Riad al-Muflih who was the Legal Counsel of the Jordanian delegation to the Rhodes and Lausanne talks in *al-Nidal,* Amman, No. 1, 15.4.54. (The paper was edited by Ahmad al-Tarawanah and al-Muflih and was closed down shortly afterwards). (The newspaper is found in Israel Shtockman's collection, Jerusalem). Similarly, interviewed property owners said Mulqi hoped to reduce their resistance to the Agreement by deceiving them and promising that the lands to be transferred to the Jews would be marginal and not cultivable, and that they would have the right to till them.

33. The bitter villagers were always criticizing the government for the hasty manner in which the Demarcation Line was established. As one interviewed notable said: "If it was the borders on the East Bank they would relate to it quite differently. Here it was not theirs. They could not care less so long as they achieved an agreement with Israel. The Jordanian officials came to our village only after the Agreement was signed. They did not understand maps and scales and that is why they had to give up even unoccupied territories".

34. For the full text see *Filastin,* 6.8.49.

35. The Islamic Christian Association with Fransis Albina as their Secretary, see *Ibid,* 2.10.52.

36. Nablus leaders also met the Iraqis in an attempt to prevent their withdrawal, see *Filastin,* 25.5.49.

37. A large "Convention" took place on 14.12., in Na'lin village, in which, it was reported, representatives of 57 villages of the Lydda-Ramallah areas participated. The delegates sent a group to thank Abdullah on behalf of "The Western part of his Kingdom" for his deeds for the Palestinians. (*Ramallah Radio,* 25.12.48). A meeting in Ramallah that included refugees and non-refugees from the neighbouring towns and villages supported the Jericho Conference resolutions and condemned the "falsified and distorted propaganda" coming from other Arab countries alleging the opposite. The Bir Saba' bedouin expressed their loyalty to the King and condemned their town's mayor who, from Cairo, announced his opposition to the union. (*Ramallah Radio,* 26/29.12.48).

38. For further details see *Mideast Mirror,* a review of the week prepared by the Arab News Agency, Bulletins May 13–August 19, 1950. For Jordan's position see Dr Shurayqi's words on *Ramallah Radio,* 17.5.50.

39. See the official commentary on the refugees' rights and the Palestinian Problem, transmitted by the Ramallah Station and presented in full in *Filastin,* daily on the 8/10/11/12/14/15 March, 1950.

40. *Sawt al-Khalil* (Voice of Hebron) (weekly, Hebron) first year, No. 3, dated 15.3.50, p. 19. (The weekly was owned and edited by Ja'bari. The petition represented the land owners of New Jerusalem, Ramleh, Lydda, Negev, Gaza area, Faluja al-Majdal and sixteen Frontier Villages (FV) from the Hebron area. A month later the newspaper praised the idea behind the Jericho Conference and denounced the Arab leaders as deceivers who allowed the towns of Palestine to fall and their inhabitants to be exiled (16.4.50).)

41. *Filastin,* 9.5.50.

42. For example, that in *Filastin* of 20.3.50 by Farid Nasir "We want the Unity and the Equality" and that by Abd al-Hafiz Muhammad of the Haifa and Galilee

Refugee Committee entitled "Voices of the Refugees: The Solution on the Jordan Banks (*difaf*)", *Ibid*, 10.6.50.

43. Arif wrote that Abdullah sent, via his officers, the text of the cables he wished the refugees to send to the Arab League and that they refused to send them, *al-Nakbah, op. cit.*, p. 1113–4. *Filastin* (daily) was closed by the authorities for 18 days after the Ba'thist Kamal Nasir suggested in a leading article that the cables and letters sent reflected the pressure exerted by the regime on their senders, rather than their own will. The newspaper was allowed to appear on 15.1.50.

44. For example: Karamah Camp had refugees originating from 104 different places in Palestine; Tulkarm–80; Arrub–52; Dahaysha–36; Mu'askar (the Jewish Quarter of Jerusalem, later transferred to Anata-Shu'fat)–48 places (about a third of the camp inhabitants were non-refugees). More cohesive camps were those of Ayda which was built practically for the Bani Hasan thirteen villages and Bayt Jibrin situated opposite it, set up for the Azzah families after which the small camp is named. (Since these were small adjacent camps UNRWA tried to amalgamate the two in 1953 but each camp preferred to retain its own elected committee and *mukhtars*).

45. I.C.R.C. and L.R.C.S. working as the UNRPR.

46. S.A. JUPR. Letters from the Jericho Regional Officer (R.O.) (Ministry of Interior) to the Committee's Secretary, No. KHN/14/886–3, dated 19.11.49.

47. *Ibid*. A letter to that effect to the Iraqi Governor challenging the authority of the local Committee and the Central Committee of Nablus, dated 16.9.48. Consequently 10 refugees representing 10 different neighbouring villages and bedouin tribes were nominated by him to form a committee. (Letter T/20/2 dated 29.9.48).

48. *Ibid*, a petition from the Tulkarm refugee committee directed to the Governor.

49. *Ibid*, a letter from the *mukhtar* of Bayt Lid who protested against the fact that his people received no relief whilst a number of local people received help they were not entitled to.

50. In the course of the field research many former members of these committees were interviewed and most of them stressed this as their main function.

51. See Gabriel Baer, *ha-Mukhtar ha-Kafri be-Eretz Israel* (The Village mukhtar in Palestine) (Hebrew), The Harry S. Truman Institute, The Hebrew University of Jerusalem (Jerusalem 1978), pp. 19–25. This work is primarily based on unpublished Jordanian records.

52. For the *mukhtar's* duties under the British Mandate, see Village Administration Ordinance, No. 23 of 1944, Supplement No. 1, *The Palestine Gazette*. No. 1352 of 17.8.44, Chapter 5.

53. Yoram Ben Porath and Emanuel Marx, *Some Sociological and Economic Aspects of Refugee Camps on the West Bank*. A report prepared under a grant from the Ford Foundation and published by the Rand Corporation, R–835–FF, August 1971, p. 23. This important paper provides a social and economic analysis of the camps, in particular that of Jalazun, which is essential to an understanding of the dynamics of the camps' development. The study, conducted in 1967–8, and later expanded, was published (October 1974) in a book by the Shiloah Institute of the Tel Aviv University. This work, entitled *Mahaneh Plitim be-Gav he-Har* (A refugee camp on the hillock) (Hebrew) contains, in addition, a political analysis written by Shimon Shamir which provides an indispensable perspective for studying the refugees' political views and attitudes on a wide range of questions relating to their problem.

54. S.A. JUPR. Refugee *mukhtar* Affairs 1949–59. Truman Centre Papers, N15–12 (1802)—conflicts and protests in the Tulkarm area.

55. S.A. JUPR File KH29/15, Letter to R.O. signed by three refugees.

56. Protest signed by the *mukhtars* of Tall al-Safi, Dhikrin and others who said the committee members there were self-appointed, and did not represent the camp's inhabitants (*Ibid,* dated 10.12.50).

57. The one of Dar al-Hijrah, *Filastin,* 20/22.1.49. In Askar Camp, for example, the authorities and the local Nablus refugee committee wanted a certain person to lead the camp committee. The refugees rejected the man for they did not consider him a "real refugee", as he had originally come from the Nablus area and only worked in Haifa (later he became a teacher in that camp). Consequently the refugee leaders were arrested and the governor had his way (*Ibid,* 1.11.50). Ridwan al-Hilu a prominent communist from Jaffa and member of the refugee committee in question, was arrested at that time. (Interview held with him in Jericho on 5.2.74).

58. *Sawt al-Laji'in* (Voice of the Refugees), Nablus, 3.10.49, p. 10. The paper was affiliated to the Muslim Brotherhood.

59. S.A. JUPR. Truman Papers (103), Report No. (220.201.50).

60. S.A. JUPR. File KH/29/16, Truman papers, (220.101.40) (AII). The Hebron D.G. reported his refusal on 22.8.49, and said that the intention of those who applied for the licence was "ill minded".

61. A report by the Secretary of the World Alliance of the YMCA written in 1959 and entitled *Survey Report on Activities for Idle Youth in Refugee Camps in the Middle East (prepared for UNRWA),* said that in Jordan, more than anywhere else in the Middle East, UNRWA failed to give any direction "to the young men who will be the refugee leaders of the future", (p. 1). It also stressed the government's unease at the establishment of youth clubs in the camps, fearing they would turn into a source of political agitation. Later, such clubs were opened but functioned under constant surveillance. This policy goes back to 1950, when the Jordanian Government was not enthusiastic about the YMCA's proposal to open refugee clubs, fearing their use by subversive elements. Smith, E. Fraser, *Report on the Provisions of Y.M.C.A. Clubs for Young Men among the Palestine Refugees*—from the unpublished records of the YMCA Archives, Geneva.

62. For the full text of the resolution, which sheds some light on the G.R.C.'s intentions to appear as a separate body in all negotiations on the refugee problem, see Appendix No. 3. (The text was typed from the original by courtesy of Aziz Shihadah who has the unpublished G.R.C. records at his disposal and who certified the document on 30.1.75).

63. Not all representatives remained there. Others joined throughout the Conference. The G.R.C. was represented by: Hawari, Shihadah, Nasib Bulus and Zaki Barakat—who replaced Yahya Hamudah when he withdrew owing to pressure from the Ba'th Party (Hawari, p. 351), and who himself resigned later, indirectly supporting the merger (*Filastin,* 19.7.49). The A.H.C. was represented by: Isa Nakhalah, joined later by Yusuf Sahyun and Raja' al-Husayni (Hawari, p. 355). "The Jaffa-Lydda Large Property and Orange Groves Owners"— refugees living in Lebanon—were represented by Sa'id Biyadis, Farid Azar, Farid al-Jalad, Edmond Bayruti and Ahmad Abd al-Rahim (*Filastin* 3.5.49). Shukri al-Taji al-Faruqi, appeared as the representative of the "Land Owners and Real Interests in Palestine" (*Ibid,* 9/16.9.49).

64. For the composition of the Jordanian delegation see Hawari, p. 354. Hawari said that Abd al-Ghani al-Karmi—Abdullah's messenger to talks with the Jewish Agency—was selected too.

65. From a debate on the reasons for the failure of the talks—an Israeli Television programme dedicated to the Rhodes and Lausanne discussions transmitted on 29.5.75. The participants included those who were involved in the talks: Gershon Avner, Eliyahu Eilat, Walter Eytan, Eliyahu Sasson, Yehoshu'a Palmon and

Aziz Shihadah. See also Eytan's article "The Lesson from Talks with the Arabs" in *Ma'ariv*, daily, Tel Aviv (Hebrew) 19.9.71. For a detailed account on the Conference—see Rony E. Gabbay, *A Political Study of the Arab-Jewish Conflict. The Arab Refugee Problem (a case study)* (Droz, Geneva 1959), pp. 240–67; and the UNCCP *General Progress Report and Supplementary Report*, G. A. Supp. No. 18 (A/1367/Rev. 1).

66. Yehushu'a Palmon "Mi Hem ha-Tsdadim Basihsuh Israel-Arav" (Who are the parties in the Arab-Israel Conflict) (Hebrew) in *Molad* Tel Aviv, No. 217, September 1968, p. 29. For additional details see Jon Kimche's article in *The Palestine Post* (later to be renamed *The Jerusalem Post*), 15.7.49., "Power Patterns at Lausanne" and his other articles covering the Conference. Also *The Economist* 27.9.49.

67. *Filastin*, 20.7.49. Hawari, pp. 389, 491–2, and interview *op. cit.* Many charges were made against him. The G.R.C. cabled him to return to Ramallah as they were dissatisfied with the way he was running things (*Voice of the Refugees*, 2.10.49., p. 7). He came eventually to his home town, Nazareth, after receiving permission from the Israeli authorities, but not before he was jailed in Syria after trying to organize a number of refugee gatherings there and in Lebanon, against the wishes of their Governments. On 16.12.49. he was "expelled" from the G.R.C. according to its Council's decision, (*Filastin*, 30.12.49).

68. No. 10/1, September 1949.

69. *Filastin*, 20.9.49.

70. *Voice of the Refugees* of 3.10.49 attacked the Arab regimes who betrayed the Palestinians and continued to ignore them, and accused those Governments whose conflicts had contributed to the refugee plight.

71. For the full text see *Filastin*, 14/17.8.49. Compare with al-Arif *al-Nakbah*, pp. 1097–8.

72. *Filastin*, 15.10.49.

73. For the original Press communiqué which contained these resolutions signed by members of the Executive Committee, see Appendix No. 4.

74. S.A. JUPR in an answer to an invitation signed by Khalid Ali al-Halabi, the Secretary of the Preparation Committee; the D.G. did not allow the Congress organized by his group to take place on 3.6.49. Letter KH/29/15/651 dated 1.6.49. The rejection triggered off more applications, and on 30.6 a licence was issued, KH29/15–1149, 115.

75. *Ibid*, File KH/29/1/7/1, entitled *Dustur Mu'tamar al-Laji'in fi Liwa al-Khalil* (The Constitution of the Refugee Congress in the Hebron Area).

76. *Ibid*. The executive included representatives from the areas of Bayt Jibrin, al-Faluja, al-Masmiyyah, Lydda and Ramleh, Wadi al-Sarar and the bedouin tribes.

77. Set up in 20.8.49 (Contr. 794/58, No. 25).

78. The short-lived united committee was called the Central Displaced Committee in the Nablus area. For further reading on its failure see *Filastin*, 18.5.50.

79. S.A. JUPR. Code dated 20.8.49.

80. A notice from Muhammad Kamal al-Huquqi who reported that the refugees in Irbid were trying to organise themselves in *Majallat al-Urdunn al-Jadid*, Amman, Vol. 1, No. 1, 10.2.50., p. 10. This weekly had, at first, a small column for refugee affairs in the East Bank which ceased after the fourth issue. The paper was edited by Abd al-Rahman al-Kurdi and existed only for a short time.

81. *Filastin*, 11.5.50.

82. For example, the local refugee committee in the remote Bala'a village set up in February 1950, approved by the authorities four months later. (S.A. JUPR. Letters T/8/2/8010 and T/19/12 of 26.6.50. to Sayf al-Din al-Nasir, the committee's chairman elect).

174   THE PALESTINIAN REFUGEES IN JORDAN

83. For the full text see *Filastin,* 7.9.49.
84. *Filastin,* 13.2.50.
85. *Ibid,* 21.2.50.
86. *Ibid,* 22.2.50.
87. *Voice of the Refugees,* 3.10.49., No. 7, p. 5.
88. See *Filastin,* 9.9.49., 4.12.49.
89. 9.9.49., No. 4, p. 4. Another article in that paper spoke about the corrupted, reactionary and so-called refugee leadership in Syria which also tried to control refugee affairs for their benefit. (*Ibid,* 3.10.49., p. 8).
90. *al-Muqawamah,* 1/8. Similarly the Ba'th blamed the refugees' apathy and egoism as a reason for their having an ineffectual leadership. See Kamal Nasir's articles "A Palestinian bloc . . . would speak in the name of the people", and "If I was a Leader" in *Filastin,* 13/14.10.49.
91. They operated also from Lebanon (Nablus A.C.'s report on Shafiq al-Hut who sent a petition to the U.S.S.R. on the 21.12.50 demanding its action against the annexation (No. TSH/422/N/11082 dated 12.3.52).)
92. An article in *Filastin,* 6.10.49 attacked the Egyptian Government for its estrangement from the *Urubah* and its attitude towards the sons of Palestine, whose honour was being trampled on.
93. Khulusi al-Khayri, former Director of the Arab Office in Washington to Minister of Agriculture and Commerce; Dr Yusuf Haykal, the Jaffa Mayor, and Edmond Rok, an editor from that town, to Ambassadorial posts in Washington and Rome; Ahmad Tawfiq al-Khalil, a Haifa Judge to Samaria Governor and Head of the Armistice Commission in 1949; Sa'id Ala' al-Din to a Minister. Others were nominated to the Senate, like al-Faruqi from Ramleh, & Husayn Raghib Khawajah from Dhuhayriyah (near Lydda).
94. Muhammad Hasan Lahham (Bayt Itab) (Interview held in Dahaysha Camp, 21.2.74.), Anwar Nusayba (interview, *op. cit.*), Hazim Nusayba (interview in Jerusalem on 7.2.75) and others.
95. Sa'id Ala' al-Din, a refugee from Ramleh who served four times as a Minister, said: "It was a temporary policy at the time to nominate a refugee Minister in the government. They wanted the refugees to be represented". He was an educated refugee and above all his family was known to be identified with the Mufti, therefore his nomination also aimed at weakening the A.H.C. (Interview with him in Jerusalem, 2.2.75.). Anwar al-Khatib, who served in the Jordanian Government said that Ala' al-Din and Khayri were selected because the Government had to include, in these early years, ministers who were refugees, and they were the best choice for the monarch. Hasan Darwish said his father, Abd al-Fattah, was offered the post of a minister twice because he was a refugee leader and represented a large portion of the refugees in the Bethlehem-Bayt Jala area. (Interview in Bayt Jala on 20.1.75).
96. Sa'id Ala' al-Din recalled that he was never even consulted on refugee affairs in the Government, although it was only natural that many refugees approached him for assistance.
97. Interviewed refugees supplied the following answers: "We who ended up in the West Bank wanted to be on good terms with the new rulers on whom we depended for good or for evil, for our basic needs, defence and food . . . the Mufti was far away and could do nothing . . . we had no say in our future . . . we couldn't care less, we were hungry . . . it was the only course we could take . . . we just could not stand up alone . . . there was a general feeling it was the right thing to do . . . at the time it seemed the only step we could support" (findings from field research held in West Bank).

Chapter II

1. Anwar Nusayba, the former A.P.G. Secretary elected as M.P., surprised the House when he advocated a delay in the process of acknowledgement. *al-Jil al-Jadid,* the Ba'th Party's weekly published in Ramallah, detailed at length the argument among the M.P.s concerning the issue. 1.5.50., from *N.E.,* July 1950, p. 303.
2. It seems that Tawfiq Abu al-Huda and Samir al-Rifa'i were regarded as Palestinians in the allocation of seats. (Ne'eman, *Abdallah's Kingdom, op. cit.* p. 73).
3. See Aziz Shihadah, "The Purposes of Jordanian Legislation in the West Bank" in *N.E.,* Vol. 20, 1970, pp. 166–70. For a more moderate view see E. Theodore Mogannam "Developments in the Legal System of Jordan" in *Middle East Journal* Vol. 6, (1952), pp. 194–206, and a Jordanian publication, *The Hashimite Kingdom of Jordan* written by Hanna Naddeh (Amman) 1973. The constitution was published in the Official Gazette No. 1093, January 9, 1952, p. 3–15 and re-published in booklet form in 1965. For English translation see *M.E.J.,* pp. 228–39.
4. This subject is discussed below in detail (see "Underground political activity and its confrontation"—Ch. VII.)
5. Compare Shimon Shamir, Rina Shapira, Eli Reches, Shira Tibon, Israel Shtockman, *The Professional Elite in Samaria* (Hebrew), the Shiloah Institute, Tel Aviv University (Tel Aviv, May 1975).
6. Preferring certain traditional leaders over other refugee spokesmen whose influence as mediators they wished to weaken, the authorities issued invitations once in a while to certain people to come and meet one of the Ministers as a "representative" of the area refugees. For example, S.A. JUPR. File T/20/1/2, letter dated 14.1.53., R.O. to Shaykh Shakir Abu Kishk to meet the Minister of Welfare in Nablus as the Tulkarm Refugee representative, blatantly ignoring the other more prominent refugee leaders.
7. See the discussion on different groups of Palestinian Refugee bourgeoisie in Pamela Ann Smith's "Aspects of Class Structure in Palestinian Society 1948–67" in *Israel and the Palestinians,* Uri Davis, Andrew Mack and Nira Yuval-Davis (eds.) (Ithaca Press, London 1975) pp. 98–118 (fn. 1).
8. Compare Don Peretz, *Palestinian Social Stratification—The Political Implications,* a paper presented to the International Conference on the Palestinians and the M.E. Conflict held in Haifa University, Israel, 1976.
9. See Na'im Sofer "The Integration of Arab Palestine in the Jordan Kingdom" (Hebrew) in *N.E.,* Vol. VI, No. 3 (23), 1955, pp. 89–196.
10. For further reading see Isa al-Nauri's article "al-Harakah al-Adabiyyah fi al-Urdunn" an *al-Urdunn al-Hadith Majmu'at Maqalat* (Modern Jordan: a collection of articles) (Amman 1972), pp. 187–191. Sawwan al-Jasir and Na'man Abu Basm in *al-Urdunn wa Mu'amarat al-Isti'mar* (Jordan and the Imperialist Conspiracies) (Cairo 1957) also examined some of the positive impacts of the annexation (which the authors condemned) on the Trans-Jordanian element: for example, the development of education, the growth of working-class consciousness, development of a student movement and the influence ideological parties had on the poor backward Trans-Jordanians (p. 21).
11. Ibrahim Walwil, Kafar Saba's *mukhtar,* said that a number of Trans-Jordanians used to work in his village up to the 1948 war, and so some of the Kafar Saba and Qalqilya people left for the East Bank. (Interview in Qalqilya on 12.3.74.)
12. Ayn Karim Christians settled at first in Bayt Jala, Bethlehem and Bayt Sahur. Later most of them moved to Amman housing Jabal al-Taji and Jabal al-Hashimi quarters. (Fransis Rahil (Ayn Karim), interview in Bethlehem, 1.7.74.).

13. According to the UNRWA unpublished map *Geographical Distribution of Refugees Eligible for Assistance in The Hashimite Kingdom of Jordan,* Scale 1: 125,000, prepared by the Engineering Branch of UNRWA, Jordan, in June 1954, (amended in 1959), the percentage of the West Bank migrants amongst the refugees equalled that of natural population increase (see Appendix No. 10). For statistical details concerning the rate of migration and emigration from the West Bank see U. Schmeltz's article, "Demographic Development of the Arab Countries" in *N.E.,* Vol. XXIII, No. 1 (89) 1973, pp. 29–46.

14. The Majalis' originated from that town in the eighteenth century. For further reading see Peter Gubser *Politics and Change in al-Karak, Jordan,* (London 1973), pp. 15, 27, 67–8.

15. Henry Knezevitz recalled that in 1953 UNRWA had to transfer 13 families of refugees back to the Nablus area and reinstate them on the ration lists, after the Majalis', who had previously agreed to allow them to cultivate some land for their mutual benefit under the responsibility of the Agency, had demanded, through Glubb, that they be evacuated. (Interview in Bethlehem on 27.1.75).

16. William Clark, UNRWA Representative in Jordan 1953–9. (Interview held in Reading, England, 3.12.73.).

17. Interview, *op. cit.*

18. Shaykh Muhammad Khalil Frayjat (interview held in the Ramadin tribelands in San' al-Jabiri on 20.2.74.).

19. Calls in this spirit were aired at the first economic congress organized jointly by the Palestine Chamber of Commerce and the Palestine Trade Committee held in Ramallah in April 1949. (*al-Jazirah,* daily, Amman 28.3./10.4.49.) The West Bankers continually hoped to receive the promised government assistance— see *al-Nashrah al-Iqtisadiyyah* (Economic and Social News) weekly, Arabic and English, edited by Yusuf Rabat, Amman, 27.6.50. edition, p. 1. The Minutes of the Congress of the Association of Chambers of Commerce held in Ramallah on 11.1.51. in which most West Bank personalities took part, repeated the demand for an immediate change in the government's West Bank economic policy. The resolutions called for paving roads, allocating money for development projects which could offer vast employment opportunity, transferring governmental departments to the West Bank, supporting the municipalities, industrialization, and opening a special office for West Bank's economic development. (From unpublished records of the Arab-Jerusalem Municipality, The Jerusalem Municipality Historical Archives, hereafter JMHA). File B/Z/42/1, text signed on 30.1.51. After such a unanimous expression of bitterness, the regime was reluctant to license similar gatherings.

20. Dr Richard Ward who was engaged in the economic development of Jordan on behalf of the U.S.A. in Amman as the Head of the AID, suggested that the East Bank needed the development far more than the West Bank. He felt that the economic potential was in the East and not the West Bank and this coincided with the government's approach to the Palestinian question. (Interview, Washington, D.C., 12.9.73.). Dr John Davis, the former Head of UNRWA recalled that the U.S.A. rejected any idea for economic development in the West Bank and wanted this to be done through the Jordanian Government. (Interview, Washington D.C. 12.9.73.). Most interviewed Palestinians refused to accept Dr Ward's economic assessment, suggesting that AID never paid attention to the West Bank's economic potential.

21. *Filastin,* 16.9.58 published a table of the areas in the West and East Banks against the respective amounts loaned and granted by the government in order to prove this discrimination, showing that small towns in the East Bank received approximately the same as, or more than, heavily populated towns in the West Bank.

22. The Jerusalem Christian Committee cabled the UN Secretary in support of that scheme. *Beirut Radio*, 8.8.49.
23. *Ramallah Radio*, 20.10.49.
24. *N.E.R.S.*, 22.10., 9.12.49. Wadi' Da'mas, Bayt Jala's mayor, cables to the UN. Isa Bandak, Bethlehem's mayor, was sent to Greece to meet the authorities, and, on behalf of the King, vouched for the safety of all Greek Churches and their congregations. *(Ibid,* 30.11.49). A number of cables were sent by Nablus people opposing the internationalization to Ahmad Shuqayri, at that time Syria's representative in the UN. *(N.E.R.S.,* 3.12.49). Special prayers were held in al-Aqsa mosque together with religious speeches (*Khutbah*) sanctioning the plan plus large meetings in Jerusalem condemning such a step. (*Ramallah Radio*, 9.12.49).
25. *Ibid*, 21.10.49.
26. Arif al-Arif presented the King with this request on 1.12.50. In 1956 Abd al-Muhsin Abu Mayzar, suggested a draft resolution against the government's policy of transferring the Education Department of UNRWA to Amman. He maintained it would harm the economy of the town the King regarded as a second capital. (JMHA, *Minutes of the Jerusalem Municipality 1956,* No. 380). In his 1956 election campaign Kamil Ariqat demanded in his extensive platform that Jerusalem be instated as Jordan's second capital. A year earlier such a call was expressed by Nablus refugees—see the part on Refugee Separatism, Ch. III, below.
27. Jon and David Kimche in *A Clash of Destinies—the Arab-Jewish War and the Founding of the State of Israel* (N.Y., 1960) maintained that Abdullah even changed the Arab invasion plan because he aspired to Jerusalem (p. 150). See Abdullah *al-Takmilah, op. cit.* pp. 88–90, 94–8.
28. The murder was followed by the "Arab Army" troops' frenzied and vicious attacks, in which people were seriously wounded and shops and stalls were smashed and robbed. (From the examined lists of claims for damages presented for compensation, it seems that the army caused severe damage to the businesses in town—found in JMHA). The whole affair left its mark on the Palestinians who have feared the unleashed ruthlessness of the Legion ever since.
29. On the occasion of the American Secretary of State, John Foster Dulles' visit to Jordan in 1953.
30. S.A. JUPR. Letters B/B/39/1/4 dated 2.2.50 from the Mayor of Jerusalem who reminded the Minister of the Interior that "Jerusalem is the first town in the West Bank and the centre of all religions and sects, the next in importance to Amman". He claimed that Jerusalem could only gain from such a transfer. A similar letter was sent by the Arab Chamber of Commerce, Jerusalem, to UNRWA Headquarters in Lebanon dated 21.12.50. (JMHA B/B/31/1369. I. Ref. No. CC/52/756). Similar protests appeared in the Press: a memorandum signed by 14 Palestinian M.P.s demanded that Jerusalem become an administrative centre for all the West Bank, with branches of all Government offices. *al-Hayat,* daily, Beirut 2.8.52. Also: *al-Difa',* 4.2.54; *Filastin,* 4/19/21/24.2.55; *al-Bilad,* 7.2.55 recorded a petition from a delegation of merchants in the newspaper's office; *al-Jihad,* 25.6., 14.8.55; *al-Difa',* 31.5., 4/15.6.56, 29/30.7.56.
    UNRWA's Area Officer (A.O.) Henry Knezevitz said that in 1952 he was asked to select three houses in Jerusalem, for the suggested transfer of UNRWA's Middle East H.Q. In so far as UNRWA was interested in a transfer there, it could not ignore the better facilities and conditions given by the Lebanese Government or the fact that the Jordanian regime wanted the Headquarters only in Amman. Shortly afterwards UNRWA abandoned the idea as it also felt politically more secure in Lebanon (Interview in Bethlehem 16.3.76).
31. Jean Chapirot said that when he joined UNRWA as Area Supervisor he

confronted many problems due to the fact that the government insisted that all essential UNRWA offices be situated in Amman, whilst 75 per cent of the refugees were in the West Bank. He said that Glubb arranged for the Agency to use the Police School in the Jerusalem "No Man's Land" area (which the Jordanians could not use) providing UNRWA repaired it. This big building enabled them to transfer a number of offices later, although the regime was unhappy about it. (Interview in Jerusalem, 10.9.74). The refugees naturally supported such action as it was extremely difficult for them to travel to Amman to protest against the Agency and arrange their business.
32. See Eli'ezer Be'eri, *ha-Palestinim Tahat Shilton Yarden-Shalosh Sugiyot* (The Palestinians under Jordanian Rule, three issues), (Hebrew), The Harry S. Truman Research Institute, The Hebrew University of Jerusalem (Jerusalem 1978), p. 54. In his work which is based on unpublished Jordanian records, Be'eri maintains that, for the ten years up to the 1962 election campaign, he found no trace of a Palestinian demand for unique political status for Jerusalem (apart from the complaints listed above), and that even at the P.L.O. Congress which was held in Jerusalem in 1964, there was no discussion of the town's position (p. 62).
33. JMHA, Letter to the Governor of Jerusalem signed by the Mayor Umar al-Wa'ari, dated 15.8.55, containing resolution No. 1480 of the Council.
34. Be'eri, *The Palestinians, op. cit.*, pp. 14–27, 44–52.
35. See his "Regime and Opposition in Jordan since 1949" in *Society and Political Structure in the Arab World*, edited by Menahem Milson (Humanities Press, Jerusalem) 1974, p. 146. This work, which categorizes the various pro- and anti-establishment elements, contributes to a better understanding of the political developments in Jordan.
36. The main theme of his work entitled "The Jordanian Entity in changing Circumstances, 1967–73", Occasional Papers Series, The Shiloah Centre for Middle Eastern and African Studies, Tel Aviv University (August 1974).
37. *Ibid*, p. 2.

Chapter III

1. S.A. JUPR File T/20/1, Tulkarm Governor, letter dated 23.10.48, concerning refugees in Taybah.
2. Announcement No. 16 of the Press and Publication Bureau in Amman co-signed by Ministers Sulayman Sukar, Khulusi al-Khayri and Musa Nasir, who was also the Head of the Supreme Refugee Committee, following their discussions with the U.N.E.S.M. members—see *Filastin* 3.8.49. The Iraqi Governor of Samaria ordered the registration of the youngsters there who were causing him security problems through their idleness— see *Ibid* 27.2.49. Announcement No. 51 following the release of a number of detainees.
3. Jerusalem's D.G. notified the Jericho R.O. to tell the refugees who were anxious about the economic situation that the Government was doing everything in its capacity to better their conditions and preserve their rights. S.A. JUPR. Letter ML/57/49/2882, December 1951.
4. S.A. JUPR. File ML/274/50 from Ramallah R.O. to Jerusalem D.G. dated 30.1.51.
5. *Ibid*, signed by Bethlehem R.O., No. B/50/34 dated 3.2.51, confiscating 200 *dunam* from the Enemy's Property.
6. *Ibid*, Ramallah R.O. report QR/50–708, dated 14.2.51.
7. *Ibid*, Tulkarm R.O. report T/20/1/1/360 dated 8.2.51.

8. *Ibid*, Cable to all A.C.'s to notify the camp Police Station Commanders (A) Q3/6/33329 dated 6.8.52.
9. *Ibid*, Report by Nablus D.G. to Minister of Interior, No. 114/1/1602 dated 17.2.54. A refugee was imprisoned for three months after beating up an UNRWA local senior official, report No. MKHT/637/53 dated 19.10.52. The Government was very sensitive to such occasional incidents.
10. *Ibid*, File titled "Police in Refugee Camps" report JT/246/133 of 24.1.54. The Bethlehem D.G. added to the expenses those spent on the new Police Station which he claimed he was forced to open in Bayt Sahur and Bayt Jala "owing to the high number of refugees living there" and advised the Minister of Interior to demand J.D. 5,000 from UNRWA for that item. 1954 report, signed by the D.G. No. B/50/34/19 dated 11.1.55.
11. S.A. JUPR Report No. KH/29/483 from R.O. to D.G. The total expense J.D. 1,840 and D.O. Minister of Interior, KH29/1753 dated 6.2.55, total costs J.D. 2,000.
12. *Ibid*.
13. *Ibid*, report No. MKH/20/28/986 dated 17.2.60. Top Secret to Head of Secret Police.
14. See Appendix No. 1.
15. See *al-Jaridah al-Rasmiyyah* (The Official Gazette), 1.2.50, No. 1009, p. 48.
16. See *ibid*, Sa'id al-Mufti on 16.10.50, p. 606; Samir al-Rifa'i on 4.12.50, p. 678.
17. Passports for Palestinians were granted under article No. 3 as opposed to article No. 1 (granted to citizens of Trans-Jordanian origin) and were therefore immediately distinguishable.
18. Infrequent articles, for example by M.P. Abd al-Qadir al-Salih, protested against the government's discriminatory policy against the West Bank which caused the emigration of its best forces. (*Filastin*, 8.6.52). See also an article in *al-Difa'*, 2.10.53.
19. For a moving description of the refugees' life in Lebanon, see Fawaz Turki, *The Disinherited, Journal of a Palestinian Exile* (N.Y., 1972).
20. A political weekly published in Amman owned by and edited by Mustafa al-Tahir. The article was published in Vol. 1, No. 25, dated 21.5.53. (From Israel Shtokman Collection, Jerusalem).
21. See also *N.E.R.S.*, 4.1.53, 27.1.53, 17.30 hours.
22. See *al-Hayat*, Beirut, 23.9.53.
23. See *al-Jaridah al-Rasmiyyah*, No. 1171, dated 16.2. 54.
24. As one interviewed man put it, "The Jews allowed unification of families, the Jordanians gave the Passport and the Arab League gave the words". See also *al-Sharq*, Lebanon, 15.3.55.
25. See Goren, *The Arab League, op. cit.*, p. 213.
26. According to a letter sent from the League's Secretariat to the Jordanian Government, the League knew very little about the refugee situation in Jordan. The letter requested basic details on such matters as numbers of refugees, health and relief affairs, Police and security problems. Arab League paper, No. FL/10/19 dated 26.9.54. S.A. JUPR.
27. See *Filastin*, 24.3.54 for the general position of the Iraqi Government regarding the issuing of a unified Arab passport for the Palestinian refugees. Also *Iraq Times*, 6.5.54. Iraq expelled refugees who were allegedly engaged in Communist subversion activities, *N.E.R.S.*, 12.2.56, 17.30 hours. *al-Masa'*, Egypt 23.2.57, Ramallah Radio, 17.4.57, 21.00 hours. The Arab Federation set up in January 1958 between Jordan and Iraq was expected to allow Jordanian emigration into Iraq. (*Filastin*, 22.6.58). When Qasim overthrew the monarchy in Iraq in July that year and took over, smashing the Arab Federation, a new era began. Nevertheless, his attitudes towards the Palestinians in Iraq seemed to be quite

positive. But it was not long before news items on refugees protesting against their treatment appeared. See *al-Fajr al-Jadid,* Iraq, 9.8.59.

28. For more details on the complaints of Palestinians in Kuwait concerning the antagonism between the Government and the people there, see *al-Difa'*, 7.3.55, 7.11.55; *Filastin,* 6.1.56; *al-Jihad,* 24.6.56. *al-Mussawar,* weekly, Cairo, 22.8.58 claimed that in 1958 there were some 18,000 Palestinians in Kuwait. That year witnessed an agreement between that country and Jordan which would "export" 200 teachers (*al-Difa'*, 10.8.58). Yet owing to the numerous Palestinians arriving illegally into Kuwait, the Government there decided to restrict the immigration (*al-Ahram,* 28.12.58). *Filastin* 12/13.1.60 announced the revision of this policy causing many to leave Jordan and enter Kuwait and all other neighbouring countries. For further reading see Moshe Efrat, *The Palestinian Refugees: A Social and Economic Study 1949–1974* (Hebrew) published by the David Horowitz Institute for the Research of Developing Countries, Tel Aviv University, September 1976.

29. Saudi Arabia notified Lebanon it would not admit refugees to enter the *hajj* as many had remained illegally during the previous year. See *Filastin,* 8.9.51.

30. Dated 21.6.55 in an open letter to the Minister of Interior signed by a "citizen". Also in *al-Difa'*, 28.11.55.

31. See *al-Jihad,* 3.10.57 and decree No. 3844 of 1958. *al-Jihad,* 5.11.58 widely publicized a very detailed law which explained the Government's entitlement to withdraw her citizenship from disloyal elements.

32. See *Amman Radio*, 25.8.59 and *Beirut Radio,* 25.8.58, 20.00 hours.

33. *Filastin,* 10.10.52.

34. *Ibid,* 25.3.52, 17.5 and 1.7.53. Ramallah refugees asked for such identity cards to be recognized by the Arab countries instead of passports, when moving around the Arab world. UNRWA announced its inability to issue such a document as it would not coincide with its definitions—See Press communiqué in *Ibid,* 6.9.53.

35. The Minister of Interior, Order No. 67 of 1954, 16–17–3576 dated 8.4.53 to all D.G.'s noted the Government's decision of 1.4.53. However, they later allowed refugees with frozen assets to go ahead with the applications, knowing that the money would be invested in Jordan. Agreement over the assets was reached in 1953/4, with refugees from the G.R.C. negotiating directly with Israel. The process of release continued through the 1950s. The Government thus gradually rid itself of some loudly critical elements, who nevertheless occasionally still signed petitions to prove their loyalty and to show that they had not been bought off.

36. On 3.6.54 the government agreed to allow refugees to sign the application forms (Ministry of Interior Order No. 95, 16/17/5467 dated 17.6.53, p. 4). For further reading on the subject of compensation and the Arab property in Israel see The Arab League, the Secretariat General, Palestine Administration—the Refugee Branch, *The Arab Property and their frozen Assets in Occupied Palestine* (Arabic) edited by Ya'qub al-Khuri, n.p.n.d.; Don Peretz's article "Problems of Arab Refugee Compensation" in *M. E. J.* No. 4, 1954, pp. 403–16; R. Gabbay, *A Political Study, op. cit.,* pp. 341–73 and others.

37. For full text see *Filastin,* 29.9.54. "We were cheated" cried *Filastin,* 20.3.55, "We followed the Arab politicians who told us we'll chuck the last of the Jews into the Mediterranean Sea . . . and we the Palestinian Arabs were thrown instead into the desert" and a column in 15.3.55 edition entitled "We . . . the sons of Palestine" says "We are your victims, the victims of your treaties, the victims of your egoism and selfishness". And again on 30.3.55.

38. They also demanded two refugees on every town council. (Report MN/17/1/1137 dated 14.6.55). The organiser of the Nablus petitions throughout the period was

Amin al-Qasim, whom the Jordanian reports suggest to have been a smooth operator liked by neither the refugees nor the authorities. In actual fact, he was not a refugee at all and came from Burqa village, near Nablus. Report MN/45/16810 from Nablus Secret Police to A.C. dated 18.9.56 and Report MN/20/28/6927 dated 15.11.60.

39. The subject of refugee demonstrations is discussed in Ch. VII.
40. *Filastin*, 17.8.49.
41. Yusuf Muhammad Dawlah, on 9.9.49.
42. Great Britain was never specifically mentioned in the petitions examined (apart from those relating to the refugees' frozen accounts or trade unions of former British Mandate clerks) and, since 1951, is perhaps covered by the wider title of "Imperialism".
43. *Filastin*, 9.8.49.
44. This conclusion derives from the Jordanian and Red Cross unpublished records examined by the author, as well as the Press of 1949.
45. For full text see *Filastin*, 24.10.52.
46. Interview with Rashid Ariqat, Deputy UNRWA A.O. (Jericho).
47. S.A. JUPR, Letter No. ML/274/50 dated 21.1.51.
48. S.A. JUPR. Nablus R.O. to D.G. 32/JM/S/17214, dated 3.12.51.
49. See *Filastin*, 9.2.52 for details of a meeting in Hebron the day before; and *Filastin*, 11.7.52 for a meeting in Arrub Camp.
50. S.A. JUPR, Report, Top Secret, MT/23/137/13510 dated 1.4.52.
51. *al-Jazirah*, 31.1.51, 3/9.2.51.
52. See an article "To Mr Dulles" published in *Filastin*, 14.5.53, also article and news item of the following two days. *al-Awdah* weekly revealed in its 14.5 and 21.5.53 editions that a group of prominent refugees (known to be associated with the G.R.C.), met Dulles and tried to interest him in an overall plan which included: Partition, the Return, Compensation and the internationalization of Jerusalem. They hoped it would appeal to the West whose consent to any possible solution had to be gained so that it could be enforced upon Israel. Aziz Shihadah recalled: "Pro-government elements did not want to show that inside the kingdom there were people who didn't see the Government as their representative. But we maintained that we are refugees and entitled to meet him". (Interview with him in Ramallah, 22.1.75).
53. S.A. JUPR, Report from Hebron D.G. to Minister of Interior, KH/29/4183 dated 3.11.52.
54. *Ibid*, KH/20/10/1160 dated 21.2.53 following Minister of Welfare to P.M. 6/2/173 dated 28.1.53 notifying the refugee's request and letter to Deputy Minister of Interior to all R.O.'s N D/14/52/468 of 31.1.53 requesting their opinion as to such an application.
55. On the 23/24.1.53.
56. See *Filastin*, 1.3.53.
57. S.A. JUPR, Letter from D.G. to Sa'id al-Azzah, MKHM/2/11/6716 dated 31.8.54.
58. *Ramallah Radio*, 5.7.54, 22.00 hours.
59. *N.E.R.S.*, 15.6.55, 18.30 hours, *al-Difa'*, 21.6.55.
60. Given by courtesy of A. Bakarjyan, UNRWA's Ramallah Area Officer.
61. S.A. JUPR. Robert Fisher's letter to Minister of Interior, RIL/11/1/7, 26.5.55 in the latter's 1/29/1/6665 of 8.6.55 to all D.G.'s notifying them of the arrangement of selection of refugee representatives in a way that would not cause uneasiness among refugees claiming they were not represented. Elections for delegating representatives to the conference were held in different places under the auspices of the D.Gs. A group of "communist" refugees had published an open letter entitled "To the Displaced" protesting against the gathering and the

manner in which it was about to take place. One of the A.Cs. suggested their arrest. Letter No. MKHM/3/3/10466 of 20.7.55.
62. See *Filastin,* 7.7.55.
63. Nevertheless, it seems that when the National Guidance Committee set up a sub-committee for refugees in Nablus, it got tangled up in the old rivalries over representation.
64. The Refugee Office opposed the new version and the suggested amendments were "to prevent UNRWA being a-government-within-a-government". This was useful to the authorities who did not want the new agreement.
65. For the full text of the speeches at the Congress, headed by Sa'id Ala' al-Din see *al-Jihad,* 12.1.57. The Conference also opposed the rehabilitation and resettlement projects.
66. A secret report revealed that many refugees in the Hebron area even supported the step of disallowing the functioning of the Leftist opposition political parties. (S.A. JUPR. File KHM/16/6/1, No. 3244 dated 25.4.57).
67. A report from Salfit A.C. to the Nablus Governor urged the dismissal of the local *mukhtar* "as he incites the inhabitants to demonstrate and therefore does not behave as expected for a man in his position whose duty is to assist in maintaining law and order. Moreover he does not enable others who wished to do so to suppress the communist demonstrations. A proof of his intentions is his refusal to *sign a cable which the villagers wanted to send expressing their loyalty for the King*"(my italics—A.P.) S.A. JUPR. No. 36 report dated 16.1.56, Truman papers, (p. 1644).
68. *al-Difa',* 12.11.57; the edition of 24.9.57 published refugees' condemnation of the smuggling of arms by traitors and demanded measures.
69. *al-Hayat* of 12.11.57 added that the refugees declared in one such 'congress' their readiness to join a Fedayyin Army under their King Husayn.
70. A cable from Jordanian students studying in the American University of Beirut was published, see *Ramallah Radio,* 12.5.57, 12.00 hours, also *Filastin,* 1.10.58. An unsigned poem titled "The Revolutionary Generation" read in one of the evening transmissions a year later emphasized the "Return to Palestine under the leadership of our beloved King". S.A. JUPR.
71. Report MKH/1/2/1439 dated 13.9.58 on a visit to Fawar Camp.
72. *Filastin,* 14.5.59.
73. *Ibid,* 24.7.59.
74. *al-Manar* described in length the various gatherings and "congresses" held on 24.10.60, the participants' names with all the resolutions, their gist being "only Husayn speaks in the name of the Palestinians . . . the West Bank is part of the Hashimite Kingdom of Jordan". Photographs of these "solidarity meetings" also appeared. See *al-Difa',* 12.10.61.
75. For further reading regarding al-Alami's Constructive Scheme See G. Furlonge *Palestine is my country: The story of Musa Alami.* (N.Y. 1969) pp. 167–211.
76. al-Alami was selected as Chairman, Anwar al-Khatib, Khulusi al-Khayri, Yahya Hamudah, Kamil al-Dajani and Wasfi al-Tall as members and Shaykh Mustafa al-Khayri, Shaykh Abu al-Sa'ud al-Dajani, Muhammad Tawfiq al-Yahya, Muhammad al-Abushi, Farid al-Anabtawi and Hajj Abd al-Rahim al-Nabulsi as the Council's members. (See *Filastin,* 9.8.49).
77. See photos in *Filastin* 26.10.51 of many stone houses in Far'a Camp.
78. See Farid Nasir's article "We want the Unity and the Equality" in *Filastin,* 20.3.50 and that of Abd al-Hafiz Muhammad, the Secretary of the Haifa and Galilee Committee. *Ibid,* 10.6.50. An article signed by a "nationalist" in *Hawl al-Alam,* No. 19 dated 1.5.51 titled "If I was the Development and Reconstruction Minister" reflected perhaps the refugees' expectations of the Government. The article suggested erecting model villages on Government-land on both sides of

the Jordan River for the resettlement of those refugees who wished to resettle. It further called for close Government supervision of UNRWA and a growing involvement in refugee affairs, for the defence of their interests and their transformation into useful citizens, to be incorporated into the kingdom's economic and social life. Similar articles, though not so explicit, are found in the daily Press of the 1950s. Compare with "His name is a Refugee and we call him a Native" by Aqil Sabiyyah in *al-Fikr,* weekly, Amman, No. 13, 17.12.50.

79. See also *Filastin,* 9.11.50.
80. *Ibid,* 28.10.50, Nablus D.G. promised to give refugees from Jenin and Janzur land near Qabatiya.
81. See Appendix No. 8. More land, however, was purchased by the Jews up to the 1948 war.
82. *Filastin,* 24.9.53.
83. Registration started in November 1954—S.A. JUPR. Letter from MDR 19/18/1260 dated 15.11.54. The project was closed down at the end of 1957. Letter from I. Duzdar UNRWA's Hebron A.O. to D.G., *Ibid,* 5/RI/1(859) dated 20.12.57 and reopened again. For further details concerning the complications emanating from the project consult letter from Duzdar to D.G. *Ibid,* 5/RI/I-A-2161 dated 12 July 1958—Appendix No. 6, 7.
84. S.A. JUPR. Eric Evans District Works Officer UNRWA to D.G. Hebron confirmation of discussion of 16.1.51, subject: *Integration of Refugees,* Ref.: WP/4/10D (716) dated 29.1.51.
85. Appeals from the Displaced Refugee Committee—see *Filastin* 8.8.51, 8.9.51— the Haifa Committee.
86. See full text in *Ibid* 16.8.51.
87. *Ibid* 20.9.50.
88. S.A. JUPR, a report on the visit of Heads of UNRWA in the Hebron camps, confronting a rejection by refugees to "lay a stone on a stone" and build anything anywhere apart from their occupied land. (Letter to Head of Political Department in Army Headquarters from A.C. MKH/3/11/9660 dated 4.9.51). Five days later, however, he reported that the refugees began building constructions in Arrub Camp—(report to *Ibid* MKH/3/1/9785). The Jericho R.O. requested the Agency to give wood to refugees in Ayn al-Sultan Camp, as the rain caused damage to their huts. (Letter AQ/5/55 dated 18.12.51).
89. The Government published in the Press the regulation for those joining the project. (*Filastin,* 27.8.52), which included the short-lived UNRWA tent factory that supplied tents for the camps (later the factory was given to the Legion—see *al-Jihad* 10.10.57).
90. For further details see *Filastin* 10.2.52.
91. See Articles in *al-Difa'* 29.8.56 and *al-Jihad* 30.8.56 warning the refugees against selling their ration cards.
92. See *Filastin,* 8.10.52.
93. *Ibid,* 22.10.52.
94. See *The Official Gazette,* No. 2 for 1952 or *Filastin,* 18/23.11.52.
95. S.A. JUPR, Letter from A.C. to Jerusalem D.G., BM/12/2353 dated 30.4.54. Visit by Henry Knezevitz and Halim Saba from UNRWA and the journalist Henry Waldi. This report's description of the Agency coming to find out the refugees' position is somewhat curious as the two local workers were surely well aware of the refugees' perceptions and moreover knew that one way of *not* finding out was to come with a journalist, especially a Western one. Moreover, UNRWA workers guided refugees as to the way they should behave and what should they say when Western guests visited the camp.
96. UNRWA's protest on the content of Anwar al-Khatib's interview on 10.7.53. (See *Filastin* 19.7.53).

97. For the attitudes of the political parties, see Chapter VII.
98. S.A. JUPR. Letter from Hebron D.G. to M.D.R., KH/29/5/2980 dated 4.9.56.
99. *Ibid,* M.D.R. to UNRWA request to postpone until further notice the beginning of the 400 shelters in Fawar Camp. (Letter No. 1/9/24/6/2339 dated 13.9.56). The file contains one petition against the erecting of shelters from the Hebron Area Refugee Committee dated 6.9.56. (Most members of this Committee were living outside the Camps).
100. See *Filastin,* 9.6.56.
101. Report entitled Family Shelter Data (Hebron Area). File B/50/34/2 signed by the Government and UNRWA Representatives.
102. Compare with Jack Lutsky's Housing proposal, *Refugee Housing in the Gaza Strip,* 1974, Architectural Association, two unpublished design proposals. For further reading see Ben Porat, and Marx, E., *Aspects of refugee camps, op. cit.* and Meir Zamir "Refugee Camps in Jordan, Judea and Samaria: A form of Settlement" in *Yehuda Ve-Shomron, Prakim be-Geografyah Yishuvit* (Judea and Samaria, Studies in Settlement Geography) (Hebrew), edited by Avshalom Shmueli, David Grossman and Rechavam Ze'evy, Geography Depts. of Bar-Ilan and Tel-Aviv Univs. pp. 350–63.
103. Compare previously unpublished maps of refugee camps before and after the shelter building—Appendix No. 11.
104. S.A. JUPR. File B/50/34/2, Letter from the lawyer Fu'ad Atallah who represented one of the land owners who came back from the U.S.A. to develop his property only to find his eleven *dunam* of land occupied by refugees and UNRWA intending to erect units. He claimed the refugees from al-Azzah Camp should be removed opposite the road to Ayda Camp or a few km. along it to Dahaysha Camp. Similar complaints came from the owners of the Ayda Camp land and from the Mayor Ayyub Mussalam (60/1102 and 1175 dated 18.6./10.7.60) who requested that both camps should be transferred to Dahaysha Camp.
105. Neither UNRWA nor the Jordanian Government wanted to meddle with this camp, in the form of demolishing the old former Jewish-owned houses or erect shelters in their place, as they both feared a combined Israeli and world wide Jewish reaction to such a step.
106. Tannus and Qaddurah squatters, Baytillu, Ayn Arik, Abu Shkhaydim, Bir Zayt, Ayn Misbah, Ayn Munjid and the Russian Compound. In Ayn Arik village the inhabitants refused to sell land to the refugees and demanded their evacuation. This occurred in a number of places.
107. Details from UNRWA minutes of meetings held on 18.4./1.5./21.9.61.
108. As early as 1952 the unofficial Qaddurah refugees feared they would be transferred from their site adjacent to the town of al-Bira to a remote site, and approached the Ba'thist Abdallah Rimawi to intervene on their behalf. *(Filastin,* 5.11.52). In 1967 the Jordanian Government intended removing the unofficial Qaddurah Camp, as it transferred Mu'askar to Shu'fat. UNRWA refused to take part in the act as it was not one of her official camps (Fisher to Governor of Jerusalem, ref: RE/C 854 dated 2.3.67). But the 1967 war put an end to the debate.
109. For further details on the project—see *The Times* 24.5.55.
110. In response to *al-Ahram* 24.6.57—see *al-Jihad* 27.6.57 recalling their cable to Nasser.
111. *Bulletin of the Palestine Arab Refugee Institution, Republic of Syria* 1958, p. 9. The projects were at al-Dab'ah near Hums and the Ramadan schemes. The first were evacuated by the army, and the latter by the refugees.
112. al-Mamlakah al-Urdunniyyah al-Hashimiyyah *Mashru' al-Ghur al-Sharqi* (Amman, 1.6.62).

113. *Taqrir an Mashru' Qanat al-Ghur al-Sharqiyyah wa madha Ya'ni Laka?* (The East Ghur Canal Project and what does it mean to you?) A colourful booklet published by the East Ghur Canal Authority (n.p.n.d.) (mostly photographs)—designed to attract refugees.
114. Evidence from two former UNRWA Representatives in Jordan who said that other kinds of payoffs were occasionally handed to Ministers in an attempt to win their active backing for certain projects.
115. The M.D.R. notified the P.M. and all D.Gs. on the arrangement with UNRWA which would pay that year the sum of $40,000 for 594 refugee secondary pupils and 153 elementary school pupils, who were prevented from enrolling in Government schools. (M.D.R. Notification No., 7/49/2492 dated 23.6.61, Minister of Interior to D.G., No. 29/17/27400 of 4.10.61).
116. See unpublished map *UNRWA Refugee Services Activities (and schools) West Bank* prepared by the Engineering Branch of UNRWA West Bank March 1969, scale 1:125,000—Appendix No. 9.
117. See Appendix No. 7.
118. For further reading on the plight of the Frontier Villagers—see Avi Plascov "Jordan's Border Inhabitants—the Forsaken Palestinians?" in Roger Owen (ed.), *Studies in the Economy of Palestine in the 19th and 20th Centuries* (Macmillan/St Antony's, Oxford, forthcoming 1981).
119. An M.D.R. unpublished booklet titled *Shu'un al-Laji'in fi al-Urdunn* (Refugee Affairs in Jordan) published in 1953 summarized the Government's attempt to arrange for those people to receive all the necessary help (p.30).
120. See also *UNRWA Reviews.* A background Information Series Information Paper, No. 6, *The Problem of the Rectification of UNRWA Relief Rolls* (1950–62), UNRWA, Beirut, 1962, pp. 11–23.
121. The combined efforts of the following organizations:

CARE:	Co-operative for American Relief Everywhere
SOIR:	Swedish Organisation for Individual Relief
LWF:	Lutheran World Federation
CRS:	Catholic Relief Services
NECC:	Near East Council of Churches
SSCF:	Swedish Save the Children Federation
CDF:	Community Development Foundation
SIRA:	Swedish International Relief Association
IRCC:	International Red Cross Committee
SFCA:	Swedish Free Church Aid
MCC:	Mennonite Central Committee
CS:	Community Services

Chapter IV

1. The various activities and operations of both sides do not come within the scope of this study. For further reading see: E. L. M. Burns, *Between Arab and Israeli*, (London 1962).
2. As one of the local people recalled: "It had a market value. At one time, in the early 1950s you had adventurous men in Ramallah who would cross over for a fee of 10 dinars, you would go to them, they were known".
3. S.A. JUPR. File KH/29 includes hundreds of petitions requesting the Jordanians to allow them to stay. Some poor West Bankers also demanded refugee status, pretending they came from Gaza, for example the case of Muhammad Jabarah Awymir, *Ibid,* file entitled "The Deportees from the Jewish Area, the P.O.W.s and the released". Letter from UNRWA to D. G. Hebron, 14.10.50. AR/5–6/3.

4. See Muhammad Nimr al-Khatib *Min Athar al-Nakbah*, (Some of the consequences of the disaster) (Damascus 1951), p. 381 and a book published in Israel by a Greek Catholic lawyer, Tawfiq Mu'amar *al-Mutasallil wa Qisas Aukhra* (The infiltrator and other stories) (Arabic) al-Rabatah (Nazareth 1957).
5. Naji Alush suggested that as far as the Qawmiyyun al-Arab activities were concerned, the Jordanians managed by 1954 to halt the operations launched against Israel from their territory. See his book *al-Masirah Ila Filastin* (The March to Palestine) (Beirut 1964) p. 145. See also Subhi Muhammad Yasin, *Nazariyyat al-Amal li Istirdad Filastin*. (A plan of action for the recovery of Palestine) (Cairo 1964), pp. 104–5, 114. Abbas Murad, *The Political Role of the Jordanian Army* (Arabic) (Palestine Books, No. 48, P.L.O. Research Centre, Beirut 1973).
6. Resolution No. 13, see *Filastin*, 30.11.51 and the Haifa and Galilee Committee resolution No. 8. S.A. JUPR. Contr. 794–58, No. 25. The Association of Chambers of Commerce in its Conference held in Ramallah 11.1.51, denounced the smuggling operation and demanded tough measures against them. (Resolutions from JMHA, File B/Z/42/1). The Economic Conference in Hebron held 11 months later, followed suit. For text of resolutions, see *Filastin*, 4.12.51.
7. *al-Ba'th* newspaper, 2.3.51, p. 5.
8. The Arabs rejected Israel's suggestion of erecting fences on the Demarcation Line, as a measure against infiltration, on the grounds that it "might imply recognition of either Israel or the existing borders". See Fred J. Khouri, *The Arab Israeli Dilemma* (Syracuse University Press, 1968), p. 185.
9. S. A. JUPR. Letter to Minister of Interior in response to Nablus D.G. recommendation No. 1/297/5/11633 and 4/8/6225 dated 17.8.50. The A.C. suggested passing a new Defence Law which would prohibit any Arab from moving into the enemy's territory and vice-versa, as he felt that the law, based on No. 55 of 18.6.48, was insufficient (*Ibid*, letter to C.O.S. 1/297/5/11633 dated 5.8.50).
10. For example, S.A. JUPR. MNM5/5N. Confd. Headquarters Arab Legion ALG/1/9/2998. Subject: *Allocation of Interrogation Duties* to Amman Police and all OsC. Districts. Signed by Glubb, C.O.S. on 1 August, 1951.
11. See *Filastin*, 1.8.49. The case of three refugees smuggling to Israel, jailed in Nablus.
12. For full text signed by the Army C.O.S., see *Ibid*, 14.6.49. The Jerusalem Police also warned the local inhabitants against infiltrating into the Jewish areas (*Ibid*, 4.8.49). An item on 6.9.49 spoke about sentences passed on those caught in smuggling relief items to Israel; *Ibid*, 18.11.49 and 25.10.52 on those punished for infiltration and espionage; 8 refugees detained for thefts on the other side. *Ibid*, 4.1.50 and 23.11.50.
13. *Ibid*, 1.8.49.
14. S.A. JUPR, Letter from Amman Police Commander to Hebron A.C., A/18/1/1884 dated 23.5.52 and 13/1/44369 dated 23.12.52.
15. *Ibid*, Report from Hebron A.C. to the C.O.S., MKH/1/38/3586 dated 14.10.50.
16. *Ibid*, Order No. 28 signed by the Minister of Interior, 2/49/2429 dated 23.2.54.
17. *Ibid*, Order MQM/7/1679, secret, dated 6.8.53.
18. In his order he drew attention to incidents of shooting at inhabitants inside Israel. *Ibid*, MQM/7/18900 dated 7.8.54.
19. *al-Difa'*, 16.11.54. *Filastin*, 18.11.56.·
20. *al-Difa'*, 14.11.54.
21. *Baghdad Radio*, 13.10.56, 13.00 hours.
22. *Ramallah Radio*, 2.12.56, 12.00 hours.
23. *Ibid*, 27.10.57, 18.00 hours.

24. S.A. JUPR. Letter from Defence Minister to Minister of Interior No. 5/1/j/6635, dated 31.8.50; and file titled "The Refugee Camps", letter from D.G. to Military Governor Assistant, KH/29/1/2387 dated 5.6.50.

25. Hilmi Shughayir, Jenin's UNRWA's Camp Leader, said he collected refugees from all the unofficial camps for the newly-established Fawar (of which he was the Camp Leader) where they tented according to place of origin. The D.G. rejected at first the erection of the Fawar Camp and demanded its transfer to another place. (S.A. JUPR Letter to Perett, ICRC delegate, No. 2627 dated 6.10.49).

26. S.A. JUPR. A detailed report on the situation in the Hebron area listed eight camps, their distance from the border and the number of refugees living there: Halhul, 18 km from border, 257 refugees from 7 villages; Haska, Bayt Kahil, 12 km, 406 refugees from Ajjur; Khirbat Kafar al-Nasari, (Hebron), 15 km, 631 refugees from 2 villages; Bayt Aula, 5 km, 577 refugees from 5 villages; Bir al-Sufla (Tarqumiya), 6 km, 1,656 refugees from 7 villages; Idna, 4 km, 593 refugees from 3 villages; and the two new Camps of Arrub, 12 km, 7,097 refugees from 47 villages, and Fawar, 15 km, 1,721 refugees from 7 villages. There were also some 15,000 scattered bedouin in that area.

27. Letter from M.D.R. to UNRWA Director 13/6/7037 dated 12.11.51.

28. One of the Agency workers recalled that UNRWA did not move into Bayt Aula unofficial camp which existed until 1953/4 and waited for all the refugees to join the new camps of Fawar and Arrub. (Fransis Rahil, and interviews in Bayt Aula, 3.4.74).

29. The D.G. asked the Area Commander to look into the possibility of transferring the refugees there to Marj Na'jah, but the answer made it clear that there was no need for the move as most refugees were renting dwellings. (S.A. JUPR File T/20/1/2, dated 13.1.51). Later the refugees presented a request for a camp to be established there or, alternatively, for their transfer to Nablus. (*Ibid*, a request to be transferred to Balata and Nur Shams Camps was presented in 1955).

30. See *Filastin*, 9.5.50, 15.11.50 and 7.12.51.

31. In May 1952, the Tulkarm D.G. added his recommendation to a request by the camp's notables for the transfer of all the camp from Nur Shams. Fearing their transfer eastwards, many Qalqilya refugees ordered to register at the local police station did not do so.

32. As was the case in Fawar Camp upon Chapirot's visit there, although others indicated their adamant refusal. S.A. JUPR. Letter from Hebron A.C. to the Political Department Army Headquarters. MKHM/1/33/835, 28.2.52.

33. Hasan Qasim Muhammad Najjar recalled upon his transfer from Idna that the refugees protested as "We were near our homes and here we were locked between two valleys". (Interview in Fawar Camp, 20.2.74).

34. In an interview (Jerusalem on 28.1.75) he said, "The Agency gave money for Rehabilitation but it was misused . . . . I was in favour of establishing villages on the border like (The Israeli) "Nahal" but got no encouragement. Glubb failed in his policy of trying to avoid any friction with Israel. We opposed his view. We wanted to fortify the border and thicken it and build villages and camps there, but Glubb was against and both Kings supported Glubb's view". (See also Khatib's interview in *al-Hayat*, 15.6.53). The Government did not accept UNRWA's proposition to set up two refugee camps for the al-Tur refugees as part of the resettlement schemes by which every refugee would receive 20 *dunam* near the Abu-Dis village, although later a modest project was established near Izariyah by one of the Voluntary Agencies.

35. On March 11, 1953 when as Minister of Development he announced the intention of building twelve model villages of 350 housing units for the refugees

in the frontier areas of the West Bank. They had been given land and equipment. It was further announced that work had begun in the first village and that this scheme was part of a large agricultural and industrial programme. A more detailed announcement was published by the M.D.R. on August 9 that year specifying the cost $11,000,000 which UNRWA allocated for this project.

36. The book entitled *Inkadh Filastin* (Salvation of Palestine), pp. 182–3. He also said that their plight should be handled on the premise that the refugees were an Arab Palestinian people *(Sha'b)* and not mere refugees.

37. Tah Muhammad al-Qadi *Masra' al-Adalah* (The Fall of Justice), (Beirut, 1954), pp. 104–5.

38. S.A. JUPR, Report MKHM/1/36/3786 dated 31.7.52. He also urged them to consider positively the role of the King as, being part of the Arab people, they should not distinguish between a Jordanian and a Palestinian.

39. The next day a few other refugee leaders gathered in Arrub Camp and called for a condemnation of Shuqayri's programme. *(Ibid)*.

40. See the article "Limadha . . . Ya Wikalat al-Ghawth" (Why . . . Oh the Welfare Agency), *Filastin*, 2.2.54. It is perhaps worth noting that some Arab Countries partially followed the Jordanian example of removing refugees from the border line. For further reading see *N.E.R.S., Ramallah Radio,* 28.9.55, 18.30 hours; *Filastin,* 9.10.55; *Beirut Radio,* 12.6.56, 13.00 hours; *al-Ayam,* 6.5.56; *al-Jaridah,* Lebanon, 16.11.57; *al-Bayraq* 21.3.58; *Filastin,* 13.4.58; *Damascus Radio,* 24.5.58, 13.15 hours; *al-Amal,* 9.8.58, 18.8.58.

41. S.A. JUPR. Letter No. 29/9/13/36 dated 29.12.54.

42. See *Filastin,* 10.8.55.

43. S.A. JUPR. 114/30/6130 dated 26.6.54.

44. *Ibid,* File titled Refugee Affairs, Bethlehem area, Order No. 145 of Minister of Interior, No. 29/9/13136 which ruled against any transfer of ration cards to Amman as they were "a risk to public security", dated 29.11.54.

45. Akif al-Fayiz, the M.D.R. denied in a Press Conference, *Cairo Radio* and *Sawt al-Arab* allegations made on 14/15 July that the government intended removing those camps. He suggested that such transmissions were made to create uncertainty and lead to chaos. *(Ramallah Radio,* 15.7.57 and *al-Hayat,* 16.7.57). An UNRWA spokesman also denied that the Agency was requested to transfer the refugees. (See *al-Difa',* 18.7.57, *Ramallah Radio,* 17.7.57, 22.00 hours).

46. The Bir Saba' bedouin were affiliated to 7 federations *(qaba'il)*: Tarabin, Tayyaha, Azazmah, Hanajrah, Jubarat, Sa'idiyyin and Ahyiwat. During the war and its aftermath most of the Tarabin and Azazmah left the areas they had inhabited in the new State and settled in the south of the West Bank. The Hanajrah and Jubarat remained on part of their lands outside Israel—in the Gaza Strip— while the Sa'idiyyin moved to Sinai, or eastwards to Trans-Jordan from where they originated. The Ahyiwat moved partly to Sinai and the rest to Trans-Jordan.

47. Some 14 tribes mostly of the Tayyaha *qabilah,* together with three Tarabin and one of the Azazmah remained in the Negev. For the composition and numbers of each tribe see Emanuel Marx, *The Negev Bedouin* (Manchester 1967).

48. For further reading on the sedentarization and the forces shaping this process see—Avshalom Shmueli *The Sedentarization of the Bedouin in the Judea Desert* (Tel Aviv, Gomeh, 1970) (Hebrew); and his work "Bedouin Rural Resettlement in Eretz-Israel" report from *Geography in Israel.* A collection of papers offered to the Twenty-third International Geographical Congress U.S.S.R., July-August, 1976, Jerusalem, 1976.

49. S.A. JUPR File 2257–35 5/12/2 and 2585–24 37/2 and 2570–26 6/16/2 contain numerous petitions from refugees wishing to be united with their families in Israel.

50. For further details read Gideon M. Kressel *Individuality Against Tribality. The Dynamics of a Bedouin Community in a Process of Urbanization* (Hebrew) (ha-Kibutz ha-Meuhad and the Hebrew University of Jerusalem, the Truman Research Institute 1976).

51. A number of Jawarish returned to Libya in 1974 aiming at settling there. In June 1975 they returned to Israel, *Ma'ariv* daily, Israel (Hebrew), 25.7.75.

52. Yosef Ginat: "The Negev Bedouin in Ayalon Basin" in *The Bedouin*, (Hebrew) published by the Councillor Bureau of Arab Affairs, Israel P.M. office, pp. 36–7.

53. The Bili tribe requested to be transferred to a place where they could engage in agriculture. (S.A. JUPR. File KH/29/9, petition signed by Shaykh Muhammad Mas'ad al-Harafi). Twelve families of the al-Sufi requested transfer from the Hebron area and land elsewhere. *(Ibid*, 13.3.52, signed by Shat Judu'a al-Sufi) and so did Awad Husayn Abu Jqim (Alamat-Tayyaha) for his 225 people (*Ibid*, 26.4.52). Hebron's A.C. report of mid-1954 said that there were only 1,384 bedouin left in the Hebron area, as most had moved to the East Bank due to the harvest season. He claimed that most of them wanted to remain there, although in a report 2 months later he added that many insisted on staying in the West Bank and he suggested settling them near the towns. (*Ibid*, letters to D.G. MKH/3/11/7383 dated 15.5.54).

54. Al-Sufi and al-Diqs bedouin approached the M.D.R. about the project of the Tarqumiya and Refugee co-operative. *Ibid*, 1.3.52.

55. One of these *Shaykhs* explained Glubb's policy as he understood it: "He wanted to transfer the Negev bedouin to the East Bank and to amalgamate them with all other bedouin there vis-à-vis the other Palestinians. Later he warned the local East Bank bedouin to be wary of the Negev bedouin as he claimed they dealt in smuggling and spying for the Jews against Jordanian interests. This he did after he realised that the Azazmah do not obey like his bedouin". (Interview, *op. cit.*).

56. Interview in Zahiriyyah on 24.6.74. The interviewed Ramadin tribe *Shaykhs'* recollection supported this version.

57. For further details see A. Mor, "The Negev Bedouin" in *The Bedouin, op. cit.*, p. 27a.

58. Report of the Arab League Council, Paper No. 1/12/5675 (60) dated 18.5.54 (found in S.A. JUPR).

59. Hasan Abd al-Malik Muhammad (Saturiyyah tribe) and Hasan Abdallah, Dayr Ammar's Camp Leader (interview held there on 7.2.74).

60. Nazzal, (Hajj) Husayn Sabri, former Mayor of Qalqilya—interview in Qalqilya on 28.2.74.

61. Fysal Saba', interview, *op. cit.*

62. Shaykh Uffi, Abd al-Raziq Irhaym—interview held in Tulkarm Camp, 2.5.74. For further reading on the Wadi Hawarith people see Dani Ayzner's work *The Wadi Hawarith Affair* (Israel, Ramat Hefer, 1973) (Hebrew).

63. The bedouin refugees of the Mansi, Lid-Awadin, Turkeman, Saidah and Wadi al-Hawarith moved with their livestock. The youngsters emigrated elsewhere.

64. Ibrahim Mustafa al-Ahmad, *mukhtar*, Rummana village (interview there on 11.4.74).

65. An unpublished extensive research *The Nomad Tribes in the Hebron and Bethlehem Subdistricts* (Hebrew) by Moshe Sharon, pp. 71–2.

66. Shaykh Muhammad Khalil Frayjat and Shaykh Sirham Sulayman Ibn Ghayad —(interview held on Ramadin lands in Khirbat San' al-Jibiri, 20.2.74). They originated from the close *Khirbah* Khwaylfah which belonged to Dura village populated partly by Ramadin-Hamzah Muhammad Khalil Abu Alan (interview held in Zahiriyyah on 10.4.74).

67. Musa Sulayman Ibn Ghayad (the brother of the *mukhtar* mentioned) a teacher, interview with him on 20.2.74, there.
68. Interview with Glubb, *op. cit.*
69. Another project initiated by the NECCRW aimed at concentrating a small part of the Azazmah near Havya—unpublished NECCRW Papers, "Proposed Tree Nursery and Settlement Co-operative", 1962.
70. Further details on this form of assistance, Willard D. Jones, *NECCRW Annual Report,* 1961 (Jerusalem 1961) pp. 12–16 and unpublished reports of the Oxford Committee for Famine Relief (Oxfam).
71. Unpublished NECCRW Report to the Executive Committee of the Near East Christian Council, March 1962, signed by W. Jones.
72. Unpublished report of W. T. Clark, UNRWA representative in Jordan, May 1958, p. 23. The report was at the disposal of the former UNRWA Representative and given to the writer of this study together with other unpublished records and diaries.
73. An unpublished report by UNRWA (Beirut 1959) (n–2), p. 27 stated the 1958 figure as 265 bedouin families.
74. The local Press reported also on the Voluntary Agencies' contribution. For details see *al-Jihad,* 9.12.58; *Filastin,* 7.12.58 and *al-Difa',* 26.2.59.
75. One of Battir's teachers put it as follows: "We wanted to live with refugees peacefully, but that was impossible because refugees were anxious to infiltrate back to their lands, and that was against the local wish because attacks from Israel would be on us. There were refugees who also did not like seeing local villagers benefit from their lands (across the border) while they could not". (Interview in Battir, 29.3.74). Interview with Dr Sab' in Qalqilya revealed the same unease amongst the local population, although they were more sympathetic to the refugees' plight.
76. Field interviews as well as contemporary reports revealed this attitude. See for example, *Filastin,* 17.8.58 which described an event where the Area Commanders visited the Hebron Frontier Villages and ordered them to be loyal to the King.
77. The people of the village of Bayt-Safafa eventually built such an access road by themselves using locally collected funds with the Government providing the tools.
78. Hasan Ali Allayan (interview Bayt-Safafa, 29.3.74). UNRWA gave the village 656 half-rations and Knezevitz's study recommended an additional allocation of 159 half-rations apart from the 650 UNICEF rations distributed through the L.W.F. The Agency set up a girls' school, and gave some scholarships and full rations to those from the "Israeli side" who moved to be with their relations in the "Jordanian part" of the village—whom the Government provided with some 300 *dunam* of land (most of it formerly Jewish-owned).
79. See *Filastin,* 28.7.55.
80. S.A. JUPR. Letter from M.D.R. to Minister of Defence, No. 1/11/20/3663 dated 18.7.57.
81. One example is Wadi Fukin. The village, partly demolished by Israeli retaliation, became an unsafe place to live or to farm. Most of its inhabitants moved to Dahaysha Camp, travelling daily to plough their fields. The Agency was troubled by this precedent as its mandate stipulated the giving of assistance only to refugees in camps, and half-rations to Frontier villagers in their respective FV. They had originally moved to the camp at the Government's request, but growing pressure for accommodation for refugees in the newly-built shelters led to the Agency demanding they move back, thus releasing the shelters they occupied. But this never happened. (S.A. JUPR. Letter from I. Duzdar to D.G. 5/SC/9-A-L (57) dated 6.1.60) and interview with Awni Manasrah in Wadi Fukin on 29.3.74.

82. S.A. *Egyptian Unpublished records,* Report SWY/T/3/2 (220) dated 21.7.58. This caused some tension between the King and his Uncle, and once in Husayn's absence his brother the Emir Hasan confiscated the contents of one of the *Sharif's* warehouses.

83. S.A. JUPR. UNRWA Letter No. S & T/5/9 (37) EWK/MJ, signed by E. W. Keast dated 3.6.52.

84. See *Filastin,* 27.11.52. The Customs seized also four barrels containing 255 kg of opium and 416 kg of hashish valued in JD150,000.

85. *Ibid,* 5.7.53.

86. UNRWA protested to the Government about renewed searches and the M.D.R. ordered that they be carried out in the Agency presence. S.A. JUPR. Letter No. D/20/7468 dated 8.8.58.

87. *Ibid,* Order MH/20/1/248 dated 29.9.58.

88. This subject is dealt with under the section on Political Parties. See Ch. VIII. With regard to the Mufti's terror operation, a secret report noted his intention as late as 1954. (*Ibid,* MN1/32/126 dated 25.4.54). A report on the renewed activities of the Mufti revealed that UNRWA's aeroplane was also used for the transfer of money and instructions.

89. *Ibid.* A letter from C.O.S. to all A.C.'s tells of three people from Dar'a who were given Refugee Cards by the Syrians which enabled them to move relatively freely between the two countries as spies and terrorists. He ordered their arrest on arrival. (Order A/4397/9075. Secret. 26.6.50).

90. See "Underground Activity and its Confrontation"—Chapter VIII.

91. See Ehud Ya'ari—*Egypt and the Fedayyin 1953–56* (Hebrew) published by the Centre of Arabic and Afro-Asian Studies, Givat-Haviva, 1975, pp. 12, 40–41. A document signed by Mustafa Hafiz, the Egyptian Commander of Intelligence, which argued against recruiting Palestinians, following Israel's attack on an Egyptian post in the Gaza Strip is given there in Supp. B (dated 20.7.54).

92. *Ibid,* pp. 19–20. In p. 21 he mentions Egyptian leaflets urging the refugees to join the Fedayyin caught in refugee camps. Also *Cairo Radio,* 16.9.57, 23.00 hours.

93. S.A. JUPR. Letter No. KH/22/4104 dated 18.11.56 tells of many "Fedayyin and Youngsters".

94. *Ibid.* Ishaq al-Nashashibi, the Chairman of the "Gaza Displaced Committee" notified the Deputy Welfare Minister that only those who arrived at Ghur Nimrin would receive aid. The date for the beginning of the operation was set at 29.12.56. (Letter No. 10/16/3606 dated 1.12.56).

95. See *al-Jihad,* 5.2.57 and *al-Difa',* 5/19.2.56.

96. See *Beirut Radio,* 26.12.57, 20.00 hours.

97. S.A. JUPR Nablus Secret Police to A.C.s mentioning the Head of the Investigation Dept. Letter MN/33/15911 dated 27.7.57, which requests a detailed list of their names, suggests concern about their being used by the Egyptians who had control of their remaining relatives in the Gaza area.

98. As late as 1962 a similar letter was sent from Amman Investigation Department Headquarters inquiring about their addresses throughout the kingdom. *Ibid,* Letter QM/20/16/3107/13300 dated 17.6.62.

99. *Ibid,* Report from Hebron A.C. to the Army C.O.S. on two refugees from Aqbat Jabr Camp caught with automatic weapons and sentenced. Letter MKH/21/50/717/58/4968 dated 9.7.58.

100. Amnon Cohen, "The Communist Party", in Amnon Cohen (ed) *Miflagot Politiyot ba-Gada ha-Maaravit Tahat ha-Shilton ha-Hashemi* (The Political Parties in the West Bank under the Hashimite Rule) (Hebrew) Unpublished. (The Hebrew University of Jerusalem, the Institute of Asian and African Studies, the Research Centre of Eretz Israel Arabs—The Truman Institute,

Jerusalem, May 1972), p. 34. This is a compilation of studies (referred to individually below) on the various political parties, based on unpublished Jordanian records.

101. An earlier report on the support the King received from amongst the M.B. in Hebron, detailed a message by one of their activists there who claimed he had arranged with the A.C. daily training for their members. Another document said that the Ikhwan group of Husayn's followers there had requested to be formed into an army unit "to defend the State" (S.A. JUPR. Report No. KHM/16/6/1/17 dated 29.11.56 and KHM/16/6/1/15 dated 22.11.56).

102. See Nabulsi, al-Takattul, op. cit., p. 52, who mentioned also the Q.S.P. in the same category (p. 53), and others.

103. S.A. JUPR. File entitled "The Activities of the Egyptian Consulate in Jerusalem", Letter AS/2/24/974 dated 4.9.57. The tariff paid for each crossing was JD.50.

104. Ibid, MQM/6/10/28756 dated 8.9.57. The file, similar to others, reviews the names of people who had visited the Consulate since November 1955, their movements, etc. Some were UNRWA workers, very few were refugees.

105. Ibid, report AS/3/6/2450 dated 12.12.58.

106. ha-Aretz, daily, Tel Aviv, (Hebrew), 11.1.57 and 15.10.57. In the 6.11.58 edition, the editor of the Amman weekly Hawl al-Alam called for arming the Palestinians living in Israel. They could then maintain their first struggle by shaking and undermining the country from within, "so the Jews would desert the country and go back to their places of origin".

107. When Maj. Gen. Ahmad Sidqi al-Jundi the D.C.G.S. and Chief of Police thoughtlessly gave his support to the Fedayyin operations (after a visit from the Egyptian C. in C. Gen. Abd al-Hakim Amir) he was summarily sacked by Glubb.

108. Shlomo Aharonson, "The Strategy of Controlled Retaliation: The Israeli example" in Medina Mimshal ve-Yehasim Bein-Leumiyim (Hebrew), a periodical of students of the Department of Political Science at the Hebrew University of Jerusalem, Vol. A, No. 1, 1971.

109. An interesting source are the memoirs of the late Moshe Sharett, the former Israeli P.M. and Foreign Minister. For example his notes on 18.1.55 considered the pressure to respond to the murder at Ajjur and described his fear of authorizing such an operation: "From the security view-point, the retaliation would serve practically nothing. On the contrary, I feared very much that it would serve as an opening link to a new outbreak of bloodshed on the frontier". See Ma'ariv, 17/21.6.74.

110. As one of the senior British put it: "They did not get the rifles and ammunition they felt they deserved, as you can never know where the gun is going to shoot to . . .".

111. See his book Politics and the Military in Jordan. A Study of the Arab Legion 1921–1957 (Cass, 1967), p. 16.

Chapter V

1. Ramallah Radio, 20.3.56, 18.00 hours.

2. Ahmad Khalil Muhammad Amir—the former head of the N.G. in al-Majd. (Interview 13.3.74 there). Glubb said "We were too poor, we could give them no more". (Second interview held on 7.2.77).

3. In Rummana village the guard did not include any refugees from the hundreds living on the village's land, as it was directed against those among them who were constantly infiltrating. In the F.V. the "returnees" (that is, people who returned in 1948 to villages they migrated from throughout the Mandate) were

considered as natives. (Muhammad Abd al-Fattah Abu Ummayir, interview, *op. cit.*).

4. *al-Jaridah al-Rasmiyyah* (The Official Gazette), 1.3.51.
5. See *Filastin*, 16.11.52.
6. *Ramallah Radio*, 11.3.53, 15.00 hours, *al-Difaʻ*, 12.3.53.
7. *Filastin*, 23.5.53.
8. See review on a meeting of Nablus area M.P.s, (*Filastin*, 11.2.53) and a presentation by the Jerusalemite Baʻthist Abdallah Naʻwas, (*Ibid*, 17.2.53).
9. *Ibid*, 12.3.53.
10. *Ibid*, 12.3.53.
11. *Ibid*, 30.3.53.
12. He added that the town folk were reluctant to guard the borders a number of km to the west of their own places. For them the Frontier Villages were the buffer they wanted reinforced, without too much effort on their own behalf (Interview, *op. cit.*).
13. For full text in English—see *Mideast Mirror*, Vol. V., No. 24, October 24, 1953, p. 2.
14. See *al-Jihad*, 15.2.54. Jordan's poor economic possibilities are emphasized in all official publications as a reason for its small army and limitations imposed on it, together with the fact that Britain did not support the N.G.—see The Supreme Headquarters of the Armed Forces. *Ishrun Aman min al-Jihad wa al-Bina' 1952–1972*. (Arabic). (Twenty years of struggle and the construction) (Amman 1972) p. 56.
15. *al-Difaʻ*, 21.2.54.
16. *Ibid*, 23.7.55.
17. See *Filastin*, 19.8.54.
18. The object of this education system was to form a young loyal Trans-Jordanian core of a political soldiers and officers, because "the Government schools were saturated with politics and many school teachers were Communist". See Glubb, *Soldier with the Arabs*, p. 263. For further details on the Legion schools see Lt. Col. Peter Young, *Bedouin Command with the Arab Legion 1953–56* (London, 1956), p. 50.
19. See Eliezer Be'eri *The Officer's Cadre and Government in the Arab World* (Hebrew) (Tel Aviv, 1966), p. 232 or his *Army Officers in Arab Politics and Society* (London, New York, 1970).
20. When interviewed Glubb noted that generally very few Palestinians had any experience as warriors, and that those who took part in the irregular Arab forces of the 1930s were one way or another too old for long service. He added that he generally refused to admit Jerusalemites, since he suspected them of being old Mufti supporters. See also Clinton Bailey *The Participation of the Palestinian in the Politics of Jordan*, Ph.D. thesis, Columbia University, 1966. University Microfilm, Ann Arbor, Michigan, 1969, p. 115. Halum in his book *op. cit.* condemned Habis al-Majali for purging the Arab Legion not only of Palestinians but also of other educated Trans-Jordanians who were all replaced by bedouin from the south (p. 43).
21. For details concerning their numbers in the different forces see Vatikiotis, *op. cit.*, pp. 84–92.
22. For example Isa Qasis, former Brigadier-General, a Christian from Ramallah who served as Finance Officer, replacing a British Officer after Glubb's expulsion, handled the promised economic aid from the Arab Countries (Interview with him, Ramallah, 22.1.75). Murad in his book *The Political Role of the Jordanian Army* mentioned the monarch's intention to promote Christians to higher ranks and even to form armed Christian units (p. 72).
23. Glubb pointed out that the East Bankers were very unhappy with recruitment of

Palestinians into the army as there was a long waiting list of Trans-Jordanians. That was especially the case when it became evident that many Palestinians were hostile to their "host country". (Interview, *op. cit.*).

24. For example, a paper of the "free officers" called *al-Jundi* (The Soldier), No. 2, titled "Who are our enemies?" attacked the American Imperialists in the service of the Jewish State since its inception (Found in S.A. JUPR. 1958). When shown such leaflets, Glubb said they were rather sophisticated for the army officers and that he himself was surprised to see how little they knew and understood when he gave lectures to groups of officers. These lectures were aimed at neutralizing the effect on the officers of the political events in Jordan. He pointed out that on the whole the political parties managed to recruit very few army officers and that informers were watching closely the officers' political involvements but did not have a great deal to report. (Interview 7.2.77). See also Young, *op. cit.* p. 59 and J. C. Hurewitz, *M.E. Politics, the Military Dimension* (New York, 1959), p. 315.

25. The Committee for Organizing the Defence of Palestine, composed of refugees as well as local Palestinian inhabitants, met in Hebron and called for the recruitment of all people from 18 to 45 years of age to receive occasional training. See *Filastin*, 23/25.6.49 which reported also that the Hebron and Tulkarm Municipalities asked for an expert from the Arab Legion to be sent to organize the scheme.

26. *al-Nahdah*, 8.6.49.

27. See his article in *Sawt al-Laji'in*, 16.7.49, p. 4.

28. For the Minutes and Resolutions of that meeting see *Filastin*, 7.9.49.

29. *Ibid*, 11.9.49.

30. The groups were named after towns in occupied Palestine to emphasize the hope for Return. *Sawt al-Laji'in*, 3.10.49, p. 8.

31. "al-Tadrib al-Askari Khayr Wasilah li Inqadh al-Watan" (The Military training is the best way for the salvation of the homeland) in *Ibid*, No. 5, dated 2.10.49, pp. 2–4.

32. Jordanian records reveal increased attempts to bribe frontier village *mukhtars* not to include names of youngsters on the list. S.A. JUPR. File KH/1/10/16/1. The government tried to control this corruption as it weakened the potential of the N.G.

33. *al-Jabhah al-Sha'biyyah* (The popular front) with Bahajat Abu Gharbiyyah as their secretary. See *Filastin*, 7.9.50.

34. "Ya Shabab Filastin" (Oh the young of Palestine) in *Sawt al-Laji'in*, 2.10.49.

35. To be in force from 26.6.50. See *Mideast Mirror*, 6.4.50 and *Filastin*, 23.11. and 19.12.51.

36. *al-Bilad*, 13.7.53.

37. *Filastin*, 24.6.53. Glubb criticized Palestinians "regarding the army as an employment Agency" (Interview, *op. cit.*). It was, however, common know-ledge that southern East Bankers were recruited into the Legion after their appeals based on their economic hardship. See *al-Jazirah*, 5.2.51.

38. See *Filastin*, 8.4.51.

39. S.A. JUPR. An item recalled when refugees and non-refugee candidates were campaigning for the 1951 elections. Report MKH/1/33/2689, Secret, dated 19.8.51.

40. See *Filastin*, 17.6.52.

41. *Ibid*, 13.12.52.

42. *Ibid*, 24.12.52, or the respective parliamentary minutes.

43. Hawl al-Alam, No. 92, 25.10.52, p. 2 and 6.6.53; *Filastin*, 17.2.53 (Rimawi's article); and *al-Qalam al-Jadid* (edited by Isa al-Na'uri) weekly, (Amman) No. 4, p. 42.

44. See *al-Difa'*, 16.10.53; *Filastin*, 18.10.53. See an article by al-Shaykh Ahmad al-Dajani in *Filastin*, 22.10.53. Rashad Miswada the Hebron M.P. in the same daily, 23.6.53.

45. S.A. JUPR. Habis al-Majali, Nablus A.C. to the Head of Secret Police. Top Secret. Report MN/58/44607, dated 19.10.53, detailed the angry protests in Nablus.

46. A. Sela, "The Ba'th Party" in Amnon Cohen (ed) *The Political Parties, op, cit.*, p. 150.

47. *Ibid*, p. 149.

48. *al-Ra'i*, weekly, 15.3.54 reminded Glubb that there was a government and a Parliament and demanded that he cease going around the frontier villages to give political talks.

49. *Ibid*, 29.3.54.

50. See *Filastin*, 29.9.54. Also an article entitled "The recruitment of the Palestinians" in *al-Jihad*, 17.9.53.

51. *The Palestinian Refugees, the Victims of Imperialism*, (Arabic) pp. 30, 105. See also Akram Zu'ytir *al-Qadiyyah al-Filastiniyyah* (The Palestinian Question), Cairo 1955, p. 265 and the Mufti's book *Haqa'iq an Qadiyyat Filastin* (Facts concerning the Palestine Question), (Published by the A.H.C.) Cairo, 1956, pp. 191–3.

52. A Communist paper published on that occasion also attacked Glubb for his use of terror methods in the suppression of the local national movement and for the way he served Western imperialist plans. The leaflet did not include any demand for recruitment of Palestinians but emphasized the need for a final and complete purge of the Legion.

53. The Ba'th party manifesto entitled "Oh the Proud Arab People" dated 4.3.56, and that "Around the Liberation of the Army (and) the Imperialism Obstructions", 5.5.56 signed by "the Ba'th in Jordan".

54. S.A. JUPR. Report No. MKHM/2/24/9354 dated 3.10.56 which reports on a large meeting in Hebron.

55. "Tajnid al-Laji'in" (Recruitment of the refugees) in *al-Mithaq* 19.4.56, p. 4.

56. S.A. JUPR. Report No. KH/M/16/6/1–9141 dated 28.9.56 and Report No. 11691 dated 27.12.56.

57. *Ibid*, Report No. 11579 dated 15.11.56.

Chapter VI

1. The political developments leading to the elections or their outcome, are extensively discussed by Abidi, Bailey, Deardern, Madi and Musa, Majali, Shwadran. M. H. Aruri, *Jordan: A Study in Political Development 1921–1965* (University of Massachusetts, Ph.D. 1967, University Microfilms, Ann Arbor, Michigan, 1967) and Kamel S. Abu Jaber's work "The Legislature of the Hashimite Kingdom of Jordan: A Study in Political Development" in *The Muslim World* LIX (3–4) July–October, pp. 220–50.

2. See a letter of thanks published in *Filastin*, 3.5.50 by a refugee who arrived from Lebanon.

3. Anwar al-Khatib the Mayor of Jerusalem and others demanded a reallocation of the seats in Parliament.

4. Representatives from occupied Jaffa, Lydda, Ramleh, Negev and the Galilee presented petitions to that effect. (*al-Difa'*, 9.1.50 in *N.E.* No. 2, p. 214). Refugees in the East Bank demanded 6 seats in Parliament to be allocated for refugees living there (3 in Amman, 2 in al-Balqa', 1 in Ajlun) and asked for one

month's postponement to enable all preparations for such a constitutional change. (*Filastin* 12.1.50). The Turkemen bedouin approached the Nablus A.C. to allocate one seat for a Haifa refugee as did a committee representing 20 villages of the Haifa area (*Ibid*, 21/23.2.50, 2.3.50), as well as the Ayn al-Sultan Refugee Committee (*Ibid* 24.2.50).

5. Interview with Na'im Tuqan a former senior government official who resigned to become a candidate of the Liberal Party. See *al-Ra'i al-Am*, Jerusalem, 12.5.50.

6. Nonetheless the Communists alleged that prior to the elections the army officers went around the villages, camps and towns and warned the people that those who did not vote would be considered Communists and arrested for 6 months and that even such threats did not help. The voting percentage was very low in the West Bank where they suggested only 40,000 out of 300,000 entitled to vote, did so. (*al-Muqawamah*, 4./2.4.50, whilst *Ramallah Radio* rated the participation as 70 per cent). Both figures, however, seem to be exaggerated.

7. Emil al-Ghuri in a Press Conference claimed those elections were a joke and the candidates did not represent the Palestinian people. (*al-Ra'i al-Am*, 24.2.50). The Mufti, from Damascus, called for the Palestinians to boycott the elections, which harmed the Palestinian interests. Leaflets smuggled through Amman to that effect carried his signature. (S.A. JUPR. File 0/297, report dated 10.4.50, from Truman Papers Card No. (H'A.1.22). The Mufti also managed to prevent his loyal supporter Muhmud Ala' al-Din, the former Ramleh Mayor, from running for election—see Ne'eman, *Abdallah's Kingdom, op. cit.*, p. 28.

8. Resolutions No. 6, in a communiqué published in *Filastin*, 15.9.49.

9. *Ibid*, 26/30.3.49.

10. *al-Ba'th*, 30.1.50, pp. 12–14, 3.3.50, p. 2 from A. Sela's unpublished M.A. thesis on the Ba'th party (Hebrew) presented in the Hebrew University of Jerusalem (draft), p. 135—reviewed with his courtesy.

11. A stencil was distributed attacking the heads of the Ba'th, "the pupils of Musa Alami", the remnants of the Defence Party (Ja'bari, Shihadah, Abd al-Rahman, al-Siksik and others). In an article in *The Popular Resistance*, 14/1:2/2, the Communists warned the Palestinians that voting would be equated with losing their right to an independent Palestinian State.

12. A policeman reported on the establishment of a special new body called "The Black Hand", which was to be responsible for such action. (S.A. JUPR. 56/794–53, dated 3.2.50 in Truman Papers. Communists Card No. (14).

13. Fu'ad Qasis (Communist) (interview held with him, Ramallah, 12.2.75).

14. Interview, *op. cit.* Isma'il Muslah al-Azzah urged the refugees in an article in *Filastin*, 11.4.50 to vote for a refugee candidate as only he felt like them and could express their pain and their problems as a full partner in their bitter destiny.

15. Interview, *op. cit.*

16. Details on the elections in the East Bank area are found in *Majallat al-Urdunn al-Jadid*, 14/21.4.50.

17. For further details concerning the candidates in all election campaigns held in the period under review—see A.O. Plascov, *The Palestinian Refugees in Jordan 1948–1957* Ph. D thesis (School of Oriental and African Studies, University of London, 1978) pp. 177–9.

18. When the number of candidates did not exceed the number of seats allocated to the area, there was no need to hold elections—a common feature in the life of the Hebron Town Council and of many places in the East Bank—avoiding the clashes and bitterness which often developed during the election campaign. Further details are found in an unpublished paper based on S.A. JUPR. by Ori Shtandel, *The Elections to the House of Deputies in the West Bank 1950–67* (Jerusalem 1969) (Hebrew).

19. In Nablus, for example, one of the competing "bodies", the United Popular Front of Fa'iq Anabtawi, Walid al-Shak'ah and Abd al-Ra'uf al-Faris included Siksik.
20. The Haifa and Galilee Committee's advertisement, *Filastin,* 28.8.51, which praised him for his various activities for the refugees. He failed to become an M.P. but was nominated again as Minister.
21. *Filastin,*25.8.51.
22. *al-Difa',* 20.5.; *N.E.S.,* 31.5.52, 14.30 hours.
23. Gad Zilberman, unpublished drafts entitled *Changes in the Economic System of Nablus Town 1949–1967* and *Nablus and Han Yunis Economic Systems* (Hebrew). (The Institute for Asian and African Studies, Hebrew University, Jerusalem, April, 1972).
24. This subject is covered extensively by two unpublished detailed works written in Hebrew by Benyamin Shidlovsky, *Ramallah—al-Bira: a social political survey* and *Bethlehem Region—a socio-political structure.* For further reading on Ramallah see Saied Assad Kassees *The People of Ramallah: A People of Christian Arab Heritage* (The Florida State University, 1970), and Mariam Zarour "Ramallah, My Home Town" in *M.E.J.,* pp. 430–9.
25. The first half of Shaul Mish'al's unpublished work *Tulkarm: A Socio-Political Account,* (Hebrew) (1970) provides details on the town's social lamination.
26. See, for example, Edward Sayyidhum *Mushkilat al-Laji'in al-Arab* (Cairo 1961) (The Arab Refugee problem), pp. 169–70.
27. According to *Filastin,* 7.3.50, the Bethlehem area had 11,749 electors (60 per cent town-dwellers) while Dahaysha Camp had 533. In the vicinity of Jerusalem there were 29 villages whose total votes were 5,326 out of the 12,587 total for the Jerusalem area, (excluding Jericho). In Nablus town there were 9,928 and in the villages 23,700 (*Filastin,* 17/19.1.50).
28. Isa Aqil on the other hand said that "the refugees were 90 per cent with me" but that "the camps were never a factor in elections as their total votes in this area did not exceed 1,000 against 32,000 from the villages and towns. What counted was the 90 villages' votes and not even Ramallah town where many never even bothered to vote". He said he only got 700 votes in the town owing to the split votes and that he "never paid much attention to the town or its refugees". (Interview in Ramallah, 22.1.75). But it should be noted that Aqil did receive many refugee votes owing to the fact that his cousin Ibrahim Aqil was a senior Ramallah UNRWA clerk.
29. A list of the Balata Camp electors of 1965 mentioned 418 names (S.A. JUPR. Contr. 635–3) compared with the 2,031 Sayyidhum presented *op. cit.,* p. 170.
30. Ya'acov Shim'oni—interview held in Jerusalem on 25.2.74.
31. Interview, *op. cit.*
32. From which possibly Ariqat, Nusayba and Husayni gained votes.
33. Hamdi Taji-al-Faruqi said Rimawi carried a letter in his pocket from the Mufti requesting those who supported the A.H.C. to vote for him. Whether this is true or not (since the A.P.G. made its position clear on boycotting the elections and such a letter, if discovered, could be counterproductive), the story shows that the candidates believed the Husayni element still carried some importance.
34. The price of a vote in 1951 ranged from JD. 1,100 in Karak to 500 Fils in Irbid (*Hawl al-Alam,* No. 36, 4.7.51). The Jordanian files suggested that Anwar Nusayba offered a Hebronite in Jerusalem some JD.100 to promote his candidacy among people living in Jerusalem and that their votes were bought by JD.1–2. (Shtandel, *The Elections, op. cit.,* p. 9). Muhammad Jarallah, UNRWA P.R. Officer, said refugees would be given a torn half of a Jordanian Dinar which was supplemented by the other matching half if it was beyond doubt that the man voted as he promised. Needless to say, some refugees collected a

number of dinars that way. (Interview in Shaykh Jarakh on 18.4.74). William Clark said that as the Communists did not spend money on votes they received little support from the poor camp inhabitants. (Interview *op. cit.*) The late Rushdi Rasas, the former Arrub and Mu'askar UNRWA Camp Leader, said that as many refugees were disappointed with all candidates, many of them voted just "because everyone did and mainly for the money they could get". (Interview with him held in Anata (Shu'fat) Camp on 5.3.74).

35. Ayyub Musallam, a former Minister of Development and Reconstruction, who took part in the 1963 elections (interview with him in Bethlehem on 20.1.75), and Dr Tuma Banurah who provided details from his unpublished manuscript on the social stratification of the three towns (interview in Bethlehem on 11.2.75).

36. He explained that his failure was due to the fact that Hasan Mustafa was popular with the refugees, being a senior UNRWA employee, whilst he, like his father, was notorious for his policy against UNRWA. He added that the Agency wanted to have "their" man inside the Parliament and that the refugees felt it was good to have someone close to their relief problems in the House. In addition he claimed the regime wanted Mustafa (and later a local Muslim) over Darwish and that the army helped them to win by allowing his opponents to vote twice. (Interview, *op. cit.*).

37. Later he was dismissed from the Parliament, tried in absentia and sentenced to ten years in jail.

38. Isa, Shihadah, Badawi, Abd al-Karim al-Alami and others complained bitterly that the elections were a fraud and that ballot boxes had been tampered with, which was the reason for the delay in the publication of results in the Ramallah, Jenin and Irbid areas.

39. Isa Aqil, who supported his explanation, said he was asked by the D.G. to drop his candidacy in favour of Kamal Nasir, as the King anticipated that the participation of Ba'th in Parliament would give a greater legitimacy to the annexation and create a more favourable atmosphere between Syria and Jordan —the Ba'thists serving as emissaries of a kind (interview, *op. cit.*).

40. Hawl al-Alam, No. 89, 4.10.52, p. 9.

41. *Ibid,* 26.3.50; an advertisement by Ja'bari urging them to vote for Isa published in *Filastin,* 6.4.50.

42. Owing to his career as a fighter and his origins—the part of the Huwaytat tribe to which he belonged came from Hijaz some 350 years ago. (Interview with Rashid Ariqat, Jericho).

43. Another local, Daud Husayni, was also popular with refugees owing to his reputation, his family connections and the fact that part of Aqbat Jabr Camp was built on his land and that he had helped refugees to gain employment (Ibrahim Abu Rish—Aqbat Jabr UNRWA Camp Leader, interview held there on 5.2.74).

44. See the unsigned articles published in *Hawl al Alam,* 8.11.: 6/13.12.52. "If I was a Member of Parliament" lists the M.P.'s duties as viewed by the electorate.

45. The former received 3,350 votes and the latter 158 votes less.

46. al-Khatib said that the Communists were the favourites owing to the Czech-Egyptian arms deal and to USSR support for the Arab cause to the extent that, even in the villages, they preferred those who support the Soviet Union and Gamal Abd al-Nasser. "They had strong active students. Our party had no base. We had good commanders with no army". (Interview, *op. cit.*) Fu'ad Qasis said the villagers learned to respect the Communists even if they did not understand what they were preaching or opposed their beliefs since they were willing to be jailed and tortured for what they advocated, without changing their position or escaping the country. (Interview, *op. cit.*).

47. Manifestos published in *Sawtal-Khalil, al-Ra'i al-Am* and *Filastin* were examined.
48. Full text in *al-Mithaq*, No. 34, dated 17.11.50, pp. 12–13.
49. For example the case of Rashad Miswada in Hebron. See also International Committee of the Red Cross *Report on General Activities* (January 1 to December 31, 1950) (Geneva 1950), p. 68.
50. The Ba'th's candidates' leaflets "From Jail to Parliament" related to their intentions to be active in changing the constitutional rights and to work for reforms in the country's political life, (printed in Amman on 23.8.51).
51. Neither the National Front nor the Popular Front, which competed against each other in Nablus, raised this subject in their first published platform although the town had a refugee contingent. (See *Filastin*, 8/12/21.8.51). Later in the campaign they began relating to the refugee problems (*Ibid*, 23.8.51). Even Tawfiq Tuqan in Amman did not relate to the issue (*Ibid*, 7.8.51).
52. S.A. JUPR. report by R.O. MKH/1/33/2263 of 8.7.51 which followed Sa'id al-Azzah's moves and speeches and No. 2689 of 19.8.51 which reported on the local candidates' tours of the area camps.
53. The conclusion of an intensive report prepared by the Jerusalem A.C. which included 41 speeches signed on 17.10.56.
54. Tawfiq Tuqan for example, who was "the only real refugee candidate in Amman, Zarqa' and Madaba", preached strongly for the refugees' conscription and their regrouping in Fedayyin groups. (*al-Jihad*, 15.10.56). This was a favourite subject amongst the refugees, yet he totally failed against Khalifah's group which hardly related to the Refugee Problem in their platform, simply because the refugees never regarded Tuqan seriously and trusted Khalifah regardless of his manifesto. Or note the example of Dr Husni Fakhri al-Khalidi (see *Filastin* 28.9.54).
55. See Khalifah's advertisement, *Filastin*, 9/10/18.10.56.
56. For its platform see *al-Jihad*, 31.5.54. The statement appeared in their manifesto of 1956 entitled *The N.S.P. One Democratic, Socialistic Arab State* signed by al-Khatib.
57. Walid al-Shak'ah and Fa'iq Anabtawi who, along with the N.S.P., defeated the Communists and the Ba'thists in Nablus. A report on Anabtawi's victory suggested that the large sums spent on his campaign were given to him by the Mufti whom he praised in his victory speech when he called for the revival and reorganization of his party. *Ibid*, report MN21 dated 24.10.56 in Truman Papers (H'A 121.4).
58. A letter from Ramallah's Mayor, K. Sallah, to Chester Page, UNRWA Chief District (ref: 17/410 dated 23.6.50) sheds some light on the problems faced in Ramallah: "the original population of 5,100 rose to about 25 or 30 thousand persons . . . the Municipality was thus forced to cater for a population of six times its original size on an annual budget of only L.P.20,000".
59. Petitions in the local Press and the government files. An article on this subject appeared in *Sawt al-Laji'in*, 15.8.49, p. 4; 9.9.49, which also tells of occasions when refugees were literally evacuated by force, depriving them of any shelter. Taj al-Din al-Bitar, who was nominated to look into the constantly rising rents, recommended that a Governmental decree should be issued to defend the homeless and restrict the house owners' greed. (*Ibid*, No. 7, 3.10.49). Apparently this problem was more acute in Nablus owing to the large number of returnees amongst the refugees and the limited space there. (*Filastin*, 5.7.49). In Hebron there was more space owing to the large migration to Jerusalem.
60. Protests registered in *Filastin*, 1.7.49. Also J.M.H.A., H/27/6/52, 564 which contains many protests to that effect.
61. J.M.H.A. File 1–79, letter from the Anglican Bishop of Jerusalem who protested to the Mayor at the abuse of the letters given by the municipality, saturating the church beyond its capacity with needy refugees and non-refugees who pretended

to be so. The latter were assisted by T.C. officials who certified people as refugees when they knew they were not.

62. S.A. JUPR. File KH/29/3. Numbers from inner governmental report were compared with those of Government-UNRWA correspondence, the Government presenting its own as well as the local authorities' reported expenditure.

63. Letter of protest was sent by Kenneth W. Clark and J. L. Kelso to Anwar al-Khatib, the Mayor, on 18.11.49. J.M.H.A., B/90/12/2.

64. Ja'bari demanded that Hebron should receive part of Britain's contribution so the TC could assist and resettle them. S.A. JUPR. letter to D.G., 4/5/49, 2.6.49.

65. The Ramallah appeal asked in addition for the setting up of a slaughter house, playgrounds, municipal buildings, schools, public library, community buildings, small industries, hotels and transport facilities. (*Ibid*). A more modest appeal came from al-Bira's T.C. on 21.6.50 and from a number of villages in the Ramallah-Jerusalem area, most of whom requested roads, schools, water and markets, as well as the building of houses for refugees along the main roads, refugee villages and work for refugees and non-refugees. (21.6.50) 18/28.8.50.

66. Jerusalem D.G. to the Minister of Refugees (ML/298/1/21/49 dated 28.8.50) stating that he supported some of these appeals from which the refugees and non-refugees and the Government could only benefit.

67. J.M.H.A. Hebron Municipality 4/5/49.

68. Meeting of 23.1.51 and al-Arif's answer to Ja'bari dated 30.1.51. UNRWA had many problems with the TC which refused even to collect the garbage from the camps in Nablus, Jerusalem and Amman as late as 1966. S.A. JUPR. Letter from Police to Nablus Health Dept. regarding Balata's garbage not being collected, MN/9/1/1627.

69. J.M.H.A., B/Z/14, letter from municipality to Governor of Palestine, dated 23.11.48, requesting him to arrange for 1,000 people to be removed to their respective houses adjacent to the border line.

70. S.A. JUPR. Ja'bari to D.G. 4/5/49 dated 15.5.50 demanding the transfer of all refugees to areas outside the town. A few months previously the Hebron Mayor warned all refugees about their behaviour towards the town's natives. (Hebron Municipality's letter No. 4/5/49 dated 7.11.49).

71. See Qaddurah refugees' appeal to al-Bira's Council to allow them to take drinking water (*Filastin*, 30.5.53). In 1952 the Jerusalem TC threatened to stop supplying the camp with water if UNRWA could not pay the demanded rate. The TC further complained about the amount of water consumed by the refugees, for which they demanded JD900 and not the JD500 paid by UNRWA to the government. The Government in turn demanded a special 50 per cent rate for the refugees. (From the *Minutes of the Jerusalem T.C. meetings* of 3.1./7.2./4.3./20.5.52). The Tulkarm TC demanded only JD90 for water supplied to the two camps. (*Filastin*, 18.12.51). The Government wanted UNRWA to pay JD20,000 as an annual fee for all the camps (*Ibid*, 14.5.52). (Compare Appendix No. 1). However it seems that whilst UNRWA paid the Government, the TCs did not receive the amount due. Furthermore the Jerusalem TC refused to cut down the rate for the refugees. (*Minutes, op. cit.* Resolution No. 1114, dated 19.11.54; 1284 of 19.3.55; 29.1.57; 841 of 4.12.56). The Government tried without success to change the Agreement with UNRWA so that the responsibility for water would be with the Agency.

72. In Bethlehem the problem was solved for the Ayda camp inhabitants when Darwish allocated his land adjacent to their camp for that purpose, whilst the Dahaysha Camp refugees complained they had to bury their dead far away in the hills as the TC refused to give them land. (Abd al-Fattah Khalil Samarah (Zakariya)—interview there on 21.2.74).

73. One of the fears of the Ramallah people was that the two towns would be amalgamated, an idea examined occasionally by the authorities.
74. Application handed to the D.G. See *Filastin*, 23.2.51.
75. Petition signed by Muhammad Khalil al-Azzah and 20 others dated April 1951. (S.A. JUPR Contr. 1046–19, No. 10 in Truman Papers). An article to that effect appeared in *al-Ba'th*, 6.4.51 signed by Rawhi al-Khatib and Hanna Ajluni.
76. For full text see Law No. 17, 1954 and Law No. 29 by *The Official Gazette*, No. 1225 of 1.5.55.
77. That enabled them to nominate an unelected Mayor—appointing as Mayor one of the two selected new members, as was the case in Hebron in 1964 when Ja'bari was installed as the head of the Municipality. Details on the system from unpublished work by Ori Shtandel *The Elections to the Municipalities in the West Bank 1951–1967* (Hebrew) (Jerusalem 1968); Shidlovsky's two works *op. cit.*, and an unpublished paper by Yosi Torpshtayn, *The Municipal System in the West Bank 1948–1967—a General Review* (Hebrew) (n.p. July 1973). Shaul Mish'al "Jehuda and Samaria: Anatomy of Municipal Elections" in *N.E.*, No. 93–4, 1974, p. 63.
78. S.A. JUPR. Jerusalem Secret Police MQM/1/3/27644 dated 11.9.55 to Head of Intelligence, report on all candidates in Bethlehem, Bayt Jala and Bayt Sahur.
79. The two competing lists there stressed in their manifestoes the need to help the refugees and promised "they would not differentiate between a relative or a stranger". One of the lists even promised to work for lowering the rent for refugees. (See *Filastin*, 27/30.6.51). In Jerusalem and Jericho there was no mention of the refugees in the various platforms.
80. Ziyadah Shamiyyah—interview in San Francisco, 25.9.73.
81. B. Shidlovsky's work on *Ramallah, op. cit.*, p. 70.
82. Ramallah interviewees said it was a painful thing to do as they were reluctant to depart from their land for symbolic reasons, although it gradually lost its economic value. They felt easier selling land to Christian refugees than to Muslim refugees and non-refugees.
83. Interview with Alfrid Kishk, Jerusalem 16.8.74.
84. As of 1953, refugees were elected to the area's Chamber of Commerce, *Filastin*, 21.6.53.
85. For further details on the previous composition of Ramallah's TC and the election campaigns preceding—See A.O. Plascov, *The Palestinian Refugees op. cit.*, pp. 203–5.
86. For further details see *Filastin*, 17/20/22/27.5.51.
87. Shidlovsky *Ramallah and al-Bira, op. cit.*, p. 97. The refugees who were elected came from Lydda, Jaffa and Jerusalem and were better off.
88. *Filastin*, 10.8.60.
89. S.A. JUPR. File MN20/28, n.d. "When will the Nablus municipality put us in her bosom and assist the refugee. And we are their brothers from the past and we count some 40,000 refugees in her area . . . and the King stipulated we were the country's sons and have equal rights like all her residents . . .", signed by Amin al-Qasim.

Chapter VII

1. Dr Taji-al-Faruqi said: "We did not give any place to the Refugee Problem as we didn't want to divide the population. We were for the people of Jordan and there was no mention of the Palestinian Entity". (Interview, *op. cit.*).
2. His "Political Parties in the West Bank under the Hashimite Regime" in Moshe Ma'oz (ed) *Palestinian Arab Politics, op. cit.*, p. 46.

3. For further reading see Shimon Shamir *Communications and Political Attitudes in West Bank Refugee Camps* (Survey) (The Shiloah Centre for Middle Eastern and African Studies, Tel Aviv University, 2nd edition, 1974).
4. For a summary of the notion of Arab Nationalism consult the term "*Kawmiyya*" written by P. J. Vatikiotis in *Encyclopaedia of Islam,* pp. 781–4. For further reading on the subject see Sylvia G. Haim (ed) *Arab Nationalism, An Anthology* (University of California Press, 1962, 1975) and Elie Kedourie's books *Nationalism* (London, Cass, 1962) and the introduction in *Nationalism in Asia and Africa* (New York, 1970).
5. A study held in the Jenin area in 1950–62 and in the Ramallah area 1962–73, revealed traces of the Qays and Yaman rivalry amongst refugees as late as 1974, alongside the more common conflicts and differentiations between bedouin and villagers, town-dwellers and *fellahin,* villagers and their *Khirbah* inhabitants, clans in the same towns or villages, Christians and Muslims and refugees and non-refugees. See Mahmud Muslah "Solidarity in Palestinian Society" in *al-Turath wa al-Mujtama'* published by the Family Restoration Society, the Committee for Social Research and National Palestinian Heritage. (al-Bira, October 1974), pp. 101–10.
6. An unpublished study of the West Bankers' attitudes following the 1967 war reveals the importance of this element in the Palestinians' identity. Rivkah Yadlin *Positions and Opinions amongst the West Bank Arabs* (Hebrew) The Institute of Asian and African Studies, the Truman Institute (Jerusalem 1973) pp. 12–14. See also Y. Harkabi "The Palestinians in the Fifties", *op. cit.* pp. 75–6.
7. See UN General Assembly, Official Records, Fourteenth Session, Doc. A/4121. Proposals for the continuation of the UN assistance to Palestine, 15 June, 1959 in which Hammarskjöld recommended that the reintegration of the Palestine refugees in the Middle East should be done "within the context of general economic development" of the area. For a Palestinian reaction see Fayiz al-Saigh *Mashru' Hammarskjöld wa Qadiyyat al-Laji'in* (the Hammarskjöld plan and the Refugee Question) (Beirut 1959), 168 pp.
8. Interview, *op. cit.*
9. For further reading see Amnon Cohen's "The Jordanian Communist Party in the West Bank, 1950–60" in Michael Confino and Shimon Shamir (ed.) *The USSR and the Middle East* (Israel Universities Press, Jerusalem 1973) pp. 420–37. W.Z. Laqueur "Communism in Jordan" in *The World Today* Vol. 12, No. 3. March 1956, pp. 109–19 and his *Communism and Nationalism in the Middle East* (London 1961) pp. 124–33, Alush *al-Masirah, op. cit.,* pp. 137–42, M.S. Agwani, *Communism in the Arab East* (Bombay 1969).
10. Apart from *al-Muqawamah al-Sha'biyyah* in its first years all other examined Communist mouthpieces had by 1953 dedicated very limited space to and had little interest in the refugee plight.
11. *al-Muqawamah,* 1/4: 1/8: 1/9: 1949.
12. *Ibid,* 1/4: 1/8: 1/10: 1949.
13. *Ibid,* 1.10.49.
14. *Ibid,* 4/1.
15. "Lebanon . . ." in *al-Ba'th,* 30.3.51, No. 171, p. 4 and *Ibid,* 2.3.51, No. 167, p. 11, which attacked that country for its treatment of the refugees, but is directed against the Jordanian regime.
16. *Ibid,* 30.3.51, No. 171, p. 4.
17. Udah Butrus Udah "Educating the refugee sons—a must", *al-Ba'th* 3.3.50, No. 166, p. 6.
18. *al-Ba'th,* 9/23.3.51, Nos. 168 and 170.
19. "This is the Agency" by Anwar al-Khatib, in *Filastin,* 19.10.52.

20. See al-Hay'ah al-Arabiyyah al-Ulya li Filastin, *An Mushkilat al-Laji'in al-Filastiniyyin* (Arabic) (On the Palestinian refugee problem) Cairo 1952, 36 pp. and *al-Laji'in al-Filastiniyyun Dahaya al-Isti'mar wa al-Sihyuniyah* (Arabic) (The Palestinian Refugees the victims of imperialism and Zionism) Cairo 1955, 112 pp. Also *al-Hayat*, daily, Beirut, 24.3.59 which published such detailed petitions.

21. Examples of this type of publication for each party:

J.C.P.: *al-Muqawamah*, 3/4.2.52; 6.6.52; 15.4.52; July 1952; 4.5.53 and March 1953; *Kifah al-Sha'b*, No. 6/1, 1955, p. 3; *al-Wathbah*, No. 3/1, April 1956, p. 3; *Sawt Jabal al-Nar*, October 1956, p. 3.

Ba'th: "To the Refugees" by Rimawi, *Filastin*, 3.6.52 and his *The Logic*, p. 50 (from Sela's summaries); Na'was's "Why we reject the Resettlement" *Filastin*, 8.6.52, "Oh Mister Blandford", *Ibid*, 26.6.52; "How we should find the solution" in *al-Bilad*, 14.7.52; "To Mister Blandford" signed by Rimawi, Na'was, Amin, Rahman Shuqayir, Bahajat Abu Gharbiyyah, and Sulayman al-Hadidi in *Filastin*, 13.7.52; Rimawi's article *Ibid*, 17.7.52. "An Open Letter to John Foster Dulles" in *Ibid*, 14.5.53. "Remembrance Day 15th of May", *Ibid*, 15.5.53; Manifesto on Abu al-Huda's Government in *al-Sarih*, 16.5.52; "Memorandum to the P.M.", *Filastin*, 26.5.53; "No Resettlement, No Rehabilitation" in *al-Difa'*, 12.7.53; Na'was and Ariqat, "We reject the Resettlement" in *Filastin*, August 1953; "Between the Rehabilitation and the Resettlement", *al-Difa'*, 23.7.53; "The Manifesto on Dulles' Proposals and Johnston's Scheme" in *Nidal al-Ba'th*, No. 4, pp. 24–32.

Muslim Brotherhood: Pamphlet of the General Islamic Congress in Jerusalem, 1956 and *al-Difa'*, 10.9.56.

Liberation Party: Leaflets against the Johnston Scheme were distributed in the camps (attached to Report MQM/4/1 dated 27.8.55—found on two refugees from Bethlehem who were caught while distributing such hand outs).

22. *Filastin*, 6.8.49.

23. See Kamal Nasir's articles "A Palestinian Block" and "If I were a Leader", *Filastin*, 13/14.10.49, *op. cit.* See also "The Palestinian . . . a Traitor" *al-Jil al-Jadid*, 8.5.49, in which ironically he attacks the Palestinians, blaming them for their fate by allowing all the Arab armies to enter their land to save them . . .

24. Like "The Perturbed on the Land", *Filastin*, 21.10.49.

25. Rimawi's article "The People's Will in the Country's Affairs" in *al-Ba'th*, 21.2.50, p. 2.

26. *Sawt Jabal al-Nar* (The voice of the "mountain of fire", that is, the voice of Nablus—A.P.), first year, No. 3, May 1956, p. 3, and *Nidal al-Sha'b*, Jerusalem monthly, No. 1/2, June 1956, p. 2, on the conditions in the Qaddurah unofficial camp.

27. Shaykh Muhammad Hasan's sermon in Nablus, Report MN1/61/27 dated 1.6.55, in Truman Papers (54). An unpublished study prepared by Avner Gil'adi *The Muslim Religious Establishment in the West Bank*, Part C: *The Khatibs' Outlook According to their Addresses in the Mosques* (The Hebrew University of Jerusalem, the Institute for Asian and African Studies 1972) (Hebrew) details at length items from some 1,000 such addresses examined in this study, carried out by Nisim Danah and Aryeh Guss. The paper mentioned a few odd cases following the Sinai Campaign when *khatibs* were calling for everyone to work for the Return of the refugees and one appeal was made in 1962 (p. 29).

28. See also Na'was "No Resettlement, No Rehabilitation" in *al-Difa'*, 12.7.53.

29. See *al-Ba'th*, 11.3.49.

30. "We Reject the Resettlement" in *Filastin*, August 1953.

31. See an interview with Na'was in *al-Hawadith*, 19.5.52 and in *Filastin* 26.6.52.

32. Rimawi in *Filastin*, 2/4.8.49.
32a. *al-Muqawamah,* 15/4 and July 1952.
33. Reports MN/72/227 and 252 dated 3.8.57 and 2.9.57 in Truman papers No. 18 and 190.
34. Signed by the Struggle's Pioneers (n.p.).
35. Signed by the Q.A. (n.d.n.p.).
36. Heads and active party members were also interviewed as the parties' records and lists of membership were not traced in the field research, and definite conclusions could not be drawn solely on the strength of the government files.
37. From Head of Intelligence to A.C.s, M'A/5/68/363 dated 13.1.57.
38. A YMCA secret report assessed that some 80 per cent of the Communists in Jordan were Christians, who became their main targets for recruitment. From an unpublished unsigned report entitled *YMCA Work as an Expression of Christian Faith in the M.E.* (strictly confidential) (n.p.n.d.) p. 3, from the YMCA Archives, Geneva. For further reading see W.Z. Laqueur "The Appeal of Communism in the Middle East", *M.E.J.,* pp. 17–27.
39. S.A. JUPR. Report No. JLN/136/M.
40. Report No. MN/17/201 dated 9.11.52, in Truman Papers (C.11.93).
41. Report No. MN/22/31 and Report MQM/5/25388 dated 17.11.52, Top Secret. The report details the contacts between the Communists in Far'a and those in Aqbat Jabr Camps. Orders were issued for their arrest.
42. Report No. MQM/6/26 of 3.5.53. The three teachers were transferred, after their incitements against the Government, to separate remote places.
43. Report MN/17/176 dated 19.8.54.
44. Report No. MQM/6/36 of 29.1.54 and No. 49 of 10.2.54.
45. Fawar Camp. 10.5.51, report KHM/16/2/263; Arrub Camp 7.8.52, report KHM/16/2/83; Aqbat Jabr and Ayn al-Sultan, 31.10.54, report MQM/3/2/89. A report in 1955 on the reasons behind the pupils strike in Arrub and Fawar revealed names of 7 Communist teachers who advocated it. Letter MKHM/2/9/2017 dated 23.3.55.
46. According to additional lists the J.C.P. had a relatively high number of Jaffa refugees in Amman: a report listed 36 names of whom 8 were refugees, 5 of whom were from Jaffa and all living outside the camps. One of them used to be active at the time in Beirut. Report MQM/4/9/12205 dated 6.5.57.
47. Another list of West Bank and East Bank activists listed altogether some 201 supporters of whom 84 were in Jerusalem, including 49 teachers.
48. Of the 32 given in Ramallah 6 were refugees; of 7 in al-Bira, one refugee; and of the two from Zarqa', one refugee.
49. From Head of Intelligence to all D.G.s, M'A/19/19/8202 dated 25.8.57. Nablus area: 46 names–2 refugees; Jerusalem and Ramallah area–91 suspects–29 refugees; Hebron, 27–6; Karak, 21–1; Ma'an, 3–none; Ajlun, 16–6; Balqa', 32–3; Amman, 28–4.
50. MN/20/1/1118, 1958.
51. SH/11/7283, 1.11.59.
52. Conclusion from Sela *The Ba'th* (M.A.), op. cit., p. 173, who examined some 24 Ba'thists, most of whom were members of its leadership on different levels.
53. A. Sela provided numbers to indicate that in the Jerusalem sector they were only 17 per cent of the total number of activists (A B & C) and in the Nablus sector they were 9 per cent—his work "The Ba'th" in Cohen (ed.), *op. cit.,* p. 134.
54. Report No. MN/21/1211 listed 67 names of whom only 3 were refugees (teachers) and 3 were non-refugees who taught in UNRWA's school in the town.
55. Out of 12 teachers affiliated to the Ba'th only 2 were refugees. *Ibid.*
56. Another list MN/7/2/31431 dated 12.5.57 showed that 3 of the teachers in Far'a

Camp were Ba'thists (though 2 of them were non-refugees) as were 2 of the Askar Camp teachers.

57. Of the 14 teachers registered as Ba'th supporters only one was a refugee employed by UNRWA.

58. Report MN/20/1/1786 of 11.5.58. A previous list there a year earlier contained 23 names including only one refugee who lived in Jenin Camp.

59. Report MQR/20/1/1038 dated 25.1.59 listed 20 refugees: 4 of them were in Jalazun Camp (one being the C.L.); 3 in Dayr Ammar Camp. Of the total 3 were UNRWA teachers, another 8 the Agency's employees and two students.

60. Rimawi made promises in the 1954 election campaign that if he were elected he would reinstate as headmasters the teachers who were transferred to the East Bank. (MQ2/4/4/74 of 6.9.54). Banajat Abu Gharbiyyah met with the ones who were fired and then approached UNRWA Education Officer, but failed to change the Agency's decision. (Report MQM/4/4/32).

61. A case of the transfer of a headmaster in Nu'yma school after he complained against the Ba'th teachers and a pupil. Report MQM/4/4/4/5 and 78 dated 25.3/4. 56.

62. Report MN22/2, 258–6, 114/2, 80 dated 2.8.56, in Truman papers (B.47). George Shapirott recalled how he was stoned in Fawar Camp and said he had arguments about this subject with Rimawi whom he tried to persuade to stop his incitement. He invited him to come and live in a tent amongst the refugees to get the feel of their grievances. Rimawi declined. (Interview, *op. cit.*)

63. The Ba'thist Hanna Ajluni said that his party did not have a strong position amongst the refugees owing to the nature of their daily worries and their apathy, which in many cases even led people to abstain from voting. "But when there was something which touched upon them, then being concerned with the issue, they became active." (Interview with him in Michigan, Southfield, U.S.A. on 3.10.73).

64. In Jenin only 5 refugees out of 74 suspects—report MN/20/1, 1958.

65. A list of 50 suspects included 2 refugees; another list of 80 names had 2 refugees. None of the 12 most active members were refugees.

66. Half of whom were from Dahaysha.

67. Six of the 7 reported refugees out of 10 suspects were from Aqbat Jabr.

68. See Walid Qamhawi, *al-Nakbah wa al-Bina'* (the catastrophe and the construction) (Arabic) (Beirut, 1956); N. Alush *al-Masirah, op. cit.,* who reviews the party's development (pp. 143–50) and G. Broyda "The Qawmiyyun al-Arab" in A. Cohen (ed), *op. cit.*, pp. 240–1.

69. Two lists of 146 names contained two refugees from Category B and 22 in C. Many of them lived in Askar Camp and some were UNRWA workers, teachers, pupils and unemployed.

70. MQ/20/1/H/64 dated 14.8.58 and MQM/20/1/F of 21.4.59. Another list on the Bethlehem activists said that most of them originated from Malha village and lived in the towns of Nablus, Amman, Kuwait and Cairo.

71. See Ribhi Jum'ah Halum *Ha'ula'i A'da' al-Taharrur fi al-Urdunn* (these are the enemies of liberation in Jordan) who suggested that Wasfi Tall was the man behind the scene organizing this connection, pp. 62–3.

72. Another list for the Ramallah area gave eight names, four of whom were refugees, and three UNRWA workers from Dayr Ammar Camp. In a 1959 list, six out of 14 names in the Ramallah area were refugees.

73. See *al-Qanun al-Asasi li jama'iyyat al-Ikhwan al-Muslimin fi Filastin* published by the General M.B. Congress of Palestine (Jerusalem 1949); The Foundation Charter of the M.B. in the H.K.J. and Palestine presents *The Message and Programme of Reform of the Muslim Brotherhood. To the People on both sides of the Jordan* (Jerusalem 1949) which reviewed in depth the M.B.'s position on

socialism, nationalism, the regime, bureaucracy, employment, sport, education, the family etc. For further reading see Rahel Simon "The Muslim Brothers" in A. Cohen (ed) *The Political Parties, op. cit.,* and others.

74. The request was signed by 26 youngsters on 23.3.54. They intended joining the already existing branch in Nablus composed also of the dispersed Refugee Affairs Committee.

75. Set up in 1955 headed by Khalifah. The school was run by Muhammad Sa‘id— letter ML/154/2/203/51.

76. Especially when their rivals, the Tahrir, were accused of receiving money from the U.S.A. and of working as "American agents".

77. Report on Sa‘id Ramadan's (The Secretary of the Islamic Congress of Jerusalem) visit to Jerusalem—MQM/KH/5–50 dated 9.7.54 in Truman papers, A.M. No. (79–82).

78. For further reading see R. Simon and A. Landau "The Liberation Party", in Cohen (ed), *op. cit.*

79. List MN/21/1277 dated 21.1.55. In Nu‘yma Camp they had five teachers and most propaganda was carried out during religion lessons and through readings from books presented by them. Simon, Landau, "The L.P." *op. cit.,* p. 463.

80. A 1957 list made in response to Order No. M‘A/5/68/363 of 31.1.57 sent by Head of Intelligence to A.C.s contained names of 7 refugees out of 26 suspected L.P. members all of whom lived in al-Bira compared with one refugee living in Jalazun.

81. A list of 118 suspected teachers in the Nablus area shows that only 9 of them were refugees. Out of 16 listed students 3 were refugees from Nur Shams. Another list of L.P. supporters gave 33 names of Category A in the northern area, of whom only one was a refugee. List B gave 83 names including 3 refugees. Another list of 353 names listed only 20 refugees and a combined list of A and B in Nablus area named 28 members including 2 refugees.

82. List MN/72/130–8 dated 3.2.57 gave 66 names in Category A of whom half were teachers, only 4 of them refugees; and 135 names of C of whom 15 were teachers, including 9 refugees.

83. An order sent by Glubb to all A.C.s requested them to classify the 172 names he supplied them with in 3 categories:
A: dangerous and smugglers; B: the ones who assisted the A.H.C. in the past; C: the Mufti's former supporters who refrained for some time from any action. It is worth noting certain numerical details. For example, 24 of the total were refugees of whom 7 lived in camps, most of them in Aqbat Jabr Camp (all from al-Abbasiyyah). The file contains lists of all fighters of *al-Jihad al-Muqaddas.* File titled A.H.C. Letters, M/S/23/1947 dated 10.7.51. Of another list of 68 Palestinians put in jail, only 3 were refugees and there were no refugees in another 12 put under surveillance. *Ibid.* List No. MN/92/11267 of 8.9.51, M/S/23/3066 dated 1.10.51.

84. *ibid,* report MN/1/83/7.

85. *Ibid,* Order No. MN/1/83/9 dated 21.10.52.

86. *Ibid,* report MN1/32/126 dated 25.4.54.

87. *Ibid,* File titled "The A.H.C. Movement Supporters", letter from C.O.S. Assistant to all A.C.'s. MN/23/797 dated 29.1.56.

88. *Ibid,* Qalqilya Intelligence Officer to HQ, QA/16/415 dated 7.2.56.

89. Such as the Mayors of Tulkarm and Qalqilya, Salah and al-Sab‘, the M.P. Abd al-Ra'uf al-Faris, Fa'iq al-Anabtawi and Yusuf Rida a refugee from Tarshiha, who is the UNRWA Nablus A.O.

90. *Ibid,* MN/7/6/3328 March 1956. Another list of the Nablus area, a similar number does not include any refugees. MN/90/3328 of 20.2.56 (of whom 6 were in Damascus, one in Cairo, 12 in Tulkarm and 36 in Nablus).

91. *Ibid*, M'A/2196/M/10588 dated 20.10.57 and again in March 1958—letter MNN/20/1/H dated 17.3.58 in Truman Papers, No. (32).
92. *Ibid*, 4 refugees out of 28 suspects from the Hebron area. None of the 52 refugees reported to be engaged in political activity in the relatively conservative Hebron area were affiliated to the A.H.C.
93. From Jericho A.C. to Ramallah A.C. dated 18.3.57.
94. *ibid*, Letter from C.O.S. and the Military Governor, MNN/20/1/H/642 dated 4.3.58.
95. *Ibid*, No. 939. The list contained 90 names and included Ishaq al-Duzdar from the Agency and Muhammad Musa al-Liftawi (Lifta). Report dated 10.3.58 in Truman Papers No. (36–41). Zaki al-Tammimi was prevented from admittance on the grounds he signed an appeal to President Nasser in the name of the A.H.C. to annex Palestine to the newly established United Arab Republic (U.A.R.).
96. Of 52 refugees 26 lived in Karamah Camp, 8 in Aqbat Jabr and 17 in al-Husayn in Amman—most of them originated from Bayt Dajan. *Ibid*, p. 12 from the Nablus with JD50,000 to be spent on organizing the activity and the establishment Muhammad Abu Shilbayah who previously was accused of Communism.
97. *Ibid*, report MNN/20/11 dated 8.7.59 in Truman Papers No. (924).
98. *Ibid*, File MNN/20/2/1/H report dated 11.11.61.
99. *Ibid*, report No. 1156 of 19.1.60 noted that a certain Mufti supporter returned to Nablus with JD50,000 to be spent on organizing the activity and the establishment of a terrorist group named "al-Salul".
100. A report of 1960 mentioned Fa'iq al-Anabtawi, Walid Salah, Walid al-Shak'ah, Hikmat al-Masri, members of the Jarar family, the Husaynis Zaki al-Tammimi, Na'im Abd al-Hadi and two UNRWA Camp Leaders in the Hebron and Bethlehem areas. The Trans-Jordanian Shafiq Rashidat was also reported to support this movement.
101. *Ibid*, 520–7–45 July 1960 in Truman papers. See E. Be'eri, *The Palestinians, op. cit.*, p. 15.
102. File MN20/1/H'A, report dated 21.3.60 in Truman Papers No. (203) and a report on his meetings with the A.H.C. members and Kamal Nasir. MQ/L/57/8376 dated 6.7.60.
103. *Ibid*, Report MQ/20/A/L/4118.
104. Letter from Assistant Head of Intelligence to Jerusalem R.O. QM/130458/M/10621 dated 20.5.62.
105. Report MN20/1/H'A dated 7.5.62.
106. Later a list was prepared in Nablus area, for example, where the Mufti had some support and showed that no refugees were included in Category A and 13 refugees out of 180 names were of Category B; most of them lived outside the camps, Report No. 14077 (top secret) dated 18.10.62.
107. Letter from Hebron R.O. to D.G. No. MKHKH/20/1/2741 dated 12.2.59. Top Secret.
108. Letter from Jerusalem Governor to Hebron and Jerusalem R.O. MKH'A/S/10/57/725 dated 25.1.59. Arrub–10; Dahaysha–8; Ayn al-Sultan–7; Nu'yma–4; Auja–5; Aqbat-Jabr–15; al-Amari–6; Ramallah and al-Bira–7; Bir Zayt–4; Jerusalem–6; Hebron and its area–28.
109. See *Tension and Peace in the Middle East, Facts that Every American Should Know about the Tragedy of the Holy Land*, published by the Palestinian Arab Refugee Office (New York, 1956), pp. 20–21; Jamal Nasser *The Resentful Arab, the Truth about the Palestine Question* (formerly entitled *The Embittered Arab*) (Jerusalem 1964) p. 119.
110. An order from Glubb to all A.C.'s, MS/9/1795 of 9.4.52, was issued to detain Communist activists for a longer period of a fortnight so that more information

could be gathered, and equally important, their activity would be weakened owing to their arrest and isolation. In another letter he rebuked the A.C.s for mass arrests on mere suspicion, and ordered them to isolate those suspected of being Communists only as long as necessary for the completion of the investigation, and then put them on secret or open trial. MT/23/221, of 13.9.52.

111. Most notorious and effective was the detention camp at al-Jafr, situated in a desert depression some 50 miles to the east of Ma'an in the south of Trans-Jordan. With temperatures reaching over 40°C. in daytime, and falling to shivering cold at night, any detainee who survived this ordeal of about six months average duration, could be released from this "reformatory institute" as a "cured person" from the regime's point of view.

112. Anwar Nusayba explained that Dr Subhi Sa'id al-Din Ghushah's popularity amongst the Jerusalem refugees was mainly because he extended free medical treatment in his private clinic and served as UNRWA's doctor in the Jewish Quarter Refugee Camp, rather than because of his political views. It was also suggested that Dr Jorj Habash initially established his position in Amman in a similar way. al-Faruqi said that the fact he was a doctor enabled him to enlist a number of important government officials, some of whom were part of the Intelligence. The Jordanian records, however, show that this was one of the methods employed by the Government to plant people in the parties, enabling the regime to follow with greater efficiency these subversive bodies' actions.

113. The N.S.P. condemned W. Clark for threatening teachers who got involved in election campaigns. See al-Difa', 4.9.56.

114. Nablus A.C. demanded information from Intelligence on 21 new applicants from refugees wanting to serve as teachers in UNRWA. (Letter No. MN/20/28/1276 dated 2.3.58). The file shows how Heads of UNRWA Education Dept. accordingly ensured the nomination of some of the people the Government recommended. Report MQ/B/213/4706 dated 21.4.60. The Governor of Jerusalem reported back personally to the Minister of Interior (Letter MD/22/24878 of 16.11.60) on UNRWA's Jericho Area senior worker, A. Bakarjyan, who, it was suggested, was a Communist (Report 28/8/18123 dated 6.12.60). The Governor said he spoke to Lucas from the Agency, following the warning issued to the suspect. In a previous document his transfer to another area was recommended. (MQ/SH/610/14484 dated 10.11.60, Top Secret).

115. In mid 1957 some 75 UNRWA employees, most of whom were teachers, were dismissed after a committee of investigation, on which UNRWA was represented, handed in its recommendations. 85 others were put under surveillance. (Report MNN/7/2/134/11495 dated 17.6.57). Eight were later returned to work, though their movements were followed (MKH/13/31 of 24.8.58). William Clark recalled numerous Government interventions and pressure put on him to dismiss many of his workers, or else not to hire those whom the Government considered to be "politically minded and dangerous people". (Interview in Reading, December 1973 and 22/23 June 1976).

116. For example out of 19 teachers arrested, 17 were Communists (Report MKHM/2/25 of 8.9.53, and another list MKHM/3/20/9774 of 8.9.57).

117. Cable from the Head of Investigation—Public Security to all Area Commanders requesting a list of all UNRWA teachers and clerks who were suspected of being affiliated to the Communist and Ba'th parties. (M'A/18/M/5361. Top secret, dated 7.5.57). Communiqué from Nablus Governor to Area Officers supplying them with lists A B and C of UNRWA personnel (totalling 162 names) to be followed and their movements watched (MN/17/11495 of 17.6.57).

118. Muhammad Musa al-Amlah, Headmaster in Bayt Aula (interview held there on 27.3.74). Khamis Wa'ari, former headmaster in Ayn al-Sultan and Nu'yma (interview held in Auja on 18.4.74).

119. Another report said he urged the camp's notables to approach Rushdi Shahin and invite him to lecture in the camp. Contr. 695–3, 13.3.57. Truman papers (C. 648).

120. A report from 1960 said another three UNRWA Camp Leaders in the Jenin and Nablus areas were Communist supporters. No. MNN/20/28/5803.

121. Letter to A.C., MN/7/1/22825 dated 6.10.56.

122. See *Filastin*, 11.5.57, where two such advertisements appeared.

123. In 1959 the J.C.P. even allowed its members to publicly disassociate themselves and temporarily join other parties.

124. When a group of refugees tried to set up a local Charity Reform Society.

125. Rahel Simon, *Associations and Clubs in the West Bank under the Hashimite Rule,* supervised by M.Ma'oz (The Truman Institute, The Institute for Asian and African Studies, Jerusalem 1974) table of activists, pp. 72–3. This extensive study details the ways in which the regime tried to control these bodies.

126. The Arab Club in Nablus was dominated by Q.A.M. though it had some Ba'thist members (Sela (MA) *op, cit.,* p. 106). R. Simon wrote that the Q.S.P. were fairly active in the Christian clubs in the West Bank. (*op. cit.,* p. 76).

127. In Nablus a meeting of the local UNRWA Teachers Trade Union was cancelled by the authorities at the last moment, when the A.C. received news that a Communist and a Ba'thist would be elected to the Executive. (Report 78/JM/S/3315 of 26.2.57).

128. A report written on 19.4.59 by the Jerusalem A.C. to all A.C.s No. MNN/20/1/A/5742 spoke of renewed smuggling assistance coming from Bayt Safafa divided village. For example, *al-Ittihad,* the Israeli Communist Weekly found its way into the West Bank every week (Report MQM/41/110 dated 24.6.51) together with other handouts and the underground newspapers such as *Tariq al-Awdah,* published in Lebanon by the Congress of Deportees (*Ibid,* MQM/4/1164 dated 26.3.51).

129. The same goes for *al-Bilad,* owned and edited by Daud al-Isa of the *Filastin; al-Sarih* and *al-Jihad* in its early days.

130. From an unpublished work by Dahir Abd al-Karim *The Press and the Regime in Jordan 1949–1967,* a work written under the guidance of Professor Uriel Dann (Tel Aviv University 1970), pp. 24–6. *al-Jihad* could serve as an example of a daily whose owners and editors (who deserted *al-Difa'*) changed the content shortly after the paper was started in August 1953, adopting generally a more pro-regime line.

131. For an analysis of this, see S. Shamir, *Communication, op. cit.*

132. In February and May 1959, the Head of Jordanian Intelligence issued similar orders (in a letter from Nablus D.O. to A.C. No. MNN/21/94/6676, dated 11.5.59). The order forbade listening to the commentator Ahmad Sa'id on *Sawt al-Arab* Radio Station. In early 1967 the regime went as far as confiscating all radio sets in cafes and other public places.

133. Report from Hebron A.C. (MKH20/1/1551 dated 23.9.58) requesting information on two refugees from Salamah working in Kuwait. A report from Kuwait said the Jordanian Communists were encouraging other Palestinians openly to reject King Husayn (MN/20/1/157 dated 20.2.58, in Truman Papers No. (C1172)). Another source of unease was the Communist activity in Iraq in which, according to a report, some 30 Jordanian students were involved. (Jerusalem D.G., MQ/20/15/5992 dated 6.5.59, Top Secret). The report sheds some light on their activity and the political developments in Iraq in which they were involved. Another report suggested that the development in Iraq in 1959 caused some uneasiness in Jordan, where people began fearing the possibility of a Communist-inspired takeover.

134. Letter from the C.O.S. to all A.C.s. M'A/19/19/1052 dated 19.5.57 giving 13

names of those tried in absentia and ordering the prevention of their exit if they
were still in Jordan.

135. Report MQ/ZO/1/0/124 dated 12.9.59 in Truman Papers (C.1060). The L.P.
also managed to send money to the families of their arrested members or
supporters, including dismissed army officers.

136. MQM/9/136 dated 19.3.51.

137. Letter from Nablus A.C. to all Intelligence Area Officers, MN/21/416, Secret,
dated 13.1.55, in *Ibid.*

138. Out of the 78 listed religious speakers in that area, the report listed 6 Tahririn of
whom only one was a refugee. The rest, 12 refugees, were classified as harmless.
(Report No. MN/21/1277 dated 23.1.55, sent to Amman HQ).

139. Dr Hamdi Taji al-Faruqi went on to say: "We could succeed only from inside.
Even from jail. My friends opposed my view. Abd al-Hamid Saraj (of the Syrian
Deuxieme Bureau) was told by Abdallah Rimawi that al-Faruqi intended to
return and feared it would cripple the image of others who had escaped Jordan,
as people would probably say 'Why did he come back and they stayed?' I was
prevented by 'delicate means' by Saraj from returning to Jordan". (Interview,
op. cit.) al-Faruqi returned to Amman in 1962 when the King declared an
amnesty. In the end even Abdallah Rimawi was allowed to return to Jordan (in
July 1970)—the last of the repentant repatriates—and became a loyal member
of the Advisory Council (set up in lieu of the dissolved Parliament in April,
1978).

Chapter VIII

1. See Rosamund Essex, *Outcasts of Today. An eye-witness report on Middle
Eastern Refugees* (London), p. 27; U.S.A. Assistant Secretary of State, George
McGhee's words in the House Committee on Foreign Affairs, 16.2.50 in Edward
H. Buehrig, *The U.N. and the Palestinian Refugees, a study in non-territorial
administration* (Indiana University Press, 1971), p. 37; Emil Samaan *The Arab
Refugees after five years, an eye-witness report* (American Friends of the Middle
East Inc., N.Y. 1953), p. 10; Najla Izza al-Din *The Arab World* (Chicago, 1953)
etc. Compare with W. Laqueur "Communism in Jordan", p. 111.

2. This assumption ignored the fact that many villagers voted for anyone of their
number running for office regardless of their political beliefs, hoping to be
rewarded by a successful candidate with some form of favouritism, for example
a governmental position, licenses etc. See Abdallah M. Lutfiyya *Baytin, a
Jordanian Village, A study of social institutions and social change in a Folk
Community* (The Hague 1965), p. 90 who gives the example of Fa'iq Warrad
who received support on those grounds. It should nonetheless also be recalled
that the Salfit village was one of the Communist strongholds.

3. Petition signed by the refugee notables in the Hebron area headed by Muhammad
al-Azzah and Qatanani requesting permission for such a demonstration on
12.8.56. (File KH/2/14, SA JUPR).

4. William T. Clark, second interview, *op. cit.* He said they were unconditional
payments which followed the monies spent on the Agency's advertisement for
distribution of rations, etc. Clark, who knew Arabic, said he decided to limit
these "subsidies . . . dished out by the Chief Public Relations Officer in Beirut
H.Q. direct to the newspapers . . . as we could not possibly have had a worse
Press . . . and there was little point to pay something for nothing, as the Press
picked up all sorts of stories from refugees about 'UNRWA's extravagances'—
and they were printing things to irritate us".

5. A YMCA unpublished report by Fraser E. Smith, *Report on the Provision of*

YMCA Clubs for the Young Men Among the Palestine Refugees, 26.1.50, Beirut, p. 2 (YMCA Archives).

6. See also League of Red Cross Societies, *Report of the Relief Operation on Behalf of the Palestinian Refugees,* conducted by the Middle East Commission of the LRCS in conjunction with the UN Relief for Palestine Refugees, 1949–50 (Geneva, 1950).

7. *Observations on the nutritional status of Arab Refugees,* February-March 1950, MH21.050, Geneva, p. 30, unpublished report.

8. *Nutritional State of the Palestine Refugees in the Spring of 1951* W.H.O., Geneva, 1951, p. 24. N.B.: To be found in Middle East Library, St. Antony's College, Oxford.

9. The Jericho refugees rejected the brown sugar and demonstrated against the Swiss-donated yellow cheese—owing to its odour and holes, which made them suspect it had been eaten by mice.

10. S.A. JUPR. Report MKHM/1/19/2415 dated 5.7.52. (The demonstrations took place on 3.7.52).

11. Letter from UNRWA's Chief District Officer, Arnold Rorholt, to the M.D.R. Ref. AD/35 (53) dated 16.11.50.

12 .The Agencies were aware that many ration cards were forged in the early days before special cards were issued. This proved to be an extremely sensitive issue. See Appendix No. 2 for a reproduction of the first trial 1948 ration cards.

13. An unpublished UNRWA document, *Consolidated Eligibility Instruction (Confidential)* (Beirut 1.11.61), 26 pp., amended on 1.3.66 and 20.11.73) reveals the complexity of judging who was a "needy refugee". The different conflicting estimates regarding the number of such people involve a basic disagreement over the term "refugee". See Avi Plascov, "Who is a Palestinian refugee? The attempts to define the refugee status and the problems that evolved around this in Jordan after the 1948 war" (to be published shortly).

14. S.A. JUPR, file T/20/7, unpublished UNWRA document, "Appeals Against Ration Cuts. System to be Followed", District Registrar's circular "C" DRC/c Amended 1, signed by T. E. Pigot District Registrar UNWRA, Jordan Jerusalem 10.11.50; the file contains many appeals and decisions of the Appeal Committee up to the census; for instance on 27.12.50 it was decided to give back 16 cancelled ration cards and to refuse 9 of the appeals examined that day. Six months later UNRWA protested to the government that it was concealing the fact that the authorities were collecting Trade and Industry Licence Fees from camp refugees who apparently earned a high income and yet UNRWA considered them "needy". According to the report, by mid-1951 there were in Aqbat Jabr 55 grocers, 15 butchers, 17 cafés, 21 bakers, 11 cloth dealers, 10 flour mills, 3 tailors, 11 laundries, 6 barbers, etc. UNRWA insisted these names "should be taken off the ration" *Ibid* File QA/5, letter AD/35/399, Amman 9.6.51).

15. UNRWA used a special column in the daily *Filastin* to explain its reasons for cancellation of ration cards (R/C): *"You are not a refugee"*—Muhammad Ali Munahi R/C No. 32602 who claimed he came from Haifa (15.11.52) and Asad Abd al-Latif Nuri who lived in the old city of Jerusalem and came from Nablus; to Subhi Isma'il Hasan of Bayt Ummar who claimed he came from occupied Dayr Iban R/C no. 168849 to Subhi Abd al-Aziz Hamad from Ramin who said he came from Haifa R/C no. 24661 (10.1.53). See also R/C no. 170655 and 16217 (31.1.53) and (14.2.53). *"The Card is not yours"* Haniha Muhammad who claimed he originated from al-Lid. UNRWA states he held the card of Abd al-Hadi-Khalil Husayn (15.11.52). *"Your friend receives your ration"* Muhammad Abu Hanna *"You are not a needy refugee"* Muhammad Isma'il Salih whom the Agency does not consider a refugee owing to the fact that he is from Silat

al-Harthiya and married there. R/C no. 43448 (22.11.52). *"You own property, you are a policeman and above all, a non-refugee"* to Musa Husayn Ali who claimed to be expelled from Haifa. (15.11.52) *"You own property"* Radi Rida al-Asali in Nablus and Amman although originating from Jaffa, R/C No. 4747 (10.1.53) *"You own 60 dunam of cultivated land"* Husayn Abdallah Husayn who claimed he came from Haifa R/C No. 129268 (6.12.52). *"Your card is forged"* to Uthman Abd al-Hadi Khashan R/C No. 154544 (20.12.52) *"You have two other Ration cards"* Muhammad Hamdan Abu Rayash (31.1.53).

16. See *Filastin*, 7.1.60.
17. See *Annual Report of UNRWA, 1 July 1954–30 June 1955*, A/2978.
18. S.A. JUPR. File UNRWA Affairs, Letter from J.B. Pruen, Deputy Chief District Officer in Jerusalem to Ihsan Hashim D.G. ref: No. 62 dated 12.8.50.
19. *Ibid*, Report No. MN20/28/12200 dated 16.7.61.
20. Amongst them rich local and refugee merchants who had at their disposal many ration cards purchased from refugees or taken against a loan. UNRWA begged the Government time and again to put an end to this black market, but the authorities, who agreed in principle to confiscate the cards (Minister of Interior Order No. 33, 29/9/3/6100 of 6.3.57.) were reluctant to carry out their promise. Also UNRWA document entitled "Conglomeration of Hawkers and Merchants around Distribution Centers" to Hebron D.G. No. 5SD/2(4207) dated 28.1.57. See article in *al-Jihad* which criticizes UNRWA for trying to discover who of the agency's personnel was behind the constant thefts of food, merchandise, tents, wood, equipment and medicine (compare with *al-Bilad* 28.12.58 and *al-Jihad* 3.3.59 which condemn these thefts).
21. *Ibid*, File MKH/6/2, Isma'il Ali Tahabub to D.G., strictly confidential, dated 24.7.61.
22. See his book *The High Tower of Refuge, the Inspiring Story of Refugee Relief throughout the World* (London, 1961), p. 102.
23. See *Filastin*, 20.6.52.
24. In al-Amari Camp the UNRWA office was just across the road, making it easy for refugees to demonstrate and force their way in. It was moved a few miles up the road to Ramallah town.
25. Interview on 7.2.77, *op. cit.*
26. M. Habab, Dahaysha's Camp Leader (interview held there on 26.6.74).
27. Interview with him in Aqbat Jabr Camp on 5.2.74. Abu Rish, a non-refugee Camp Leader, held considerable influence over the camp's notables. He accounted for this through his being a villager and "one of them", as opposed to urban Camp Leaders before him who, he claimed, could not succeed with the refugees. Up until his arrival there in 1956, he served in Karamah Camp.
28. Hazza' al-Majali *Hadha bayan lil nas. Qissat Muhadathat Templer* (a statement for the people—the story of the Templer talks) (Arabic) (n.p.n.d.) pp. 17–8.

Appendices

Appendix No. 1

AGREEMENT BETWEEN THE GOVERNMENT OF THE HASHEMITE KINGDOM OF THE JORDAN AND THE UNITED NATIONS RELIEF AND WORKS AGENCY FOR PALESTINE REFUGEES

14 March 1951

WHEREAS the General Assembly of the United Nations at its Fourth Session, by Resolution 302 (IV) of 8th December, 1949, established the United Nations Relief and Work Agency for Palestine Refugees in the Near East hereinafter referred to as The Agency, to carry out the terms of the said Resolution;

WHEREAS the relief for Palestine refugees was formerly the subject of an agreement between the Hashemite Kingdom of Jordan and the Director of the United Nations Relief for Palestine Refugees and that this agreement has been continued by grace of the Hashemite Kingdom of the Jordan pending the conclusion of a new agreement between that Government and the Agency;

WHEREAS the Hashemite Kingdom of the Jordan identifies itself with the above quoted Resolution of the General Assembly and with the Resolution adopted by the General Assembly at its 315th Plenary meeting of 2 December, 1950, which Resolutions have been agreed to by the Arab member nations, and whereas the Hashemite Kingdom of the Jordan at the same time introduced legislative measures which permit the reintegration of Palestine refugees within the Kingdom of the Jordan at the request of the refugees concerned, the Hashemite Kingdom of the Jordan and the Agency have agreed that the present machinery established by the Ministry of Development and Reconstruction and the Agency for the consideration and implementation of reintegration and other projects shall be maintained;

WHEREAS the supplies to be distributed and the funds to be expended represent gifts of member states of the United Nations and others for the implementation of the provisions of the above quoted Resolutions;

WHEREAS the Agency as a matter of policy will endeavor to utilize its funds to the maximum advantage of the refugees;

WHEREAS the Hashemite Kingdom of the Jordan has expressed its desire to cooperate with the Agency in giving effect to the provision of the above quoted Resolutions with which the Hashemite Kingdom of the Jordan has identified itself, the Hashemite Kingdom of the Jordan and the Agency have agreed that the following facilities and immunities are necessary for the successful continuation of the Agency's program;

ARTICLE 1

The Hashemite Government of the Jordan agrees to grant the Director of the Agency, the members of his Advisory Commission and the senior officials of the Agency as may be agreed upon in writing between the Hashemite Government of the Jordan and the Director of the Agency the privileges and immunities normally granted in accordance with international custom to Diplomatic Envoys of equivalent rank. The Hashemite Government of the Jordan further agrees to grant all internationally recruited members of the Agency's staff the privileges and immunities including freedom from income and other taxes provided for under the convention on the Privileges and Immunities of the United Nations with which the Hashemite Government of the Jordan identifies itself, a copy of the Convention is annexed to this agreement.

ARTICLE II

The Hashemite Government of the Jordan agrees to grant the international and local staff of the Agency whose names are communicated to the Hashemite Government of the Jordan certificates of identity or travel permits which will authorise them to:–

(1) move freely at any time throughout the Hashemite Kingdom of the Jordan in and between areas in which substantial groups of refugees may be found, or where reintegration projects are proposed or undertaken;

(2) move freely between the Hashemite Kingdom of the Jordan and the neighbouring Arab states;

(3) such certificates or permits may be withdrawn by the Minister of Foreign Affairs for international staff and by the Minister of Reconstruction and Development for local personnel at any time for reasons connected with public security or for unlawful actions which may have been committed, but in all cases not before notification has been made to the responsible officers of the Agency;

(4) the Government further agrees to issue permits which will permit passengers, cars and freight vehicles of the Agency to move freely at any time within the Kingdom and to grant facilities for speedy crossing of the frontiers; it being understood that the freedom of movement described above shall be subject to regulations pertaining to military security in areas where such regulations are in force;

(5) The Hashemite Government of the Jordan agrees to issue to the Director of the Agency, the members of his Advisory Commission and all members of his staff, appropriate visas which will permit them at all times to enter and leave the Hashemite Kingdom of the Jordan, and agrees to exempt all such persons, when travelling on official business of the Agency, from quarantine, customs, visas or other fees or taxes of a

similar nature collected for the profit of the Kingdom or any administration or society whatsoever.

ARTICLE III

The Agency agrees to pay to the Jordan Government, with effect from 1st priority in the selection of personnel and in the utilization of services will be given to refugees or to services operated or owned by the refugees; and further agrees, all conditions being equal, to purchase such supplies as may be required and are available from local markets.

The appointment of local staff shall be made upon the recommendations of an Agency selection board in which the Government shall be represented.

ARTICLE IV

The Hashemite Government of the Jordan agrees to pay to the Agency, with effect from 1st March, 1951, contributions amounting to five thousand Jordanian Dinars per month for all relief and administration purposes.

The Government further agrees to provide safe conduct of goods, produce, stores and equipment at all times within the Hashemite Kingdom of the Jordan.

The Agency agrees to pay to the Jordan Govenment, with effect from 1st March 1951, the sum of five hundred Jordanian Dinars per month towards all costs arising out of rents for land occupied by refugee camps and for charges of water consumed by refugees within the Hashemite Kingdom of the Jordan; it being understood that the responsibility for the provision of camp sites and of water and for resolving all questions arising out of their procurement shall rest with the Government.

The Hashemite Government of Jordan agrees to bear all costs arising out of rents for land occupied by refugees in excess of five hundred Jordanian Dinars per month.

ARTICLE V

The goods, stores, produce and equipment including petroleum products destined for the refugees in the Jordan shall be admitted exempt of all customs duty, taxes or import duties of any sort collected for the profit of the Kingdom or any administration or society whatsoever.

The Hashemite Kingdom of the Jordan, without prejudice to reasonable security requirements, waives the right of inspection of the aforementioned goods, stores, produce and equipment and further grants exemption from the need to obtain export permits and import permits; it being understood that the Government reserves the right to withdraw this exemption upon the submission of evidence to the responsible officers of the Agency that it has been abused.

ARTICLE VI

The goods, stores, produce and equipment including petroleum products brought into the Hashemite Kingdom of the Jordan by virtue of the preceding Articles shall remain the property of the United Nations until delivery to individual beneficiaries or formal transfer by the Agency to the Government.

ARTICLE VII

The Agency agrees that a schedule of refugees shall be established upon the completion of the current census of refugees within the Hashemite Kingdom of the Jordan to which the Government has given its support, and thereafter agrees that this schedule may be amended by *eliminations* and *additions* by the Chief District Officer of UNRWA in Jordan after *consultations* with the Hashemite Minister of Development and Reconstruction; keeping in mind the necessity of encouragement of able-bodied refugees to find employment as well as the responsibility of the Agency to spend its funds in conformity with its mandate.

ARTICLE VIII

The Hashemite Government of the Jordan agrees that any funds which are the property of the Agency at the end of its program and which are on deposit or current account within Jordan as the result of an official transfer, may at the request of the Director of the Agency be reconverted into the original foreign currency at the current official rates obtaining at the time of reconversion.

The Agency further agrees that all transfers of Agency funds into the Hashemite Kingdom of the Jordan shall be effected through official channels.

ARTICLE IX

The specific conditions under which works and reintegration projects are to be carried out shall be laid down in special agreements between the Government of the Hashemite Kingdom of the Jordan and the Agency.

ARTICLE X

The Hashemite Government of the Jordan undertakes to accept responsibility for guarding within the Kingdom the stores, warehouses, water and other installations of the Agency and generally undertakes to give all such facilities which may assist the Agency in achieving the objectives set out in the Resolutions of the General Assembly which are annexed to this Agreement and to which the Hashemite Government of the Jordan now adheres and supports in common with the action taken by other Arab Governments at the fourth and fifth sessions of the General Assembly.

ARTICLE XI

The terms and obligations of this Agreement shall be regarded as being binding upon the contracting parties from the date of signature. The provisions of Articles IV and V concerning contributions and service to be given by the Government of the Hashemite Kingdom of the Jordan save when otherwise indicated shall be binding as from 1st May, 1950.

Signed this 14th day of March, 1951.

(Signed) Howard Kennedy,   (Signed) Anastas Hanania
    Director

On behalf of the United Nations   Minister for Development and
Relief and Works Agency for   Reconstruction The Hashemite
Palestine Refugees in the Near   Kingdom Of Jordan.
East.

NOTE: Agreement in Arabic signed on 14 March, 1951, by Anastas
      Hanania, Minister of Reconstruction and Development, on behalf
      of the Hashemite Kingdom of the Jordan, and by John H.
      Blandford, Jr., Director, on behalf of the United Nations Relief
      and Works Agency for Palestine Refugees in the Near East on 20
      August, 1951.

Appendix No. 2

Photocopy of 1948 prototype Refugee Ration Cards

Appendix No. 3

RESOLUTIONS

On 17th March, 1949, a Congress representing all refugees residing in the Arab areas of Palestine was convened at Ramallah to consider the refugee question in all its aspects. After lengthy deliberations the following resolutions were passed:

1. The refugees insist on their return to their homes as of right without awaiting the ultimate settlement for the Palestine question.

2. The refugees ask to be fully compensated for all material losses suffered by them before and after the end of the mandate.

3. That adequate safeguards be taken to ensure that refugee property is returned to the refugees immediately upon their return.

4. Adequate guarantees be given to insure the re-establishment of the Refugees in their homes and their liberties.

5. That the General Refugee Council elected hereafter shall have the exclusive right to represent the refugees in all matters and that no other body shall have the right to represent them.

6 .The General Refugee Council shall be constituted as follows:—

   a. The General Council shall consist of forty members to be elected by this Congress. (In implementation of this resolution the Congress elected thirty members, whose names were inscribed in the Refugee Office. Ten seats were reserved for ten duly elected representatives of those refugees residing in the Hashemite Kingdom of Transjordan).

   b. An Executive Committee of ten members of the General Council to be elected by the Council. (The General Council duly elected ten members whose names were inscribed in the Refugee Office).

   c. The Executive Committee shall elect from its members the required staff for the Congress Refugee Office.

   d. The Executive Committee shall be bound by the resolutions of the General Council.

   e. The Congress further empowers the General Council to increase its members from time to time to provide the fullest possible representation of refugees in all Arab countries.

7. The Congress empowers the General Refugee Council to contact all political and international organisations for the purpose of attaining the resolutions of this Congress.

Secretary,
General Refugee Congress
(two signatures)

Appendix No. 4

A STATEMENT OF THE AIMS AND POLICY OF
THE PALESTINE ARAB REFUGEE CONGRESS

Introductory:

The Arab refugees resident in Irbid and in Arab Palestine, excepting those in the Gaza enclave, are as fully and as constitutionally represented as circumstances will permit by the Palestine Arab Refugee Congress, first called at Ramallah on 17 March, 1949 and expanded to full representative capacity in September, 1949.

1.   The Palestine Arab Refugee Congress upholds most strongly the right of the refugees to return to their homes, to regain their property, both movable and immovable, and to their right to obtain compensation for loss or damage to such property as defined in the General Assembly resolution of 11th December, 1948. The Congress affirms that these rights are inalienable and cannot be fettered, relinquished, conditioned or waived by any Government, authority or body other than themselves.

2.   The Palestine Arab Refugee Congress believes that the alteration of the present armistice lines in conformity with the United Nations Partition Plan for Palestine of November, 1947 would facilitate the repatriation of large numbers of refugees to their former homes and would constitute a major and effective step towards the satisfactory settlement of the refugee problem.

3.   The Palestine Arab Refugee Congress recognises the possibility that some refugees, for varying reasons, may not wish to return to their former domiciles and that they may wish to be settled temporarily or permanently elsewhere.

4.   In order to preserve as far as possible the entity of Arab Palestine, and in order to satisfy the natural longing of a people for its native soil and climate, the Palestine Arab Refugee Congress affirms that it will not concur in any proposal to resettle Palestine Arab refugees in any of the other Arab countries until the maximum number possible has been resettled firstly in Palestine as a whole and secondly in the Hashemite Kingdom of Jordan.

5.   The Palestine Arab Refugee Congress rejects the Israeli contention that the resettlement of the refugees in Israel or Israeli occupied territory is a matter for the Israelis alone, and holds that it is a matter for the United Nations authority to carry out such resettlement in consultation with the competent authorities and the refugees themselves.

6.   The Palestine Arab Refugee Congress affirms the inalienable right of the refugees to dispose of their former property as they see fit and their right to claim and receive full and equitable compensation for any property

relinquished, destroyed, lost or damaged as a result of their flight or ejection. It also affirms that the assessment of and payment of compensation, where it is applicable, be carried out under the strict supervision of the United Nations and in close consultation with the refugees themselves.

7.   While the Palestine Arab Refugee Congress is not wanting in gratitude and appreciation for the direct assistance that has so generously been afforded to the refugees until now, it fully welcomes the Economic Survey Mission's intention to replace it by relief through employment and offers its full and complete co-operation with the reservation that the refugees shall not be bound by any decision that may conflict with the aims of the Congress or prejudice the rights of the refugees as defined in the General Assembly resolution of the 11th December, 1948.

8.   The Palestine Arab Refugee Congress proposes to set up the necessary machinery for the registration of the refugees in Arab Palestine by professions; former occupations and property holdings as well as former places of origin. This vital information will be made available to the Economic Survey Mission with a view to opening an employment exchange as soon as employment schemes are approved and with a view to facilitating the later payment of compensation where this is applicable and the subsequent return of refugees to their homes. The Palestine Arab Refugee Congress asks the Economic Survey Mission for its full co-operation in return.

9.   The Palestine Arab Refugee Congress proposes to incorporate in the Congress, General Council and Executive Committee duly elected representatives on behalf of those refugees in the other Arab countries not already represented in the Congress.

The above statement of the aims and policy of the Palestine Arab Refugee Congress was considered and approved by the Executive Committee in a meeting held at Ramallah on 9th October, 1949.

Mohammed El-Yehia   Aziz Shihadeh
Member   Secretary
Executive Committee   Executive Committee

Nassib Bulos
Member
Executive Committee

Appendix No. 5

UNITED NATIONS
RELIEF AND WORKS AGENCY
FOR PALESTINE REFUGEES

NATIONS UNIES
OFFICE DE SECOURS ET DE TRAVA:
POUR LES RÉFUGIÉS DE PALESTIN

وكالة هيئة الامم المتحدة
لاغاثة وتشغيل اللاجئين الفلسطينيين

Telephones: { Amman 125
Jerusalem 145

Cables : UNRWADO

Field Office
P. O. Box 484
Amman - JO:D:

Ref: 5/R/11-A-2161

12 July, 1958.

His Excellency,
Mutasarref of Hebron.

عطوفة متصرف لواء الخليل المحترم •

Reference is made to the petition submitted
to you by Mohammed Darwish, Ahmad Mohammed
Darwish and Ismail Ahmad Saqer, all of Hubeileh
project, about which you have requested
information.

You are most probably aware that sometime
ago the Agency and the Government cooperated
together to build up agricultural projects in
particular like Marj Na'je, Jisr-Il-Majame' and
Hubeileh to provide eligible refugees with a
means of income and thus make them independent
not relying on rations which eventually are
cancelled. The first number of refugees
amongst whom petitioners were considered as
eligible for Hubeileh project, all received
considerable sums of money, a piece of land,
a house and a large number of sheep and one
mule per family. With the above each family
was considered by the government and the Agency
as having become self sufficient and their
rations were cancelled. It must be kept in
mind that the lands of Hubeileh belong to the
custodian of enemy property and all through
the Agency was paying to the said custodian the
rent agreed upon with the government. It goes
without saying that the buildings on Hubeileh
were all erected by the Agency.

However a few months after petitioners and
other refugee families have settled there, they
claimed to the Government that what they were
given was not sufficient to make them independent
particularly since the lands of Hubeileh are
somewhat rocky. After considerable investigation
and checking, in addition to the continuous
complaints of these refugees and at their head
the three petitioners, the Government and the
Agency together decided to close down the
project and return the rations to each and every
family who had entered the said project. This
was done and each family had to go back to its
place of origin or the place from where it came
from before the project was started. The
government and the Agency decided to consider
the project as having failed with a loss of
almost a quarter of a million dollars.

صاحب العطوفة •

اشير الى الاستدعاء المقدم •

بمعروفتكم من محمد درويش واحمد محمد درويش
اسماعيل احمد صقر وهم من مشروع الحبيله
وانك تطلبون بيان معلومات عنه •

ان عطوفتكم ولاشك تعلمون بان
الوكالة والحكومة قد تعاونتا منذ مدة سابقة لانشاء
مشاريع زراعية وعلى الخصوص في مرج نعجه وجسر
المجامع والحبيله وذلك لتزويد اللاجئين المستحقين
بوسائل دخل حتى يتسنى جعلهم مستقلين لا
يعتمدون على مخصصات الاعاشة التي تلغى نهائيا
وان عدد من اللاجئين اعتبروا مستحقين لمشروع
الحبيله كان بينهم المستدعون وكل عائلة
منهم تسلمت مقادير ارا لا بأربعه من النقود وقطعة
ارض ومسكنا وعددا كبيرا من الماشية وبغلا.
وبهذه الاشياء اعتبرت كل عائلة من قبل
الحكومة والوكالة انها قد غدت تكتفي ذاتيــا
وقد اظطرت بحاجتها. ويجب ان لا يغرب عن
البال ان اراضي الحبيله تخص الحارس على
املاك العدو وان الوكالة كانت طيلة المدة
تدفع للحارس المذكور الايجار المتفق عليه
بالحكومة • ولا حاجة للقول ان كل بناء
في الحبيله قامت بتشييده الوكالة •

وعلى كل حال بعد اشهر
نزل من استقرار المستدعين وبعض العائلات
اللاجئة الاخرى في المشروع ادعوا للحكومة
ان ما اعطي لهم لم يكن كافيا لجعلهم
مستقلين خصوصا وان اراضي الحبيله صخرية
زيادة ما • وبعد اجراء تحقيقات وتدقيقات واسعة
بالاضافة الى شكاوى مستمرة من هؤلاء اللاجئين
وعلى رأسهم المستدعون الثلاثة قررت الحكومة والوكالة
بالغاء المشروع واعادة مخصصات الاعاشة لكل منهم
وكافة العائلات التي دخلت المشروع المذكور •

Appendix No. 5 (cont'd)

I believe that your excellency agrees with me, in view of the above, that the families who had benefited from this project namely the three petitioners, have received very much more than they are entitled to since their rations were returned to them and they can neither have any claim on the lands which belong to the custodian of enemy property and are leased to the Agency; nor do they have any right to any of the installations erected by the Agency with the agreement of the Government on Hubeileh site.

Recently we have decided as an Agency to reactivate the project on a particularly different basis than previously done and have chosen what we believe are refugee families who would be a success. This was done in complete agreement with the Government who undertook to clear the site and the buildings from all refugee and non refugee families living there. As a matter of fact this was done and military families and some of the refugee families who have entered without our permission were cleared out from the site. The three petitioners with three other families refused to leave and the Ministry requested the police authorities of Hebron to clear them out. Unfortunately this action was delayed for one reason or another and our work on the project was hindered.

I hope that after this detailed explanation, your Excellency would take the necessary action to clear them out as soon as possible to enable us to continue our work keeping in mind that if what they have said is true in respect of some plantations on Hubeileh lands, they must be considered as having encroached upon property not belonging to them and making use of it. I believe this action is punishable by law.

With my respects.

I. K. Duzdar,
Area Officer, Hebron.

اسحق الدزدار
مدير منطقـــــة الخليـــــل .

Appendix No. 6

to

Appendix No. 11

at back of

book

Appendix No. 12

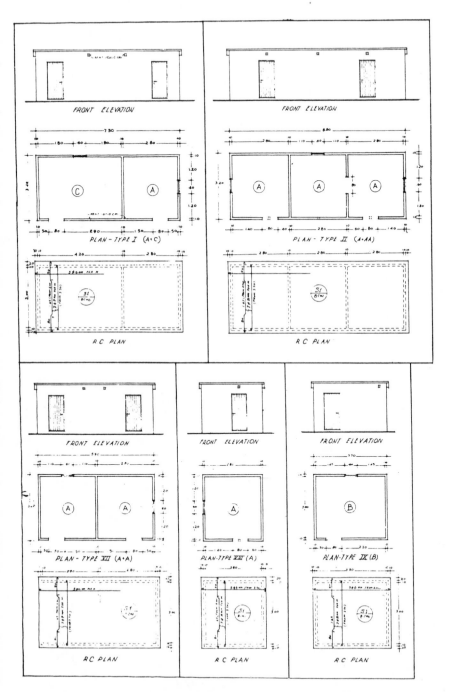

UNRWA's scheme of different types of the UNRWA built shelters

Appendix No. 13

at back of

book

Bibliography

PRIMARY SOURCES

A. ARCHIVES

British Red Cross Society Archives, Barnet Hill (Guildford). Unpublished records of the British Red Cross Commission's work in Transjordan 1949-1950. (and photographs)
British Council of Churches Library
Christian Aid Library, London
Public Record Office, London
    Colonial Office, Foreign Office, Cabinet Papers 1944-1946
St Antony's College, Middle East Library, Private Papers
Harry S. Truman Research Institute Archives, The Hebrew University of Jerusalem, Mount Scopus, Jerusalem.
Archiyon Z.H.L. (The Israel Defence Forces Archives)
Israel State Archives, Jerusalem
    Jordanian Records, Section No. 65(114) and 17/3
Jerusalem Municipality Historical Archives
The Shiloah Research Centre, Tel Aviv University
Near East Christian Council Committee for Refugee Work East, Jerusalem Head Quarters
International Red Cross Library, Head Quarters Geneva
League of Red Cross Societies, Head Quarters Library, Geneva
World Alliance of Young Men's Christian Associations (YMCA) Archives, Geneva
World Council of Churches, Geneva
UNRWA Head Quarters, Jerusalem, Geneva, New York

B. PRIVATE PAPERS

William Clark (UNRWA Representative in Jordan 1953-1959) Private papers, (diaries, documents and photographs)
Henry Knezevitz. Former ICRC and UNRWA Area Officer

C. OFFICIAL RECORDS

1. UNITED NATIONS

(a) UNRPR

American Friends Service Committee, *Quaker Work Among Arab Refugees undertaken for the United Nations, December 1948–April 1950.*

ICRC,   *Report on General Activities, July 1, 1947–December 31, 1948* (Geneva, 1949).
        – *The International Committee of the Red Cross in Palestine* (Geneva, July 1948)
        – *Rapports général d'activité du Commissariat pour l'aide aux Refugiés en Palestine, 1.1.49–30.4.50.* (4 pamphlets)
        – *General report on the activities of the medical services* (Geneva, 1949)
        – *Health Conditions among the civilian population of certain countries affected by the War*, No. 5 (Geneva, August 1949)
        – *Report on General Activities, Jan 1–Dec 31, 1949* (Geneva, 1950)
        – *Relief scheme for the poor of Jerusalem* (Geneva, 1950)
        – *Report on General Activities, Jan 1–Dec 31, 1950* (Geneva, 1951)
        – *Report on the work of the International Committee of the Red Cross Jan 1–Dec 31, 1951* (Geneva, 1952)
        – *Summary report for July 47–December 51, given to XVIII International Red Cross Conference, Toronto, July–August 1952* (Geneva, 1952)
        – *Report on the work of the ICRC Jan 1–Dec 31, 1952* (Geneva, 1953)
        – *Commissariat of the International Committee of the Red Cross for relief to Palestinian Refugees: General report on the activites of the Medical Centre* (n.p.n.d.) 189p.
LRCS,   *The Red Cross World*, XVIIth International R.C. Conference XXth meeting of the Board of Governors of the LRCS. Vol. XXIX, No. 3 (Geneva, October 1948)
        – *Monthly Report* No. 25 (Geneva, June 1949)
        – *Report of the Relief Operation on behalf of the Palestine Refugees 1949–1950* (Geneva, 1950).
        – *Report of the Relief operation on behalf of the Palestine Refugees* (Geneva, 1951)
        – Dr Z. S. Hantchef, *The Refugees Throughout the World*, P.4932/m.l.c./13.10.53 (Geneva, 1953)
        – *Personnel location list as at 6.7.49*
BRCS,   *Report for the year 1948, Refugee Relief in the Middle East, year ending 31 December 1949*
        – *Relief Overseas, 1950*
        – *Relief Overseas, 1951*
        – *Relief Overseas, 1952*
UNRPR, Doc. A/1060 of 4.11.49: *Report of the Secretary General on the Activities of UNRPR–submitted to the 4th session of the General Assembly.*
        – Doc. A/1060/Add. 1 of 4.11.49: *Financial Statements of UNRPR for the period 1.12.48–30.6.49*
        – Doc. A/1452 of 24.10.50: *Report of the Secretary General to the 5th session on the activities of UNRPR for the period 30.9.49–30.4.50*
        – *First interim report of the UN Economic Survey Mission for the Middle East*
        – *Final report of the UN Economic Survey Mission for the Middle East* (Clapp's Mission) 2 vol. 1950
        – *Middle East–Work amongst Refugees*, Nos. 5 & 179
HIGH COMMISSIONER FOR REFUGEES, *The Red Cross and the Refugees* (Geneva, 1963)

(b) WHO
        – *A Report on present conditions of the Palestine refugees and WHO Aid* (by Dr J. D. Cottrell) (7.2.49)

–*Palestine refugees–Health needs* (1.9.49) (by Dr J. D. Cottrell)
–*The UNRWA Health programme for Palestine Refugees* (7.8.50)
–*Report on visit to the Hashemite Kingdom of the Jordan February 20–March 5, 1951* (by E. Magnussen, April 1951)
–*Bilharziasis Survey in some countries of the Eastern Mediterranean Region* by Dr M. Abdel Azim, June 1951
–*Report on the Mission to Arab Refugees in Palestine on behalf of WHO (2–30 December 1950)* by Prof. G. B. Bietti 6.6.51
–*Report on the mission accomplished from 26.3.51 to 15.4.51 among the Arab refugees in Palestine on behalf of WHO* by Prof. G. Bietti, 6.6.51
–*Nutritional State of the Palestinian refugees in the Spring of 1951.*

(c) UNRWA

–Doc. A/1451/Rev. 1 *Interim report submitted to the 5th session of the General Assembly (G.A.)*
–Doc. A/1905 *Annual report of the Director for the period 1.5.50–30.6.51*
–Doc. A/1905/Add. 1 *Special report of the Director and the Advisory Commission*
–Doc. A/1931 *Accounts for the period 1.5–31.12.50*
–Doc. A/2171 *Annual report of the Director for the period 1.7.51–30.6.52*
–Doc. A/2171/Add. 1 *Special report of the Director and the Advisory Commission*
–Doc. A/2207 *Accounts for the period 1.1.51–30.6.52*
–Doc. A/2470 *Annual report for the period 1.7.52–30.6.53*
–Doc. A/2470/Add. 1 *Special report of the Director and the Advisory Commission*
–Doc. A/2497 *Account for the period 1.7.52–30.6.53*
–Doc. A/2717 *Annual report for the period 1.7.53–30.6.54*
–Doc. A/2717/Add. 1 *Special report of the Director and the Advisory Commission*
–Doc. A/2760 *Accounts for the period 1.7.53–30.6.54*
–Doc. A/2978 *Annual report for the period 1.7.54–30.6.55*
–Doc. A/2978/Add. 1 *Special report of the Director concerning other claimants for relief*
–Doc. A/2989 *Accounts for the period 1.7.54–30.6.55*
–*Special Report by the Advisory Commission for Palestine Refugees in the Near East, December 21, 1956: The Problem of Palestine Refugees, 1956*
–Doc. A/3129 *Accounts for the period 1.7.55–30.6.56*
–Doc. A/3212 *Annual report of the period 1.7.55–30.6.56*
–Doc. 3212/Add. 1 *Special report of the Director for 1.11–15.12.56*
–Doc. A/3686 *Annual report for the period 1.7.56–30.6.57*
–Doc. A/3836 *Accounts for the period 1.7.56–31.12.57*
–Doc. A/3931 *Annual report for the period 1.7.57–30.6.58*
–*The Unified Development of the water Resources of the Jordan Valley Region* (Boston, 1953)
–*Refugee Congress–Jerusalem 20 July 1955*, 20pp. (unpublished)
–*Vacancy Advertisements* (unpublished)
–*Figures of vocational training graduates 1955–1968* prepared by Harry Howard (unpublished)
–*Staff regulations*–applicable to Area Staff Members (Beirut, 1 July 1957) (unpublished)
–*Information Sheets* (on each refugee camp)
–*Consolidated Eligibility Instruction* (Confidential) (unpublished) UN

Relief Headquarters (Beirut, 1.11.1961) amended 1.3.1966, amended 20.11.73, 26pp.
–*Summary data on assistance to the Palestine Refugees 1 December 1948–30 June 1961*
–*Information on the operation of UNRWA in the Jericho Area* (1964)
–*Explanatory memorandum made by host countries representatives on UNRWA Commission, 1965* (original: Arabic)

UNRWA Reviews: A Background Information Series Information Paper No. 1. *A brief history of UNRWA 1950–1962* (Beirut, 1962)
–Information Paper No. 2. *Summary data on Assistance to the Palestine Refugees (December 1948–31 December 1962)* (Beirut, 1962)
–Information Paper No. 3. *The UNRWA Education and Training Programme 1950–1962* (Beirut, 1962)
–Information Paper No. 4. *The UNRWA Health Programme 1950–1962* (Beirut, 1962)
–Information Paper No. 5. *UNRWA Experience with Works projects and self-support programmes: An historical summary 1950–1962,* (Beirut, 1962)
–Information Paper No. 6. *The Problem of the rectification of the UNRWA Relief Rolls 1950–1962* (Beirut, 1962)

(d) UNITED NATIONS GENERAL ASSEMBLY

United Nations Special Committee on Palestine, *Report to the General Assembly.* 5 vols. General Assembly Official Records: Second Session. Supplement No. 11. (NY, 1947)
Official Records: 3rd session, 1st part Paris 21.9–12.12.48 2nd part, NY 5.4–18.5.49: Supplement No. 11. *Progress Report of the UN Mediator on Palestine,* Doc. A/648, 1948/9–Supplement 11A. *Progress report of the UN Acting Mediator on Palestine: Assistance to refugees.* Doc. A/689; A/689/Corr. 1; A/689/Add. 1.
Technical Assistance for Social Progress, No. 3: *UN Social Welfare Seminar for Arab States in the M.E.* (Beirut, 15 August to 8 September 1949) E/CN.5/175/Rev. 1.
Review of Economic Conditions in the Middle East, Supplement to World Economics Report, 1949–1950, Doc. ST/ECA/9/Add. 2; 1950–1, E/2193/Add. 3; 1952–3, ST/ECA/25; 1953-4, E E/27–40; 1954–5, E/2880; 1955–6, ST/ECA/45.

(f) UNESCO/UNRWA

Documents relating to the Middle East in *International Social Science Bulletin,* Vol. V, No. 4, 1953, pp. 671–858
Flight and Resettlement, by Henry Murphy & Brian Meggett, (Paris, 1955).
In Human Terms: the 1959 story of the UNRWA–UNESCO Arab Refugee Schools, by Robert Faherty (Paris, 1959)
UNRWA/UNESCO Education Service for Palestine Refugees (Beirut, 1970)
Photoscope 10,*UNRWA/UNESCO work together for Palestine Refugees*

(g) UNESCO

Studies on Social Development in the Middle East, UN Publication Saber No. E.70 IV2, "Report on the Social Survey of Amman, Jordan 1966"
Foreign Trade Statistics of Jordan 1960–63 (NY, 1967)

2. GOVERNMENTS

(a) The Hashimite Kingdom of Jordan

al-Kitab al-Urdunni al-Abyad, al-Watha'iq al-Qawmiyyah fi al-Wahdah al-Suriyyah al-Tabaiyyah (The Jordanian White Book, the National documents on the unity of Natural Syria) (Amman, 1947).

al-Jaridah al-Rasmiyyah lil Mamlakah al-Urdunniyyah al-Hashimiyyah 1952–58 (The HKJ Official Gazette)
–"Constitution of the H.K.J." No. 1093, Jan. 8, 1952, pp. 3–15 (published in 1965 in a booklet, 60 pp.)

Majlis al-Ummah: Mulhaq al-Jaridah al-Rasmiyyah, Mudhakarat wa Munaqashat Majlis al-Ummah (the Parliament: Supplement to the Official Gazette, Records of discussion of Parliament) 1952–58. Majlis al-Nuwab (the Chamber of Deputies). Majlis al-A'yan (the Senate)

Ministry of Development and Reconstruction, Shu'un al-Laji'in al-Filastiniyyin fi al-Urdunn (Palestinian refugee affairs in Jordan) (Amman, 1956).

The Supreme Headquarters of the Armed Forces. Ishrun Aman min al-Jihad wa al-Bina' 1952–72 (Twenty years of Struggle and Construction) (Amman, 1972)

Ministry of Culture and Information, al-Urdunn fi Khamsin Aman 1921–1971. (Jordan in fifty years) (Amman, 1972).

Foreign Ministry's Press and Publicity Bureau, Jordan and Its Growing Importance in the Middle East (Amman, April 1951).

Ministry of Foreign Affairs, The Rising tide of terror (Amman, 1952).
–al-Urdunn wa al-Qadiyyah al-Filastiniyyah wa al-Ilaqat al-Arabiyyah (Jordan, the Palestinian Question and Arab Ties) (Amman, 1964).

Husayn, Bin Talal King of Jordan, The Palestine Question Department of Culture and Guidance, Ministry of Information (Amman, 1965).
–al-Urdunn wa Qadiyyat Filastin (Jordan and the Palestine Question) (a special speech delivered by the King) (Amman, 1966)

Jordan Co-operative Control Union, The Co-operative Movement in Jordan (Amman, 1961)

Department of Statistics, First Census of Population and Housing, 18 November, 1961. Interim report No. 1 (Arabic and English text) pp. XV 37 (VI) tables, illustrations (Amman, 1962)
–Interim report No. 9, Distribution and Characteristics of Population, Ajloun District, (Amman, 1963)
–Jordan 1962 (maps and tables) (Amman, 1962)

The East Ghur Canal Authority, Special pamphlet on the occasion of inauguration of East Ghur Irrigation project (October 1961) (Arabic and English)
–Mashru' Qanat al-Ghur al-Sharkiyyah wa Madha Y'ni Laka (The East Guhur Canal Project and what it means to you) (np.nd)
–Mashru' al-Ghur al-Sharki (The Eastern Ghur Project) (Amman, 1962)

al-Urdunn al-Hadith, Majmuat Maqalat (Modern Jordan–a collection of articles) (Amman, 1962)

al-Wizarat al-Urdunniyyah fi Khamsin Aman 1921–71 (The Jordanian Cabinets during 50 years 1921–71) (Amman, 1971)

Thiqafatuna fi Khamsin Aman (Amman, 1972)

Safhat Matawiyyah min Tarikh al-Mamlakah al-Urdunniyyah al-Hashimiyyah (Unrevealed pages in the history of the H.K.J.) (Amman, n.d.)

Risàlat al-Urdunn (Jordan's mission) (Amman, n.d.)

Director of Culture and Guidance, Preparatory notes for the Palestine Problem: A White Paper, (Amman, n.d.)

El-Farra, M. H. The Palestine Question–The Refugee Problem (Amman, 1968)

El-Kurd, A. A. *The Hashimites* (Amman, 1967)
Hadawi, Sami. *The Palestine Refugees 1948–1967* (Amman, 1967)

(b) League of Arab States

Arab Office London, *Human Disaster: The Arab Refugees* (London, 1948)
al-Amanah al-Ammah, Lajnat Ta'lim Abna' al-Laji'in, *Taqrir an Ta'lim Abna'
    al-Laji'in wa Riayat Shu'unhum al-Ijtimaiyyah wa al-Sihhyyah* (report on the
    refugee children's education, social affairs and health) (Cairo, 1952)
 –Idarat Filastin–Shu'bat al-Laji'in, a report by Ya'qub al-Khuri, *Amlak al-Arab
    wa al-Amwal al-Mujammadah fi Filastin al-Muhtallah* (The Arab Property and
    frozen assets in occupied Palestine) (Cairo, n.d.)
Arab Information Centre, *Border incidents: a background* (by Fayez Sayegh) (NY,
    1955)
 –*Arab-Israel Conflict* (by F. Sayegh) (NY, 1956)
 –*Arab property in Israeli-controlled territories: Israeli measures for the disposal of
    Arab property.* 2nd edition (NY, 1956)
Arab Palestine Office: *We are returning back* (Arabic) (Beirut, 1955)
 –*Important decisions by the refugees* (Arabic) (Cairo, 1955)
 –*Unity will safeguard Refugees' interests* (Arabic) (Cairo, 1958)

(c) Egypt

Information Department, Cairo: *The Palestine Problem and the case of the
    Refugees*
 –*The Problem of the Palestine Refugees* (Cairo, 1964)
al-Matbaah al-Salfiyyah, *Watha'iq Khatirah an Ittisal Wali al-Ammr fi Sharq al-
    Urdunn bi al-Yahud Qabl Harb Filastin wa Ba'daha* (Crucial documents on the
    contacts of the ruler of Transjordan held with the Jews before and after the war)
    (Cairo, 1950)
Gamal Abd al-Nasir, *Filastin* (Palestine) statements of the President Gamal Abd
    al-Nasser) (Arabic) (Cairo, n.d.)

(d) Syria

al-Jumhuriyyah al-Suriyyah, *Wizarat al-Dakhiliyyah, Mu'asasat al-Laji'in al-
    Filastiniyyin al-Arab Ma'lumat wa Ihsa'at an Awda al-Laji'in al-Filastiniyyin*
    (Arabic) (Information & Statistics on the situation of the Palestinian refugees)
    Damascus, August 1952, 89pp.
Bulletin for the Palestine Arab Refugees' Institution, Republic of Syria (monthly,
    Arabic and English) 1952-6.

(e) Israel

Office of Information: Eban, Abba S. *The Arab Refugees* (Jerusalem, 1952)
Israel Foreign Office–*Arab Refugees,* Serial Nos. 1–14 (Jerusalem, 1959)
Central Bureau of Statistics, *Moslem, Christian and Druze in Israel,* Population
    and Housing Census, 1961, Publication No. 17 (Jerusalem, 1964)
 –*East Jerusalem, Census of population and housing 1967,* published by Central
    Bureau of Statistics, (Jerusalem, 1968)

Israel's Prime Minister's Office, the Authority for Economic Planning, *Hagadah Hamaaravit, Skirah Klalit* (The West Bank–general outlook) (Jerusalem, 1967) Parts I and II (unpublished)

Israel Defence Forces. *West Bank of the Jordan, Gaza Strip and Northern Sinai, Golan Heights: Data from full enumeration publication No. 1 of the census of population, 1967,* published by the Central Bureau of Statistics (Jerusalem, 1968)

–*Housing conditions, household equipment, welfare assistance and farming in the administered areas.* Publication No. 2 on the Census of Population, 1967 published by the Central Bureau of Statistics (Jerusalem, 1968)

–*Demographic characteristics of the population in the Administered Areas. Data from sample enumeration,* publication no. 3 of the Census of population 1967, published by the Central Bureau of Statistics (Jerusalem, 1968)

–*Labour Force,* Part 1. Publication No. 4 of the Census of Population 1967, published by the Central Bureau of Statistics (Jerusalem, 1968)

–*The Administered Territories. Additional data from the sample enumeration,* publication No. 5 of the Census of population 1967. Central Bureau of Statistics (Jerusalem, 1970)

Bank of Israel Research Department: *Omdany ha-Mekorot ha-Shimushim ve-Kishray ha-Gomlin bayn Anfy ha-Meshek ba-Gada ha-Maaravit* (Sources estimates, usages and mutual relations between the West Bank's economy and branches) (Jerusalem, 1967)

–*ha-Matsav ha-Monitary ba-Gadah ha-Maaravit* (The monetary situation in the West Bank) (Jerusalem, 1967)

Ministry of Agriculture-Water Commission, *Yehuda ve-Shomron luhot Shtahim Shel Admot-Kefar* (Judea and Samaria, tables of village land) (December 1969)

(f) Great Britain

Command Papers on Palestine and Transjordan.

Report presented by the secretary of state for the colonies to Parliament by command of His Majesty, July, 1937 Palestine Royal Commission, London, H.M.S.O. (British Blue Book, Command 5479 of 1937)

Report, Palestine Partition Commission, London, H.M.S.O. 1938 (British Blue Book, Command 5854 of 1938)

The Palestine Gazette, No. 1352 of August 17, 1944 "Village Administration Ordinance", No. 23 of 1944 pp. 49–61

Palestine: General Bulletin of Monthly Statistics. "Survey of Social and Economic conditions in Arab villages, 1944", Vol. 10 (1945–6).

A Survey of Palestine, 3 vols. (Jerusalem, 1946)

The political history of Palestine under British administration. Memorandum by H.M. Government presented in July 1947 to the UN Special Committee on Palestine (Jerusalem, 1947)

Progress Report of the UN Mediator on Palestine, Rhodes, 16 September, 1948. Command 7530 (London, 1948)

(g) U.S.A.

Department of State, Working Group on Legislation:
  The Palestine Refugee Programme, Publication No. 3757
  Near and Middle Eastern Series 3, Released February 1950
–*Working group on legislation for the Arab Refugee Problem* (Washington, Dept. of State, Dept. of Publication, Office of Public Affairs, 1950)

US Congress: House Committee on Foreign Affairs. *Palestine Refugees.* Hearings before the Committee on Foreign Affairs, House of Representatives, 81st Congress, 2nd session, on S.J. Res 153, February 16 and 17, 1950 (Washington, US Govt. Printing Office, 1950)

–*The Arab refugees and other problems in the Near East* Report of the special Study Mission to the Near East, Lawrence H. Smith Chairman and Winston L. Prouty, of the Committee on Foreign Affairs, pursuant to H. Res. 113 (Washington, U.S. Govt. Print. Office 1954)

Department of State, *Report of the Administration of the Refugee Relief Act of 1953* (Washington Govt. Print. Off. 1956)

Government Printing Office, "The Problem of Palestine Refugees" from *US Policy in the Middle East,* pp. 399–417, September 1956–June 1957. Documents

–*United States Policy in the Middle East,* September 1956–June 1957. *Documents,* Ch. VII "Problem of Palestinian Refugees", p. 398–416 (Greenwood Press, NY, 1968, Library of Congress)

Humphrey, Sen. H.H., Report to the 55th Congress

US Congress: House Committee on Foreign Affairs. *Arab Refugees from Palestine.* Report of a special study mission to the Near East of the Committee on Foreign Affairs, by Leonard Farbstein, pursuant to H. Res. 55, 88th Congress (Washington, US Govt. Print. Office, 1963)

House Committee on Foreign Affairs. Subcommittee on the Near East. *The UN Relief and Works Agency for Palestine Refugees in the Near East* (UNRWA). April 19, 1972 (Washington US Govt. Print. Off, 1972)

Howard C. Reese, et al. *Area Handbook for the Hashemite Kingdom of Jordan* co-athors) (Washington D.C.)
(US Govt. Printing Office, 1959)

3. NON-GOVERNMENT ORGANIZATIONS

American Near East Refugee Aid, Reports and publications

British Council of Churches, *Annual Reports*

Lutheran World Federation, Dept. of World Service Vocational Training Centre (Unpublished reports) (Jerusalem, 1971)

Lutheran World Federation, *Booklet on activities,* Geneva

The Middle East Council of Churches, Service Department, Unit on service to Palestine Refugees, *Annual Report 1974* (Jerusalem, 1974)

Near East Christian Council Committee for Refugee Work: *Annual Report 1961* prepared by A. Willard Jones (Jerusalem, n.d.)

Near East Ecumenical Committee for Palestine Refugees *Annual Report 1973*

International Christian Committee, Jerusalem. West Bank Area Committee of Middle East Council of Churches Service Department, *Annual Reports* by Elias Khoury

Union of Charitable Societies in Jerusalem Governorate (established in 1958) *Annual report of activities 1966* (Arab Press Co. Jerusalem, 1966)

World Council of Churches, *Palestine Refugees–Aid with Justice: The report of the consultation on the Palestine Refugee Problem* (Nicosia Cyprus, September 29–October 4, 1969)

–*Palestine refugees –aid with justice* The World Council of Churches (Geneva, 1970)

YMCA, Reports and publications

D. MEDIA

1. RADIO STATIONS

  a) Ramallah   e) Cairo
  b) Amman   f) Sawt al-Arab (Voice of the Arabs)
  c) Beirut   g) Damascus
  d) Near East   h) Baghdad

As monitored by: Israel's *Liket Shidurim Arviyyim,* the BBC and U.S.A.'s
Information Service, Daily Radio Bulletin

2. PRESS

 (a) H.K.J.

 1. Dailies and Weeklies
 al-Akhbar
 al-Asa
 Al-Awdah
 al-Bilad
 al-Difa'
 al-Fikr
 al-Hawadith
 al-Jazirah
 al-Jihad
 al-Mahd
 al-Manar
 al-Nashrah al-Iqtisadiyyah
 al-Nathir
 al-Nidal
 al-Qalam al-Jadid,
 al-Ra'i al-Am
 al-Sarih
 al-Sha'b
 al-Tariq
 al-Urdunn
 Bulletin of Arab Chamber of Commerce, Jerusalem,
 Filastin
 Fatat al-Ghad
 Hawl al-Alam
 Jerusalem Times
 Majallat al-Khalil
 Majallat al-Urdunn,
 Sawt al-Khalil
 Sawt al-Laji'in
 Wathbat al-Jaysh

2. Political Party Publications

Ba'th Party: *al-Ba'th*
                    al-Hadaf
                    al-Jil al-Jadid
                    al-Yaqzah

J.C.P.:   *al-Fajr al-Jadid*
                    al-Haqiqah
                    al-Jabhah
                    Jabal al-Nar
                    Kifah al-Sha'b
                    Nidal al-Sha'b
                    al-Muqawamah al-Sha'biyyah
                    Sawt al-Jamahir
                    al-Tariq

Muslim Brotherhood: al-Lajnah al-Ulya lil Ikhwan al-Muslimin fi al-Mamlakah
                    al-Urdunniyyah wa Filastin
                    – *Risalat al-Ikhwan al-Muslimin wa Manahijhum fi al-Islah.
                    Ila al-Ra'i al-'Am fi daffaty al-Urdunn* (The message and
                    program of reform of the Muslim Brotherhood to the
                    people on both sides of the Jordan) (n.d.n.p.) 45pp.
                    – *al-Qanun al-Asasi li Jama'iyyat al-Ikhwan al-Muslimin fi
                    Filastin* (Jerusalem 1949)
                    – *al-Mu'tmar al-Islami al-Amman al-Maktab al-Da'im* lil
                    Mu'tmar, Jerusalem, Bulletins 1954, Vol. 1 and 2.

N.S.P.:   *al-Mithaq*

The Liberal Party: *al-Nahdah*

(b) Egypt
     al-Ahram
     al-Akhbar
     al-Salam (Gaza)

(c) Lebanon
     al-Hayat
     al-Nahar
     al-Tha'r

(d) Israel
     al-Anba
     Davar
     ha-Aretz
     Jerusalem (Palestine) Post
     Ma'ariv

(e) Great Britain
   The Economist
   The Guardian
   Manchester Guardian
   Times
   and others

(f) U.S.A.
   Newsweek
   New York Times
   and others

3. *BULLETINS AND OTHER PUBLICATIONS*

The Bible Lands Society, *The Star in the East*
British Council of Churches, *The Church in the World*
British Red Cross Society, *Quarterly Review*
ha-Mizrah-ha-Hadash, (The New East) Quarterly of Israel Oriental Society
International Affairs (Moscow)
Journal of Palestine Studies, Beirut
Ma'arachot (Tel Aviv)
Mideast Mirror
Middle East Record 1960,
Middle East Report
Middle Eastern Studies
Palestine Refugees Today, UNRWA monthly newsletter
The P.A.R. Newsletter, 1958-9, Palestinian Arab Refugee Office, New York
Refugee News, 1954, published by Inter-Church Aid and Refugee Service, London
*Revue International de la Croix-Rouge et Bulletin International des societies de la
   croix-rouge*
Shu'un Filastiniyyah, Beirut
Skirah Hodshit, Tel Aviv.
The Middle East, 1948, Europa Publications Ltd. London
The Middle East Royal Institute of International Affairs, (London 1950)
The Red Cross World, published by LRCS
United Nations Monthly Chronicle:
UNRWA, Quarterly Bulletin of Economic Development (Beirut)
World Truth, Jerusalem, Jordan
YMCA, *Work with Refugees*, Geneva

E. UNPUBLISHED WORKS

Abbas, M. *The Impact of the November 1956 Events on the Economic Situation of Jordan* (Jerusalem, May, 1957)

al-Khatib, Rawhi. *Development of Jerusalem during the years 1948–62.* (Speech delivered by the Mayor of Jerusalem at a meeting of the Rotary Club of Jerusalem, 5.5.63)

–*Development in Jerusalem from 15 May 1948 to March 15, 1956,* (lecture delivered in a seminar in Beirut)

Aruri, Hasan Naseer. *Jordan: A study in political development 1921–1965* (A dissertation submitted to the Graduate School of the University of Massachusetts in partial fulfilment of the requirements for the degree Ph.D. June 1967)

Bailey, Clinton, *The Participation of the Palestinians in the politics of Jordan* (Columbia University, Ph.D. 1966, Political Science, general)

Ben-Ami, Stockman. *Situation analysis in a Samaria Village* 1.2.68

Berlinsky, Uzi. *Survey of the Development and Structure of UNRWA 1948–1967,* part of the study conducted by Doron, A; Moses, R; and Rosenfeld, J. (Hebrew University of Jerusalem 1968)

–*Aspectim Nivharim ba-Mivneh ha-Formali shel ha-Irgun* (Selected aspects in the formal composition of the organisation UNRWA)

Bandak, Isa. *Bethlehem Stories and Traditions* (Lecture by the Mayor of Bethlehem given at the YMCA Jerusalem December 17, 1946)

Cohen, Ammon (ed): *Miflagot Politiyot ba-Gada ha-Maaravit Tahat ha-Shilton ha-Hashemi* (Hebrew) (The Political Parties in the West Bank under the Hashimite Rule) (The Hebrew University of Jerusalem, the Institute of Asian and African Studies, the Research Centre of Eretz Israel Arabs, Jerusalem, May 1972)

Cohen, Aric. *Markivy ha-Uhlusiyah be-Yerushalaim Hamizrahit* (Hebrew) (East Jerusalem's population components).

Dahir, Abd al-Karim. *The Press and the Regime in Jordan, 1949–1967* (Hebrew), a work written under the guidance of Prof. Uriel Dann. (Tel Aviv University 1970)

Danah, Nisim *ha-Mimsad ha-Dati ve-Hayye ha-Dat ba-Hevrah ha-Muslemit be-Yehuda ve-Shomron* (Hebrew) (The religious establishment and the religious life in the Muslim West Bank community) (The Institute of Asian and African Studies, Hebrew University of Jerusalem, n.d.)

Doron, A. Moses, R. and Rosenfeld, J. *Welfare Services for Arab Refugees: UNRWA as a partner in the development of Welfare Programmes for the refugee population* (October 1967–February 1968), Summary of research report (draft) (Hebrew University of Jerusalem, 1968)

Etgar, Michael. *Mashmautah ha-Kalkalit shel Peilut Sasut be-Azory Yehuda ve-Shomron u-Rutsuat Aza* (Hebrew) (The economic significance of UNRWA's activity in Judea, and Samaria and the Gaza Strip), supervised by Klinov, Ruth. Part of a study conducted by A. Doron, R. Moses and J. Rosenfeld. The Paul Baerwald School of Social Work (Hebrew University of Jerusalem, 1970)

Goren, Asher. *The Arab Refugee problem;–News from the Middle East Countries; –The Palestine refugee problem;–The Palestine refugee problem* (February 1948–April 1949) (Hebrew)

Guss, Aryeh. *ha-Mimsad ha-Dati ba-Gadah ha-Maaravit–Ezor Shhem* (The religious establishment in the West Bank–Nablus area) The *Khatibs'* outlook as reflected in their sermons in the area's mosques between 1954 and 1965) (Hebrew) Hebrew University of Jerusalem, Institute of Asian and African Studies (Jerusalem, 1971)

Guss, Aryeh and Giladi, Avner. *ha-Mivneh ha-Hevrati shel Hevron* (Hebrew)

(The social composition of Hebron). Supervised by Prof. Haim Blank (Jerusalem 1973)

ha-Hevrah ha-Geografit ha-Israelit, *Annual meeting–Lectures dedicated to Judea and Samaria,* Tel Aviv University 26–27.8.74 (Hebrew)

Hurvitz, Dan and Mishal, Shaul. A report on the West Bank's leadership (Hebrew University of Jerusalem, n.d.)

Husni, Gama Abid. *The UN and the Palestinian Refugee: An analysis of the UNRWA for the Palestinian Refugee in the Middle East.* (May 1950–30 June, 1971) (University of Arizona, Ph.D. 1972) University Microfilms, Ann Arbour, Michigan.

Howard, Harry. *UNRWA and the Problem of the Arab Refugees* (n.d.n.p.)

Kassees, Saied Assad. *The People of Ramallah: A people of Christian Arab Heritage* (The Florida State University, 1970)

Knezevitch, Henry. *Explanatory notes on frontier villages in the UNRWA Area of Hebron/Bethlehem* (unpublished, 1955)

–*UNRWA Vocational Training Programme 1952–69* (a lecture delivered at the R.W.T.C. on 2.7.73)

Lutsky, Jack. *Refugee Housing, the Gaza Strip.* A study carried out in the summer of 1974.

Matt, Dani and Baydes, Uri. *ha-Mishpahot ha-Mehubadot ve-ha-Manhigut ha-Aravit be-Eretz Israel be-Tkufat ha-Shilton ha-Briti Bayn ha-Shanim 1917–1947.* (Hebrew). (The notable families and the Arab leadership in Palestine under British rule between 1917 and 1947). A paper written in a seminar under the supervision of Y. Arnon (Tel Aviv University, 1973)

Mishal, Shaul. *The Conflict between the West and East Banks under Jordanian rule and its impact on the Government and Administrative patterns in the West Bank 1949–67* (Hebrew). Thesis submitted for the degree Ph.D. (Hebrew University of Jerusalem, 1974).

–*Tulkarem: Social and Political Composition* (Hebrew n.p.n.d.)

Michaelis, M. and Zilberman, A. *ha-Uchlusiyah ha-Aravit be-Tekufat ha-Mandat* (Hebrew) (The Arab population under the Mandate period) (n.p. 1961) (found in the Israeli Foreign Office Library, Jerusalem)

Peres, Yohanan. *A Study on the position and values of the West Bank Arabs* (Hebrew)

Peretz, Don. *Palestinian Social Stratification–the Political Implications* (Paper delivered in a symposium on the Palestinians in Haifa University, 1977)

Refaeli, Nimrod. *ha-Hagirah le-Yarden–Herkeva u-Meniayha* (Hebrew) (The emigration to Jordan, its composition and motives) (November 1967)

–*Mehqar al ha-Plitim be-Mahaneh Jabeliyyah* (Hebrew) (A study on the refugee camp of Jabaliyyah–the Gaza Strip) (Hebrew University of Jerusalem)

Richardson, Channing B. *The UN and Arab Refugee Relief 1948–50. A case study in international organisation and administration.* Ph.D. Columbia University 1951. University Microfilms International.

Sela, Avraham. *The Ba'th Party.* Draft of M.A. thesis (Hebrew) Hebrew University of Jerusalem, 1976)

Settlement Study Centre. *Tochnit le-Yisuv 50,000 Plitim be-Azor al-Arish* (Hebrew) (a resettlement project of 50,000 refugees in el-Arish region). The National and University Institute of Agriculture (Rehovot, Israel, 1969)

Shamir, S., Shapira, R., Reches, E., Tibon, S., Shtokman, I. *ha-Elita ha-Miqtsoit ba-Shomron* (Hebrew) (The professional elite in Samaria) (Shiloah Institute, Tel Aviv Univeristy, 1975) (and the first draft of this study)

Sharon, Moshe. *Shivty ha-Beduim ha-Nodedim be-Nafot Hevron u-Bayt-Lehem* (Hebrew) (The nomadic Bedouin tribes in the Bethlehem, Hebron regions) (n.p., August 1970)

Shidlovski, Benjamin. *Nafat Bayt-lehem: Mivneh Politi Hevrati* (Hebrew) (Bethlehem region–a socio-political structure) (n.p., n.d.)
  –*Ramallah–al-Birah, Skirah Hevratit Politit* (Hebrew) (Ramallah–al-Birah, a socio-political survey) (n.p., n.d.)
Shtandel, Uri. *ha-Behirot la-Iriyot ba-Gada ha-Maaravit 1950–1967* (Hebrew) (The elections to the municipalities in the West Bank) (Jerusalem, n.d.)
  –*ha-Behirot le-Bayt ha-Nivharim ha-Yardeni* (Hebrew) *1950–67.* (The elections to the Jordanian House of Deputies) (Jerusalem, n.d.)
Shtokman, Israel. *Mivneh u-Peilut ha-Moatsah ha-Ironit Salfit* (Hebrew) (The composition and activity of Salfit Municipal Council) (n.d.n.p.)
Simon, Rahel. *Agudot Umoadonim Ba-Gada ha-Maaravit Betkufat Hashilton ha-Hashemi* (Hebrew) (Associations and clubs in the West Bank under the Hashimite rule) Supervised by M.Ma'oz. The Institute of Asian and African Studies, the Truman Research Institute (Jerusalem, 1974)
  –*Maamad Politi Shel ha-mukhtar* (Hebrew) (The *mukhtar's* political position)
Stok, A. *Hitpathut ha-Mandat shel ha-Irgun ba-Shanim 1948–50* (Hebrew) (the development of the organisation (UNRWA) 1948–50) (Part of the unpublished study on UNRWA held by the Social Work School, Hebrew University of Jerusalem, n.d.)
Torpshtayn, Yosi. *Ha-Maarechet ha-Monitsipalit ba-Gadma 1948–67–Sqirah Klalit* (Hebrew) (The Municipal System in the West Bank 1948–67–a general survey). (Draft July 1973)
Tsimhoni, Daphnah. *Tmurot ba-Mivneh ha-Aydot ha-Notsriyot u-ve-Maamadan be-Yehuda ve-Shomron 1948–67* (Hebrew) (Changes in the composition and position of the Christian sects in Judea and Samaria) Written under the supervision of Prof. G. Baer, (Jerusalem 1971)
Ward, Richard. *Opportunities for employment of Middle East Labour, Summary of conclusions.* A.I.D. (Washington DC, 1969)
Weigert, Gideon. *Hatnuah ha-Shitufit be-Yehuda ve-Shomron u-Rutsuat Aza* (Hebrew) (The co-operative movement in Judea and Samaria and the Gaza Strip) Kaplan School, Hebrew University (Jerusalem, 1970)
Yadlin, Rivka. *Emdot ve-Dyot be-Qerev Arveye Hagadah* (Hebrew) (Positions and opinions among the West Bank Arabs) (The Truman Institute, Hebrew University of Jerusalem, 1973)
Zilberman, Gad. *Shinuyyim ba-Maarechet ha-Kalkalit shel Shhem 1949–1967* (Changes in the economic system of Nablus town) (The Institute for Asian and African Studies) Hebrew University of Jerusalem, 1972)
  –*Maarehet Kalkalit shel Khan Yunis ve-Shhem* (Hebrew) (Khan Yunis and Nablus' economic systems) (n.p., n.d.)

F. MEMOIRS

Abdallah Ibn al-Husayn. *Mudhakkirati* (Arabic) (My memoirs) (Jerusalem, 1946)
  –*Memoirs of King Abdullah of Transjordan.* Edited by Philip R. Graves (London, 1950)
  –*al-Takmilah min Mudhakkirat Hadrat Sahib al-Jalalah al-Hashimiyyah al-Malik Abdallah Ibn al-Husayn* (Arabic) (A supplement to his Hashimite Excellency King Abdullah Ibn al-Husayn's memoirs) (Jerusalem, 1951)
  –*My memoirs completed.* Tr. by Harold W. Glidden (Washington DC, 1954)
Abd al-Hafiz, Muhammad. *al-Nahar aladhi wahhada al-Arab* (Arabic) (The river which united the Arabs–the river Jordan and the diversion schemes) (Amman, 1964)
al-Ghuri, Emil. *Filastin Ibra sittin Aman* (Arabic) (Palestine during Sixty Years) (Beirut, 1972)

al-Husayni, Muhammad. *Personal Notes.* (Translated by Rahamim David from Arabic, French, German and English) Found in the Archiyon Z.H.L. (Israel's Defense Forces Archives)

al-Khuri, Iskandar. *Dhikrayati* (Arabic) (My Memoirs) (Jerusalem, 1973)

al-Majali, Hazza'. *Mudhakkirati* (Arabic) (My memoirs) (Jerusalem, 1960)

al-Qauqji, Fawzi. "Memoirs, 1948", *Journal of Palestine Studies,* pt. 1, No. 4 (1972)

al-Saba', Hashim. *Dhikrayat Suhufiy Muddahad* (Arabic) (Memoirs of an oppressed journalist) (Jerusalem, 1951)

al-Tall, Abdallah. *Karithat Filastin Mudhkkirat Abdallah al-Tall Qa'id Maarakat al-Quds* (Arabic) (The calamity of Palestine–the memoirs of Abdallah al-Tall, the commander of the battle of Jerusalem) (Cairo, 1959)

Azcarate, Pablo de. *Mission in Palestine, 1948–52* (Washington, DC, Middle East Institute, 1966)

Bernadotte af Wisborg, Folke. *Till Jerusalem* (Stockholm, Norstedt, 1950) (English version–London, Hodder, 1951)

Glubb, John Bagot. *A Soldier with the Arabs* (New York, 1958)

–*The Story of the Arab Legion* (London, Hodder and Stoughton, 1948)

Hussein, King of Jordan. *Uneasy lies the head: an autobiography* (London, Heinemann, 1962)

Johnston, Sir Charles Hepburn. *The brink of Jordan* (London, 1972).

Kirkbride, Alec Seath. *A Crackle of Thorns. Experiences in the Middle East* (London, 1956)

–*From the Wings, Amman Memoirs 1947–51* (London, Cass, 1976)

McDonald, *My mission in Israel* (N.Y. 1951)

Perowne, Stewart, *The One Remains: A report from Jerusalem* (London, 1954)

Sharett, Moshe, *At the threshold of Statehood* (Tel Aviv, 1966)

–*Diaries for the years 1953–5* (part of which appeared in *Maariv,* daily (Hebrew), April–June, 1974)

Turki, Fawaz. *The disinherited: journal of a Palestinian exile* (New York, Monthly Review Press, 1972)

SECONDARY SOURCES

A. BOOKS

Abcarius, Michel F. *Palestine Through the fog of Propaganda* (London, Hutchinson and Co., 1946)

Abd al-Mun'im, Muhammad Faysal, *Asrar 1948* (Arabic) (The Secrets of 1948) (Cairo, 1968)

Abidi, Aqil Hyder H. *Jordan, a political study, 1948–1957* (N.Y. Asia Publishing House, 1965)

Abu Haydr, Ali. *Tariq Filastin* (Arabic) (The Way to Palestine) (Beirut, n.d.)

Abu-Lughod, Ibrahim, (ed) *The Transformation of Palestine: essays on the origin and development of the Arab-Israeli conflict* (Evanston, Ill. Northwestern University Press, 1971)

Abu Shilbayah, Muhammad. *Al-Tariq Ila al-Khalas wa al-Huriyyah wa al-Salam* (The road to settlement, liberation and peace) (Jerusalem, 1972)

–*La Slam bi ghair Dawlah Filastiniyyah Hurrah* (Arabic) (No peace without a free Palestine State) (Jerusalem, n.d.)

Agwani, M.S. *Communism in the Arab East* (Bombay, 1969)

A.G.M. (Israel's Defence Forces) *Lekah ha-Aravim mi-Milhemet ha-Shihrur* (Hebrew) (The Arabs' lesson from the 1948 war) (Z.H.L., 1952)

Agra, *Tsvaot Arav Beyamynu* (Hebrew) (The Arab armies today) (Tel Aviv, 1948)

al-Alami, Musa. *Ibrat Filastin* (The lesson of Palestine) (Arabic) (Beirut, 1949)

al-Aqad, Ahmad Khalil. *Man Huwa li Rijal Filastin 1945–6* (Arabic) (Who's who in Palestine) (Jaffa, 1946)

al-Ashkar, Musa. *Mashahir al-Rijal fi al-Mamlakah al-Urdunniyyah al-Hashimiyyah li Am 1955–6* (Arabic) (Famous personalities in the HKJ) (Jerusalem, 1956)

al-Dajani, Ali. *Muhadarat fi Iqtisadiyyat Urdunn* (Lectures on the economy of Jordan) (Cairo, Arab League Institute of Higher Arab Studies, 1954)

al-Dur, Niqola. *Hakadha Daat wa Hakadha Taud* (Arabic) (So it was lost and How it could be regained) (Beirut, 1964)

al-Ghuri, Emil. *al-Mu'amarah al-Kubra* (Arabic) (The great conspiracy) (Cairo, 1955)

–*al-Shuqayri fi al-Mizan, Abatil Tadhaduha al-Haqa'iq* (Arabic) (Shqayri on the scales–lies contradicted by the facts) (n.p., n.d.)

al-Hawari, Muhammad Nimr. *Sir al-Nakbah* (Arabic) (The secret of the disaster) (Nazareth, 1955)

al-Hay'ah al-Arabiyyah al-Ulya li Filastin. *The Palestine Arab case. A statement by the Arab Higher Committee, the body representing the Palestine Arabs. April 1947.* (Cairo, 1947)

–*An Mushkilat al-Laji'in al-Filastiniyyin* (Arabic) (On the Palestine Refugee problem) (Cairo, 1952)

–*al-Laji'in al-Filastiniyyun Dahaya al-Isti'mar wa al-Sihyuniyah* (Arabic) (The Palestine Refugees the victims of imperialism and Zionism) (Cairo, 1955)

al-Husayni, Muhammad Amin, *Haqa'iq an Qadiyyat Filastin* (Arabic) (Facts concerning the Palestine question). Published by the Arab Higher Committee (Cairo, 1956)

al-Jasir, S. and Abu Basm, N., *al-Urdunn wa Mu'amarat al-Istiamar* (Arabic) (Jordan and the imperialist conspiracies) (Cairo, 1957)

al-Kaylani, Subhi Zayd. *Qabl An Nansa* (Arabic) (Before we forget) (a text book with al-Alami, Haykal and others writing in it) (Jerusalem, 1952)

al-Khatib, Muhammad Nimr. *Ahdath al-Nakbah Aw Nakbat Filastin* (Arabic) (The Tragic events or the Palestine disaster) (Beirut, 1967)

–*Min Athar al-Nakbah* (Arabic) (Some of the consequences of the disaster) (Damascus, 1951)

al-Madi, Munib and Musa, Sulayman. *Tarikh al-Urdunn fi al-Qarn al-Ishrin* (The history of Jordan in the 20th century) (n.p., 1959)

al-Majali, Hazza'. *Hadha byan lil Nas: Qissat Muhadathat Tembler* (A statement for the people: Story of talks with Templer) (n.p., 1955)

al-Nabhani, Taqi al-Din. *Inqadh Filastin* (Arabic) (Salvation of Palestine) (Damascus, 1950)

al-Nabulsi, Fysal Abd ad-Latif, *al-Takattul al-Raj'i wa Awdat Filastin.* (Arabic) (The reactionary grouping and the return of Palestine) (n.p., n.d.)

al-Nashashibi, Nasir al-Din. *Tadhkirat Awdah* (Arabic) (A return ticket) (Beirut, 1962)

al-Nauri Isa. *Bayt Wara' al-Hudud* (Arabic) (A house behind the border) (Beirut, 1959)

al-Nimr, Ihsan. *Tarikh Jabal Nablus wa al-Balqa'* (Arabic) (The history of the Mountain of Nablus and al-Balqa'), Part II (Nablus, 1961). Part III (Nablus, n.d.)

al-Qadi, Tah Muhammad. *Masra' al-Adalah* (Arabic) (The fall of justice) (Beirut, 1954)

al-Qusri, Muhammad Fayiz. *Harb Filastin Am 1948* (Arabic) (The Palestine war 1948) Part II (Damascus, 1962)

al-Rushydat, Shafiq. *Filastin, Tarikhan, wa Ibrah wa Masir* (Arabic) (Palestine, a history, a lesson and destiny) (Beirut, 1961)

al-Rusan, Mahmud Ahmad. *Maarik Bab al-Wad* (Arabic) (The battles of Bab al-Wad) (n.d., n.p.)

al-Shumali, Ya'qub. *Qafilat al-Shuhada' Majmuat min al-Qisas wa al-Riwayat* (The Convoy of Martyrs, a collection of stories and tales) (Bayt Sahur, 1953)

Alush, Naji, *al-Masirah Ila Filastin* (Arabic) (The march to Palestine) (Beirut, 1964)

Antoun, Richard. *Arab village; a social structural study of a Transjordanian peasant community* (Bloomington, Indiana University Press, 1972)

Arif al-Arif. *Tarikh Bir Saba' wa Qaba'iluha* (Arabic) (The history of Beir Sheva and its tribes) (Jerusalem, 1934)

–*al-Nakbah* (Arabic) (The disaster) (Beirut, n.d.)

Ashkanta, Muhammad Sa'id. *Asrar Suqut Yafa* (Arabic) (The secrets of the fall of Jaffa) (n.p., 1964)

Ashkenazi, Touvia. *Ohaly Kydar le-min Ha-Yarkon Ad Ha-Karmel* (The tents of Kydar) (Tel Aviv, 1932)

Assaf, Michael. *Hitorerut ha-Aravim be-Eretz Israel u-Brihatam* (Hebrew) (The Arab movement in Palestine) (Tel Aviv, 1967)

Atiyah, Edward. *The Arabs* (Harmondsworth, 1955)

Avnery, Arieh. *Pshitot ha-Tagmul* (Hebrew) (Israeli commando 1950–1969) Vol. I and II. (Tel Aviv)

Ayzner, Dani. *Parashat Vadi Hawarith* (Hebrew) (The Wadi Hawarith affair) (Ramot Hefer, 1972)

Baer, Gabriel. *The Village mukhtar in Palestine* (Hebrew) (Jerusalem, 1978)

Beaynay ha-Oyev (Hebrew) (In the eyes of the enemy: Three Arab publications on the 1948 war) (Tel Aviv, 1954)

Be'eri, Eliezer. *Army Officers in Arab Politics and Society* (N.Y., 1970)

–*The Palestinians Under Jordanian Rule–Three Issues* (Hebrew) (Jerusalem, 1978)

Ben Porat Yoram and Marx Emanuel. *Some Sociological and Economic Aspects of Refugee Camps on the West Bank* (Rand, Santa Monica, 1971)

Ben Porat Yoram, Marx Emanuel and Shamir Shimon. *Mahneh Plitim be-Gav he-Har* (Hebrew) (A refugee camp on the hillock) (The Shiloah Institute, Tel Aviv University, 1974) (and the first draft of this study)

Bitar, Nadim. *Qadiyyat al-Arab al-Filastiniyyah* (Arabic) (The Arabs' Palestinian Question) (Beirut, 1954)

Buehring, Edward H. *The UN and the Palestinian refugees; a study in non-territorial administration* (Bloomington, Indiana University Press, 1971)

Bulus, Salman. *Khamsat A'wam fi Sharq al-Urdunn* (Arabic) (Five years in East Jordan) (Jerusalem, 1929)

Burns, General E.L.M. *Between Arab and Israeli* (Harrap, London, 1962)

Carr, Winifred. *Hussein's Kingdom, of Jordan* (Leslie Frewin Publishers Ltd. London 1966)

Cattan, Henry. *Palestine and international law, the legal aspects of the Arabic-Israeli conflict* (London, Longman, 1973)

Chandler, Edgar, H. S. *The High Tower of Refuge: The inspiring story of refugee relief throughout the World* (London n.d.)

Cohen, Abner. *Arab border-villages in Israel: a study of continuity and change in social organisation* (New York, Humanities Press, 1965)

Cohen, Arik and Grunau Hermonah. *Seker ha-Miutim be-Israel* (Hebrew) (Survey of the minorities in Israel) (Hebrew University of Jerusalem, The Institute of Asian and African Studies, Truman Research Institute, 1972)

Conference on the refugee problem today and tomorrow, (Geneva, May 27–28, 1957)

Copeland, Paul W. *The land and people of Jordan,* 2nd ed. Revised by Frances Copeland Stickles (Philadelphia, J. B. Lippincott, 1972)

Council of Europe, Committee of experts on the problems of refugees. Report presented on October 8, 1951 (Strassburg, 1953)

Darwazah, Muhammad Izzat. *al-Qadiyyah al-Filastiniyyah fi Mukhtalif Marahiluha* (Arabic) (The Palestinian problem in its various stages). Part II (Beirut, 1960 (1951)).

Davis, John, H. *The evasive peace: a study of the Zionist-Arab problem* (London, Murray, 1968)

Dearden, Anne. *Jordan* (London, Robert Hale, 1958)

Dodd, Peter and Halim Barakat. *River without bridges: a study of the exodus of the 1967 Palestinian Arab refugees* (Beirut, Institute for Palestine Studies, 1968)

Efrat, Elisha. *Judea and Samaria, Guidelines for regional and physical planning.* (Hebrew) Ministry of the Interior and Planning Dept. (Jerusalem, 1970)

Effrat, Moshe. *ha-Plitim ha-Paleshtinaim, Mehqar Kalkali ve-Hevrati 1949–74.* (Hebrew) (The Palestinian Refugees, an economic and social study) (The David Horowitz Institute for the research of Developing Countries, Tel Aviv University, 1976)

Elath, Eliahu. *Shivat Tsion ve-Arav* (Hebrew) (Zionism and the Arabs) (Tel Aviv, 1974)

ESCO Foundation for Palestine. *Palestine: a study of Jewish, Arab and British policies.* 2 vols. (New Haven, Yale University Press, 1947)

Essex, Rosamund. *Outcasts of Today, An eye witness report on Middle Eastern refugees* (London, n.d.)

Forsythe, David P. *United Nations peacekeeping: the conciliation commission for Palestine* (Baltimore and London, The Johns Hopkins Press, published in co-operation with the Middle East Institute, 1972)

Forrest, Alfred C. *The unholy land* (Toronto/Montreal: McClelland and Stewart, 1971)

Furlonge, Geoffrey. *Palestine is my country. The story of Musa Alami* (London, 1968)

Gabbay, Rony E. *A political study of the Arab-Jewish conflict: the Arab refugee problem (a case study)* (Geneva, E. Droz, 1959)

Goren, Asher. *haliga ha-Aravit* (Hebrew) (The Arab League 1945-54) (Tel Aviv, 1954)

Granovsky, A. *ha-Mishtar ha-Qarqai be-Eretz Israel* (Hebrew) (Land order in Eretz Israel) (Tel Aviv, 1949)

Gubser, Peter. *Politics and change in al-Karak, Jordan. A study of a small Arab town and its district* (London, New York, Oxford University Press, 1973)

Habibi, Amirah. *Al-Nuzuh al-Thani* (Arabic) (The second exodus) (The 1967 exodus of Palestinian refugees: a study in reactions to disaster) (Palestine Liberation Organisation Research Centre, Beirut, Lebanon, 1976)

Hacker, Jane. *Modern Amman: A social study* (University of Durham, Durham, England, 1960)

Hadawi, Sami. *Bitter Harvest; Palestine between 1914–1967* (N.Y. New World Press, 1967)

–*Village statistics, 1945; a classification of land and area ownership in Palestine, with explanatory notes* (Beirut, Palestine Liberation Organisation Research Centre, 1970)

–*Palestine: loss of a heritage* (San Antonio, Texas, The Naylor Co., 1963)

Haim, Sylvia. *Arab Nationalism: An Anthology* (Berkeley and Los Angeles: University of California Press, 1964)

Halum, Ribhi Jumah. *Huwala'i A'da' al-Taharrur fi al-Urdunn* (Arabic) (Those are the enemies of liberation in Jordan) (Cairo, 1962)

Hammerskjold, Forum, 13th. *The Middle East: prospects for peace: background papers and proceedings.* Quincy Wright, author of the working paper. Isaac Shapiro, editor. Dobbs Ferry, N.Y. (published for the Association of the Bar of the City of N.Y. by Oceana Publications, 1969)

Hamza, Fuad. *The United Nations Conciliation Commission for Palestine, (1949–1967* (published by the Institute for Palestine Studies, Beirut, 1968)

Hareuveni, Emanuel. *Yishuvy ha-Miutim be-Yisrael* (Hebrew) (The minority settlements in Israel) (Tel Aviv, 1973)

Harkabi, Yehoshafat. *Arab attitudes to Israel* (New York, Hart Publishing Co., 1972)

–(ed) *Arab Lessons from their defeat* (Hebrew) (Tel Aviv, 1969)

–*Fedayeen Action and Arab Strategy,* Adelphi papers, No. 53, December 1968. Institute for Strategic Studies, London.

Harris, George L. *Jordan, its people, its society, its culture* (Grove Press Inc. New York)

Hattis, Susan Lee. *The bi-national idea in Palestine during the mandatory times* (Tel Aviv, Shikmona Publishing Co. 1970)

Hijazi, Na'if and Atallah, Mahmud.*Shakhsiyyat Urdunniyyah* (Arabic) (Jordanian personalities) (Amman, 1973)

Hilal, A. and Akif, A. *al-Laji'un* (Arabic) (The Refugees) (Cairo, 1957)

Hochstein, Philip. *The Arab refugees, a report on this 15 year old problem.* Advanced News Service (Washington DC, n.d.)

Hopkins, John. *The Economic Development of Jordan* (Johns Hopkins Press, Baltimore, USA, 1957)

Howard C. Reese, et al. *Area Handbook for the Hashemite Kingdom of Jordan* (co-authors) (Washington DC, Superintendent of Documents, US Govt Printing Office, 1959)

Hurewitz, J. C. *Middle East Politics: The military dimension* (N.Y., 1969)

–*The struggle for Palestine* (N.Y., 1950)

Hutchinson, Elmo H. *Violent truce: A military observer looks at the Arab-Israeli conflict, 1951–1955.* (London, John Calder Ltd. 1955. New York, Davin-Adair, 1956)

Hutchison, Frank L. *Refugees from Palestine, the church's continued concern* (New York. National Council of Churches, 1963)

Hykal, Yusuf. *Filastin, Qabl wa Ba'd* (Palestine Before and After) (Beirut, 1971)

Institute for Mediterranean Affairs and the Roosevelt University, Chicago, *The Palestine Refugee problem–a new approach and a plan for a solution.* (N.Y., 1958)

Institute for Palestine Studies, *The Palestine refugees: a collection of United Nations documents* (Beirut, 1970)

–*The partition of Palestine, 29 November, 1947: an analysis* (Beirut, 1967)

International Bank for Reconstruction and Development. *The Economic development of Jordan* (Baltimore, Johns Hopkins Press for IBRD, 1957)

Iyzuli, Abd al-Aziz. *Izat Karithat Filastin al-Arabiyyah* (The lesson of the Arab Palestine disaster) (Damascus, 1963)

Jam'iyyat Inqadh Filastin, *Karithat Filastin 15 Ayar 1948* (Arabic) (The Palestine tragedy, 15 May 1948) (Baghdad, 1949)

Jansen, Michael E. *The United States and the Palestinian people* (Beirut, Institute for Palestine Studies, 1970)

Jarvis, Claude S. *Arab Command: the biography of Lt. Col. F. G. Peake Pasha* (London, Hutchinson, 1942)

Jiryis, Sabri. *The Arabs in Israel 1948–64* (The Institute of Palestine Studies, Beirut 1969)

John, Robert and Sami H. Hadawi. *The Palestine diary.* 2 vols. (N.Y. New World Press, 1970)

Jum'ah, Sa'id. *al-Mu'amarah wa maarakat al-masir* (The conspiracy and the battle of destiny) (Beirut, Dar al-Kitab al-Arabi, 1968)

Jreisat, Jamil E. *Provincial administration in Jordan: a study of institution building* (Pittsburgh, Inter-University Research in Institution Building. University of Pittsburgh, 1968)

Kadi, Leila S. *Arab summit conferences and the Palestine problem 1936–1950, 1964–66.* (Beirut, Research Centre, Palestine Liberation Organization, 1966)

Kaplan, Deborah. *The Arab refugees, an abnormal problem* (Jerusalem, 1959)

Kanovsky, E. *Economic development of Jordan. The Economic implications of peace in the Middle East* (The David Horowitz Institute, Tel Aviv University, 1974)

Karmon, Yehuda and Shmueli, Avshalom. *Hevron-Demutah shel Ir Hararit* (Hebrew) (Hebron–the image of a mountain town) (Tel Aviv, 1969)

Kedourie, Elie. *Nationalism* (London 1962, 1966)

Kerr, Malcolm H. *The Arab Cold War 1958–67: a study of ideology in politics* (Oxford 1967)

Kevatsim Ayzoriyyim be-Geografyah shel Eretz Israel u-Sevivata, Yehuda ve-Shomron, Prakim be-Geografyah Yishuvit (Hebrew) (Judea and Samaria, a compilation of studies in urban geography), by Geography departments of the Bar-Ilan and Tel Aviv universities *(draft)* (to be published by Kenaan, Jerusalem)

Khalidi, Walid, (ed) *From Haven to Conquest: readings in Zionism and the Palestine Problem until 1948* (Beirut, Institute for Palestine Studies, 1971)

Khijazi, Arafat. *15 Ayar Am al-Nakbah* (Arabic) (15 May the year of disaster) (n.p., n.d.)

Khouri, Fred. *The Arab-Israeli dilemma* (N.Y. Syracuse University Press, 1968)

Kimche, Jon and David. *A clash of destinies; the Arab Jewish war and the foundation of the State of Israel* (New York, Praeger, 1960)

Kressel, Gideon, M. *Individuality Against Tribalism. The dynamics of a Bedouin community in a process of Urbanization* (Hebrew) (Hakibutz Hameuchad Publishing House, Hebrew University of Jerusalem, The Truman Research Centre, 1976)

Kurzman, Dan. *Genesis 1948* (A Signet book from New American Library, 1972)

Lacey, Janet. *Refugees–Still they come.* Christian Focus (London, 1963)

Laqueur, Walter Z. *Communism and Nationalism in the Middle East* (London, third edition, 1961)

–The Soviet Union and the Middle East, (London, 1959)

Lewis, Bernard. *The Arabs in History* (Harper, 1950)

–The Middle East and the West (Harper, 1964)

Lias, Godfrey. *Glubb's Legion* (London, Evans Brothers, 1956)

Loroh, Natanel. *The Edge of the Sword: Israel's war of Independence, 1947–1949* (New York: Putnam, 1961)

Lutfiyya, Abdullah M. *Baytin, a Jordanian village: A study of social institutions and social change in a folk community* (The Hague, Mouton, 1966)

MacDonald, Sir Murdoch and Partners. *Report on the proposed extension of irrigation in the Jordan Valley* (London, Cook, Hammond and Kell, 1951)

Main (Charles T.) Inc. *The unified development of the water resources of the Jordan*

Valley Region (Prepared for the UN under direction of Tennessee Valley Authority. Boston, 1953)

Marlowe, John. *The seat of Pilate: an account of the Palestine mandate* (London, Cresset, 1959)

Marx, Emanuel. *Bedouin of the Negev* (Tel Aviv, 1974)

Meahory Hapargod, (Hebrew) (Behind the curtain, the Iraqi Parliamentary Commission Report on the war with Israel). (Translated) (ZHL, Maarachot, Tel Aviv, 1954)

Murad, Abbas. *al-Dawr al-Siyasi lil Jaysh al-Urdunni 1921–73*, (Arabic) (The political role of the Jordanian army) (Palestine Books, No. 48, Palestine Liberation Organization Research Centre, Beirut, 1973)

Morris, James. *The Hashemite kings* (New York, Pantheon, 1959)

Musa, Sulayman. *Ta'sis al-Imarah al-Urdunniyyah 1922–25* (Arabic) (The establishment of the Jordanian Emirate) (Amman, 1972)

Naaman, H. *Abdallah Amir Ever Hayarden* (Hebrew) (Abdullah Emir of Transjordan) (Jerusalem, 1942)

Nasser, Jamal. *The embittered Arab; the bitter story of the Holy Land* (Jerusalem, Commercial Press, n.d.)

Nation Associates, *The Arab Higher Committee: its origins, Personnel and Purposes* (A documentary record submitted to UN, 1947)

Ne'eman, Zvi. *Mamlehet Abdallah le-Ahar ha-Sipuah* (Abdullah's kingdom following the annexation) (Jerusalem, 1950)

Nevo, Yosef. *Abdallah ve-Arviyye Eretz Israel* (Hebrew) (Abdullah and the Palestinian Arabs) (Based on MA thesis) (Shiloah Institute, Tel Aviv University, 1975)

Nimrod, Yoram. *Mey Meriva, ha-Mahloqet al Mey Hayarden* (Angry water, controversy over the Jordan River) (The Centre of Arabic and Afro-Asian Studies, Givat Haviva, 1966)

Nuseibah, Hazem Zaki. *The Ideas of Arab Nationalism* (Ithaca: Cornell University Press, 1956)

O'Ballance, Edgar. *The Arab-Israeli War 1948* (London, 1956)

Oliver, Beryl. *The British Red Cross in Action* (London, n.d.)

Palestine Arab Refugee Office, *Tension and Peace in the Middle East. Facts every American should know about the Tragedy of the Holy Land* (N.Y. 1956)

Parkes, James W. *Whose land? A history of the peoples of Palestine* (N.Y., Taplinger, 1971)

Patai, Raphael, *The Kingdom of Jordan* (Princeton University Press, 1958)

Peake, Frederick G. *A History of Jordan and its Tribes* (University of Miami Press, 1958)

Peretz, Don, Evan M. Wilson and Richard J. Ward. *A Palestine entity?* (Washington DC, Middle East Institute, 1970)

Peretz, Don. *Israel and the Palestine Arabs* (Washington DC, Middle East Institute, 1958)

–*The Palestine Arab refugee problem* (Santa Monica, California, 1969)

Phillips, Paul Grounds. *The Hashemite Kingdom of Jordan: prolegomena to a technical assistance programme* (Chicago, The University of Chicago Press, 1954)

Pinner, Walter. *The legend of the Arab refugees. A critical study of UNRWA's reports and statistics* (Tel Aviv, Economic Social Research Institute, 1967)

Porath, Yehoshua. *The Emergence of the Palestinian Arab National Movement 1918–1929* (Frank Cass, London 1974)

–*The Palestinian Arab National Movement*, Vol. II *1929–1939: From Riots to Rebellion* (Frank Cass, London 1977)

Pryce-Jones, David. *The face of defeat: Palestinian refugees and guerillas* (London, 1972)

Qalylat, Kamal Amin. *Filastin Mahd al-Masih wa Qiblat Muhammad* (Arabic) (Palestine, the cradle of Jesus and the Prophet Muhammad's amulet) (Beirut, 1948)

Qamhawi, Walid. *al-Nakbah wa al-Bina'* (Arabic) (The catastrophe and the construction) (Beirut, 1956)

al-Qasim, Anis. *Min al-Tih Ila al-Quds* (Arabic) (From wilderness to Jerusalem) (Tripoli, Libya, 1965)

Qatish, Hashim. *Jawlah Hawl al-Jaysh al-Arbi al-Urdunni* (Arabic) (Tour around the Jordanian Arab Army) (Amman, n.d.)

Quandt, William. Faud Jabber and Ann Mosley Lesch. *The politics of Palestinian nationalism* (Berkeley, University of California Press, 1973)

Rashid, Harun Hashim. *Maa al-Ghuraba'* (Arabic) (With the exiles) (Cairo, 1954)
–*Awdat al-Ghuraba'* (Arabic) (The return of the exiles) (Beirut, 1956)

Rees, Elfan. *The Refugees and the United Nations* (N.Y. Carnegie Endowment, 1953)
–*Century of Homeless Man* (N.Y. Carnegie Endowment, 1957)
–Report, *Refugee Problem, We strangers and Afraid,* (Carnegie Endowment for International Peace, World Refugee Year 10.6.1959)

Research Group for European Migration Problems, *Report,* 1957

Safran, Nadav. *From war to war: the Arab-Israeli confrontation 1948–67* (N.Y. Pegasus, 1969)

Sakik, Ibrahim Khalil. *Dirasat al-Mujtama al-Filastini wa Mushkilan* (Arabic) (Studies of the Palestinian society and its problems) (Gaza, 1963)
–*Tarikh Filastin al-Hadith* (Palestine's modern history) (Gaza, 1964)

Saliba, Samir N. *The Jordan River dispute* (The Hague, Martinus Nijoff, 1968)

Sanger, Richard H. *Where the Jordan flows* (Washington DC, Middle East Institute, 1963)

Sayigh, Anis. *al-Hashimiyyun wa Qadiyyat Filastin* (Arabic) (The Hashimites and the Palestine question) (Beirut, 1966)

Sayigh, Fayiz. *Mashru' Hammarskjöld wa Qadiyyat al-Laji'in* (The Hammarskjöld plan and the refugee question) (Beirut, 1959)
–*The Palestine Refugees* (Amara Press, Washington DC, 1952)

Sayyidhum, Edward. *Mushkilat al-Laji'in al-Arab* (The Arab refugee problem) (Cairo, 1961)

Schechtman, Joseph B. *The Arab Refugee Problem* (NY 1952)

Shamir, Shimon. *Communications and political attitudes in West Bank refugee camps* (Shiloah Centre for Middle East and African Studies, Second edition, October 1974)

Sharabi, Hisham. *Nationalism and revolution in the Arab world,* (NY, 1966)

Shimoni, Yaacov. *Arveyy Eretz Israel* (The Arabs of Palestine) (Tel Aviv, 1947)

Shirdan, Musa. *al-Urdunn bayn Ahadyn* (Jordan between two eras) (Amman, n.d.)

Shmueli, Avshalom. *Hitnahalut shivtay ha-Bedouin be-Midbar Yehuda* (Hebrew) (The Settlement of the Bedouin tribes in the Judea desert) (Tel Aviv, 1969)

Shulman, Yona. *Abdallah* (Hebrew) (ZHL, n.d.)

Shuqayri, Ahmad. *al-Nizam al-Urdunni fi Qafas al-Ittiham* (Arabic) (The Jordanian regime in the dock) (Beirut,1972)
–*Min al-Qimmah Ila al-Hazimah* (Arabic) (From the zenith to defeat) (Beirut, 1971)

Shwadran, Benjamin. *Jordan: a state of tension* (NY, Council for Middle Eastern Press, 1959)

Sirhan, Bassem. *Palestinian Children: The generation of Liberation,* PLO Research Centre, Palestine Essays No. 23,

Snow, Peter John. *Hussein, a biography* (London, Barrie and Jenkins, N.Y. Robert B. Luce Inc., 1972)

Sparrow, Gerald. *Hussein of Jordan* (London, George G. Harrap, 1960)
–*Modern Jordan* (London, Allen and Unwin, 1961)

Stevens, Georgiana. *Jordan River Partition* (Board of Trustees of the Leland Stanford Junior University)

The Arab refugee problem, how it can be solved, 1951, Proposals submitted to the General Assembly of the UN, signed by 19 religious, labour, education and liberal leaders

Thicknesse, Sibylla G. *Arab Refugees: a survey of resettlement possibilities* (London, Royal Institute of International Affairs, 1949)

Tokun, Baha Uddin, *A short history of Transjordan* (London, Luzac, 1945)

Tawfiq, Muamar, *Mudhkkirat Laji' aw Hayfa fi al-Maarakah* (Arabic) (Memoirs of a refugee of Haifa in battle) (Nazareth, 1958)
–*al-Mutasalil wa Qisas Ukhra* (Arabic) (The infiltrator and other stories) (Nazareth, 1957)

Tuqan, Qadri. *Ba'd al-Nakbah* (Arabic) (After the disaster) (Beirut, 1950)

Udah, Butrus Udah. *Masra' Filastin* (Arabic) (The Fall of Palestine) Part I (Jerusalem, 1950)

Vatikiotis, P. J. *Politics and the military in Jordan: a study of the Arab Legion 1921–1957* (NY, Praeger, 1967)

Warriner, Doreen. *Land and poverty in the Middle East* (London, Royal Institute of International Affairs, 1948)

Washitz, J. *The Arabs in Palestine,* (Hebrew) (Tel Aviv, 1947)

Witkamp, F. T. "The Refugee Problem in the Middle East" in the *R.E.M.P. Bulletin* (Hague, 1961)

Yaari, Ehud. *Mitsraim ve-ha-Fedain* 1953-1956 (Hebrew) (Egypt and the Fedayeen) (Centre for Arabic and Afro-Asian Studies, Givat Haviva, 1975)

Yasin, Subhi Muhammad. *Nazariyyat al-Amal bi Istirdad Filastin* (Arabic) (A plan of action for the recovery of Palestine) (Cairo, 1964)

Young, Peter, Lt. Col. *Bedouin command with the Arab Legion, 1953–56* (London, W. Kimber, 1956)
–*The Arab Legion* (London, 1972)

Zibyan, Muhammad Tyasir. *al-Malik Abdallah Kama Araftuhu* (Arabic) (King Abdullah as I knew him) (Amman, 1967)

Zaghib, Mishal Ilyas. *al-Mamlakah al-Urdunniyyah al-Hashimiyyah, Lamhat Tarihyiyyah an al-Awdai' al-Qadimah wa al-Hadithah* (Arabic) (The HKJ, an historical glance at the situation in the past and present) (Beirut, 1950)

Zarkali, Khayr al-Din, *Aman fi-Amman* (Two years in Amman) (Cairo, Maktabah al-Arab, 1925)

Zuaytir, Akram. *al-Qadiyyah al-Filastiniyyah* (Arabic) (The Palestinian question) (Cairo, 1955)

Zuqan, al-Hindawi. *al-Qadiyyah al-Filastiniyyah* (Arabic) (The Palestinian question) A text book for secondary school (Amman, n.d.)

Zuraiq, Qustantin K. *Palestine: the meaning of the disaster* (Beirut, Khayats, 1965)

B. ARTICLES

Abidi, A. H. H. "Survey of source material: select Arabic source material for the modern political history of Jordan", *International Studies,* V.4, No. 3 (Jan 63), pp. 317–328.

Abu-Ghazaleh, A. M. "The impact of 1948 on Palestinian Arab writers: the first decade", *Middle East Forum,* 46, No. 2–3 (1970), pp. 81–92

Abu-Jaber, K. S. "The legislature of the Hashemite Kingdom of Jordan: a study of political development", *The Muslim World,* 59, nos. 3–4 (July–Oct 69), pp. 220–50.

Alami, M. "The Lesson of Palestine", *M.E.J.* 3, 1949, pp. 373–405

al-Dajani, Shukri Zaki. "I was a refugee" (series of articles) in *Western Mail,* Cardiff, 1955

al-Tabi'i, Muhammad, "A story on Hajj Amin al-Husayni–The *Mufti* of Palestine" (Arabic) *Akhbar al-Yawm,* Cairo daily, 12 Oct 1963

Alexander, D. "ha-Umm ve-ha-Plitim" (Hebrew) (The UN and the refugees) in *N.E.* Vol. 5, 1953, pp. 1–13

Amiran D. H. K. and Ben-Arieh Y. "Sedentarization of Bedouin in Israel" in *Israel Exploration Journal,* Vol. 13, No. 3, 1963, pp. 161–181

Anabtawi, Samir N. "The Palestinians as a Political Entity" in Moor, John Norton (ed) *The Arab Israeli Conflict,* Vol. I, Readings Princeton University, New Jersey, 1974, pp. 506–517

Arlozorov, Haim. "Abdallah and the Jews" (Hebrew) in *Molad,* July 1948, pp. 189–192

Asad, Talal. "Anthropological texts and ideological problems: an analysis of Cohen on Arab Villages in Israel" in *Review of Middle East Studies,* 1976, pp. 1–400.

Awad, M. "Living conditions of nomadic, semi-nomadic and settled tribal groups" in *Readings in Arab Middle Eastern Societies and Cultures,* (ed) A. M. Lutfiyya and C. W. Churchill, 1970, pp. 135–148

Baer, Gabriel. "Land tenure in Transjordan", *ha-Mizrah,* Spring 1952, pp. 233–241

Baster, James. "Economic aspects of the settlement of the Palestine refugees", *M.E.J.,* 8, No. 1, 1954, pp. 54–68

Brawer, Moshe, "The frontier villages in western Samaria" in *Yehuda ve-Shomron–Prakim be-geographia Yishuvit* (Hebrew) (Judea and Samaria–chapters in Urban Geography) *op. cit.*

Bruhns, Fred C. "A study of Arab refugee attitudes", *M.E.J.,* 9, No. 2 (Sept 1955) pp. 130–38

Cnaan, Haviv. "ha-Atsula ha-Aravit 1969" (Hebrew) (The Arab aristocracy) (eleven articles) in *Haaretz,* Nov–Dec 1969

Cnaan, Haviv. "Mihu Hajj Amin al-Husayni" (Who is Hajj Amin) in *Ibid,* 1, 2, 6 March, 1970

Canaan, Taufiq. "The Saqr Bedouin", in *Journal of the Palestine Oriental Society,* Vol. XVI, 1936, pp. 21–32

Carter, William. "Musa Alami's miracle", *Geographical Magazine,* 39, No. 4, (Aug 1966), pp. 268–82

Childers, Erskine B. "The other exodus, 1948: Why the Arabs left Palestine", *Middle East Newsletter* (Beirut) 2, No. 7 (Aug–Sept 1968) pp. 3–5. Reprinted from *The Spectator,* London, May 12, 1961

Clapp, Gordon. "An approach to economic development", *International Conciliation,* April 1950

Coate, Winifred. "The condition of Arab refugees in Jordan", *International Affairs,* 29, Oct 1953, pp. 449–56

Cohen, Aharon, "Mi Hechshil Hakamat Medinah Paleshtinit?" (Who prevented the establishment of a Palestinian State?) in *Mariv,* daily (reprint)

Cohen, Ammon. "Political Parties in the West Bank under the Hashemite Regime" in Moshe Ma'oz (ed), *Palestinian Arab Politics* (Truman Institute Studies, The Hebrew University of Jerusalem, Jerusalem 1975), pp. 21–49

–"The Arab population in the Israel-administered West-Bank" in *The Arabs and Palestine,* Institute of Jewish Affairs, London 1972, pp. 40–8

–"The Jordanian Communist Party in the West Bank 1950–60" in Confino, M. and Shamir, S. (ed), *The USSR and the Middle East* (Israel Universities Press, 1973), pp. 420–437

Council for the Advancement of Arab-British Understanding, CABU "A just settlement of the refugee problem?", *Records of a Seminar on the Palestine Refugee Problem,* held on Dec 12, 1973, House of Commons

Dann, Uriel. "The beginnings of the Arab Legion", *Middle Eastern Studies,* 5, No. 3 (Oct 1969) pp. 181–91

–"Regime and opposition in Jordan since 1949" in *Society and Political structure in the Arab World* edited by Menahem Milson (Humanities Press, Jerusalem 1974), pp. 145–181

–*The "Jordanian Entity" in changing circumstances 1967–73,* occasional papers, the Shiloah Centre for Middle Eastern and African Studies, Tel Aviv University

–"The United States and the recognition of Transjordan 1946–49" in *Asian and African Studies,* Vol. LL, No. 2, 1976, pp. 213–239

Dayan, Moshe. "Israel's border and security problems", *Foreign Affairs,* 33, No. 2 (1955), pp. 250–67

Dees, Joseph L. "Jordan East Ghor Canal Project", *M.E.J.* 13, No. 4, 1959, pp. 357–71

Efrat, Elisha. "Change in the pattern of settlement in Judea and Samaria 1947–67" (Hebrew) in *N.E.,* No. 91, 1973, pp. 283–295

–"The distribution of settlements in Judea and Samaria" in *Ibid,* No. 79, 1970, pp. 257–265

Eytan, Walter. "The lesson from talks with the Arabs" (Hebrew) in *Maariv* daily, Tel Aviv, 19 Sept 1971

Forsythe, David P. "UNRWA, the Palestine refugees, and world politics", *International Organisation,* 25, No. 1, 1971, pp. 26–45

Furlonge, Geoffrey. "Jordan today", *Royal Central Asian Journal,* 53 part 3, Oct 1966, pp. 277–285

Galloway, Lt. Gen. Sir Alexander, "What can be done about the Arab refugees?" in *Daily Express,* 29 Aug 1952

Gershuni, Israel, "The Arab Nation, the Hashimite Dynasty and the greater Syria in the writings of Abdullah" in *N.E.* Vol. XXV, 1975, No. 1–2 (97–8), pp. 1–26 and No. 3(99), pp, 161–183

Glubb, J. B. "The Arab Legion", *Statesman,* 25 Sept 1948, p. 261

–"Violence on the Jordan-Israeli border: A Jordanian view", *Foreign Affairs,* 32, No. 4 (July 1954), pp. 552–562

Gosenfeld, Norman. "Changes in Business Community of East Jerusalem" in *N.E.* No. 4(96) 1974, pp. 261–279

Gottheil, Fred M. "Arab Immigration into pre-state Israel: 1922–1931" in *Middle Eastern Studies,* Vol. 9, Jan 1973, No. 1, pp. 315–324

Harkabi, Yehoshafat. "The Palestinians in the fifties and their awakening as reflected in their literature" in Ma'oz, M. (ed), *Palestinian Arab politics* (Truman Institute Studies, Jerusalem 1975), pp. 51–89

Holborn, Louis. "The problem of refugees–an analysis and UNRWA's efforts to handle it", *Current History,* 1960, pp. 342–346

Hourani, Cecil A. "Experimental village in the Jordan Valley" in *M.E.J.* 5, No. 4, Aug 1951, pp. 497–501

Howard, Harry N. "UNRWA, the Arab host countries and the Arab refugees", *Middle East Forum,* 42, No. 3, 1966, pp. 24–42

Hurvitz, Dan and Aahronson, Shlomo. "The strategy of controlled retaliation: the Israeli example" in *Medina, Mimshal ve-Yehasim Bein-Leumiyim* (Hebrew) Periodical of students of the Department of Political Science in the Hebrew University of Jerusalem, Vol. A, No. 1, Summer 1971

Ionides, M. G. "The disputed waters of the Jordan", *M.E.J.* 7, No. 2 (Spring 1953), pp. 153–164

Jarisati, Jaqlin F. "The Palestinian people–numbers and characteristics" in *Shu'un Filastiniyyah,* Feb 1975

Jones, Christina. "Ten years of service", *The Near East Committee for refugee work,* Jerusalem 1958
–"The frontier villages", *M.E.F.,* 1961, Dec, pp. 1–13

Jones, Willard. *The work of the voluntary agencies for Palestine refugees* (unpublished report), Nov 1961

Kallner, D. "Durah–a typical village on the Bedouin frontier" (Hebrew) *Bulletin of the Jewish Palestine Exploration Society,* Vol. XIV, 1–2, Oct 1947–March 1948, pp. 30–37

Kanafani, Ghassan. "The different kinds of tents" (short story) from the *Arab Palestinian Resistance,* monthly magazine, Palestine Liberation Army–People's Liberation Forces, Vol. II, No. 6, March 1970, pp. 24–8

Kanev, Itzhak. "UNRWA, the Arab refugees and research on their real number" from *Economic and Social Research Institute,* Press conference at Bet-Sokolov, Tel Aviv, Jan 24, 1968

Kapeliouk, M. "King Abdullah's Personality" in *N.E.,* Winter, 1952, pp. 127–133

Khalidi, Usama. "The Diet of Palestine Arab refugees receiving UNRWA rations", published by the *Institute for Palestine Studies,* Beirut, 1970

Khalidi, Usama and Amin Majaj. "A special report on the Palestine refugees", *Middle East Forum,* 41, No. 2, 1965, pp. 31–39

Khalidi, Walid. "Why did the Palestinians leave?", *M.E.F.* July 1959, pp. 21–15
–"The fall of Haifa", *Middle East Forum,* 35, No. 10, Dec 1959, pp. 22–32
–"Plan Dalet, the Zionist master plan for the conquest of Palestine", *Middle East Forum,* 37, No. 9, Nov 1961

Khouri, Fred J. "The policy of retaliation in Arab-Israeli relations", *M.E.J.,* 20, No. 4 (1966), pp. 435–455

Laqueur, Walter Zev. "Communism in Jordan" in *The World Today,* Vol. 12, No. 3, March 1956, pp. 109–119

Lazarus-Yafeh, Havah. "The Study of Arab textbooks" (Hebrew) in *N.E.* Vol. XVII, No. 67–8, 1967, pp. 207–221
–Jerusalem's holiness in the Muslim tradition (Hebrew) in *Molad,* No. 231, Oct–Sept 1971, pp. 219–227

Lewis, Bernard. "The Palestinians and the P.L.O.", in *Commentary,* Jan 1975

Liskovsky, Ahron. "Resident 'Absentees' in Israel" (Hebrew) in *N.E.* Vol. 10, 1960, pp. 186–192

Marx, Emmanuel. "The Social structure of the Negev Bedouin" (Hebrew) in *N.E.* Vol. VIII, No. 29, 1957, pp. 1–18

Midrashat Sde-Boker, Field Studies School, *Reshimot be-Noseh ha-Bedouim.* (Hebrew) (Notes on the Bedouin), Vol. I–IV, 1973

Mishal, Shaul. "Anatomy of Municipal elections in Judea and Samaria", (Hebrew) in *N.E.* No. 93–4, 1974, pp. 63–7

Mizan, "Soviet writings on Jordan", 2, No. 10, November 1960, pp. 2–12.

Mizra, Khan. "The Arab refugee–a study in frustration" in *Midstream,* New York, Spring 1956

Moe, Sherwood G. "Conditions among the Palestinian refugees", *Jewish Social Studies* XXI, Oct 1959, pp. 228–237, 219–227

Mogannam, E. Theodore. "Development in the legal system of Jordan", *M.E.J.,* 6, No. 2, Spring 1952, pp. 194–206

Monroe, Elizabeth, "The Arab–Israel frontier", *International Affairs* 29, Oct 1953, pp. 438–48

Muhiddin, Sabah. "The Return" (short story) in *Arab Palestine Resistance*, Vol. II, No. 4, Jan 1970, pp. 58–62

Muhsam, H. V. "Sedentarization of the Bedouin in Israel" from *Integration and Development in Israel*, (ed) Eisenstadt, Ben Yosef, C. Adler, (Jerusalem, 1970) Ch. XXVI, pp. 618–633

Nassar, Fuad. "Jordan's road to complete liberation, democracy and social progress", *World Marxist Review*, 9, No. 1, Jan 1966, pp. 48–52

Pa'il, Meir. "The Problem of Arab Sovereignty in Palestine 1947–1949: Arab governments versus the Arabs of Palestine", offprints from *Zionism*, Institute for Zionist Research, Tel Aviv University, pp. 439–489

Palestine Pictorial News, "Sands of sorrow", published by Christian Approach Mission, Bethlehem, 1951

Palmon, Yehushua. "Who are the parties in the Arab-Israeli conflict" (Hebrew) in *Molad*, Tel Aviv, No. 217, Sept 1968

Paz, Y. "The Jordanian National Guard" in *Maarachot*, March 1956, pp.35–41

Peretz, Don. "The Arab refugee dilemma", *Foreign Affairs*, 33, No. 1, Oct 1954, pp. 134–48

–"Problems of Arab refugee compensation", *M.E.J.*, 8, No. 4, Autumn 1954, pp. 403–416

–"Detente in the Arab refugee dilemma", *Orbis*, 1961, pp. 306–20

–"The Arab refugees: a changing problem", *Foreign Affairs*, 41, No. 3, April 1963, pp. 558–70

Perowne, Stewart, "The Arab Legion", *The Geographical Magazine*, XXVII, 1954, pp. 352–58

Porath, Yehoshua. "Revolution and terrorism and the Palestinian Communist Party (P.C.P.) 1929–1939", and "The Origins and Nature and Disintegration of the National Liberation League ('Usbat at-Taharrur al-Watani) 1943–1948" (Hebrew) in *N.E.* Vol. 18, 1968, pp. 255–267, and Vol. 14, 1964, pp. 353–366

–"Al-Hajj Amin al-Husayni, Mufti of Jerusalem, his rise to power and the consolidation of his position" in *Asian and African Studies: The Ulama' in Modern History*, Israel Oriental Society, Vol. 7, Jerusalem 1971, pp. 121–156

–"The political organisation of the Palestinian Arabs under the British Mandate", *Palestinian Arab Politics, op. cit.*

Qarman, Suad. "al-Bayt al-Mahjur" (The abandoned home), in *Mifgash*, Arab-Hebrew Bulletin for Literature and Art, Vol. C., p. 112, Acre, May 1968

Qutub, Ishaq. "Social change in rural Jordan: The rise of the middle class", *Middle East Forum*, 37, No. 10, Dec 1961, pp. 40–44

Rabia, Walid "Emigration and alienation in Palestinian Society" in *al-Turath wa al-Mujtama'* (Heritage and Society), Vol. I, No. 3, Oct 1974, pp. 31–81, published by the Palestinian Folklore and Social Research Society, Inash al-Usrah Society, al-Birah.

Reddaway, John. "UNRWA: a second look at the record–were the critics mistaken?" *New Middle East*, No. 16, Jan 1970, pp. 20–27

Roman, Michael. "The economic development of Jerusalem" (Hebrew) in *Atlas Yerushalaim*

Rosenfeld, Henry. "Processes of structural change within the Arab village extended family", *American Anthropologist*, 60, No. 6, Dec 1958, pp. 1127–39

Samaan, Emile. *The Arab refugees after five years, an eye witness report*, published by American Friends of the Middle East Inc. New York

Samarah, Adil. "Aspects of Palestinian migration from the end of the 19th century to the 1940s" in *al-Turath wa al-Mujtama'*, Vol. 1, No. 2, July 1974, pp. 4–8.

Sayegh, A. Fayez. "A Palestinian view" in *Time Bomb in the M.E.*, The Friendship Press, New York, 1963, pp. 44–72

Schmeltz, U. "Demographic developments of the Arab countries" in *N.E.* No. 89, 1973, pp. 29–60 (the part on Jordan)

Shaath, Nabil. "High level Palestine manpower", *Journal of Palestine Studies,* Beirut, Vol. I, No. 2 (Winter 1972)

Sharabi, H. "The crisis of the intelligentsia in the M.E.", *Muslim World,* 47, 1957, pp. 187–193.

Shihadah, Aziz. "The purpose of Jordanian Legislation in the West Bank" (lecture in the Hebrew University, Jerusalem, Jan 17, 1970) in *N.E.* No. 78, pp.166–170

Sherf, Ze'ev. "Negotiations with King Abdullah", *Outlook,* June 1958, p. 19–22.

Shimoni, Yaacov. "The Arabs and the approaching war with Israel 1945–1948" in *N.E.* Vol. XII, No. 47, 1962, pp. 189–211

Shmueli, Avshalom. "Bedouin Rural Settlement in Eretz-Israel", reprint from *Geography in Israel,* a collection of papers offered to the 23rd International Geographical Congress, USSR, July–Aug 1976, Jerusalem 1976, pp. 308–326

Shtandel, Ori. "The Arab population in East Jerusalem–leadership and political groups" (Hebrew) in *Yehuda ve-Shomron, op. cit.,* draft, 1977

Shufani, Elias. "The fall of a village", *Journal of Palestine Studies,* 1, No. 4, 1972, pp. 108–121

Shwadran, Benjamin, "Assistance to Arab refugees", *M.E.A.,* 1, No. 1, Jan 1950, pp. 2–11

–"Jordan annexes Arab Palestine, *M.E.A.,* 1950, pp. 99–111

–"Israel-Jordan border tension", *M.E.A.,* Dec 1953, pp. 385–402

Smith, Pamela Ann. "Aspects of class structure in Palestinian Society" in Davis (ed), *Israel and the Palestinians, op. cit.,* pp. 98–118

Sofer, Naim. "The integration of Arab Palestine in the Jordan Kingdom", *N.E.,* 1955, pp. 189–196

Stevens, Georgiana G. "Arab refugees: 1948–1952", *M.E.J.* 6, No. 3, Summer 1952, p. 281–298

St Aubin, W. de. "Peace and refugees in the M.E." *M.E.J.* 3, 1949

Ticknesse, S. G. "The Arab refugees: their position today", *J.R.C.A.S.* Jan 1951, pp. 29–30

Tibawi, Abdul Latif. "Visons of the return. The Palestine Arab refugees in Arabic poetry and art", *M.E.J.,* 17, No. 5, 1963, pp. 507–526

Tokan, B. "Transjordan: past, present and future", *J.R.C.A.S.* July–Oct 1944, pp. 253–264

Tweedy, O. "The Arab refugees: report on a M.E. Journey", *International Affairs,* 28, 1952, pp. 338–343

World Today, "King Abdullah's assassins", Oct 1951, pp. 411–419

World Today, "Jordan's frontier villages (The scene of border tension)" Nov 1953, pp. 467–475

Wright, Esmond. "Abdullah's Jordan: 1947–1951", *M.E.J.,* 5, No. 4, Autumn 1951, pp. 439–460

Wright, L. L. "The Arab refugees", *Foreign Notes,* Jan 14, 1949

Yinam, Sh. "The assassination of Abdullah", *Molad,* June–July, 1954, pp. 72–3

Zamir, Meir. "Historical, organisation and physical aspects in the development of the refugee Camps between 1948–1967" (Hebrew) in *Yehuda ve-Shomron, op. cit.,* Draft, 1977

Zarour, M. "Ramallah: My home town", *M.E.J.,* 7, 1953, pp. 430–439

Zimmerman, John. "Radio propaganda in the Arab-Israeli War 1948" in *The Wiener Library Bulletin,* 1974, Vol. XXVII, New Series, No. 30–1

Zurayeq, Constantine K. "Today and yesterday–two prominent aspects of the new meaning of the disaster", *Middle East Forum,* 43, nos. 2–3, 1967, pp. 13–20

Index

Abd al-Rahim, Ahmad, 172n, 196n
Abda, Yusuf Niqula, 116
Abdullah Ibn Husayn, King of Jordan, 8, 23, 55, 106, 165n, 166n, 168n; All-Palestine Government and, 7–9; annexation policy and relations with Palestinians, 10–16, 26–8, 29; Greater Syria goal of, 1, 5, 14; internationalization of Jerusalem and, 37–8; Israeli relations with, 5; murder of (1951), 9, 34, 38; 1948 War and, 4–5, 6, 7; spontaneous demonstrations against, 149; "stick and carrot" policy of, 29–32
Abu Shkhaydim Camp, 82, 184n
al-Abushi, Muhammad, 182n
agricultural projects, 34, 62, 63, 68, 70
al-Ahmad, Ibrahim Mustafa, 169n, 189n
Ahyiwat bedouin, 86, 188n
Ajjur, murder at, 192n
Ajlun, 195n, 204n
Ajluni, Hanna, 201n, 205n
Alamat tribe, 81
al-Alami, Abd al-Karim, 12, 112, 198n
al-Alami, Musa, 62, 129, 182n, 196n
Albina, Fransis, 170n
All-Palestine Government (A.P.G.), 7–9, 11, 28, 55, 197n
al-Amari Camp, 207n, 212n
Amarin tribe, 82
Amir, Ahmad Khalil Muhammad, 192n
Amir, General Abd al-Hakim, 192n
Amman, 7, 8, 35, 155, 175n, 205n, 207n; Communists in, 204n; demonstrations against king (1948), 149; economic development, 37, 38–9; elections, 107, 116, 195n; escalating rate of migrants to, 78–9; First Palestinian National Congress (1948), 11; Jabal al-Nazif Housing Project, 64, 65; Jerusalem as rival to, 37, 38–9; Palestine Office, 11; Palestinians in, 33, 34, 35, 52–3, 78–9, 162; Refugee

Office, 57–8, 59; transfer of ration cards to, 79, 188n
al-Anabtawi, Fa'iq, 197n, 199n, 206n, 207n
al-Anabtawi, Farid, 182n
Annexation, 8, 31, 32, 44, 174n; Abdullah's policy of, 10–16, 26–8; impact on Trans-Jordanian elements, 175n; official (April, 1950), 16, 29; recognition of, 105, 169n
Aqbat Jabr Camp, 93, 100, 132, 133, 134, 136, 155, 191n, 198n, 204n, 205n, 206n, 207n
Aqil, Ibrahim, 197n
Aqil, Isa, 169n, 197n, 198n
Arab Abu Kishk tribe, 82, 84
Arab al-Sidrah tribe, 82
Arab Army of Deliverance, 3–4, 9
Arab countries, 61–2; Jordanian citizenship and relations between, 46–50; Palestinians' role and situation in, 162–3; recruitment of refugees in armies of, 87–8, 100, 101; refugees' disillusionment with, 58; restrictions imposed on entry of refugees by, 45; see also Egypt; Iraq; Jordan; Saudi Arabia; Syria
Arab Countries Conference on Refugee Affairs, Jerusalem (1956), 58–9;
Arab Federation (1958), 179n
Arab Higher Committee for Palestinian (A. H. C.), 2, 3, 6, 10, 22, 100, 101, 105, 110, 128, 138–9, 166–7, 168n, 172n, 174n, 197n, 206n, 207n
Arab-Israeli conflict, 46; 1948 War, 2–7, 14, 15, 49, 73, 97; Sinai Campaign (1956), 58, 70, 88, 161
Arab Land Owners, Farmers and Citrus Grove Growers' Congress, Nablus (1948), 15
Arab League, 2, 3, 5, 6, 7, 8, 22, 28, 47–8, 100, 179n; Abdullah's strained relations

al-Nabhani, Muhammad Taqi al-Din, 78, 137
Nabil, Shafiq, 105
Nablus, Nablus refugees, 13, 14, 15, 19, 37,
    49, 55, 56, 57, 94, 98, 99, 195n, 209n;
    Arab Club, 209n; Central Displaced
    Committee, 173n; Committee for
    National Guidance, 59; District Gover-
    nor, 43, 62–3; demonstrations, 149, 152;
    elections, 105–6, 107, 108, 109, 110,
    116, 120, 122, 197n, 199n, 201n; Haifa
    Cultural Association, 19; Jaffa Refugee
    Committee, 16, 18; National Congress
    (1957), 129; P.A.W.A., 23–4; petitions,
    49–50, 180–81n; political parties' sup-
    port, 132, 134, 135–6, 138, 146, 204n,
    205n, 206n; refugee committees, 23–4,
    25; "returnees", 199n
al-Nabulsi, Abd al-Rahim, 182n
al-Nabulsi, Faysal, 167n
al-Nabulsi, Radi, 15
al-Nabulsi, Sulayman, 58; attempted coup by
    (1957), 59
Nahhalin village, Israeli attack on, 100
al-Najjadah, 10
Najjar, Hasan Qasim Muhammad, 187n
Nakhalah, Isa, 172n
al-Nashashibi, Anwar, 105
al-Nashashibi, Ishaq, 191n
al-Nashashibi, Raghib, 168n
Nashashibi faction, 1, 10, 13, 110
Nasir, Kamil, 21, 171n, 174n, 198n, 203n
Nasir, Musa, 47, 178n
Nasir Bin Jamil, *Sharif* (king's uncle), 86, 89;
    tension between Husayn and, 191n
al-Nasser, Col Gamal Abd, 48, 60, 70, 117,
    135, 207n; demonstrations in support of,
    149, 156; popularity among refugees, 48,
    58, 88, 90, 91, 95, 145, 156, 160, 198n
Nasserism, 113
National Congress, Nablus (1957), 129
National Front, Jordan, 114
National Guard, Jordan (N.G.), 76, 85, 92–6,
    137, 160; amalgamation with Arab Leg-
    ion (1965), 93; budget allocation to, 94,
    95; donations by local people to, 94;
    Frontier Villages' attitude towards, 95–6;
    king's view of, 91; M.B. members among,
    136; recruitment of refugees into, 93, 94,
    160; refugees' attitudes towards training
    and recruitment, 98–100, 102; training,
    93, 94, 96, 98, 99; National Guidance
    Committee, representation on, 182n; *see
    also* Fedayyin
National Liberation League (Communist)
    (N.L.L.), 6, 132, 165n, 166n
National Socialist Party, Jordan (N.S.P.), 89,
    107, 111, 116, 129, 134, 141, 144, 199n,
    208n
Narionality Law, Jordan, *see* Jordanian citi-
    zenship

Natural Syria, 13, 14; *see also* Greater Syria
al-Na'uri, Isa, 194n
Na'was, Abdallah, 105, 112, 130, 193n, 203n
Nazareth, Israeli occupation of, 5
Nazzal, (Hajj) Husayn Sabri, 189n
Near East Radio Station, 145
N.E.C.C.R.W., 190n
Negev, 6, 8, 166n, 170n, 195n; bedouin in,
    10, 80, 86, 105, 189n
New Arab Party, 116
non-refugees, 7, 12, 13, 67, 68, 161, 185n,
    199–200n, 201n; in Mu'askar Camp,
    Old Jerusalem, 118; tension in towns
    between refugees and, 117, 121
Nur Shams Camp, 43, 77, 137, 139, 187n,
    206n
Nusayba, Anwar, 78, 105, 106, 166–7n,
    175n, 197n, 208n
Nusayba, Hazim, 167n, 174n
Nuwayhid, Ajaj, 11, 12, 169n
Nu'yma Camp, 82, 206n, 207n, 208n

Palestine Arab Refugee Congress (1949),
    statement of aims and policies, 222–3;
    see also General Refugee Congress,
    Ramallah
Palestine Arab Workers Association
    (P.A.W.A), Nablus, 23–4, 105
Palestine Communist Party (P.C.P.), 166n
Palestine Office, Amman, 11
Palestine Trade Committee, 176n
Palestinian Arab Congress(es): First
    (Amman), 11, 12; Second (Jericho Con-
    gress), 12–14, 15, 29, 169n, 170n; Third
    (Nablus), 14–15
Palestinian Arab Villagers League, 19
Palestinian Army *see* Refugee Army
Palestinian Entity, 29, 39, 40, 48, 61, 72, 88,
    129, 135, 137, 138–9, 152, 160, 201n;
    see also Palestinian separatism
Palestinian Identity Card, 47, 180n
Palestinian Government, Jordan govern-
    ment's opposition to idea of, 138–9
Palestinian National Guard *see* Fedayyin;
    National Guard
Palestinian refugees, 6, 7, 9, 16–26; Ab-
    dullah's relations with, 10–16. 26–8;
    agricultural projects for, 34, 62, 63, 68,
    70; Arab passport for, 179n; Area
    Committees, 20–26; attitude towards
    military training and equipment, 98–102;
    burying of dead, 118–19, 200n; camp
    committees, 17–19; cancellation of
    ration cards, 55, 63, 64–5, 114, 128,
    151–2; census opposed by, 152; cheap
    labour, 80; compensation for abandoned
    property in Israel, 52, 62, 70, 126, 128,
    181; demonstrations and protests by,
    50–51, 90, 95, 105–6, 124, 148–57; in